To: Dale
my truly best friends — to the
from the urinal to the bake.
Jacuzzi to the
Always the best.
times —

NO PLACE TO HIDE

Gary Christensen

Previous Book by Christensen

NO SAFE PLACE

Echo Company 2nd Battalion, 1st Marines

NO PLACE TO HIDE

Foreword

In May of 2003, I received an email from another Marine Vietnam veteran. He asked me what unit I was with and where I was stationed in Vietnam. I responded by saying that I had spent about ten months at Con Thien, with Echo Company, 2nd Battalion, 1st Marines (2/1) in 1967-68. I quickly received an email reply from him saying "No, you weren't". At that moment I knew I was wrong. It turned out he was also with 2/1 and said we only stayed at that base 77 days. I also realized that I didn't remember much else about my nearly 13 month tour of duty.

Some of my memory has slowly come back, as I discuss my time in Vietnam with others or am told of events from that period of time.

I wrote this book for three reasons:

First, to regain my lost memory regarding my time in Vietnam, to understand where I was, who I was with and what I did during the war.

Second, as a memoir for my family, should they have an interest in this period of time and how it affected the rest of my life.

Third, to acknowledge the many others who fought in this war and so many still fighting the war every day.

Even though many guys from 2nd Battalion, 1st Marines will relate their stories during their tour in Vietnam during 1967-68, there are ten main characters, all with Echo Company, who carry the story: My sincere thanks to each of them for their contribution.

Listed in alphabetical order:
• Sergeant Steve "Bernie" Bernston, Combat Reporter
• Corporal Gary "Chris" Christensen, 2nd Platoon
• Corporal Mike Coates, Combat Photographer
• Corporal Chuck Estes, 2nd Platoon
• Corporal Roger Goss, 3rd Platoon
• Corporal Mike House, 2nd Platoon

- Lieutenant Jim Kirk, 1st Platoon CO, then 3rd Platoon Commander
- Corporal Dennis Knobby, 3rd Platoon
- Lieutenant Lee Suydam, 3rd Platoon CO, then Executive Officer
- HM3 John "Doc" Turner, Company Senior Corpsman

Additional contributors in alphabetical order:
Captain Robert Black, Echo Company
Clinton Davis, Echo Company
Dave Dillberg, Golf Company
Bob Dunbar, Echo Company
Lt. Col. Duncan, Echo 2/1 CO
Captain Thomas Eagen, Echo Company
Tony Gallasso, Golf Company
Lt Haaland, Hotel Company
Terry Halloran, Echo Company
Roy Hannon, Hotel Company
Doc Mike Hill, Hotel Company
Dave Stromire, Echo Company
Paul Rangel, Golf Company
Lathan Williams, Echo Company

The narrative that follows is based on my letters home, House's squad leader book and our memories, which have been refreshed by our discussions. Our recollections have been stimulated and sometimes corrected by reading the 2nd Battalion, 1st Marines Command Chronologies, made available by Texas Tech University's Virtual Vietnam Archive.

Note: Military time is used throughout the book. Military time uses a 24 hour clock: 1am is 0100 hours, 2am is 0200 hours, noon is 1200 hours, 1pm is 1300 hours, 2pm is 1400 hours, midnight is 2400 hours.

Preface

During WWII, Japan invaded and occupied Vietnam, a nation on the eastern edge of the Indochina Peninsula (Vietnam, Cambodia and Laos) in Southeast Asia. This area had previously been under French control. Ho Chi Minh formed the Viet Minh to fight both the Japanese and the French. Japan withdrew its forces in 1945 and Ho's Viet Minh forces rose up immediately, seizing the northern city of Hanoi and declaring a Democratic Republic of Vietnam (DRV) with Ho as president.

Seeking to regain control, France set up the state of Vietnam (South Vietnam) in July 1949, with Saigon as its capital. Battles continued until a decisive defeat of the French forces at Dien Bien Phu in May 1954. Subsequent treaty negotiations at Geneva split Vietnam along the latitude known as the 17th parallel and a Demilitarized Zone (DMZ) was established. This created North and South Vietnam as separate countries.

With the Cold War intensifying, the United States hardened its policies against any allies of the Soviet Union and by 1955 President Eisenhower had pledged his support to President Diem and South Vietnam. Diem's forces cracked down on sympathizers in the south and by 1957, the Viet Cong (Vietnamese Communists) intensified its actions and war escalated.

In 1961, a team was sent by President Kennedy to report on conditions in South Vietnam. They recommended a U.S. military presence and economic and technical aid in order to help confront the Viet Cong and the communist threat. They worked under the "domino theory", which held that if one Southeast Asian country fell to communism, many would follow. By 1962, U.S. troop strength had reached 9,000.

In August 2, 1964, after Democratic Republic of Vietnam (DVR) torpedo boats attacked a U.S. destroyer in the Gulf of Tonkin, President Johnson ordered retaliatory bombing of military targets in North Vietnam. Congress gave the President broad war-making powers, and U.S. planes began regular bombing raids, later code-named Operation Rolling Thunder.

In March 1965, Johnson made the decision, with solid support from the American public, to send U.S. combat forces into battle in Vietnam. The Marines were chosen to lead the offensive into the country with an offensive code-named Operation Starlight. By June, 82,000 combat troops were stationed in Vietnam, and General William Westmoreland was calling for 175,000 more by the end of 1965 to shore up the struggling South Vietnamese Army. Johnson authorized the immediate dispatch of 100,000 troops at the end of July 1965. Another 100,000 troops were sent in 1966. In addition to the United States, South Korea, Thailand, Australia and New Zealand also committed troops to fight in South Vietnam on a much smaller scale, as part of the allied forces.

The U.S. - South Vietnamese war effort sought to kill as many enemy troops as possible, rather than trying to secure territory, as was done in World War II. By 1966, large areas of South Vietnam had been designed as "free-fire zones", from which all innocent civilians were evacuated and only enemy remained. Heavy bombing by B-52 aircraft or shelling made these zones uninhabitable. Even as the body count mounted steadily, the enemy refused to stop fighting, encouraged by the fact that they could easily reoccupy lost territory. The North Vietnamese strengthened their air defenses with support from China and the Soviet Union.

As the war stretched on, U.S. soldiers came to mistrust their government's reasons for keeping them there, as well as Washington's claims that the war was being won. Territory was not conquered or taken over. No matter how many of the enemy were killed, they were replaced. The U.S. and its allies continued to tally enemy killed or wounded. Rules of engagement and restricted territory access limited the scope of the U.S. fighting men. The war was definitely being fought out of Washington D.C. and its political machine and not by the generals on the ground in Vietnam.

By the end of 1967, Hanoi's communist leadership was growing impatient as well and sought to strike a decisive blow aimed at forcing the better-supplied United States to give up hopes of success. On January 31, 1968, the NVA and Viet Cong launched the Tet Offensive. This was a coordinated series of fierce attacks on more than 100 cities and towns in South Vietnam.

The Quang Tri Province, in the I Corps area, (where this story takes place) was more heavily bombed than all of Europe during WWII. The 3,500 villages in the area were reduced to a mere 11 by the end of the war. The intense bombing campaign, combined with the constant artillery and mortar firing and the use of Agent Orange, turned much of the land into a virtual moonscape, with only a fraction of the original triple jungle canopy forest remaining.

For military purposes, the U.S. divided South Vietnam into four military areas: I Corps (up north and next to the DMZ), the II Corps Area, the III Corps and the IV Corps area down at the southern portion of the country.

This story begins in the southern part of Quang Nam Province in the late summer of 1967. The countryside surrounding the city of Da Nang was patrolled by the Marines, in order to keep enemy forces away from the main U.S. Marine airbase and staging headquarters for the many supporting units of the Marine Corps. The Marines slowly moved closer to the Demilitarized Zone (DMZ) and by Christmas of 1967 found themselves positioned in the northernmost U.S. combat base of Con Thien, just in time for the Tet Offensive - January 31, 1968 and the Bloodiest Year of the War.

Table of Contents

1

THE REUNION

It was July, 2008 and five of us were gathered in the living room of a rented beach house on the Oregon coast. We hadn't seen each other for 40 years when we served together as combat Marines in Vietnam, in 1967-1968. Actually, Doc John Turner, our corpsman, was U.S. Navy, but serving as our platoon corpsman. Even though he was in the Navy, we thought of him as a Marine and I don't think we ever let him think differently.

We all arrived at the beach house within a few hours of each other. John "Doc" Turner, our Senior Corpsman, now living in Louisiana, and his friend, Jerry "Shotgun" Slater, also a corpsman, from California, were the first to arrive. They were followed by Mike House from Washington, our squad leader, then Chuck Estes, from Texas, our radioman and second in command, and me, Gary "Chris" Christensen, from Oregon. We greeted each other with warmth and excitement. It was as if no time had passed, but it had. Our lives had changed so much since the time we spent in Vietnam. We learned how to survive and return home. In conversation, we reintroduced ourselves to those we'd met along the way, the places we'd been and our experiences, not only in Vietnam, but events since we had parted from that war.

We talked about Con Thien, the Marine's northernmost outpost on the Demilitarized Zone (DMZ). The DMZ was six miles wide and nearly 60 miles long, stretching from the ocean on the east, following the Ben Hai River initially, and then west in a straight line to the Laotian border. Con Thien was a hill in the middle of nowhere, barely elevated enough at 158 meters to see into the enemy's country, a mere 2,000 meters north of our position, and south to Dong Ha. 2nd Battalion, 1st Marine Regiment, 1st Marine Division was positioned along the first line of defense along the DMZ. In front of us was the North Vietnamese Army (NVA). We were not allowed to cross the DMZ. We did travel into the DMZ, just weren't supposed to. We spent more time at this combat base than any other unit during the war. It was truly a 77 day visit to hell as we endured nearly 3,000 rounds of incoming enemy artillery, mortars, rockets and recoilless rifle fire. We were exhausted by platoon and squad size patrols, night and day, sometimes extending thousands of meters from our base. Some of our fellow Marines could not last through the continuing daily harassment of incoming rounds, explosions, wounded friends being dragged or carried to either the aid station or to the copter pad in nondescript black body bags. They were sent home.

Someone brought up Operation Medina which occurred under the triple-canopy cover of the Hai Lang National Forest. It was a long and exhausting slog through the deep jungle on a search and destroy mission. We were in search of the enemy in area known as Base Area 101, which was a North Vietnamese Army (NVA) staging area for the replacement troops traveling into South Vietnam. The NVA felt safe hidden deep in the jungle as they staged their personnel and supplies. Planes overhead were unable to spot the large gathering areas, as the jungle foliage hid their activities. We found an NVA hospital deep in the dark jungle, fired our way in and destroyed it, along with all the munitions and food and supplies we could find.

We fought side by side for 13 months, guarding each other's safety so we all could return home. That was really our goal. It was simple. Do what it took to get home.

Our lives truly changed during our tour, not only as individuals, but as a team. We had given everything we had. We had been blessed with a return trip to our families. Dreams of those killed in this far off land would haunt each of us the rest of our lives.

As we talked with each other, the old times returned. We felt safe in the living room and shared all we could.

This is our story...

2

PREPARE FOR WAR - GOING TO VIETNAM

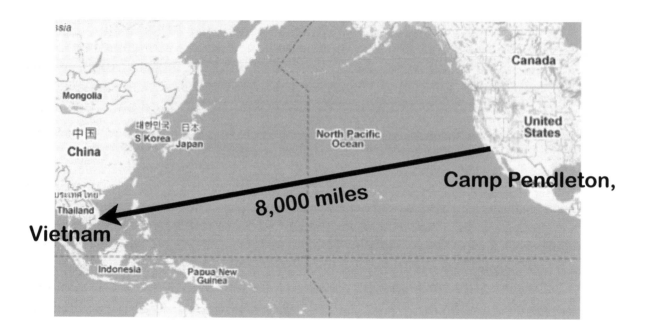

The nearly 8,000 mile trip from Camp Pendleton, California
across the Pacific Ocean to Wake Island and
then on to our final destination -
Da Nang, South Vietnam.

We were all so very young: the average age of the fighting Marine in Vietnam was 19 years old. Most of us were just out of high school or had left school early. There were a few, a very few, with a year or so of college. A common belief is that most Vietnam Veterans were drafted. The fact is that three-quarters of the men who served in Vietnam were volunteers, and nearly all of the Marines were volunteers.

The Vietnam War escalated in the northern section or I Corps area of South Vietnam during the autumn of 1967, especially along the Demilitarized Zone (DMZ). We learned later that the North Vietnamese Army (NVA) was using this period of time to build up their supplies of food, ammunition and troops. This was their preparation for the upcoming 1968 Tet Offensive, the plan to bring down the U.S. forces throughout the country and to turn over South Vietnam to the hands of the North Vietnamese Communists.

We had been trained to the nth degree in either the U.S. Marine Corps Boot Camp located at Parris Island, South Carolina or at MCRD, San Diego, California. After the initial phase, most of us were sent through the Advanced Infantry Training (AIT) program, then without much delay, sent to a country we knew nothing about, except it was full of communists and it would be our job to kill them. Kill them and set the South Vietnamese people free. It's a frightening thought for young men, many being away from home for the first time in their lives.

This story focuses on Echo Company, 2nd Battalion, 1st Marines, and the infantry squads, how they met and were woven into a fighting team, supporting each other throughout a very difficult time. The table of organization for a rifle squad called for a strength of 14, but squads often had only 7-10. Second squad of the second platoon is the focus of the story.

The display that follows shows the normal strength of a regiment of Marines. In wartime, because of injury, sickness and death, actual strength was often much lower.

Some of the guys we met would be remembered forever, some of them would live - some wouldn't. Some would be able to face battle and return the next day and do it again, others wouldn't. We all learned to support each other, every day, every single day. It was this act of bonding that saved us physically, as well as mentally.

11

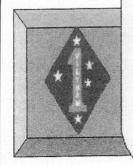

Regiment

(Known as "Marines")

Consists of 3 Battalions

Battalion - 1,100 men

4 letter rifle companies plus Headquarters & Service

Company - 225 men

3 letter rifle platoons and a weapons platoon plus HQ section

Rifle Platoon - 45 men

3 squads 14 men each

Squad 14 men

3 fire teams

Company - 4 platoons and HQ section

Rifle Platoon 45 men	Rifle Platoon 45 men	Rifle Platoon 45 men	Weapons Platoon	H&S Section
3 rifle squads	3 rifle squads	3 rifle squads		

Rifle Squad

14 men

- 3 fire teams

Weapons Platoon

- Machine gun teams
- Rocket Teams
- 60 mortars

We were a "meat and potatoes" company - riflemen. No, we didn't see USO shows..., some didn't get R&R (rest and relaxation) to Hawaii or Australia, we didn't get a beer run on Fridays, we didn't get three square meals a day, didn't shower for weeks at a time, didn't always have the comfort of socks or clean clothes, but settled for the 1.4 meals a day in the bush and the friendship of those around us. We did fine. We had each other.

Each Marine would enter the service and the war with different backgrounds, religions and education. We had some that could shoot the eyes out of a running squirrel at 100 yards and others that had never left the city, done a lick of work or been close to a gun.

The experience that would be unfolding soon and the individuals we met would change our lives forever.

We were soon to "ship-out" to a country nearly 8,000 miles away, somewhere south of China and Japan and far to the west of California. The country was only the size of the state of Washington, yet more than a 1,000 miles in length, but very narrow, measuring from 300 miles wide to less than 50 miles at its narrowest.

Helicopters were of vital importance for medical evacuations, transport in assault operations, insertion and extraction of reconnaissance units and direct fire support for engaged infantry. We never had enough helicopters.

Movement of the Marines over long distances was normally accomplished by marching, or the 6x6 or "six by" (so-called because it has 12 wheels) transport truck when available or the occasional UH-34 copter, known as "the Dog". Much of the delivery of Marine supplies of mail, food, ammo and water was held back while the wounded were transported. The Marines received old style meals called C-rations. We were often short of C-rations and water and sometimes ammunition. We sometimes had to wear our utilities (fatigues, as the Army called them) until they disintegrated. We had a Spartan life, particularly in comparison with the other branches of military service.

The U.S. Army troops fighting mainly in the II, III and IV Corps areas were well supplied with their large inventory of UH-1 ("Huey") and CH-47 Chinook helicopters toting the load. Their supply of ammunition, food, water, beer, hot meals, clothing, mail and medevac copters seemed almost never ending.

13

The Navy pulled duty anywhere there was water, along the country's shoreline, in the coastal ports, riverboat patrols and their supply runs and most important to us - they supplied the men to patch us up when we were injured - the U.S. Navy Medical Corpsmen, the Marines' best friends. The Corpsmen were the exceptionally well-trained and well-disciplined medical personnel responsible for keeping wounded Marines alive until copters could get them to the safety of the med-centers. The aid stations were dispersed throughout the torn and shredded jungle landscape. The corpsmen had the power to stop an infantry company of Marines dead in their tracks and force them to shower if they believed those individuals had been seriously rained upon by Agent Orange. They had the ability to send troops out of the field for any mental or physical issues they deemed necessary. They had the power and they used it whenever necessary to aid the welfare and health of the Marines they served. They were enlisted men, but nicknamed "Doc" by all the troops. It was a term that showed respect to these men who displayed bravery each and every time they were called on - firefights where thousands of rounds of ammo were zipping through the air. They immediately responded to the wounded Marines, without regard for their own safety.

The Navy Seabees also supported us. Seabees (Construction Battalions) were engineers who operated the heavy equipment necessary to build bridges, aircraft support facilities, camps, fill sand bags, and pave roads. They often had to jump off their equipment, return fire to the enemy and then jump back on the equipment and finish the job.

We also were supported by our own Marine engineers.

1966

CPL GARY "CHRIS" CHRISTENSEN
Salem, Oregon

Corporal "Chris" Christensen

In 1966 I was sitting at my desk at Southern Oregon College doing some studying, when big Mike Kellis (tailback on the football team) rips the door open and with a big grin on his face he says, "You and I are going to join the Marine Corps, buddy." I was absolutely baffled by his approach to the subject and remember laughing. Number one, we had it made where we were – 19 years old, away from home, in college, playing football and on a campus loaded with gorgeous girls, most we hadn't even met yet. Number two, why in hell would we do something so bizarre, as go into the service? Wasn't there a war going on somewhere over there?

In 1967 neither Mike or myself were setting the world on fire with our grades. At least when we got out, we would have our college paid for by the government G.I. Bill. We said good-bye to our girlfriends, our family and neighbors. A very short and quick three months later, we were processed through the Portland Oregon Recruiting Depot and were on a plane to Marine Corps Recruiting Depot (MCRD), San Diego, California. The plane was full of guys the same age as us, many talking big, acting big, but truly clueless. One guy that I met on the plane was a biker – a tough guy. Only time would finally show this guy for who he really was – weak, really weak.

Boot Camp – Sure it was tough. It was supposed to be tough. We really didn't understand the training regimen until we got to Vietnam. There was truly a purpose in the training, every bit of it. If you understood the fact that the minority, the 10%, the weak…they would break first. They would be first to fail in any of a hundred exercises, marches, and tests that were put in front of us. They would be used by the drill sergeants to set an example, they were the ones that would receive the brunt of the difficult physical and mental work, they were the weak. If the rest of us were scared enough to do what we were told, we would survive. That's it! Be the average guy…survive, hide among the group, don't be noticed, learn to blend in and don't volunteer for anything!

The three Drill Instructors' first objective in Boot Camp was to tear each of us down, physically and mentally. We were told we were nobody. That's what they wanted and that's when the real work started.

Now that we were nobody, we would be shown how to be Marines. There was a Marine Corps way for everything we did - how to walk, how to march, how to sit, how to eat, how to speak and the list went on for the next thousand weeks, it seemed. There was "Semper Fidelis" or "Semper Fi" for short, the Marine Corps motto - "Always Faithful". We were shown how to work as a team, to be winners, how to depend on guys to help you, to watch out for you and to watch your back. Damn, it was tough. We didn't really know these other guys, not really…but, in time we would. The Marine Corps taught you the lessons that just might save your life in Vietnam and without anyone saying anything, we learned to trust each other…it was all we had.

The Marine Corps pressed and stressed the basics – discipline and teamwork, that's right. Were you disciplined enough to know your job, to carry it out as told and work as part of a team? No one really knew as we left for Vietnam. We didn't talk to each other about it. There was a fear of the unknown. How would we fare when faced with battle? Would we able to do what was going to be asked of us when the firing started? Could we kill someone? So many questions left unanswered, yet we felt prepared. We were Marines! We were well-trained and tough, just not tested. Do our job. Do what we were told. We'll be all right, won't we?

We finished Boot Camp and went on to Advanced Infantry Training (AIT). Everything began to get more serious at this point. The Advanced Infantry Training time was an "at ease" time. We really didn't have any responsibilities, other than to respond to the daily regimen of classes and schedule. Soon, we were to have a purpose. It was getting close. It was scary. We were all so young. Up to this point in our life, we really didn't have a purpose, yet now we did. We would carry a rifle in battle in a foreign country. That's a lot to absorb. We had daily lessons about how to survive in combat – how to spot a booby-trap, how to disarm a booby-trap, how to setup perimeter flares, so no one could sneak up on your position and kill you, how to pop a smoke grenade so the medevac copter could rescue your injured,...the list went on. Everything had a serious tone to it. The instructors yelled every day that if we didn't learn this stuff, we would die in a foreign country. We would die, because the guy next to us didn't listen and for this, he would die and maybe take others with him. It was a sobering experience. Time was getting short and soon we would leave. Soon we would leave everything...our families, our friends.

CPL MIKE HOUSE
Bremerton, WA

Corporal House

As a kid, I dreamed of being an oceanographer/engineer, but my divorced mother worked three jobs just to keep me and my brother fed and clothed. I did manage to become a certified scuba diver at age 15 with the help of a Navy Master Diver who had two cute daughters in my school.

There was no money for us to attend college so, during my senior year of high school I took a competitive exam for a civil service apprenticeship at Puget Sound Naval Shipyard. I managed to place 40th out of 800 taking the eight hour exam, and was offered a four-year apprenticeship as a ship fitter (steelworker). Although I received extensive drafting and math and physics training, building Navy ships and sport diving was as close as I would get to being an oceanographer. I did get my associate degree in engineering.

I was really into hot-rods, and built and drove a '34 Ford Tudor Sedan with "suicide" doors, and a built '48 Mercury flathead motor that would do a 14 second quarter-mile at the local drag races (I still own it!). I also crewed on a friends' Gas Dragster for a while, but broken parts just got too expensive!

With a solid job and a future ahead, I married my high school sweetheart, who was a student nurse at the time. We had been married for six months when I received my draft notice from the Army, and since we both had relatives who had

17

been Marines, I joined up, hoping to get some engineering training. The shortest tour was two years, and that only got me as far as the infantry or, in Marine jargon, a "grunt."

My first duty station was Kaneohe Bay, Oahu, Hawaii. I was stationed with a new Amphibious Assault Battalion, the 27th Marines, 5th Marine Division. I had been awarded platoon "high shooter" in boot camp, and quickly won promotion from private to private first class to lance corporal, and was a squad leader during our time training in the jungles of Hawaii and our two amphibious assaults of other islands and the beaches of California. We trained together for almost a year and thought we were prepared for combat, but nothing can really prepare you for that shock of actually being shot at by people who want to kill you!

I took a lot of correspondence courses from Marine Headquarters (HQ) Training Division on subjects such as infantry tactics, map and compass navigation, improvised weapons and explosives, camouflage, and topographical mapmaking. I was able to score highly on all, and this was brought to the attention of my Battalion HQ, where they needed a draftsman/mapmaker for operational planning and coordination with air and other ground units, such as armor and artillery. I was assigned to headquarters, sent to NCO School and promoted to the rank of corporal in short order. My boss was a captain and I traveled with our colonel to carry and prepare maps and operational plans for training.

I was able to move Nancy to Hawaii where she found a small apartment right on the beach outside the base. It was like a long honeymoon for us, but when she was eight months pregnant with our first child, the battalion was disbanded, and I received orders for Vietnam, following a thirty day leave.

A month later, I was in line waiting to board my flight at Travis Air Force Base, California to Da Nang when I was summoned to the phone and heard my wife tell me we had a son. Boarding that plane was really bitter-sweet, proud I had a son, but dreading being sent into combat, never having seen him, or held him in my arms. It was even worse having to return to Vietnam six months later, after being with my wife and infant son for only five days on my Rest and Relaxation (R&R) in Hawaii. I knew that I would not see or hold him until I returned from my tour.

We flew to Da Nang Airbase, Vietnam. The whole scene could have been from an episode of "The Twilight Zone". There I was in a big Boeing 707 filled with men from all the military services and pretty stewardesses. Four of the "stews" had swapped their uniforms with same-sized guys and they all served sandwiches and soft drinks to the rest of us on the flight into Da Nang Air Base, South Vietnam. The stews looked cute in military uniforms, but the guys looked like real ugly women in the stewardess uniforms, especially the guys with mustaches wearing the blonde wigs the gals provided! They took pictures during the flight and joked around like we were flying into some vacation resort, instead of a country at war.

"DOC" JOHN TURNER
Pollack, LA

Doc Turner

The U.S. Navy chose me to be a corpsman and to be a part of a Marine combat battalion in Vietnam. I was just home from Marine Field Med School at Camp Pendleton learning how to be a Marine. Ha. I was having a good time with my daughter Shawn, eight months old and learning a lot of stuff, like who were the ones she could wrap around her finger. Everybody. I was trying to find out where my wife, Brenda, would be staying and such. I was catching up with old friends...finding out we weren't really friends anymore, not like we were before. I think we all changed. Them and me. I wanted to have a good time at home, thinking all the time that I may never be back. I was also determined that come hell or high water that I was gonna be coming home. It was a confusing time. Momma and Daddy were themselves up to about three days before I was to leave, then I could tell the mood was changing. Mom was easily at the edge of crying and Dad was more somber looking and acting. There were scads of pictures taken with all of our family. I guess for old times' sake.

In mid May of 1967, I was sent to California for more training. We would be leaving from the West Coast to the only little war we had. It took two days to get out of Santa Barbara, California. Our plane kept having engine problems. All of us stayed drunk for two days. We were all U.S. Navy Hospital Corpsmen. There were about two hundred of us and about forty or fifty other guys from the other services. I was almost broke and of course, everybody else was too. I did buy a bottle (pint) of Blackberry Brandy. I was saving it for a special occasion. The plane was finally repaired and we left. Our flight was headed west and over the Pacific Ocean.

When we arrived in Hawaii, we were given the opportunity to get off the plane to stretch our legs. The flight had been long and we quickly exited. I didn't see or hear anything there that impressed me. We got back on the plane and flew on to Okinawa. I liked that place. There were lots of things to do that were cheap - girls, massages, more booze. I got my first ever massage and it was great. She walked on my back, after bathing and massaging me all over. There was no sex involved. I just got a great massage. Mike Trample and I had a great time. He was a good guy and was kind of my chaperone. He was from Kansas. Jerry Slater was another friend. Jerry and I first met in Field Med School and were together throughout our training in the states. We developed a good friendship and were hoping we would be together in the Nam.

Corporal Steve Bernston "The Storyteller"

The Marine Corps' motivation for having combat correspondents was not a big secret. The Marine Corps Correspondents' Association goes back to World War II, when it was first formed as a pickup bunch by a guy by the name of Colonel Danzig who told the Commandant of the Marine Corps, "You know, you need a little publicity, because you're not getting any for your Marines."

So, originally, it was PR. The old story is that the Marines are the best covered and the best publicized landing organization in the world, because every third one on the beach is either a reporter or a photographer. That's an overstatement, of course, because we never had that many in the whole MOS (Military Occupational Speciality).

Besides all the other things, being a combat reporter meant it was the chance to record history. They'd stand up there and tell us, "You're there to make sure that you tell the story properly for all time." It was also good PR with the national news media. And, finally, it was a morale issue. The *Sea Tiger* (a military

CPL STEVE BERNSTON
Hope, Idaho

newspaper given to the troops) was a morale thing. And, it was important. It was the only paper the troops had.

By January 1966, I was a lance corporal (L/CPL) and co-editor of the weekly base newspaper, *The Flight Jacket* at El Toro, CA. I didn't have it bad but I put in requests for Vietnam. Nothing happened. I got married and decided to stay on base when I got orders to FMF Pacific. The orders were for 18 month unaccompanied tour to Fort Smedley Butler, Okinawa. I protested as now I had a wife, with a child on the way. On the evening of April 26, 1967, I kissed my pregnant wife good by and boarded a midnight 707 flight out of El Toro headed to Okinawa and then onto South Vietnam. I promised my wife we would meet in Hawaii.

After spending my first night in Okinawa at the replacement depot at Tensin, I was told to get on a 6BY (standard GI truck with benches to seat troops) and I would be dropped off at gates of Camp Smedley Butler further down the island. Clutching my orders and Service RecordBook (SRB) and trying not to drag my sea bag filled with all my clothes and everything I owned, the Marine at the gate of Camp Butler pointed toward the headquarters building, where I would check in.

I walked into the administration office and found no one was there (noon chow), except in a glassed office in the corner sat a lieutenant colonel with "Executive Officer" on his desk plate. I turned to leave when he shouted out, "What do you want in here, Marine?" "I'm reporting in, Sir", I replied. Then I added "but I can come back later after chow." "No, step in here and I'll sign you in Lance Corporal." When I entered his office, my whole future and life changed in about 15 minutes!

I gave the XO my orders and Service Record Book (SRB) and he thumbed through them without saying anything for a couple of minutes and then he said, "Hey, what's your MOS (military occupational specialty), again?" "4312, Combat Correspondent, Sir", I replied. He said "I remember a getting an administrative memo marked for priority reading somewhere last week about somebody urgently needing 4312's." The XO turned to paper loaded clipboards hanging on the wall behind him and in a minute or so, he spun back around to face me witha clipboard open to a page. "Here it is! The 1st Marine Division ISO is requesting immediate assignment of any excess 4312's to replace their 4312's ready to rotate home." The XO looked directly at me for what was seconds, but it felt like an hour and then he said, "We don't need you here Lance Corporal Berntson!

We got more than enough 4312's hanging around this place.

OFFICIAL
U. S. MARINE CORPS
REPORTER

PRESS

STEVEN L. BERNTSON

is assigned to obtain news of military interest for publication
and to assist the members of the civilian press. All personnel
are requested to cooperate with the bearer in carrying out his
duties. The bearer is authorized to have in his possession camera equipment and to pass from the base with such equipment
as is necessary for the performance of his duties.

CPL STEVE "BERNIE" BERNSTON
Tacoma, WA

Do you have a brother serving in Vietnam or are you a sole surviving son?" he asked with eyes looking right into mine. "No, Sir. I don't fall into either category," I replied, as his next question was "Any reason you can't serve in Vietnam?" "My wife is expecting our child in couple of months", I said. "Sorry, but a lot of Marines in Vietnam have a wife expecting, so I can't let you off for that one," he said. "Sergeant Cummings. Take this Marine's orders and cancel his assignment here and reassign him to 1st Marine Division HQ in Chu Lai, South Vietnam. "Good Luck to you son," ending our meeting with a wave toward Sergeant Cumming's desk.

Two hours later, I was on another 6BY (troop transport truck, with a steel cargo bed, wooden sides and troop bench seats) headed to Camp Tensin with my sea bag, SRB, and a set or orders assigning me to 1st Marine Division ISO, Chu Lai SVN (South Vietnam).

I volunteered to go on the next Vietnam manifest, which was that evening. This

6BY Troop Transport Truck

delighted the sergeant doing the manifest because he was tired of listing reasons why a Marine couldn't go that night. Shortly after midnight on April 28th, I was flying south to Da Nang, Republic of South Vietnam (RSV) having spent little more that 24 hours at my 18 month duty assignment on Okinawa.

Chris

We're flying out this afternoon. Dick and I went to the gym and worked out...karate and boxing. Got in a good workout and afterwards, we walked to the base-service station at El Toro Air Field in California and met with Bob and Rick. We met a girl that was lonely and wanted to write someone in Vietnam. Geez... what a time to meet a lonely girl.

The trucks finally came for transport to the plane. I swear most of the company was drunk or trying to get that way. Dick Stafford, Tom Borges, and I flew to Wake Island. There's not much there. We walked around and stretched our legs while the plane was being refueled and readied for the last leg of this trip. The stop lasted 20 minutes. Many died here protecting this airstrip during World War II. We were getting close to our destination and another war zone area. Anticipation of our next stop kept the mood quiet.

I don't know why, but I began to think about my good friend Mike Kellis, actually Private Mike Kellis now. He and I met when we started college our freshman year. We both had made the football team and became best friends from that time on. He was also the guy that got me into this situation. I laughed remembering how Mike would entertain us at parties by playing the guitar and singing songs that he had written. His girl friend, Chris, was a pretty red-head, and lots of fun. She was also the niece of General James Doolittle, the famous WWII flyer. We all thought that was pretty cool.

My mind wandered to an event that occurred at the Edison Rifle Range, at Camp Pendleton, during our Boot Camp days. My good friend, Mike, was probably bored, so he bent down, picked up a rock and threw it at the fence some 30 yards away. The sergeant saw Mike's move and called him on it. He ripped him up one side and down the other using language only a Boot Camp Gunnery Sergeant could. It didn't help that Mike had a slight grin that he couldn't seem to get off his face. A few days later was Sunday and I couldn't find Mike. In fact, I didn't see him until chow was served that evening. When I asked Mike where he had been, he laughed and told me he had been playing baseball with the platoon gunnery sergeant and the Marine Corps baseball team. The sergeant had noticed something about how Mike threw the rock at the rifle range and nabbed him. Mike ended up playing baseball for the Marine Corps – I went to Vietnam. Good for him.

We flew from Wake Island to Camp Hansen, Okinawa. Upon our arrival, we were directed to the Receiving Area and then to the barracks. We filled out forms all night long...name, address, next of kin, etc. We were truly going into a war zone. You could feel the quiet, sober demeanor that was present. There wasn't any question to why we were asked to fill out forms asking for next of kin. If we were killed in Vietnam, they wanted to know where to ship our bodies. Wow! Pretty scary thoughts. When all the paperwork was finished, we were then given a pillow, a sheet and assigned to a tin Quonset hut for sleeping the few hours left in the night.

August 8 - We had most of the day to ourselves, so I tried to find Roesch Kispaugh. He was Rick Grabenhorst's friend (my buddy from Salem) and supposed to be stationed here. No luck finding Roesch. The night was quite eventful, though. Tom, Dick, Glen and I went to the enlisted club. We drank a large amount of beer. Tom was not used to drinking much. He got drunk and got our group into a fight. We did some damage on the other guys, they reported us to the Military Police (MP's) and they came looking for us, ten of them. They saw Dick, thinking he was me. Well,...another scrap. We faired quite well and headed back to our barracks for sleep. Tom, Dick and I were mighty proud of ourselves, as we left for Vietnam, the next morning.

Lieutenant Lee Suydam

We kids grew up on cowboy movies and WW II films. Shows like Combat and Victory at Sea were popular on television. When we played, we played cowboys and Indians, or war.

LT LEE SUYDAM
Montgomery, Alabama

Every young man in my day had, by law, a six-year military obligation to satisfy. If he did not choose, then he would be subject to the draft. I liked the military stuff. I joined the drill team. We marched and paraded, we gave and took orders and we considered the possibility of a career in the U.S. Military.

I went to Auburn University, where graduates with four years of ROTC, were guaranteed a commission, if they went into the service.

The Marine Corps had a program called the Platoon Leaders Class (PLC). It consisted of two boot camps, one after the freshman year and one after the junior year. I joined up. In the summer of 1965, I spent 10 weeks of boot camp at Quantico, Virginia. I returned to college for the first quarter of my sophomore year, but I was not doing well. I had no direction or interest and my grades were failing. Having flunked out, I received a draft notice in a matter of weeks. As it was, I had already enlisted in the Marines and was on my way to Paris Island, South Carolina.

Paris Island Boot Camp was 8 weeks long followed by another 12 weeks of Infantry Training at Camp LeJeune, North Carolina. With my previous training, I was a standout. I was selected for an enlisted commissioning program. So, from Infantry Training, I went to another boot camp at Quantico for ten weeks of Officer's Candidate School (OCS). Upon graduation, I was commissioned a 2nd Lieutenant and sent off to 26 weeks of The Basic School (TBS) at Quantico, Virginia. TBS was intense training in tactics, logistics, map reading, military law and history, leadership, and command. My classmates were mostly college graduates, including some from the Naval Academy in Annapolis. I graduated 56th in a class of 250. I was 176 pounds of twisted blue steel and sex appeal, we liked to say.

Upon graduation, I took leave and was to report from leave to San Francisco for a flight to Vietnam. At home, I received an extension of my leave. I was to ship out on my 21st birthday, June 29, 1967. I believe someone noticed that I was only 20 and did not want me in Vietnam, as an officer at that age.

The night before my departure, I tried to get into a bar in San Francisco. Wouldn't you know it? I got carded. The bouncer was so apologetic, but firm in denying me entrance. I gave up. It wasn't worth it. We flew a charter jet to Da Nang. On the way, we refueled at Wake Island. What an experience. I've since read a lot about Wake Island. From the air it looks like a dot in the Pacific. The Island is only a little bit longer than the runway and so narrow, you can seen the surf lapping on both shores just by turning your head. There are only a few junky looking buildings there.

When we got to Da Nang, they put us into some barracks at the end of a runway. Jet planes took off over our heads all night. Did they do that just to scare the hell out of us? The next day we were put on trucks to take us to our respective units. I can still remember that day, like it was yesterday. Never before or since have I seen such a deep lush green everywhere I looked, bamboo and rice. Beautiful young girls walking to market, with a duck and some vegetables to sell, squatted by the roadside to pee. When they smiled, their teeth were black surrounded by blood red, the indelible stain of the peasant narcotic chew - beetle nut.

CPL. CHUCK ESTES
Dallas, Texas

Corporal Estes
Although I graduated from high school in Victoria, Texas, I didn't consider it home, as I had attended over 20 schools. I never got to know anyone very well. I became a bookworm, reading every history and war book I could. Without money to attend college, I began building pipelines in Virginia, North Carolina, Texas, Louisiana and Colorado. We

worked in snow, mud and heat...lived in cheap motels and run down apartments 6-7 days a week. It wasn't much of a life, but I found out that if you worked hard, people took notice of you and went out of their way to kid around with you...there was no social stigma being the new kid in school any more...I came out of my shell with the laughter and jokes of the men working around me. Somewhere in those 10 hour work days, I discovered I wanted an education. I was tired of leather gloves and dirty clothes and a life of only work. With the money I had saved, I enrolled in Arlington State College in 1964. I lived in a dorm and for the first time in my life discovered everyone was new and wanted to make friends with each other. It reinforced the social awareness that I had learned on the pipeline and gave me a whole new outlook on life. Taking after my father's master mechanic background, I chose to study Mechanical Engineering. I read everything in those days...2-3 newspapers a day and even learned of the Marines landing in Vietnam, in March of 1965. I felt guilty about sitting out the war and in December 1965, I went to the Marine recruiter in Fort Worth. I then reported in for a physical and finally to the Dallas Induction Center, which was a dirty place. The people were cold and very unfriendly and I decided against joining.

I returned to my college life, the apartment with a swimming pool and the girls that were everywhere. It felt pretty good. After enrolling back into college in January of 1965, with a new semester, new classes, etc, I still felt guilty about not signing up. With the new term, tests started, also. I was taking a full load, including four hours of physics. The first test just killed me and I dropped the class and without thinking about it. My status was now part time.

Two weeks later, my mother called...she was crying...saying she had received a notice from the Draft Board and for me to report for a physical. I called the same recruiter I had talked to earlier. He told me to be in Dallas at 5 am the next morning and they would swear me in. I was now 20 years old and in the Marine Corps. I had a year of construction work, a year of college behind me, had only one girl friend, but was beginning to experience life...eager to be a Marine.

Before I left Arlington for boot camp, five of my friends and I piled into a car after a few six packs of beer. We drove half the night to a whorehouse across the border in Mexico. I think it was the first time I had ever been drunk. It was fun....we took turns on the ride down, throwing half empty beer cans at highway signs, along the highway....laughing and joking all at 60, 70, and 80 miles per hour. It's a wonder we lived. The ride back the next morning was hell, as we all had hangovers. It wasn't near as much fun as the ride down. I went home after that and spent a week with my family. It broke my Mother's heart, when I left for Marine Corps Depot, San Diego. And, then... Vietnam.

Chris

Each of the guys to whom I would later place the safety of my life in their hands were as ignorant as they were young regarding the situation that would soon unfold. We were headed to war. We didn't even know what that meant. We would just follow directions and tried as hard as we could to stay alive. Doc Turner was the oldest non-com (non-commissioned officer was an E-4 rank or higher) among us at 25 years old. Estes, House and I followed at 21, 20 and 20 years, respectively. Most of the others that would form our squad would be a few years our junior. They would be right out of high school, some as graduates, some not. Not many years to gain any experience in life itself, let alone going into a war.

I remember going to my first college class at Southern Oregon College. I had signed up for Introduction to Physics and since I was a freshman I knew I needed to get my science credits out of the way as soon as possible. It wasn't a class I was particularly looking forward to attending, as I knew it would probably be one of the more difficult classes my first term.

Class began an, I mean, it began. There was no "How is everyone doing"? It was a lecture with questions being fired back and forth among the students and the professor. It was as if everyone had been together for the past year and that they had class the day before. As the professor spoke, I tried to take notes. I found it extremely difficult to put anything down on paper. I didn't have a clue what the class was talking about. Everyone in class was attentive and the majority of the students were participating. There wasn't any doubt in my mind that I didn't have what it took to be a college student. I just didn't have what it took. I was not smart enough. I did not belong in this class or in this college.

When the physics class was over, I felt drained and lost. I quickly returned to my dorm room and placed a call home. Home was only four hours north on the highway, but it felt a million miles away. I explained my first day to my parents and about my experience in the physics class. I let them know I would be packing up my bags and leaving college immediately. I just wasn't cut out for college. As we talked, my parents listened carefully, then proceeded to suggest that I at least attend another class or two and get a better perspective on what college was all about. It was true, I was basing my decision to leave on one hour and half class. I had been brought up to learn to make my own decisions, (with a bit of guidance at times). So, with the pep-talk from my parents and a small trace of confidence, I took off across campus to my next college class. I don't remember what the class was or what the next class after that was. I understood the subjects and was greatly relieved and excited to realize that, "yes, I could do this college thing".

The next day, I walked across campus to see my academic advisor. I felt lucky that I had caught him in his office and that he would see me. I explained my predicament. I learned that I had accidentally been assigned to an upper-division physics class for juniors and seniors. My class schedule was changed and I left his office, relieved and probably with a smile. College might be okay.

Now we were headed to war, with somewhat the same feeling as I had experienced when I first went off to college - unprepared. At that time, I was 18 years old, just out of high school, three months prior. I didn't know anything. I sure didn't know if I was prepared for the task before me. Now, the same feelings of being under-prepared were being felt by each of us as we left out for a country so far away. We sure didn't understand the political ramifications or policy of our presence in Vietnam.

For me, it took longer than I wanted to feel as if I could take care of myself and help with the safety of my squad. There was so much to learn and it had to be done right the first time. At the beginning of my combat tour, I was totally lost. And scared. It was a comfort later on to learn that those around me had exactly the same feelings.

Doc Turner
July 20 - After a few days, and seemingly a thousand shots later, we are on our way to the war. It was seemingly one of the longest airplane rides that I ever took. As we approached Vietnam, we began circling the Da Nang Airfield and noticed there were flares everywhere. You could look out the airplane window and see explosions and smoke on the ground throughout the area around the airfield. I was scared. Brandy time. I pulled out that bottle of brandy and asked the stewardess for a couple of glasses of ice. She ask me "what for?" I told her it was for a special time. She brought three glasses of ice and sat on my lap and we drank to the USA, me, Mike and her. She was absolutely a beautiful person, inside and outside, from Georgia, of course. We killed that bottle before the plane touched down on the Da Nang airport runway.

We got off the plane and onto a couple of cattle trailers that hauled us to a terminal. Once there, we unloaded and walked inside. They brought in our seabags, filled with clothing items we had packed stateside and laid them on the floor. I had none. My seabags had been lost in Okinawa. We were told to line up against the wall. After a while, we laid down and went to sleep, probably just passed out. The airplane that brought us here was refueled and reloaded with new troops that were going somewhere, probably back to the states. The plane took off before we were settled down for the night. I watched the plane disappear. It somehow made the night feel even more lonely.

Slater and I were assigned to Echo Company under the leadership of Doc John Weed. We were both in the same platoon and didn't see many of the other corpsmen, as we were kept busy "learning the ropes and tricks...keeping our heads down and not up our rectums."

Jerry Slater became a super planner and always had everything ready ahead of time. He quickly acquired a large box, 4x4x6 square, and had it filled with all, and I mean all the supplies that we, as line-corpsmen, could possibly use - bandages, medication, IV replacement fluids with tubing, ointments...you name it, he had it.

LT JIM KIRK
Rocky River, Ohio

Lieutenant Kirk

I was attending Kenyon College in Gambier, Ohio, a highly selective men's liberal arts college. The last night of the semester before Christmas break two fraternity buddies of mine and I had a little too much to drink. We stayed up all night raising hell and showed up in the dining hall for breakfast the next morning with no shirts and a six pack of beer under each arm. It wasn't the first time I got into trouble. The Dean of Students once told my identical twin brother, who also attended Kenyon, that if he had to put one more letter of reprimand in my record, he would have to get an accordion file. It didn't help that a few weeks earlier my friends and I introduced a box of toads into his office. You, see, he looked like a toad and so we called him The Toad. The Dean suspended us for six months. My parents were really angry and not willing to pay for me to enroll in another college. I wound up enlisting in the Marines.

30

Somehow, I always knew I would join the Marines, even as a little boy when I would sing the Marine Corps hymn in the shower. The catalyst was my father's stories about the Marines he encountered during WWII on Saipan (my father was a supply officer in a B29 squadron in the Army Air Corps).

I enlisted in February, 1968. I completed boot camp in San Diego and infantry training at Camp Pendleton. I was ordered to the Engineer School at Camp Lejeune, North Carolina where I completed the electrician's course. However, I didn't want to be an electrician. I wanted to fight. So I applied to Officer Candidate School and was accepted. I was commissioned as a 2nd Lieutenant upon graduation and attended The Basic School, infantry officers' training, at Quantico. When filling out my "dream sheet" indicating my first three choices of assignment, I put down infantry for my first, second and third choices. I got my wish.

The first leg of my trip from Cleveland to Vietnam was a flight to San Francisco. In the airport I ran into Mike Jackson, who had been in my platoon in Basic School (infantry officer training) at Quantico. We decided to get a hotel room together. Mike was booked on a flight out of Travis Air Force Base the next morning, as was I, but his flight was earlier.

Mike got up and left early in the morning. I overslept and realized I had only a short time to catch my flight. I was too late for the military transportation that had been arranged. My only choice was to take a cab, which cost me almost $100, a lot of money in those days. I caught the flight. We stopped in Anchorage, Alaska to refuel, then again in Tokyo, before landing in Okinawa. We spent a week or so at Camp Hansen, getting shots and briefings. The night before we were to leave for Vietnam, three of us (Jack Hewitt, my big, tough, football player roommate from Basic School at Quantico and "Grady" Harreld) went into town and stayed out late. When we returned to our quarters at Camp Hansen, we told a corporal on duty to wake us at a certain hour. He didn't and we missed our flight. Our superiors could have charged us with "missing movement," a serious offense. However, they accepted our excuse and booked us on a flight the next day.

As we were waiting to board the airplane in Okinawa to go to Vietnam, soldiers and Marines returning from Vietnam were milling around, looking at us and calling us "fresh meat." You could tell who the grunts were as opposed to the pogues (the guys in the rear with the gear) – the grunts were lean, sun-tanned and hard looking.

We got on the plane, a chartered commercial aircraft, only to turn back half way there because of bad weather. Jack Hewitt sat next to me on the plane. Jack had too much to drink at the officers club before we left and he was also very scared. He believed we turned back because something catastrophic had happened in Vietnam. When we got back to Okinawa we went back to the officers club.

The next day we finally made our way to Vietnam.

Following article is written by PFC Roger Goss to his home newspaper -
"The Pauls Valley Daily Democrat."
Pauls Valley, Oklahoma

PFC Roger Goss reports from South Vietnam

(EDITORS NOTE: Pfc. Roger Goss, son of Earl Goss, Pauls Valley jeweler, is now in Vietnam with his Marine unit. This is his first report from the war zone.)

Phoun Loc, RVN
18 miles south of Da Nang
28 March 1967

A Marine arrives in Vietnam anxious and apprehensive from the start.

He left the states in the middle of night. Two days later he arrives over the coast of Vietnam in the middle of night.

The pilot announces that the airfield has been under mortar attack and the plane must circle while the runway is inspected.

As the plane circles, the Marines can see the shadowy countryside below forecasting things to come. Magnesium flares light up scattered scenes of conflict. Red streaks of tracer rounds slice the darkness. Little areas seem to sparkle and glitter with muzzle flashes from rifles, grimly beautiful.

"Man I never thought there was so much stuff going on all the time," one Marine comments.

Marines are silent as the plane finally lands.

At the Marine air terminal, men are herded into an open air auditorium and separated according to their assignments in Vietnam. The rest of the night is spent filling sandbags and building bunkers.

Next day representatives from various commands come to the terminal to take charge of replacements and transport them to their new assignments.

Marines load into trucks and begin the ride to their outposts. Marines load their weapons as the truck drives off the airbase.

Although the ride is uneventful the replacements are nervous. They point out to each other some of the sights that bore men who've been in Vietnam for months.

There are real pagodas, rice paddies, little farmers in coolie hats, bamboo forests and countryside that seems rich and lush. But the villages and people are so poor. One new Marine asked why. The answer: "Viet Cong tax collectors." A characteristic of the countryside that seems especially ominous; what land isn't being farmed is graveyard. And the graves seem endless.

Arrival at the outpost is hectic and surprising to the new men.

The hectic part is drawing new gear. Rifles and ammo, flack jackets, canteens, shelter halves, cots, blankets, ad infinitum.

The surprise is that facilities are available and in quantity. There's electricity, showers with plenty of hot water, a PX, a club with soft drinks and beer rations, movies at night. The chow is good and plentiful.

After the new men have put up all their gear they are given an indoctrination lecture by their new company commander. He ends his lecture with this advice: "Men don't ever lapse into a false sense of security; never relax men, never relax."

Later at the club his lesson is graphically and poignantly illustrated.

A patrol comes in. The Marines are filthy with sweat and dusty. Their faces are drawn and set. Their eyes stare from hollow eye sockets.

At the sighting of the patrol, one Marine yells to them: "Hey, hurry up. Tell Olsen I've got his beer waiting for him." The men in the patrol just stare at the man. They say nothing.

Then the Marine realized what the stares meant.

"No! No! Not Olsen! Not Olsen!"

Other Marines gather around the patrol and talk in hushed tones. Several turn away cursing. One kicks over a trash can. Another smashes his fist against a wall.

"How?"

"One crummy round from one cruddy sniper!"

The new men uncomfortably watch the scene. They are beginning to understand.

Corporal Olsen's best friend on the same patrol collapses from exhaustion on a bench, his face buried in his hands. He can't be more than 19, but he is a man.

3

The Enemy...the Cong...the NVA

Charlie knew the true purpose of their booby traps, as they weren't made to kill, but to maim.

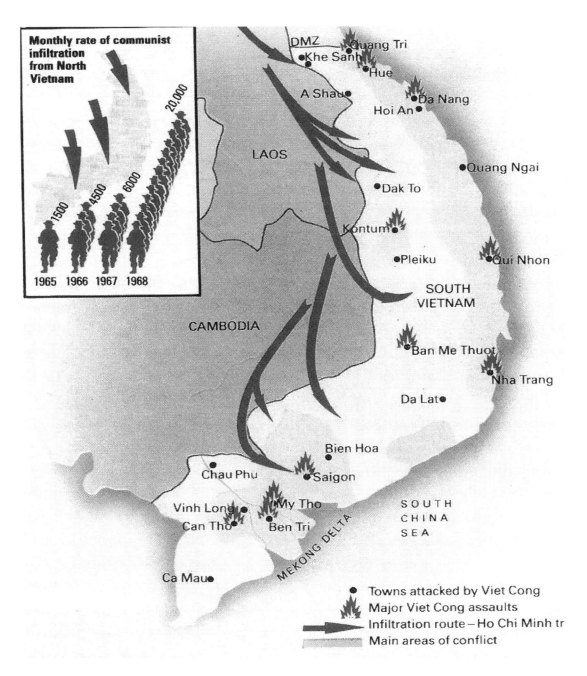

Monthly rate of communist infiltration from North Vietnam

20,000

1500 4500 6000

1965 1966 1967 1968

DMZ
Quang Tri
Khe Sanh
Hue
A Shau
Da Nang
Hoi An
LAOS
Quang Ngai
Dak To
Kontum
Pleiku
Qui Nhon
SOUTH VIETNAM
CAMBODIA
Ban Me Thuot
Nha Trang
Da Lat
Bien Hoa
Chau Phu
Saigon
Vinh Long
My Tho
Can Tho
Ben Tri
SOUTH CHINA SEA
Ca Mau
MEKONG DELTA

● Towns attacked by Viet Cong
Major Viet Cong assaults
Infiltration route – Ho Chi Minh tr
Main areas of conflict

By putting one Marine down, others were required to administer aid, therefore, rather than kill one guy, they took 2-3 men out of the battle, thus reducing the action of their enemy. Anytime we ran across areas that we thought might have booby traps, we were slowed down considerably. We ran into a wide range of booby traps: sharp bamboo sticks or punji sticks (with a sharpened tip one would liken to a piece of broken glass, then dipped in excrement to effectively poison them), trip wires with attached grenades, pressure devices, activated by stepping on and then releasing your foot from the device, a bamboo whip with punji sticks attached, dud unexploded artillery shells and aircraft bombs.

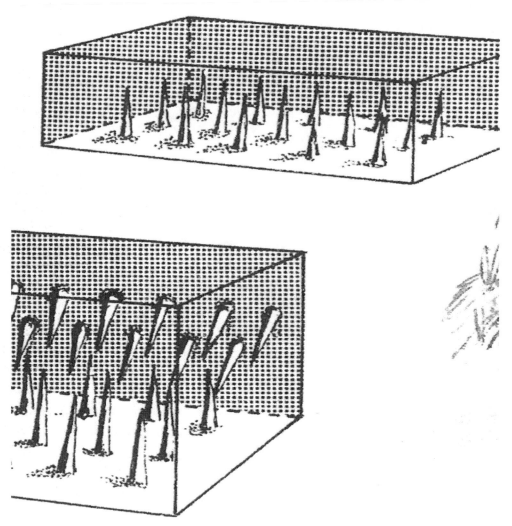

History would call them a formidable enemy - a tireless and ingenious enemy...an enemy that had been through war with other outsiders before. They had fought the French in the 50's and sent them home, not long before the U.S. invaded their land - they were the Viet Cong. They were the field workers and the storekeepers, but they were also the enemy. You couldn't look at them and tell if their alliance was with the United States and the South Vietnamese government in the effort to turn back the communist troops from North Vietnam. They worked their crops of rice during the daytime, working at all the tasks of providing for their families, yet at night, it all changed.

The uniform of the Viet Cong was a floppy jungle hat, rubber sandals, and green fatigues without insignia. Quite often the Viet Cong wore a black top and bottom pajamas. Both of these types of clothing worked well for blending in the jungle. They carried very little other than the necessary weapons for the specific mission they were on at that time. With little to carry, their movements were stealthy and well executed.

Marines patrolled the villages in order to show support for the South Vietnamese people and their crops. The continued patrols around Da Nang kept the Viet Cong from harassing the villagers - capturing or recruiting the young men or stealing their rice. The patrols also supported keeping the Viet Cong weaponry far enough away from harming the airfield in Da Nang. Day time patrols had to slowly explore their route down each and every trail leading up to the villages. The villagers knew where the explosives were buried and for this their cows were captured and led down many trails to clear the trail and make safe the route for the Marines. The Vietnamese didn't like this, but it happened. If their cow stepped on a mine and was blown up, they would be paid for their loss, most of the time.

The VC were especially ingenious in booby-trapping the paths the Marines would travel during both day and night patrols. The VC planted numerous devices in the path of their enemy - trip wires crossing the pathways and hooked up to grenades and pressure sensitive explosives, which were armed when someone would unknowingly walk on top of a mine and ignited when the foot released the downward pressure, as they continued to walk. In any type of action, the first move was either to return fire or to hit the ground in a defensive move. Often a move to the ground resulted in leaving the trail and diving off to one side. By leaving the trail, we subjected ourselves to the possibility of landing on punji sticks. The VC planted these stakes everywhere. You didn't see them until it was too late.

Whenever a U.S. grenade fell into VC hands, it usually ended up as a temporary booby trap. It was used in the same way as the night alarms. The grenade was secured to a bamboo splint with string or rubber bands. The grenade pin was replaced with a safety pin (like those used with baby diapers). After nightfall, the grenade could be set with a string across a trail and the safety pin unclasped. So now, the sleeping VC would hear a BLAM! ... instead of a clatter. Hopefully, the VC would also achieve a few U.S. casualties in the process. The safety pin arrangement facilitated the retrieval of the booby trap before dawn. Re-clasping the safety pin rendered the grenade safe until it was used again.

The Viet Cong were ingenious guerrilla fighters who were adept at developing simple homegrown devices and techniques to thwart the might and technology of the US war machine. The VC Security Alarm was an excellent example of that ingenuity. At nightfall, VC who took refuge in a village, or simply returned home, would set out alarms to keep from being surprised by marine night patrols.

The alarm is built with a tin can. Two bamboo splints are lashed to its sides with rubber bands or string. One splint is longer than the other, so that it can be pushed into the soft rice paddy mud to hold the device about 12 to 18 inches above the ground. The two splints extend above the can top, actually the can bottom now facing skyward. A washer or a flattened bottle cap with a hole in it is suspended between the two upright splints by rubber bands so that it can be twisted up like a propeller on a toy airplane. Now a small stick is placed through the hole in the washer to keep it from spinning. A string tied to the stick is pulled across a trail and tied off in the brush.

Now when an intruder hits the string in the darkness, the stick comes out of the washer and the washer spins, striking the tin can with a loud metallic chatter. It's like a fire alarm bell in the middle of the night when maximum stealth is being applied. The chatter of one of these alarms will flatten a marine patrol and bring their hearts into their throats. The beauty of these alarms is that they can be taken up before dawn, hidden and no one is the wiser. The NVA and the VC used the AK-47 automatic rifle as their primary weapon. The AK-47, first developed by the Russians in 1946/47, was one of the first true "assault rifles". The People's Republic of China, the main supplier of weaponry to the enemy, manufactured this weapon throughout the war. The AK-47 was especially suited for jungle warfare - it could be submerged while crossing streams, gathering sediment throughout the working areas of the rifle and would fire without delay, when needed. It was extremely durable, had a low production cost, very easy to use and held a 30 round magazine.

When night time fell, the rules changed. The men of the villages, plus others that lived in the forests became guerrilla fighters and planted booby traps, punji sticks and other maiming devices in the entrances to their villages and other avenues of approach - the rivers, stream beds, etc. Anyone, even children, were taught how

to set-up the explosive mines that ultimately caused injury to so many young Marines. Nightfall meant everyone was to be in their hooch (a thatched hut). If a villager was seen outdoors at night, he was shot. It was a free-fire zone. The rules of engagement had changed. It was war.

The VC harassed the villagers continuously to support their cause or they were punished - beat-up or killed, women raped and crops taken. The Vietnamese were in a difficult situation, being pulled in both directions, to either support their present government or support the communist led Viet Cong. Either way, they lost. Showing support for one side led them to be an enemy of the other side.

It did not take long before combat Marines lost trust in the villagers. We learned we could not trust anyone. It was a fact. We had been burned too many times. Too often we would enter a village, only to lose a man to sniper fire. As soon as the shot sounded and the man hit dropped to the ground, there were no signs of the attack. The Marines dropped to the ground and waited, searching the

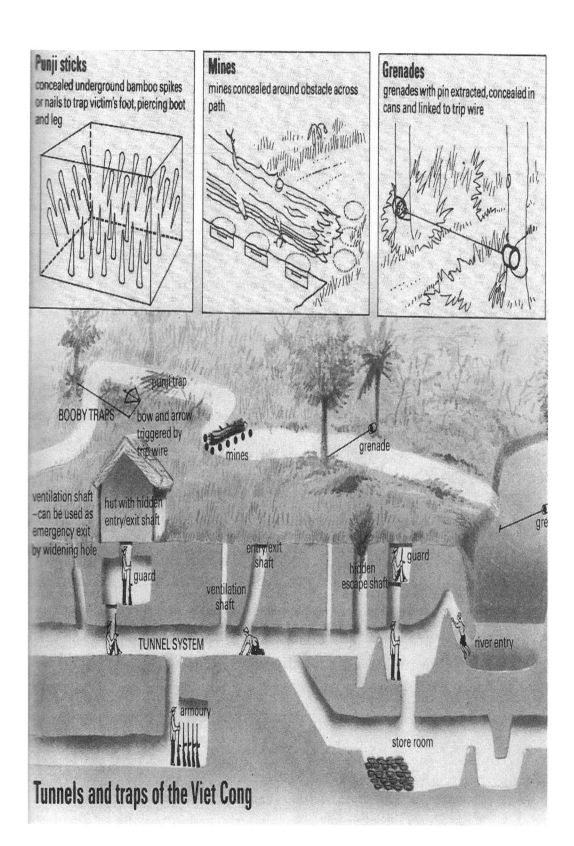

Punji sticks
concealed underground bamboo spikes or nails to trap victim's foot, piercing boot and leg

Mines
mines concealed around obstacle across path

Grenades
grenades with pin extracted, concealed in cans and linked to trip wire

punji trap

BOOBY TRAPS — bow and arrow triggered by trip wire

mines

grenade

ventilation shaft – can be used as emergency exit by widening hole

hut with hidden entry/exit shaft

entry/exit shaft

hidden escape shaft

guard

gre

guard

ventilation shaft

river entry

TUNNEL SYSTEM

armoury

store room

Tunnels and traps of the Viet Cong

landscape for some sign of where the killing round had come from. It was silence. No additional firing. There might not be any more action that day. The next time we would visit the same village, the same thing would happen - one round, one dead Marine. It wore terribly on us. Anger built up, frustration was evident and sometimes inappropriate action might occur - a full squad might open up on one villager seen running, unloading a tremendous amount of ammo. A hooch might be blown up. Interrogation might be a bit forceful. It was so difficult to continuously go through the same scenario. The villagers knew so much more than we could get out of them, at least we thought they did.

The sly, quick and deadly actions of the VC agitated the Marines daily. The VC disappeared as soon as their shots were fired. The tunnel systems used by the VC were complex. It hid the fighters, its ammo, food and supplies, sometimes for hundreds of VC. The underground tunnels turned and twisted, creating a complex maze that was extremely difficult to penetrate. When a tunnel was found, one individual would enter the tunnel, armed only with a .45 automatic pistol and a flashlight. Those tempting to take this position of "tunnel rat" were small in stature and the bravest we had. Quite often the tunnel rats might be met by a snake, coiled and in-wait. A trip wire or other explosive devices were common. As the tunnel rat entered the hole, the enemy could easily move themselves a 100-200 yards away and be gone. Anything of value that was found would normally be blown up where it laid. Living quarters were partitioned to allow for cooking, living and storage of supplies. Destroying the tunnels was extremely difficult.

NVA
(NORTH VIETNAMESE ARMY)

The big brother and partner of the Viet Cong was the North Vietnamese Army (NVA). These were the professionally trained soldiers from up north - North Vietnam. They had history. Their families had fought, their grandfathers had fought, they were well organized and battle tested through the generations - it was a matter of "national pride".

They would come *en masse*, to the lower area of South Vietnam, with a mission and under the direction of their President Ho. They would travel by truck, bicycle, or walk the entire trip to reach their destination below the Demilitarized Zone (DMZ). Elephants were utilized to help move supplies.

The troops would carry their rifles, ammo and food the entire trip, stopping along the way at base camps or staging areas for rest, nourishment and supplies. They would travel the Ho Chi Minh Trail to cross the DMZ and either into South Vietnam at the border or travel south in Laos and into South Vietnam further south. The triple canopy jungle provided cover from the US planes overhead, as well as the well-established wooden built camps.

The U.S. troops were prohibited from crossing into Laos or Cambodia to chase the NVA, which allowed the continuous movement of thousands of troops and their supplies to strategic areas throughout South Vietnam.

The NVA were supplied tanks, artillery, mortars and ammo by China, Russia and North Korea. Additional battlefield advisors were also brought in to aid the NVA in their quest.

Bicycles carried up to 400 pounds of weight and were thus effective transport vehicles bringing in weapons, ammo, rice and medical supplies down the Ho Chi Minh Trail.

Corporal Goss wrote to his hometown newspaper throughout his tour. The following article is one of many to follow where Goss shares insight through his writings. This article is regarding Booby Traps.

(EDITOR'S NOTE: Roger Goss, a serviceman from Pauls Valley writes another letter from the war front in South Vietnam.)

VIET CONG booby traps. Sometimes they seem to be everywhere. Some are deadly; some only maim. Some are primitive and crude, others are ingenious and sophisticated. They are all dreaded.

Aside from the injuries they inflict, they are also a nemesis to the nerves. Sometimes you think each step may bring the blinding flash, noise and pain—or the indescribable black nothingness.

The crude V. C. traps are merely stone age animal traps set for man. The Chinese man trap is a deep pit with sharpened stakes at the bottom to impale a man who might step through the camouflaged covering. The spikes are called punji stakes and are usually covered with a crude poison; human defecation, deadfalls, a weighted platform with punji stakes, are suspended above a path. Trip the wire strung across the path and it falls on you.

The Malay gate is a strong sapling bent back into the brush alongside a trail. Spring the string across the trail and the sapling with punji stakes snaps into you.

+ + +

THE TRAP may be just a small hole filled with downward pointing barbed stakes. Step into it and you're caught and can't get out. Then there are the cross bows and plain old bear traps plus hundreds of other variations.

One of the V. C. favorites is to insert a grenade into a tin can. Tie a wire to the grenade a n d stretch i t to something across a path, then pull the safety pin on the grenade. A soldier catches the wire on his foot, pulling the grenade out of the can, letting the spoon fly and the grenade explodes. Or they may suspend a mortar round in a tree. A wire is tripped allowing the round to fall to the ground and explode on impact. A mine may be electrically detonated when it would do the most good by a V. C. hidden at a safe distance.

The entrances to Charley's caves are especially dangerous. If the bottom is not booby-trapped there may be deadly cobras or bamboo vipers hung by their tails from the ceiling and anxious to strike at anything entering the cave.

+ + +

THE VIET CONG know where to set the traps to take advantage of American traits; places of comfort (a shady spot on a trail), objects of value or curiousty, or a short cut through the jungle. And they are experts at camouflage. A trip wire may be only a vine.

The only defense is extreme caution. Watch each step. Carefully inspect each thing you touch. Step in the tracks of the man in front of you.

Try to second guess Charlie. If I were Charlie, where would I put a booby trap?

Sometimes even the greatest care isn't enough. Sometimes all you can really do is hope.

ROGER GOSS

4

First Days – First Combat

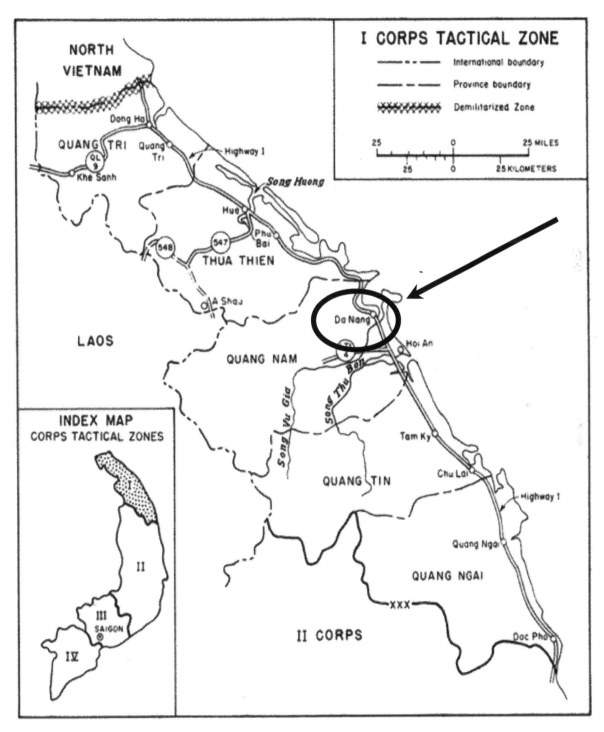

Along with other Marine units, the 2nd Battalion, 1st Marines, were in the I Corps Area, the northernmost area of Vietnam.

Near the city of Da Nang, we spent our time patrolling around small villages, and hopefully keeping the NVA and Viet Cong from establishing themselves in these areas. We were there to keep the VC troops far enough away, so they couldn't fire rockets onto the Da Nang Air Base and the runways. The NVA were using this time to buildup ammo and supplies for the Tet Offensive, which would begin early the following year.

Initially, our job became one of overseeing the villages and the inhabitants and keeping a watchful eye on enemy movement, especially at night. The enemy was initiating terrorist activities in the rice growing areas around Da Nang. They threatened Vietnamese farmers in order to obtain a portion of the rice harvest that the individual farmer stored on his property. The enemy frequently moved confiscated rice over waterways to avoid land patrols and check points. We were to seek out the Viet Cong, their arms, food caches and destroy it all, while preserving the peace for the villagers. Also, what we learned early on was that the Vietnamese often tilled the fields in the day and planted booby-traps and mines at night. Our job at night became one of setting up ambush sites at likely entrances to villages and meeting and destroying the enemy. The daytime conflicts were always dealing with snipers, booby-traps and small groups of Viet Cong. The North Vietnamese Army (NVA) presence at this time was light in this area, during the months of August and September, but would dramatically increase in the months that followed.

Constant day and night patrols kept the VC from launching major operations against the base.

Press releases were constantly being sent out to the U.S. mainland, and also were published in military newspapers like the Sea Tiger and the Stars and Stripes for the troops to read. The following is an example of an episode where Echo Company encountered VC attacks five times during a short operation.

L/Cpl Dennis Knobloch (Knobby)
July 18 - We just got done chasing a bunch of jailbirds. 1,400 VC prisoners broke out of a prison camp about 10 miles south of here and Echo and Hotel companies from our battalion. were sent down to find them. We didn't do anything too out of the ordinary but I did get a taste of close air support. Our

platoon had just crossed a river and we were receiving enemy fire from our front. We couldn't see the gooks because the undergrowth was too thick but we knew they were only about 250 meters in front of us. Our Lieutenant had us stop moving forward and then he radioed for an air strike. Within 10 minutes we had two jet phantoms softening up the area in front of us. I have a lot more respect for jets now. Those guys have a big bag of tricks.

July 21 - Late in the afternoon about 3 days ago we were trucked about 10 miles south of the battalion. area to a place that was referred to by our Captain as simply "District". It was a pretty big village by Vietnamese standards. The platoon sgt. told me that it housed a lot of records on tax collections, etc. and acted somewhat like a county courthouse in the U.S. Our intelligence reports said that about 100 NVA regulars had moved to the area and banded together 1,000 plus local VC Our battalion commander moved Echo and Hotel companies down into the village to try to prevent the VC from over-running it. We waited for 2 nights and one day but the goods never showed up. I think it was probably a bad intelligence report which would be par for the course. We've been going out after companies, battalions and regiments of VC ever since I got here but I've yet to see more than 15 or 20 at one time. It's getting to be a joke anymore whenever the Captain or the Lieutenant says there is a battalion of gooks in the area, we just laugh. It isn't that we're over-confident because 2 or 3 snipers can cause a lot of damage, but these intelligence reports are ridiculous. If they say we are going out after 2 or 3 snipers we had best watch out because there will probably be a regiment waiting for us.

Our Company was supposed to return to the battalion area this morning, which I imagine they did. I don't know for sure though since I was medevaced from the field yesterday morning with the chills, nausea and a high fever. They brought me to the 1st Battalion medical station (1 mile west of Da Nang air base) and that is where I am right now they thought I might have had malaria at first, but all the tests turned out negative. This afternoon Doc told me I would be able to go back to Echo in another day or so. I think I just had another touch of the dingy fever. I feel real good now.

Doc Turner

July 21 - In the morning, we were awakened by explosions, far off, and were told to go down the road about four hundred meters to a mess tent and eat breakfast. I ate like a horse. I was starving. Anything they put in front of me was gone in a second. We washed up the mess gear and came back to where we had been. Later on, we lined up and waited to be assigned to a Marine unit. The first thing was roll call. The second thing was to ask for volunteers for Force Recon (FR). One wormy looking little guy did and the sergeant nearly died laughing. He gently pushed him back in line and walked down and stopped in front of Mike and me. We said, "No" in unison. Then he said he would call out some names and that they were to step forward and would be classed as FR volunteers. Our names weren't called. Mike was assigned to 3rd Battalion, 1st Marine Regiment, 1st Marine Division (3/1) and I was assigned to 2nd Battalion, 1st Marine Regiment, 1st Marine Division (2/1). We grabbed our gear and said goodbye. That was the last time I ever saw or heard from Mike. I hope and pray he made it.

The first few days in the battalion compound of 2/1 were uneventful, except for the frickin' big artillery guns going off at all hours of the night. Extremely loud. The first time it happened, I jumped (fell) out of the cot.

We spent the next few days getting field gear and learning what we needed in our first aid kits. I remember getting issued my Colt .45 automatic sidearm. It was still in the cosmoline petroleum packing material, meaning it was new. It took me three days to get it cleaned. Ithaca was the model. I loved it.

After we were there in the battalion area about a week, I got assigned to go on a road mine sweep detail. It was with Echo Company. They called themselves the Echo Raiders. Boy! They were so cool. Or, so I thought. They had just returned from Operation Canyon City, where they had killed quite a few NVA that had tried to sneak up on them. They were really pissed about the new M-16 rifles they had been issued.

The rifle had problems because of the weapon jamming problem. Most of the Marines had their own personal weapons. It wasn't long after I arrived (couple of months) that Marines having personal weapons were forced to give them up (.45 caliber grease guns, .45 automatic pistols, and .38 caliber pistols) and to send them home. Hanoi Hanna advertised on radio what kind of weapons were used and the Top Brass got pressure from the 'crats in Washington D.C. to use only government issued weapons. One of the guys had twin pearl handle .38 specials that were truly a prize to look at. Another had a grease gun, another had a Thompson Machine Gun and the list went on.

After about one hour into our search for land mines, we found one. It was on the roadway to regimental headquarters. It was also, the first time that I think I was personally shot at. The bastard missed. I had a real hard time getting down closer to the ground. The Marine uniforms have the very thickest buttons on their shirts. I kept waiting for somebody to holler "corpsman up", but it never happened, thank God.

After that shot, I think every one of the Marines returned fire. Anyway, we never got another shot from the sniper and we finished the road sweep without incident. We, Slater and I, went several more times on mine sweep patrols with Echo Company and never were shot at again. I guess we started to trust the guys in Echo Co and we began to feel the Marines were becoming comfortable with us and our ability to aid them, if they incurred battle injuries. We were assigned to Echo after we were there about three weeks in country. I'll never forget the confidence that the company had in Jerry and me and the confidence we had in them as our protectors.

After joining Echo, there was a big black sergeant assigned to guard me and teach me how to walk and move when sweeping a rice paddy field and moving in line with the others in the company. He soon had confidence that I would make it. We had many discussions about the woods, nature and stuff. I was his last assignment and he shipped out for the states shortly after. After joining the company, Jerry and I found that a whole bunch of us were in Field Med School together, including Miller and McArthur. There were four more, but I can't remember their names.

I had not gotten my gear stowed and put up, when along come two Marines, Keller and Dodd. They look me over real good and critically and say, "Could you kill somebody?" What? You heard us. I answered 'em. "If he was trying to kill me or you, yes"! They said ok, and turned around and walked away.

The following press release was written by Corporal Steve Bernston, Combat Correspondent, known to his friends as "Bernie". Corporal Bernston was assigned to Echo Company for most of his tour.

It was always "out there somewhere" that if Bernie wrote a story about you, you'd be a "hero" in your home town. Articles were often sent to a Marine's hometown. It was good for morale, good for the family, and good for the town to see one of their own doing well.

Bernie enjoyed talking with each of the guys, as we also enjoyed his time. He was someone with more information about where we were or what we might be doing, as he spent some of his time with the command group. He was always listening, so therefore he picked up info all the time and shared the news with us. He became one of the only "sources" we had.

FORCE INFORMATION OFFICE
III MARINE AMPHIBIOUS FORCE
MILITARY ASSISTANCE COMMAND VIETNAM
C/O FPC SAN FRANCISCO
CALIFORNIA 96602

Release No: 2058-67   Da Nang Press Center
1st Marine Division Release No: 899-67   Da Nang, Vietnam
By: Cpl Steve L. Bernston   Tel: Puma

<u>FOR IMMEDIATE RELEASE</u>

Da Nang, Vietnam.   July 4----Using the Viet Cong's favorite tactic---night movement----the 2nd Bn., 1st Marine Regiment, 1st Marine Division, accounted for two confirmed VC kills as they moved into position for Operation Calhoun.

The lead element of the battalion was "E" Co., commanded by Capt Thomas Pratt, (Raytown, Missouri).

The battalion moved seven miles in the morning darkness June 25, to position themselves for the five-day operation which took place 17 miles south of Da Nang.

During their night march, "E" Co., was ambushed 5 times by a small VC force.

The first enemy ambush occurred at the gate leading into the village of Chien Son (1) at 5:30 am.

This time the Viet Cong, using an AK-47 automatic weapon and an M-1 rifle fired almost point blank into the point fire team, killing 1 Marine and wounded 3 others.

The VC were unsuccessful in setting up a Claymore mine found later by Marine's searching the area.

As the VC attempted to escape, the 1st platoon killed 1.

-

--USMC--

Doc Turner

July 24 - We went several times out on patrol that included those at night to try to find out who was planting the road bombs. One night we were set up and nothing happened until just before dawn. A group of kids came down the road, playing, and we actually watched a 12-year old girl plant a booby trap. None of us believed it, until the patrol found it where we had watched the kids play. We got our butts chewed for that one. None of us could believe that it was done in front of our eyes. Sgt. Bob Cummings, New York City, said that wouldn't happen again on his watch and it didn't. We found her a few days later. I don't know what ever happened to her, but we never saw her again.

Echo was a young company, full of new Marines straight from stateside training. We were given close-to-base patrols that would only last a day or two away from the battalion area. As the guys became more experienced, the patrols became longer and more hazardous, digging deeper into the forest and further from the security of our base.

Bernie

July 25 - I arrived at the Da Nang in-processing center early on the morning of the 27th. After I had my C-rations for breakfast, I was sent up the hill to 1st Marine Division HQ (Task Force X-ray at that time) and eventually found my way to checking in at the half of the Quonset hut that served as a division office for Combat Correspondents (CC).   Eight days later, I was assigned to an experienced CC, Sgt. Bill Christofferson, located at the Chu Lai ISO. I found him just as he was leaving the compound to chopper in on Operation Union II with 3rd Bn, 5th Marines and so began my first combat experience. Six days later, I had learned what life was going to be like as a field Combat Correspondent. After Operation Arizona in late May with 1st Bn, 7th Marines, I was assigned to be the

51

field CC for 2nd Bn, 1st Marines. I had been living in an old villa located off the highway on the way to the coastline Hoi An village. After going out on several platoon three day sweeps of the TAOR (Tactical Area Of Responsibility), I selected Echo Company as the "go get them" group of Marines I felt most comfortable with and thus started my six month journey with Echo Company, from south of Da Nang to Christmas in Con Thien. I got my first purple heart traveling with Echo Company on Operation Calhoun when our platoon was ambushed as we completed an all night march to an observation point in the Arizona Territory.

The July Command Chronology for 2nd Battalion, 1st Marines reports that an emphasis was placed on night patrols. Contact was light. 2nd Battalion, 1st Marines casualties for July: 4 enlisted KIA, 2 officers WIA, 73 enlisted WIA.

Knobby
August 2 - Nothing too exciting has happened here lately. Tomorrow morning we are going out on a 4-5 day patrol a couple of miles southwest of here. We've got a new Lieutenant that is going to take charge of the platoon. He is fresh from Quantico (OCS) and from the way he talks I don't think he knows the first thing about being in the bush. We call him the boy wonder. He has some crazy ideas but I think his attitude will change after he gets shot at a couple of times (especially if it's by his own men – ha!).

Lt. Suydam
August 5 - The 2nd Battalion, 1st Marines (2/1) were in a perimeter in an abandoned village called An Tu 2. South of An Tu, on either side of Highway 1, were the villages of Phong Ngu 1 and Phong Ngu 2. Our purpose was to prevent enemy forces from bringing rockets into range ofthe air base at Da Nang. I joined 2/1 as a newly commissioned 2nd lieutenant and was assigned as platoon commander of the third platoon of Echo Company.

I took over the third platoon from Lt. Pannicci who was like a god to his Marines. He trained me for several weeks and then turned the platoon over and it was mine. The first few weeks were difficult physically, the heat, the sweat, and the realization that you couldn't carry everything you wanted on your back all day, every day. Some things had to be discarded. For example, after struggling unsuccessfully with my Marine Corps skivvy drawers, one day, I just dropped my pants and cut them off with my bayonet. That way I didn't have to take off my boots. Anything that didn't do its job had to go. I didn't wear underwear again until I got back to Okinawa. And then, it just didn't seem natural.

Chris

August 6 – When we landed in Da Nang, we were immediately moved directly to the Transit Receiving Area. We handed in our orders and waited all day for our personal assignments to be called out. It was an actual cluster. Hundreds of guys, with nowhere to go. Not one of us knew what was in store for us. We were so young, inexperienced and sat around waiting for our number (name) to be called. Finally, someone yelled for everyone to fall-in and then the whole group was assigned to working parties, cleaning up cigarette butts and papers on the ground and other activities to kept the group busy and out of trouble. Tom, Dick and I decided that we should skip this activity, so we just silently slipped away. Heck, if they were going to bust us for not going on a working party, what could they do - send us to Vietnam? We decided to take a nap. We slept on the ground. Actually, we ended up spending the night sleeping on the ground, outside the huts and we didn't mind at all.

Early the next morning, formation brought a taste of reality to the picture. Everyone had been fed and assignments were now being given out. Finally, I received my orders. I am being split up from the guys I had trained with. I am going to 2nd Battalion, 1st Marines. I hate the thought of leaving my friends, especially Dick, as we had gotten to be good friends in AIT (Advanced Infantry Training), Camp Pendleton, California. I had even taken Dick up to Santa Ana, to meet Uncle Max, Grace and of course, my cousin, Linda Lee, on a couple of occasions.

The trip out to my new unit, which is located 12 miles SW of Da Nang, was a wild ride, with all the other new guys, plus a few coming back from Rest and Relaxation (R & R) and a small amount of supplies being transported. The open 6BY truck, carrying 8-10 of us, started out at a quick pace, and kept it until we got to the battalion area. The convoy of three trucks traveled as fast as it could through the city streets. Highway #1 is the main north-south road in Vietnam, with offshoots into the bush. It was a very strange feeling, as we passed hundreds of Vietnamese walking next to the road, out in the fields, working in the shops, etc. They were everywhere. Hundreds of them. We were definitely the minority and it felt like it. The looks we received as we traveled along were not those of comfort and joy but cold stares. No cheers for the Marines, who were there to save them from Communism. I felt numb. Everything was unknown – I felt very suspicious of everyone I saw. I was a bit in fear of the unknown. No rifle! I can't imagine we were out somewhere, where ever that was and really without much support. The driver probably had a rifle, didn't he? Geez, better not to think about it, just hope we hit camp soon…some type of security.

What would it be like, how would I do in the face of battle, would I make it back to the states, which seems so far away? I have few thoughts of anything in my past, as each minute I am, again, seeing something new for the first time. Not having a rifle is uncomfortable. What's next?

All the new guys spent the night in the battalion headquarters area, ate chow, watched a movie in an outdoor theater and tried to mentally prepare for the next day. Before the movie started, guys are talking about where they're from and where they're going. Some of the guys, are heading home, others for R&R or those like me, are waiting to be assigned to a combat company, where they'll be for the next 13 months, if they make it that long. The scuttlebutt is about the event that happened last night.

Note: Chris - A Shot in the Dark. One of the first stories I remember being told, shortly after getting to the 2/1 Battalion in August of 1967, was the story about a group of Marines watching an outdoor movie. Those attending, included both the incoming replacements and their counterparts, those lucky enough to be going home. As the Marines watched the movie, some imbibed any alcohol they could get their hands on. One Marine went unnoticed, as he slumped in his chair and assumed to be drunk by those around him. It was only after the movie was over that it was discovered that he (a short timer with only two days left) was a victim of a stray round. The name of the movie – "A Shot in the Dark."

Doc Turner
August 10 - Doc Miller opened Austin's airway (throat incision) yesterday when we got hit by the VC. We spent one more night out, minus one Marine and Birdie, both of these with fragmentation or blast injuries and Austin wounded by a sniper. Doc Miller and Fisher were the only ones in the squad not hurt by the sniper / booby trap inside the house. I believe that either 7 or 8 were medevaced. Bad day for the squad.

Knobby
August 10 - We just got back this morning from a 3 day patrol. We're going out tonight at 0600 hours but we're coming back in at 0900. Tomorrow we'll probably go on one or two short patrols close to the battalion area. We are supposed to go on an operation on the 12th, but no one really knows for sure.

'Doc' Saves Marine With 'Big Decision'

By Cpl. Steve Berntson

DA NANG — A tracheotomy performed by a corpsman in the field in enemy terrain saved the life of a seriously wounded Marine.

HM Norman E. Miller Jr., (Lawrence, Mass.), "E" Co., 2nd Bn., First Marine Regiment, made the throat incision during an operation August 9.

A squad which Miller was with had moved into a hut for observation after receiving sniper fire while moving into a village. As one Marine moved to a window he tripped a mine under the floor.

"There were five Marines injured in the explosion," recalled "Doc" Miller.

"Right after the explosion, another squad moved to our position along with another corpsman. While he took care of the less seriously wounded, I moved to aid the Marine nearest the explosion," he said.

The most seriously wounded man had several pieces of fragments in his face and neck and was unable to breathe.

"At first I tried the mouth to mouth resuscitation but I found the air was escaping from the wounds in his neck," explained

"I immediately decided he needed a tracheotomy. It was the first one I had ever performed and was the biggest decision I've had to make since I've been a corpsman," said Miller who has been in Vietnam three months.

A medevac helicopter was called in to take out the wounded man despite heavy sniper fire. Miller went along to continue administering aid.

At the hospital Miller spent four hours assisting the doctor in the operating room.

The Marine is now recuperating and awaiting return to the States.

Chris

August 10 - I get my regular pay and now that I'm "in-country" I receive combat pay and overseas pay. It's not much, but it will help when I get home and go back to college. It seems like a long time away from now, but I will get back. I know I will. I somehow feel I will get hurt in 'Nam, but I'll make it home.

My first impressions of Echo Company are good. I was signing papers all day, getting more gear, receiving orientation classes and talks from the doc, chaplain, and Major Joy, a mustang (an individual who started as an enlisted Marine, then became an officer). He explained that Captain Pratt (also a mustang from the Korean War) was the company commander (CO) of Echo Company. We seem to have leaders with good combat experience. It definitely helps us feel more secure.

SGT "SPANKY" BALDWIN
Cuba, New York

August 12 - Sgt. "Spanky" Baldwin is our squad leader. I am assigned to 2nd platoon, 2nd squad, 2nd fire team. He's a hard looking guy who doesn't smile much. He has a leathered face, tanned and unshaven. He seems like a nice guy, a little nervous, but understandably, I find out later, as he has seen continuous action in the field and he is a short-timer (almost ready to rotate home).

The weather is hot. Even when it's raining it's about 95-100 degrees. I feel sweaty all day long, even if I just got out of a shower.

I've got more classes to attend today. All of us new guys are rushed through indoctrination classes on everything - the village people, the jungle, the VC, our rifle, water, water tabs for sanitation, malaria pills, interrogation techniques. It will continue each day, all a part of the process of getting us ready enough to get in the field

August 13 – I will be going out into the field in two days. I have been issued gear for the field, a couple of canteens, a flak jacket, boots, a mess kit and a lot more. Around our neck, we wear our dog tags, our personal identification with name, serial number, religion and our blood type (for obvious reasons) and a P-38 can opener for our C-ration cans. A very few had watches and a few wore glasses, but normally no jewelry, nothing shiny to catch a reflection from the sun, moon or flares in the air…nothing to give an advantage to the enemy. Some carried salt tabs, Zippo lighters with some type of macho saying imprinted and a pack of cigarettes. Most guys smoked. It was a nasty habit picked up in boot camp. Weather is in the high 90's with a cool breeze.

August 14 – I am told by others, that I am lucky to be in Echo Company. It's supposed to be a good company…it makes a guy feel a little bit better, yet still scary. Our captain is Tom Pratt and is well thought of by the men, it seems.

I'm getting to know my squad leader, "Spanky" a little bit better. He always looks salty or a bit dirty, doesn't ever look clean-shaven, has a deep tan and has eyes that are dead – no life. I'm told that this look is the 1,000 yard stare. It completely lacks emotion and tends to focus on nothing. He's been around awhile and I think I'm lucky to be with him.

No nonsense type of guy, nice, quiet, battle-tested. He makes sure I have what I need and then tells me I'll be going with them tomorrow, so be ready.

We received our weapons today and fired, cleaned and again fired our M-16 rifle, the standard 7.5 pound gas-operated assault rifle, which fired most of the time, but not always. The rifle fired a .223 caliber round that was carried in 20-round magazines and in a bandolier across your shoulders which carried an additional 10 magazines of ammo. We received some pay, about $20.00. Not much money, but very little to buy, except cigarettes, writing paper, shaving creme and toothpaste.

Lt. Suydam
August 14 - We were in a line walking along a dike crossing a rice paddy. We came to an intersection of dikes and the men in front of me were jumping across the intersection. It was all heavy with grass. I just didn't see the need to jump so I just walked through. It was an irrigation well. I splashed in over my head and had to be pulled out. I couldn't help thinking, what must my guys be saying? Is this guy going to make it?

Chris

August 15 - My first day in the field was pretty hairy, lots of sniper fire, and mortars, etc. Booby-traps are everywhere. Many mines are set off by tripping or stepping on a wire, which is setup across a path and waiting for someone to drag their boot across the wire. The wire has been hooked up to some type of explosive device or bomb. As the trip wire is pulled, the mine is activated and explodes. Often the device will not kill, but rather will maim the individuals' lower extremities. Another explosive device is triggered by stepping on a pressure sensitive pad, which then actives a bomb.

While walking on the narrow paths, incoming fire may cause Marines to fall off the path looking for cover in the grass or tree line. This is where the gooks place the "punji sticks". There might be 40-100+ of these in one spot. They are very difficult to avoid if you suddenly have to hit the ground or go off the path for cover.

We received fire, hit the ground and returned fire to where we thought the VC were hiding. The gooks know we're around, so we ditched them and later setup an ambush and waited for them. Without getting into any action, we decided to make camp and set up watches for the night and hope we would get a chance later this evening to confront the enemy. We are individually positioned around the perimeter of our ambush site by the squad leader. Individual watches are for two hours at a time. The VC hit us again with small arms fire and a couple of grenades. Unless you see the flash of a rifle, you absolutely don't know where they are hiding. We sprayed an area out in front of us with automatic fire, hoping to hit or hear something. No one is getting much sleep tonight.

We're going to be out for three days. We carry our C-Rations, along with enough ammo, grenades, smoke, claymore mines, C-4 and shoulder rockets for the whole trip, as we won't be resupplied. With everything we have to carry, this heat and constant sun bears down and makes it tough walking. The older guys don't seem to be bothered by the heat. No one really complains about it. It wouldn't change anything. Attitude and morale seem good with the guys.

Lt. Suydam

August 15 - It was in Phong Ngu where our platoon sized missions roved for three to four days at a time. It was a place for snipers, booby traps, occasional firefights and ambush. Each night we would set up in a village, either that or sleep on top of graves in the rice paddies, but after nightfall, we would slip away and set up again under cover of darkness. Invariably, the place we left was fragged during the night. Once during daylight, I left a squad hidden in a village, walked out to Highway 1 and doubled back by a more northern route. The Viet Cong (VC) closed in behind us and our hidden squad was able to ambush them successfully, capturing one VC, which we took to battalion HQ.

Knobby
August 15 - The operation that was rumored didn't come off. We rode security on a truck convoy today. There were over 75 trucks loaded with supplies going to the 5th Marines. We took some sniper fire going down Highway 1, but nobody got hit.

My squad leader's Mother sent him a clipping from his hometown newspaper and I am going to send it home. He sent home some pictures he had taken on a patrol and his Mother send them to the paper. We were on our way back to the battalion area when they guy hit the mine. It was a 60 mm mortar round, well concealed and placed right in the middle of the main trail. Myself and 8 other men in the column walked right over it; the 10th tripped it off. That is one of the reasons why I don't believe that being point or being a machine gunner is any more dangerous than any other job in the field. Many times the guys that try to skate and pick the easy or "safe" jobs are the ones that get hit.

We're going on a 2 day patrol early tomorrow morning, so tonight I need to clean my rifle, pick up chow and a number of other things.

Doc Turner
August 15 - We ran small patrols around the Pagoda and looked over the river. The villages were then booby-trapped and had been discovered by another squad and we never returned to that area. Sometimes it's best to avoid the bad areas, if you are allowed.

Lt. Suydam
August 16 - The Vietnamese peasants work the land for a living. The land is everything. Ancestor worship is also part of their culture. Therefore, they bury their dead vertically in the rice paddy, so it would require as little crop yielding land as possible, leaving a grave mound above the water in the paddy. Grave mounds were usually covered in thick grass and offered good cover. These graves were here and there but most often in clusters. When we slept on patrol, one man out of four stood his turn at watch.

Chris

August 16 - We spend most of the time going on patrols in and around small hamlets (villages) in the Da Nang area. Our job is to be present in the villages, make them feel secure and to like us. If we accomplished our goal, they would be less likely to fight against us or plant booby-traps. They also would be less inclined to want to go over to the VC side. Right. No one believes that. The older Marines hate the Vietnamese, don't trust any of them. After numerous stories regarding the villagers and their hate for the Americans, the distrust factor gets deeply imbedded in all of us. We learn not to trust anyone.

Part of being on patrol though the villages during the day time is to check all villagers for good government-issued ID cards. These cards are supposed to show us that they belong where they are and are registered with the local authorities. If they don't have any ID, we assume they are the enemy and send them to headquarters for interrogation. We check ID's looking for VC and look into some of the field stocks (bound lengths of straw standing upright) and hooches (straw huts) to make sure they aren't storing guns, ammo, etc. We search outbuildings and stacks of straw in the fields. Quite often we find weapons and confiscate them. Trying to determine who the owner is can be a real problem, unless the weapons are next to a hut. Then, it's all over for the owner. After a small bit of interrogation, intimidation and a few threats, the person is arrested, hands bound and taken to the rear area for the brass to deal with.

Before nightfall, we setup at the seamstress' house on Anderson Trail. Kids wanted cigmos (cigarettes). I gave one to a kid about three years old. He smoked it like a pro. The women are hurtin', with their black teeth and bleeding gums from chewing "beetle nut" (a local leaf) and smoking smelly cigars. The young girl's name is Bi. We were lucky tonight since we had clean water, a clean house and we could sleep all night. They had dogs to awake us should someone approach. We pull perimeter security watch, only two hours at a time, then go back to sleep and the next guy would take his turn "on watch". Sometimes watch duty could be pretty tough. Staying awake at night, after walking many miles through villages and countryside in the terribly hot days, could make a guy pretty tired. We have to sit up straight in order to have a good view of anyone approaching. We have to be totally quiet, in order not to give away our position. A watch is passed from Marine to Marine until morning. Falling asleep is not a problem. You have to trust the next guy to be vigilant.

I hated leaving my friends when I was assigned to Echo Company, but am feeling better all the time, as I seem to feel more comfortable with my squad. The area I'm in is fairly secure, they say. Who knows where my buddies ended up? I seem to think about them less and less, as time goes by. Being part of a team now and getting to know each of them better, day by day captures time. Nothing is more important than the guys around me.

August 17 - I have sent a picture of our company on a mission, using a Vietnamese boat, loaded with ammo, big guns and mortars, to help with the crossing. The river is deep and crossing it was difficult. I am now carrying an M-16 automatic rifle, .45 automatic pistol, M-79 grenade launcher - my weapons. I always find I am carrying more ammo than anyone else. I do have a fear of not having enough ammo, if we should get into a major firefight.

Marines Use Vietnamese Boat for Crossing

A Vietnamese woman allows members of "E" Co., 2nd Bn., First Marine Regiment to use boat to transport ammunition, radios, mortars and other equipment across river during an operation near Da Nang. Cpl. M. C. Nelson (Wichita, Kansas) guides the boat.   (Photo by Cpl. M. J. Coates)

Note: - Chris – This is a picture of our company on a mission, using a Vietnamese boat, loaded with ammo, big guns and mortars, to help with the crossing. The river is deep and crossing it was difficult. I am carrying an M-16 automatic rifle, .45 automatic pistol, M-79 grenade launcher - my weapons. I always find I am carrying more ammo than anyone else. I do have a fear of not having enough ammo, if we should get into a major firefight.

Chris

August 18 - We were sent back into the bush for patrols at 1800 hours and we set up for an ambush. During the day, we are visiting the hamlets, checking ID's and looking for VC suspects. Lots of patrolling, keeping the area secure. It's pretty scary walking around in the rice fields at 2300-0600 hours. It's very dark. It's too quiet most of the time and time passes very slowly. We must be aware of every sound, smell, change in the trail, something out of place, so hard to see anything at night. It's very hard to learn everything, but I know it's so very important, not only for me, but for the safety of those in my squad.

Finding clean water is very difficult, if not impossible. If we get water out of a river or creek, the water buffaloes have been dumping in it, the people have been washing clothes and peeing in it, dead animals and people have been left in it. The water is so nasty, we have to put purification tablets in our canteens to kill the bugs or we will get dysentery for sure. If we get the bug, we are "dropping trou" (trousers) immediately. No one wears underwear or skivvies, as they scrape the skin on our legs. It also makes it easier when we get out of streams to drop trou check for leeches. No matter where we are, when the dysentery hits, it hits. You feel like the flu hit your stomach with a 4 x 4 post. We can't trust the water anywhere.

As we walk our patrols, we know the odds are stacked against us – we're in their back yard, they can travel light, maybe only a rifle or a grenade – hit and run. There is lots of harassment, day and night. It really gets on your nerves, day after day. We have to stay so alert. A slight "tell" of something off or different may save our life. The birds may stop chirping, you may smell something.

I notice that one of the guys in my squad, named Speck, has a decal plastered to his M-79 grenade launcher "Richard Speck Kills". He finds humor re: the Richard Speck at home in Chicago that killed 6-8 nurses in 1966. It's weird, no one says anything.

August 19 - Back to base camp this morning and not too soon. I got almost no sleep last night. They are 40 men in my company and 12 in my squad. We all live in the same hardback tent, which is built off the ground to protect from the monsoon rains. The weather is hot, even the rain is hot. I feel sweaty all day long. We're going to some kind of orientation classes, about six people at a time, including the company XO. Then we fire weapons and clean weapons.

August 20 - We're told a USO show is coming to our camp. I hope I'm not in the field, so I at least have a chance to go. There should be all sorts of good-looking girls, music, basically a big party. I know my chances of going is very close to zero, but something positive to think about today.

I've met a bunch of really cool guys in the company lately, which is great. It seems that the newer guys are the ones that you talk with more. The older guys are a bit standoffish. They have their friends and it doesn't seem like they want any more. The monsoon season is supposed to start soon, which will make traveling more difficult. Everything gets wet and stays that way, at least that what the guys that have been here are saying.

Everyone is going through a training exercise on how to use our gas masks. This is a dreaded procedure, but evidently an exercise that is needed or at least someone up the command thinks so. We enter a tent with the sides down and exits closed, the gas grenade is activated and then, after a few seconds, we are given permission to put on our gas masks. We breathe for a while and then are given permission to leave, which everyone does immediately. As soon as we get out of the tent, the masks come off, our eyes are watering something terrible. Everyone bitches about the exercise. We are told to clean the masks, have our mask size recorded and turn them in. We are done with that.

I just met Doc Turner. He's our senior corpsman. He seems like a good guy, a little older than most of us, probably about 27 years old, a southern guy with a great slow drawl, from Louisiana. He's a very serious sort, but that's probably has to do with his job. It can't be easy trying to save lives during the heat of the battle, with bullets and explosions going off everywhere. It's so hectic when the firing starts. You can't hear anything. Often the enemy is so well hidden it's difficult to get a bearing on his position.

August 21 - Attended classes in the morning and then spent time cleaning my rifle, my pistol and my new acquired M-79 grenade launcher. I now hold the position of grenadier. It's a responsible position and the lieutenant told me I did a good job when we were practice shooting. I enjoy firing a grenade across the paddies a couple of hundred yards and seeing the explosion. The weapon can really make a difference in a firefight.

I noticed some of the guys tape their dog tags together, so they don't clang together when we're out in the bush. Dog tag, what a crazy name for these things. Everybody has to wear 'em, as they have all our personal info. We wear them around our neck on a chain and it stays there. The first tag is attached to a long chain and the second tag is on a shorter chain and attached to the long chain. If a guy is killed, the second tag is collected and the first remains with the body. Some of the guys have their second tag laced into their boot.

Tomorrow is going to be a hard day. We will be constantly walking all day, so we can get into position for an upcoming operation, starting later in the day. I better take advantage of being in the tent and being able to get some sleep.

We are told today that no one is allowed to have a sling on their rifle. It accounts for wasted ammo and poor shooting. Additional training on the cleaning of the M-16E1 rifle is conducted. The rifle has a history of not firing correctly, if you can imagine that. We are told "to recognize every possible reason the rifle has jammed or will not fire and we need to know it as well as we know our name". That bit of news doesn't sit well.

Our 3rd squad got into some action today while out on patrol. None of our guys were hurt, yet we got some gook KIA's, so everything is good.

August 22 – We left Delta 6 at 1530 hours, late afternoon and made our way into the village of Phong Ngu. We quietly slide our way through the night and into our position – a well-hidden place off the way of the path, open to firing in both positions, protecting our rear position, with everything in front of us. No action. We ran patrols all day long. and then set up a camp for the night. Anything moving at night was to be shot. We watched the river for gooks. We saw them coming in small canoe-type boats and as they closed in on our position, we fired everything we had. We have taken so many casualties lately. It felt good to get a couple of VC. Their days of hunting us had ended.

The next night, we moved up the river and away from our previous position, away from the church toward the pump house. I set out a trip flare, which was the normal procedure to give us an advanced warning, should someone try to sneak up on us. The trip-flare has a low lying trip wire strung across a path or point of entry. If the intruder's foot pulls on the trip wire, the burning flare will ignite and illuminate the area, thus exposing the position of the enemy. I threw one grenade. Everyone else threw about the same. Something or someone was out there and probing our perimeter. Pretty scary, no one could sleep. Occasionally, a sniper round would whistle through our position. We wanted daylight so badly – it couldn't come quickly enough. The next morning, I noticed someone had messed around with the trip flare I had set out. One of the more senior guys made it a point of ridiculing me and my inability to do something correctly. His way of telling me to "get it together or you'll kill us all." It definitely made an impact on me. I don't know what I did or didn't do, but I accepted the tough-lashing. I really felt as if I had let the squad down. I didn't hear anything else about it, but I sure learned my lesson about something?

L/Cpl David Aasen, one of the guys in our squad, was KIA today.

**Lance Corporal David Aasen, Longview, Washington
(panel 25E, line 27 on The Wall)**

Doc Turner

August 23 - At times, the Battalion Aid Station would request supplies from Slater. He kept a working list of "needs" and if any of us got to Da Nang and came back without some of the needs, we made his fecal roster. On more than one occasion, when we were going on a long extended operation, some of us corpsmen would go over to his hooch, where he lived and "juice up". We never got to practice a lot of the time on how to start IV's in the field, except while under fire in a firefight. So, we practiced in Jerry's hooch under his watchful eye. Since it was considered a waste of supplies to discard the unused supplies, we used the fluids to administer to each other needed Vitamins, C, K, B12, antibiotics and other mineral salts that would be sweated out the next few days. This built up our personal reservoir of needed vitamins. We would infuse those fluids until we could taste the salt and such. As a result of this, we as corpsmen could easily perform extremely well in our care for the Marines we were in charge of, especially those having problems with heat exhaustion. It would normally take about three days for us to "run out of gas", whereas the grunts (enlisted Marines in a rifle company) would already be really dragging their butts. There was such a difference in humid heat and the dry heat. It seemed the humid heat just sapped everything out of a man, no matter what kind of good physical shape he was in.

Lt. Suydam

August 24 - I was wounded in the Phong Ngu area. It was night and we were trying to gain a position of advantage before dawn. BLAM! That's all the warning you get. A small metal fragment hit me on the last rib on my left side. Grenades are funny. The M26A1 has an effective casualty radius of fifteen meters but the killing radius is quite a bit smaller. The grenade had a smooth thin metal cover and is designed to throw shrapnel that comes from a coil of serrated wire. The theory is that the serrated wire will break up more consistently in a regular spherical pattern. Older grenades like the cast iron pineapple looking grenade of WW II, the MK2, would break up in irregular patterns. So, the piece of wire about the size of a broken pencil lead hit me giving me a pinprick and a minor thud on my rib. I was far enough away from the blast that it was not a serious wound.

Chris

August 24 - It just seems to continue each day - you must stay very alert – watch the ground, so you don't trip any wires and always watch the tree line. You need to hit the ground, as soon as the first round goes off or you're not coming back the next day. You watch for anything on or next to the path that is out of place… stress, yeah,…a bit, but everyone has the same amount. You just want to make it through today. The squad operates very calmly as it patrols, sets up ambushes or engages in firefights. The adrenalin level definitely rises during a firefight or any firing or explosion.

Estes hates this Phong Ngu area and with good reason, as we get into a bad firefight every time we come here, and we leave with more guys hurt.

Our squad leader, "Spanky" Baldwin, set us up in a small straw hooch, about 20 feet from the trail. The people were very unfriendly. You could easily tell they didn't want us there. We didn't seem to care, as we needed a good place to hide out for the night. We stayed outside the hut on the front porch, allowing them the privacy of the inside. Late that night, 6 VC came walking up to the hut, dressed in camouflage and appeared to look like Marines. Spanky was on "watch" at the time. As the VC turned off the main path and approached the hut on a small walkway, they saw us sitting on the front porch and immediately turned and ran. Spanky didn't fire, and instead said "Oh, shit!" This was a common expression of his. Spanky yelled, they turned and ran, we fired into the jungle, probably out of fear and the high-level stress caused by a nervous squad leader. I awoke, but couldn't fire, as I had the M-79 as my weapon. The jungle was extremely thick with vines and thick foliage hanging down in front of us. The branches could have actually caused a M-79 round to detonate before going but a few feet in front of us.

We carefully watched the people of the hut the next morning. We searched the area of the hut, both inside and outside. I had used a metal bucket to rest my feet on that night. Upon inspection, I found the bucket contained six grenades, hidden under a pile of leaves. Spanky went nuts. He started screaming at the family, where we were staying. We gathered our now four VC prisoners. Spanky called the captain at command post and he sent an interpreter, a Chieu Hoi (a VC that had converted over to our side) to our position. The Vietnamese interpreter absolutely went off on the people, yelling and screaming. He backed one of them into a tree. He grabbed a large piece of wood and swung it at her head, only barely missing, yet scaring the hell out of her. He beat the young VC up pretty good to make her talk. They all started talking as fast as they could, definitely fearing for their lives. The kids were all watching and crying. Her husband was one of the men coming up to the hut that night. Outside we found flake TNT, chicom (Chinese) grenades, Z-10 mines, block mines, cans filled with explosives and a 155mm artillery round! We did good. We captured four VC and closed down a small weapons supply hut.

It was too bad we weren't set up better to fire on them last night. Not very good planning on our part. We returned to CP for a well-deserved night's rest. We've been out too long, too tense, too much action, too many guys hurt, and all in a short period of time.

Lt. Suydam

August 25 - Phong Ngu area. We had reached our position under cover of darkness and we were undiscovered. Dawn came. A trooper told me that three armed VC were crossing our front in the shoulder-high rice. I went to the M-60 machine gun. When the time was right, I signaled for them to open up. Click! The gun jammed. There was only a rifleman and a 3.5-inch rocket team. The rifle would have been a waste of a good ambush. The rocket team was loaded with a White Phosphorous round. They begged me for permission to shoot.

White phosphorous is a chemical that burns when exposed to the air. The shell explodes in a 35 meter bursting radius. Unfortunately, it leaves an enormously heavy cloud of white smoke that takes forever to clear. I knew if we fired the rocket that would be the end of the ambush. Firing the rifle would be the same. Maybe we would hit one, but the others would duck under the rice and run out of the killing zone.

I gave the rocket man the nod and he put the round exactly where they were. Blam! White smoke. We waited. When we entered the killing zone to check for damage, there was nothing, not a sign, not a clue. Did we kill? I don't know.

Terry Halloran – Cincinnati, Ohio, Echo Co., 3rd platoon

August 25 - It was late into the night when we changed our position after nightfall. This was a common practice in the Phung Ngu area because it reduced the likelihood of night attack if we could set up under darkness. The rear guard heard noises from the position we had just vacated. There was gunfire. We stopped to figure out what was happening. Turns out Terry had the radio, so he told us that he had just been fired on. I asked if he was alone. He said, "yup." I told him to just be quiet and not to shoot and that we'd send someone back to fetch him. We waited for awhile to insure ourselves that whoever was out there had left. We slowly returned to Terry and departed deeper into the forest.

Chris

August 26 - I hated sleeping on the Vietnamese graves. Sometimes it was the only place we could find to hide and provide some cover. If the grave site was at all recent, the smell of the recently dead would gag you. You would be lying

Mission Proves Profitable

DA NANG—A two-day search and destroy mission 15 miles south of Da Nang, Aug. 22-23, turned out to be profitable for Marines of "E" Co., 2nd Bn., First Marine Regiment, 1st Marine Division, and costly to the Viet Cong.

Moving into the village of Lanh Dong (3) in the early morning hours, the Marines met no contact. However, just before dawn, LCpl. Lewis A. Kukav (Marble Head, Ohio), killed a VC as he ran past the company command post.

"I was just leading a patrol out to check some nearby huts when the VC dressed in black ran onto the trail. Apparently he didn't see us as he kept coming down the trail almost as if he were charging me," said Kukay.

Another VC killed by members of the 1st platoon, was carrying an M-26 grenade, a poncho, transistor radio, gray utilities and a bag of rice.

Two more Viet Cong were spotted running across a paddy by men of the 2nd platoon. The Marines opened fire and killed one.

Three "Charlies" were caught in the open and killed by 3rd platoon Marines.

The operation ended with eight Viet Cong confirmed killed, two detainees, and four weapons captured—a M-16, a M-1 rifle, a carbine, and an Ak-50.

The Marines also discovered and destroyed a Viet Cong mine factory complete with tools, forge and anvils, 41 mines and booby traps, and explosives and small arms ammunition.

August 23 *Sea Tiger* Newspaper Article by Cpl "Bernie Bernston

directly on top of the mound, with nowhere to go.   A mound might be approximately 8 feet across and 3 feet high. There might be 1-5 or more buried in the same grave.

If you had 6-8 hours in one location, waiting, you probably wouldn't have anything to eat because of where you were. Bad JuJu (bad medicine or bad luck). Once daylight was approaching, we would gather our belongings and head out of the hamlet area and back to our base.

August 27 – I've just gotten back from patrols out in the bush and went directly to church, which says something about how happy I was to get back safely. Mail and packages from home are so important to everyone. When mail call happens, everything stops – some get letters from family or girl friends and packages with all sorts of things, like socks, camera film, magazines, newspapers, chocolate cake, cookies and list goes on and on. I haven't received anything yet, but I am told it takes anywhere from 10-30 days, if we get it. Sometimes the gooks shoot down copters or blow up trucks coming to the bases. One guy got a "Dear John "letter from home. No one talks to him.

One of the senior NCO's walked around to all the guys and asked if they had any old pictures of girls or girlfriends from back home. Most of the guys tried to find some extra pictures and threw them into the hat. The NCO told the guy that had just received his "Dear John" letter to write a letter to his old girlfriend and to include all the pictures the guys had collected. He said to thank the girl for the letter, but would she mind picking out her picture from the stack and sending it back, as you just couldn't remember which one she was. The guys all got a kick out of the joke and the new guy actually was smiling as he was composing the letter.

Estes
August 29 - Everyone was breaking down their weapons when two Vietnamese men approached. We noticed there were strap marks on their shoulders which indicated they were VC. We knew the strap marks were from carrying packs, not working in the rice fields. The squad took custody of them. They asked for something to drink and we gave them coffee and salt to drink. Then the gooks were put under a poncho and were gassed with heat tabs, when they asked for

food. The heat tablets that we normally used for heating up food gave off a terrible gas and smoke. I hadn't been here very long and everyday something was new was happening. We had just taken more prisoners. We took them back to camp and gave them to the interpreters and the brass to get worked over.

Chris

August 30 - It's been bad lately. A friend of mine was killed today when he tripped a booby trap (grenade) mine. The fragments just missed me. I was so lucky. I said a quick prayer to thank God for looking out for me. I could have easily received a wound from the flying fragments. It's starting to seem like this is the way it's going to be every day. Are you in the wrong place at the wrong time? My friend was walking point and missed seeing the trip wire across the path. It all happened in an instant moment. I felt so lonely. The mood was quiet.

An additional four men were hurt before that by a trip wire activated mine, including a San Antonio guy whose name I can't remember. It just continues to happen. You can't have the state of mind that allows you to rethink or go over the bad situations or it will take you down and away from being totally alert, which is the very most important thing we all must do. We must always be looking around the landscape, down where we are placing each step and again around the landscape...

For the last 2-1/2 days, we have walked in swamps, mud holes, rice paddies, streams, etc. The constant rain causes our feet to rot. I'm told it'll get worse in Sep, Oct, Nov, Dec. You can't imagine how bad our feet smell. No wonder they know we're coming. I try to dry my feet at night by taking my boots off (could be bad idea if we get hit), ringing out my socks (if I have any on), and hang them in the breeze for my two hour watch. I put them back on, wake the next guy and go to sleep, normally for four hours each night. The same people we see in the daytime are the ones we shoot at in the evening. You learn very early not to trust

anyone, kids included. It's the end of August, which means I only have 12 more months and I'm out of here.

Knobby

August 30 - When it rains here it gets COLD – down in the 40's. It isn't too bad as long as we're moving around but when we stop to set in, the cold, damp air really shoots through us.

**L/Cpl Dan Dowling on the right, Mac in the
middle, Zack Williams on the left.**

We're supposed to be on an operation right now but it was cancelled. Da Nang got hit by rockets the other night and we had to go out and beat the bush, looking for the VC that were firing the rockets. We didn't find anything but we didn't expect to since it was raining so hard we could hardly see two feet in front of us. About the only way we could have found the gooks that night would have been to have them flash a neon sign reading "Victor Charlie Launching Site". I don't know whose idea it was to send us out.

I get to choose what month I want to go to Hawaii to see my parents. I'll have 4 days and 5 nights.

The platoon sergeant just came in and told me to come see him and he would give me a razor blade. I think he is hinting because I haven't shaved for 2 weeks.

House

August 31 - I am a combat-ready Marine, trained and experienced in infantry tactics, and here I am in my nice, tropical uniform: unarmed landing in a hostile country with nothing but a sea bag! I was expecting to get shot at as soon as we landed, but this is like landing at any military base in the U.S. This place is huge! There are lots of construction trucks running around the base with "Brown-Root & Johnson Construction" signs on the side –which is a big government contractor out of Texas! What a surprise – I think I read the President's wife, Linda Bird Johnson, owns part of the company. Since it is the last day of August, I am officially entitled to $65.00 of combat pay, plus my $173.00 monthly pay as an E-4 Corporal! Wow! Big raise for me! The aircraft door flies open at 1515 hours. I have officially arrived in the Republic of South Vietnam to start my tour of duty with only nine months remaining in my enlistment. I did not think I would be sent here, if I had less than thirteen months left. The standard tour is the standard tour, but HERE I AM.

It is hot, sticky, smelly, crowded and noisy as fully loaded combat aircraft keep taking off into the sky. There are big commercial jets, military cargo planes and small trucks with fuel, ammo, security, all service forces vehicles, guard towers with search lights located everywhere around the perimeter, and lots of concrete and steel revetments surrounding the planes up and down the flight-line.

From the 31st of August to the 4th of September, I am stuck in the transit barracks at Da Nang Airbase, awaiting assignment to my new unit. Due to the South Vietnamese elections that are underway, all outer roads are shut down for polling security by ARVN (Army of the Republic of Vietnam) and U.S. forces to keep VC (Viet Cong) from stealing the voting boxes and killing the poll workers. Nice guys! Huh?!

I hear they have machine-gunned buses full of voters and blown-up government schools where people try to vote. I am supposed to go to 2nd Battalion, 1st Marines somewhere south of Da Nang, but the roads are still closed. I try to scope-out the airbase layout and get my bearings, as to what is located where.

Chris

August 31 - Many of the villages we patrol are mainly made up old papa-sans and mama-sans (men and women). It is very important for all of us to notice any subtle changes in the mood of the villagers. They may have VC in the village, as we are moving through or they may may have hidden rifles, ammo or supplies for returning VC. We never know, yet it is so important to be observant of everything. Village unease or unfriendliness seems to equate to trouble. If this seems to be the case, it is normally a place we will move away from. If we really feel something is not right, we may put a prize bull in front of us as we exit the village. A villager cannot lose this farm animal. He will tell us not to go that way - bad juju. The good move on his part saves the Marines and also saves the man's bull.

On daytime patrols, we travel light: M-16 rifle, 1-2 bandoliers of ammo (200-400 rounds), bayonets or knives hanging loosely at our hips, 1-2 grenades, a canteen of water, maybe a snack of some sort, smokes and mosquito repellant.

Note: The August Command Chronology for the 2nd Battalion, 1st Marines reports 60 VC initiated contacts during the month, most in the Ky Minh and Than Phong villages. The most serious incident occurred on the 28th of August, when an estimated 25 VC attacked the Cau Do Bridge position, dropping part of the bridge into the water. Eleven VC bodies were left behind. Blood trails and drag marks indicated there were more enemy casualties. Water supply was a problem. It was discovered that one Marine is illiterate. The chaplain is teaching him to read and write. Lt. Col. Archie Van Winkle assumed command of 2/1 on August 6. Captain Thomas Pratt commanded Echo Co. 2nd Battalion, 1st Marines. Casualties for August: 10 enlisted KIA, 7 officers WIA, 73 enlisted WIA.

Chris

September 1 - We went out to Phong Ngu again. The platoon split up for a while, going separate ways and trying to cover more ground. We all came back together later in the day, neither unit having any action on patrol.

All the sudden, I heard an explosion that scared the hell out of me. It was a block mine that went off and hit and injured three Marines. One of the guys came to the 'Nam with me and was also stationed in California with me. Everyone stopped, the corpsman was called up to the explosion site and the rest of us took a knee and faced outwards toward the area we felt most dangerous. Then Levine was told to watch the rear of the column. He wandered off the trail and sat down on a mine. An M-26 grenade went off killing him instantly. Geez, we did it to ourselves, again. Cpl. Brian List got hit in the neck, wounded in action (WIA) and Levine was killed in action (KIA), Estes got knocked back and down. This was Estes' birthday. Boy, is he nervous.

September 2 – Patrolling Phong Ngu all day, taking sniper fire. All the people leave their huts and hide when the Marines come around. We know whose side they're on and it's not ours. They're scared of us. They think we eat babies and worse. Patrols during the day, fight 'em at night. Don't trust anyone. We move back to the rear area for the night and sleep in our own tent. First good sleep in a long time.

September 3 – We left for an operation today. Supposed to sweep quite a bit of territory. Other companies from our battalion will be out here helping. We went into the area at night and all was well. As we started to set up positions, we got hit - sniper fire all around us. We couldn't fire back, as we couldn't tell where the fire was coming from. It's so frustrating not being able to return fire and take 'em out. They hit us and run. Then they do the same thing again. It really wears on your nerves, making it difficult to relax, even for a short time.

House

September 4 – I ran into Alexander and Halster, guys from my Infantry Training Regiment (ITR) and they tell me that our friend, Frank Endicott and two of our other guys from Bravo Co., 1/27, in Hawaii were just killed at the Khe Sanh Combat Base up by the Demilitarized Zone (DMZ). Halster told me that he had been shot in the back a couple weeks before this and his scar still bled, big, ugly and red.

I finally got my orders from the Desk Chief at Da Nang Airbase late in the afternoon. The trip out to my new unit was a wild ride doing about 50 mph in a 6x6 truck approximately 8 miles from Da Nang, along Highway #1, the main paved road all the way along the coast from South Vietnam to North Vietnam.

About 15 minutes later we turned off the main highway, going just as fast (or faster) onto a dusty dirt road called Anderson West, and pulled into the CP (command post) of 2nd Battalion, 1st Marines. As we drove through the gate, a truck going the opposite way ran over a land mine and two Marines were wounded. My welcome to Vietnam by the Viet Cong! This tells me they must be close-by every night. I am in Indian Country!

2/1 has been in this location for two years and had a strong fortified compound. It was hot, but the sun felt good, with numerous tall trees and bamboo around the area for shade.

I was sent to the "short-timers tent" to stow my gear. These guys are all close to rotating back to the world, so they have been pulled out of the field and they do jobs like collecting garbage and help fill the drinking water bags and stuff like that, but they don't care, they are "short". They are going home soon!

Marines on disciplinary action get the ugly job of "burning shitters". The human waste from the outhouses falls into 55 gallon oil drum bottoms and must be pulled-out, doused with diesel fuel, and burned every day. It is the worst job, and nobody wants that punishment, if they can avoid it, but there is a full crew hard at it. Oh, what a stink!

There were lots of hardback tents (canvas tents over wood framing) with raised wood floors, a chapel, an outdoor movie theater, PX of sorts, stocked and run by Vietnamese civilians, a motor pool and HQ buildings, guard towers, lots of barbed wire, sandbagged bunkers, and trenches. The base was an old Japanese fighter strip from WWII, named Phong Luc on the maps.

One of the stories I hear is about one night shortly before I arrived. It was about the showing of a movie called "A Shot in the Dark". While the Marines were watching a movie, a single round was fired into the movie crowd, and killed one of the Marines sitting on a bench in the open-air theater. I wonder if it is really true.

The company gunnery sergeant is Nathaniel Webster (black dude, really cool guy). He interviewed me and asked me all about my previous service. I tell him I am a fully qualified 0311 squad leader, having trained nine months for AMFIB Assaults, and I have a secondary MOS of 1400 – a Topographical Draftsman/ Mapmaker and I am compass certified. He says, "Let's go see Lt Col Van Winkle". I am presented to the colonel, who says he would be able to use me in his S-3 in sixty days, when his current guy rotates back "to the world". Wow! I would be his right-hand draftsman at headquarters!

Gunny then says, "For now, you get assigned to a rifle company under the wing of somebody that can teach you to stay alive and keep everyone else around you the same. "OK?" "Yes, Sir!" "House, things are changing fast around here now, we are not sticking around, so stay flexible for a little bit. We will get you placed

Snake Bites His Shelter

**Written by
Cpl Steve Bernston,
Combat Correspondent**

DA NANG, Vietnam (ISO) — All the snake wanted to do was get in out of the pouring rain and stay dry and warm—just like the Marines.

Unfortunately for Lance Cpl. Daryl B. Plueger, the snake chose Plueger's pants leg to seek refuge.

A fireteam leader with E Co., Plueger was among the Marines of his platoon manning an observation post atop a mountain overlooking the Khe Phu Loc river valley.

The platoon was setting in for its second night on the rough, treeless, rock-strewn mountaintop. Up until that time no one had seen any type of snake, although the terrain was a perfect home for them.

A heavy rainstorm, coupled with strong winds, began around 10 p.m. The storm apparently drove the snake to the "shelter" of Plueger's pant leg.

When the Marine reached down to investigate the "funny feeling around my knee" the snake bit him.

"When I got to him, paralysis had already set in around the knee and Plueger didn't even feel me lance the teeth marks to suck out the venom," said Navy Hospitalman Jerald L. Slater, 20, the platoon corpsman.

Plueger was later medevaced by helicopter despite the heavy rainfall and recovered from the poisonous bite.

in S-3 ASAP (as soon as possible). It is not that often they send qualified staff. Carry on Marine!"

That was it! I was going to be the battalion S-3 draftsman, just like I was with the 27th Marines in Hawaii. I would be a part of the C.P. (Command Post) and I would know what was going on at all times! The battalion S-3 officer is Captain Deegan. The current strength of the battalion is 37 officers and 1035 enlisted Marines and 50 Navy (mostly corpsmen).

The Gunny walks me over to the armory and says, "House, you take this new M-16 and a box of 500 rounds of ammo and these 6 magazines and you load 1 tracer for every 5 ball and shoot all this ammo at the range to break it in right and limber it up. Then you spend at least one hour cleaning your rifle and bring it to me and show me before you reassemble it." That is all I do all day, for three days! He is right; it breaks-in the rifle, as it loosens up the mechanical parts and makes it "battle-field" ready. The rifle zeros (hits the target) correctly, and gets nice and loose on full automatic fire. After a few jams and extraction failures it functions flawlessly. I think it is a great weapon for close-in, but for long shots past 300 yards I would want my M-14 rifle, anytime. This is the first time I have ever handled an M-16 rifle, as they are new weapons to Vietnam. They weigh less than our other rifles, which is nice and they are supposed to be much better for automatic firing. It is all new to me. Some training, huh? Here – go shoot it!

The Gunny gives me the opportunity to shoot all kinds of other weapons the unit has captured. The Range Master is only too willing to oblige and have someone get rid of the old ammo that he has collected. I get to shoot a Thompson .45 submachine gun, full automatic and old M-1 Garand .308 rifle, .45 pistols, M-60 machine guns, PKM, AK-47 & SKS assault rifles.   There are Chinese RPG's (rocket-propelled grenades) French rifles and Chi-Com fragmentation grenades and booby-traps. I also get to clean each of these weapons! But, man, what an education, which I never got in all that training time I had back in the States.

<u>Chris</u>
September 4 - The only accountability was "death". How many confirmed kills, bodies on the ground, or portions of bodies accounted for. The "body count". It was everything. It told someone up the line how well your unit was doing. Were you killing more than you lost? Did your kill count justify the amount of men on the mission? It wasn't about taking the next piece of ground, as was the direction in WWII. It wasn't about liberating a town. It was just about "killing". It was all about the body count. It's what Washington wanted to know. If we reported the

body count of four, it well might be passed up the line as six and then higher and by the time it was actually a "number", it was probably much higher, maybe even doubled. It's what they wanted. We knew this as a fact. Yes, it was confirmed by those that worked in the Marine Headquarters in Da Nang. We were all a part of the big machine – Washington politics. They ran the war, not the generals, it was very evident. We all knew it, we hated it. The "brass" had their hands tied… and it meant the war was being dictated by the politicians. We couldn't do the things we all knew we should be doing, the things that would enable us to win the war. Confirmed kills, did we care? I don't know. We got some of them, that was good, at least 'til tomorrow, at least it wasn't us. Most of us were 18-19 years old. It was our first war and we were scared. After the skirmish, the ambush, the attack, it all was bad and the only release was the temporary halt in firing. You were alive! The feeling never got old. We had honestly survived…Pvt. X was killed, L/Cpl Y had lost his both legs, Sgt Z lost his sight and one arm, but we killed two. All that really mattered was we had survived again. We felt so lucky. We didn't tell each other we were lucky… we didn't say anything.

September 5 - We started the day with a memorial for Cpl. Levelle, Cpl. Yanez, Cpl. Adams and L/Cpl. Aasen. Lavelle was a well-liked guy in my squad and also lived in my tent. The mood was quiet. Lavelle's death hit most everyone. He had been in 'Nam a long time and was to be going back home soon. This is the only time I would be present for an actual memorial service during my tour in Vietnam.

A VC leader that had been killed was found to be carrying important documents. Another Marine was KIA in first platoon.

Now, we're at Ven Tu outpost. I carried the M-79 grenade launcher last week, this week - I'm walking point. Point is, without a doubt, the most difficult position of a rifle squad, (other than that of a corpsman). Point is the safety leader, he's the first one to walk the path or move through the jungle. He's probably the first to take a round or set off a booby trap.

He is the one that says, "I don't like the area ahead, let's go around it", or "stop, we're going back to the river." He must watch out for any signs of the enemy or for that "something" that just doesn't look right ahead of him or off to either side. His ears and eyes are continuing to search the 180-degree view in front of him, as he slowly moves ahead. Everyone in the squad is depending upon his careful execution that day, to get them back to camp alive. Some guys like to walk point, for the pure adrenalin rush. Most squads switch men on point each day and thus spread the risk.

Knobby
September 5 - I am at China Beach in Da Nang – I lucked out on in-country R&R. I hope my luck still holds when I go to take out of country R&R in Hawaii. China Beach is pretty cool. There is a movie or a band playing every night, pool tables, cafeteria, library, gymnasium, and a big PX. The racks have mattresses and the toilets are indoors. I guess they serve beer here too, but I haven't checked into it – since I'm not 21.

The weather has been good so far. It has rained a couple of times, but it has never lasted very long.

Lt. Suydam
September 5 - The Headquarters and Service Company (H&S) manned the 2/1 perimeter at An Tu south of Da Nang at night. Sometimes, we'd return from patrol at night. When approaching the perimeter, we'd establish radio contact, ask permission to come in and then agree upon a visible signal such as a green star cluster (pop-up flare).

The troops were always a little indignant about the H&S "pogues" (those who didn't venture into the forest or jungle, but stayed behind) staying in the comfort of the wire. So, this one time, some old "salt" takes the green star cluster and shoots it level at the H&S bunker on the perimeter lines instead of up in the air. The H&S "pogues" were manning a 50-caliber machine gun. Taking enormous umbrage to our offense, they open up on us. Actually, safely over our heads, but no matter, we still dive face-first into the paddy water. Are we scared? Yes, but at the same time, we're alternately laughing and cursing at the salt that shot the cluster. When no one was bleeding, it was all fun and games.

House
September 5 – I attended a memorial service today, at the little chapel for a Cpl. Lavelle and two other Echo Company Marines who were killed recently. A sign outside the chapel said "Memorial To Our Lost and Fallen". One of the names listed is Pfc. Dennis Pawlowicz. That used to be my last name, before I was adopted by Frank House, when my mom remarried. I wonder if it is a relative from my dad's side in Minnesota. I will write and ask if there's any connection.

Note: I find out later Dennis is my real father's son from his second marriage. He was killed by small arms fire. He was 18 years old. How weird is that? The half-brother I never met, killed in the same outfit I end up serving in. He was one of thirty Fox Company Marines killed in action on April 21, 1967. It must have been a real battle!

Private First Class Dennis Pawlowicz
(panel 18E, line 063 on The Wall)

I have a cot at the far end of the short-timers' hooch. There are two bare light bulbs and a big cable spool, used as a poker table at the other end. They gamble, drink and smoke all night long. They spend most of their time drinking Primo, Anchor-Steam or Lone-Star beer, munching on Cheetos, and badgering each other to raise bets. They are a really happy bunch, but all have the "thousand-yard stare" from combat.

Some nights pot smoke slowly fills the tent and I can watch it descend like a cloud. It edges down the inside, because we can't show any lights outside the tents past dark and we must close all openings. It really gets hot inside, with no circulating air. When the smoke gets low enough to cover me in my cot, I have to breathe it, I cough a bit, then it gets really smooth, after a while and I fall asleep pretty easy. It smells like alfalfa hay.

Chris

September 6 - Last night was bad – I was as sick as a dog all night long – stomach cramps, high blood pressure, high temperature. Haven't eaten since yesterday, noon. I stayed in bed all day, unable to do anything. Who knows what I got.

I studied my Vietnamese language booklet, hoping to advance my language skills enough to be picked to go to Okinawa for schooling. Anything is better than what I've been through, lately. Bad news, one of our guys was test firing his M-16 on the rifle range and his rifle blew up. Another injury, another guy lost. Echo was used as the blocking force near Phong Ngu today on a small operation.

Battalion Bulletin 3574 states that all Marines will participate in Marksmanship Training of the Quick Kill Method. This method of "instinct shooting is currently

81

taught to U.S. Army recruits at Fort Benning, Georgia. Very remarkable results have been claimed using this method, such as consistently hitting a penny in mid-air, or even a "BB" shot with another "BB". The secret is in making the weapon an extension of the arm, bringing the butt plate up into the shoulder and sighting along the top of the sights, not through them. This method of shooting is not a substitute for accurate fire. It is only intended to be used for fleeting targets at relatively close range. It is also far superior to "hip shooting" or aimed fire against fleeting targets. Every officer, staff NCO and squad leader will attend. It starts 17 September.

House
September 7 - We got word the VC blew up one of the main bridges into Da Nang, using underwater swimmers, and attacked the helicopter base at Marble Mountain. The battalion loaded up on trucks and was sent out to find them. I have not been assigned yet and was left behind.

Chris
September 7 – The VC blew up main bridge to Da Nang, along with blowing up 11 copters from the helicopter-staging base. We were awakened at 0200 hours to go look for the VC responsible for the attack. By the time we got there, they were gone. Monsoon time will be starting soon and I'm told it will really be bad. I don't know what this means, but the guys are all convinced it's going to make it tough on us. Rather than ask someone what it means, I keep my silence, as I know I'll understand in a short while.

Loneliness sets in occasionally. We're separated from our families and friends. Everything seems so far away. I feel okay, probably because I have accepted the fact that I will be here with my unit, until I either get hit or get rotated home. I don't spend much time at all thinking about being injured. If it's going to happen, it will happen. There really is nowhere else to go with these thoughts. I have a job to do. I need to do that job and take care of myself and those around me.

Knobby
September 8 - My squad leader woke me up this morning and said the Lieutenant wanted to see me. I halfway guessed what he wanted since my parents' letter said they took Ma (my Grandmother) to the hospital and she wasn't doing well. The lieutenant handed me the radio message, which I suppose came while I was at China Beach. The top (1st Sgt.) said that they didn't try to contact me at China Beach, as the message said nothing of my presence being requested at home. The message said she died at 08:34 on

September 3, and the funeral was at 10:30 on September 5th. I'm sorry it had to happen and I'm sorry I couldn't do anything to help. I'm glad she didn't have to suffer for any great length of time. I know what a loss it was.

Chris

September 8 - I have just spent the last three days in the field and leave tomorrow for three more days, going to Phong Ngu. One of my best friends, Larry Herfel, almost got shot by another Marine, but his rifle jammed. I can see how easily it is to screw up and get yourself killed. I'm sure I'll see a lot more of the dumb mistakes that end up going bad. We fought our way in - no casualties. We were told by the lieutenant to go down by the river, which was about 1,000 meters away and follow it quite a way (at night). This is absolutely stupid. It is pitch black and the VC are everywhere around us. Our squad leader changes this plan and we only went out a few hundred yards and set up an ambush site for the night. We do this often, as it's safer to stay close to the base camp versus going out 1,000 meters where we're all alone, it's dark as can be, with no support available. It's just another way you learn to survive.

The old guys that have been here awhile have been trying to throw a bit of a scare into us new guys. They were telling stories about all the wild animals around us. The krait, even though a small snake at 3' long, carries some of the deadliest poison of any snake in Vietnam. The python could get above thirty feet long and weigh more than a fully grown man. The key on snakes is to leave them alone and don't back them into corner.

Indochinese tigers range from about 8-9' in length and weigh 330-550 lbs. Stinging red ants, hanging on branches and on vegetation, used by some cultures for torture.

Monkeys (rock apes) tend to be pets for those in rear areas. They're dirty and nasty and can have bad tempers. They can actually be quite funny as all hell and do the damnedest things like trying to copy you. I don't have a clue how much of this is just bull. I guess I'll find out. Snakes do happen to bother me, but I'll be the last person to share that info.

Tomorrow is going to be another hard day. We will be doing a ton of walking. Operation Bald Eagle will start the following day. Down to battalion supply, to draw 7 more magazines, to bring my total to 22 magazines, plus additional ammo boxes, grenades, a rocket launcher, and more. The 5th Marines have been suffering a large number casualties in the nearby Que Son Valley - 109 KIA and over 400 WIA, probably more by now. They were nearly overrun before artillery delivered teargas and drove back the enemy. We don't ever get much information about the other units around us, just enough to count our blessings. Just got my indoctrination into fragmentation grenades, M-18 colored smoke grenades, C-4 plastic explosive, and Claymore mines.

I was given a KA-Bar knife, an E-Tool (to dig your sleeping or fighting hole), a butt pack, which I preferred to carry our C-rations, TP, pictures of girl friends and family, a camera, set of glasses which I didn't wear, as they fogged up in the heat, the frame of the glasses seemed to bother my field of vision. There's a lot going on every day. Something new is always being pointed out. I so hope I can remember most of it. Since the extra weight of shaving cream and razor, I have switched to shaving with my KA-Bar knife. I always have it with me and it is kept sharper than any knife I've ever had. If soap is not available, water and works just fine.

September 9 – We saw the VC running about a 100 meters from our position. We fired our rifles, M-79's, and had mortars called in. While the machine gun crew was firing the mission, one of the assistant gunners suffered traumatic amputation of both hands, as the result of double-feeding of his machine gun. (The machine-gun rounds were being hand-fed into the gun and a mis-feed of ammo caused an explosion).

We left the Delta 6 area and made our way to the village of Phong Ngu. We patrolled the immediate area and watched the river for gooks. We fought our way in and got a few VC. We moved to another position that night, away from the church and toward the pump house. We always stay away from the church, as the area is heavily mined. The VC count on Marines looking for an easy shelter. We know their tricks, at least a few of them. We know that even though it may not be mined, the best thing to do is to play it safe and stay clear. I set out a trip flare in front of our position. The gooks were out in front of us all night. We mainly threw grenades, both sides trying to get an advantage. We could hear them, but their position was difficult to find. No sleep. Damn, they were close. I threw grenades that night, as did everyone - too damn close. A few sniper rounds were fired off. Still no bead on their position. We're in deep low brush, very dark hillside and as scary and tense as any night we've had in the past few weeks. We held the uphill position, that was good. Finally, morning came and we moved on, but cautiously.

House
September 9 - I keep hearing about lots of action at a village named Phong Ngu. There are always firefights, prisoners, ambushes, mines, booby-traps and snipers. Sounds like a bad spot close by that belongs to us.

Note: Chris – The fact is House didn't understand that we did not own Phong Ngu. If anyone owned this village, it was the enemy. House wrote this after he was in-country only five days. This was the place that Estes hated the most and for good reason, as we got hit every time we went there, making it more likely you would get hit with each continuing trip. This place scared the hell out of everyone.

House
September 11 - Sick - bad stomach, fever, probably water at Phong Ngu. I am feeling better than yesterday. One of our mascots in the rear area was called "Damn-it", who goes into the field on patrols. The other dog is "Sarge." He's the office dog, lazy.

The platoon left yesterday and came back in this afternoon. No real contact with the enemy.

Chris
September 11 – When we set up ambushes, they are normally along known trails or avenues of approach to villages. The Rules of Engagement describes procedures we need to follow before opening fire during the daytime. At night, if someone is walking around, the assumption is they are VC and we fire on them. The night is open to all.

Word is that the VC have our radio frequency, know our call signs and are trying to make contact with us, keying the handset and blowing into it. I'm sure we'll hear more about it tomorrow and procedures will change.

"Chris" and the second squad crossing a paddy

FULLY EXPOSED TO ENEMY FIRE IN TREELINE

House

September 11 - I notice that some of the trucks are going out with armed escorts and some without. I asked the Gunny if I could ride along as security with one of the trucks, since I still hadn't been assigned to a platoon. He said sure, make yourself available to the motor pool officer. So, looking for a little adventure, I did.

Out at 1000 hours, here I am riding "shotgun" in a 6X6 truck, while the rest of the company went out at 2300 hours last night to look for a VC rocket site that was shooting at the airbase. All the rest of the guys that stay behind are either, sick, injured, or too close to going home. The first place we drive to is Phong Ngu, to drop-off a water tank on wheels (called a "water buffalo"), a 55 gallon drum of gas and all is quite peaceful. Loaded with boxes of C-rations and crates of grenades for the next stop along the road up Anderson Trail West, we are blowing red dust all over the local folks struggling along the rutted road at 60 mph in this bouncing, jerking monster truck, with a screaming diesel pounding and gears grinding away! This is just another wild ride with another crazy driver.

At 1130 hours, September 11th, I get officially shot at by the enemy, for the very first time! We are cruising along at a good clip and Blang! The sound is an unforgettably clear "rattle" that is an AK-47, loose bolt on full automatic. Bullet impacts are kicking up dust in front of us and then hitting the truck! A dual rear tire bursts, but we keep on going, even faster. The steel plates and sandbags tied to the sides of the truck absorbed the bullets like it was nothing. The only place I could figure the fire was coming from was good 100 meters away in a tree line, because it was all open ground around us. Then I saw a green tracer round from the trees parallel to the road and had something to shoot at! I am sure I did not hit anything at that distance and speed and the way we were bouncing around, but at least I got to return fire, and give him a taste of his own medicine.

We did not stop until we got all the way into the Da Nang Motor Pool and both the driver and I were a little shaky in the knees. The tire and the steel rail on the bed were the only hits, no problems! The driver changed the tire, joined about eight other trucks and we went back without incident. Nobody got hurt, and I had a good story to tell the guys when I got back. When I related my adventure, they were not impressed. The rest of the company was out all night and didn't find anything of the rocket sites they had been searching for.

The tent mascot is a dog, called Ho Chi Minh, she is pregnant. There are also cats and kittens all over this place. Fox Company even has a monkey for a mascot!   The mutt had her puppies under the company office and Gunny Webster is all smiles, he loves them!   He can't count them all because she is nervous and snaps at him.   The Gunny is going to actually post a guard on the puppies.

Chris
September 12 – We're at an outpost, which is guarded by the Army of Republic of South Vietnam (ARVN) and we are providing security for them.   The ARVN troops aren't worth much.   They have terrible leadership and organization.   They expect the Marines to guard them.   When they go out on patrol, they carry radios, wear thongs, cooking pots and rice.   Not very serious about their job, they won't go where they're not supposed to go, so no risk.   We don't trust them.   Never!

I understand I'm going to be up for corporal in October, which would be good.   Actually, I would be surprised, as I haven't been here very long and to tell the truth, I would just as soon learn more before I have command of a squad.   My pay would go from $128.90 to $178.90, which would be great.

House
September 13 - Gunny hauls me out of the short timers tent after breakfast, "Cpl. House, gather all your gear, you will be following me to your new quarters with 2nd platoon!   Off we go, finally assigned!   I am part of a real unit today, after almost two weeks of being adrift.   Nice!   We walk into an empty hardback tent - nobody there.   He says, "Stow your gear in the corner.   When they come back, the platoon Sgt. will show you where to bunk.   Now, follow me."   We then continue to walk out the gate and down Anderson West to the ARVN Compound.   The Gunny has nothing, but his 45 pistol and 3 mags (21 rounds) and I have my M-16 (120 rounds) and 6 grenades (and, knees knocking, waiting to be ambushed).

Our platoon commander, Lt Reydel, greets me with a big smile, handshake and a canteen cup of cold pineapple juice and a big "Welcome aboard"!   It was terrific!   I was quickly assigned to his second squad leader, Sergeant "Spanky" Baldwin, a scruffy, salty, maybe 25 year old with a hard stubble beard, 5'8 tall, 130 lbs., square jaw, squinty eyes, hard tan, scars on the backs of his hands and forearms, stone-cold black eyes, small hard grin on the sides of lips only.   It looked like his back hurt him when he walked.   He had the look of someone that had seen some action!   He shook my hand hard, long and strong, and he looked at me square in the eyes and asked me, "Can you keep up and pull the trigger when I say so?"   I replied, "Yes, sergeant!"   He says, "Yes, sergeant is good enough for me" and slaps me on the back. Welcome to the 2nd squad!" And, he grins a big toothy smile!

We are at a little village down the road from our tactical position called "AnTu", and in a house the guys have named the "Seamstress House". She has a sewing machine (foot-powered), she makes clothes and repairs uniforms for the guys in the area. We stay there until dark and before going out on night patrol, we allow our eyes to get our night vision adjusted, then we begin to move slowly out of the protected stone house. We try to not let the local VC see us move out during daylight or they will try to set up an ambush on us. Is night time better for us? I don't really know.

Now, I am on my first real patrol with my own unit, I am told to follow the lead of L/Cpl. Speck, the M-79 grenadier. He will show me the ropes. This is the 1st fire team, with Cpl. Teebo, as our fire team leader. Nothing happens as we move quietly through trails and often we slow down, stop, and drop to one knee, look

out both ways, and listen. The point man sweeps with a flexible tree branch for a trip wire across the trail in front of him as he again moves, slow and easy. Crickets, birds, moon, but no bullets. We get all around the village, disturbing nothing except some chickens (can't help that) and by morning, are all setup at a pre-designated rendezvous point in a low ditch waiting for an engineer team with mine detectors and two K-9 dogs. We are to provide them with security, as they sweep the dirt road back into our area, for the start of a whole new day of adventure. The guys say tomorrow night we go to the place of evil called "Phong Ngu." Someone always gets hurt there, as they're all VC in that village!

We received a new CO today, a negro guy named Captain Clay Baker. He's taking over for Captain Pratt. I wonder how long we'll have him? Personnel seem to change frequently. Officers have some type of rotation policy, like every six months or so.

Chris
September 13 - We quickly moved to the pump house, (which was a diesel operated pump drawing out irrigation water from the river). The guys yelled about some VC running away from us. I fired an M-79 round at one VC running away. At that point, everyone in the squad opened up. The person was never seen again. Our new lieutenant, Lt Graffam, told us to stop firing. He yelled until we stopped. He's getting mad, as our squad has been shooting up things lately - in a heavy way. He's gonna have to learn. It's an outlet for us, after storing up so much adrenaline, to finally have the opportunity to fire our weapons in some kind of retaliation. We started receiving sniper rounds, again. We fired back, again. The lieutenant was a pretty sharp guy and I'm sure he understood our feelings after a while.

We sat around waiting for the new CO to figure out what he wanted to do. Some of the older guys started talking about snakes. "There's the 8-second snake," says one guy. "That's the one that bites you and you only have 8 seconds to live". The large and ugly python snake gets its time, also. They say it will wrap its body around you so fast your eyes will pop out, right before you're squeezed to death. Geez...the guys that were talking about the snakes just laugh, as they know they're scaring the hell out of the new guys. I'm one of the new guys. I try not to let it show or bother me, but crap...there probably were snakes and probably everywhere around us. Every day we walk through water, through jungles. Oh, yea, snakes...probably. I'm sure the new guys will talk about this one later, when we aren't around. I'm sure I'll think about them tonight, when I go to sleep on the ground. Shit!

We escorted the new CO back to the highway to pick up tanks. It had just started raining, again.

We are receiving more pressure be applied regarding "Body Count". This is how we labeled those of the enemy we killed. Confirmed kills, did we care? I don't know. We got some of them, that was good, at least until tomorrow, at least it wasn't us. General Westmoreland had us adding up numbers, numbers of "confirmed kills" (those of bodies in front of us on the ground) and "probable kills" (those leaving a pool of blood and enough of it for us to assume they would die). These numbers were supposed to act as a gage regarding how the war was going - were we winning? Did our "confirmed kills" outmatch those of our fallen brothers? If so, we were probably winning. There were no lines to cross, no territory to capture, nothing but these numbers. The pressure to send larger numbers to our commanders continued to increase. It was all about the numbers. Were our numbers increased? Of course. Our squad of 7-9 Marines might report 2 "confirmed" and 2-3 "probables". By the time those numbers went through our platoon, then though our company and on to battalion the numbers might be doubled or more. The general would send these numbers back to the United States for the politicians in Washington to review. The news media would probably throw out all sorts of numbers to the public. It seems to be some sort of game. The politicians don't seem to understand that these numbers mean so very little.

First platoon just came in from their patrol. While they were out, their last man noticed four VC attempting to fall in at the end of their column. He opened fire with 10 rounds of his M-16 rifle. Then he went back and checked the area. He found a blood pool and a large piece of a human head, a chicom grenade and assorted documents. Reported 1 KIA confirmed. Just another day.

Chris

September 14 - Last night, when we were walking across lake-like paddies at 2400 hours, midnight, dark and cold and very scary, I popped out a piece of gum that Mom sent me. It sounds silly, but it made everything seem better.

The rice paddies are large plots of land where the crops are grown in standing water. The paddies are bordered and divided by dikes, which are very narrow, allowing a little more than room to walk. When we receive fire, we immediately drop into the paddy and seek protection behind the paddy dike. We may only have 12-20" of water and another 12" of dike above the water line to hide behind.

It's a terrible place to have to fight, so we try not to spend any more time than necessary to cross these areas safely. The entire squad is exposed, so fire from the bordering tree lines comes way too often. The moon, at night, will expose a squad of Marines moving across the paddy dikes. Travel at night is difficult.

The 1st squad of Golf/3 observed a female, which they ordered to halt. She kept running, and an M-16 round was fired at her, hitting her left thigh. She was detained. It just continues, as here is someone that didn't have to run, she had an ID card. She ran. We shot her. Can't trust anyone. And, it gets worse day after day.

House

September 14 - We are out at a South Vietnamese ARVN Outpost called, "Tiger 3." They were overrun by VC last week and these particular "Tigers" got their M-60 machine gun taken away! We are now supposed to run a three day patrol out of here! This is officially a CAP (combined action platoon) with the local PF guys (popular forces) and the villagers hookup with the ARVN (South Vietnamese regular army) and share weapons, ammo and stand guard in these outposts and are at the mercy of attacks by the VC at any time!

I do not know how they can work their farms, rice fields and take care of their families, when these killers can just come in at night and slaughter them at will! It is crazy. They have fought the VC so long and hard for so many years. Brave little farmers! You have to respect a man who will defend his family and land like that. I sure do. The commies just want to kill them and take everything they have ever built or improved and enslave them forever. Worth fighting and dying for in my book.

The villagers had two choices - follow the way of the VC, their own countrymen or follow the way of the other intruders, the U.S. Marine forces.

The food the P.F. (Popular Forces – South Vietnamese Army) guys cook is mostly spicy meats of any kind and every description: chicken, pigs, fish, goats, beef, our C-rats, and rice, but it is too much for me to choke down. So, I pretty much decline, unless I can catch it before they add the hot stuff, which is hard to do because they like it to "simmer" over the open fire. They had recently caught a medium-size turtle in the river and made a soup stew out of it.

Lance Cpl. Gary Christensen sat down and ate it with them and he made up some Kool-Aid and passed it around. He is like the surfer-dude from Oregon. He is a cool guy, always cracking jokes and smiling! They all sat around after dinner, and hand rolled cigars, from dry tobacco leaves they grew in their fields and Gary joined in, puffing-up a storm! The whole building smoked like a chimney! Thank God, the hut was tall and had plenty of ventilation. It smelled like crap, but they all thought it was very refined, I am sure. I saved my cigs (cigarettes) for trading stock later.

The M-79 was a popular weapon used to destroy hootches, fire into brush and move out the enemy. Launching a grenade is much easier than trying to throw one, especially at a distant target.

We are approximately seven miles south of our base, and se tup in a building that is a very old crematorium with mud/brick walls up to eight feet thick in some places! There are hundreds of black bats hanging up in the roof beams and along the chimney, maybe 20 feet above us, and rats scurry around behind the ammo boxes stacked in the shadows along the walls. The dirt floor is covered with ashes. I wonder what kind?

About a week ago, the guys said one of our tanks shot at the building with its 90mm gun and hardly damaged the wall. It just punched a neat round hole, straight through, and exploded out in the field behind. Some windows have iron bars, some don't. Some have low sills, and there are no doors. Not the best fortifications, but the walls will sure stop bullets and give us some degree of cover in a firefight. I guess it is better than digging a hole and it is always better than being out in the open in the rain…and then it starts to rain…hard, then harder!

Then comes the deluge and a flood from the sky! I have never seen rain like this!   It is dark, cold, black rain-slamming and pounding with thunder and lightning! Buckets and rivers, and torrents fall from the sky flooding the ditches in front of us so fast the road disappears and we are looking out at a virtual sea of water surrounding us with only tiny islands of land off in the distance!

Well, after dark, one of the trip flares the ARVN put out by the wire, goes off on my side of the building and I zero-in on the movement of a man crawling in a ditch. I draw a bead on him and slowly pull back on the trigger, slow—breathe, relax, aim, draw up slack, squeeze…and I hear, "Don't Shoot! He is one of ours! It's our scout! He has been out trailing the local VC and does not have any flares to let us know he is coming in!" Isn't that great communication? I was so close to pulling the last of the trigger slack on his life, it was too much! I got the shakes so bad, I was sick!

It rained so hard all night and all the next day that some bricks started to fall on us inside the building! All the ammo and grenade boxes were soaked and sandy from the brick mortar weeping water and the roof leaking. But, it was still better than being outside!

Finally, it was good to see the sun again, but the standing water did not recede much all day. At dusk, we got a report that a VC force had come back to take over the area again. We spotted three men with weapons moving in the open field across the road and paddies. They fired a couple rounds at us and they disappeared into a tree line out about 100 meters. My squad had to go out to try to find them after all got quiet, and we were not very happy! Dark, rain, unknown area, flooded rice paddy, mines and booby-traps, and everything under water! We all got our feet wet that night, right up to our ears! The mud in the rice paddies was so sticky your boots were like suction cups trying to pull off your feet.

Linares, our point man from New Mexico, found a 60mm mortar round booby trap. But, it was a dud, so he just dug a deep hole in a dike wall and buried it, so they could not find it again. We got back to the outpost about 1100 hours to find all the ARVN troops were gone.   They went out after the VC patrol from the opposite direction and killed the three VC in an ambush. It happened on the trail they took back to camp after shooting at us! Pretty good!

We sat and watched one of the twin engine C-47 "Spooky" or "Puff the Magic Dragon" gunships. They were equipped with three electric Gattling-guns working the area for about an hour, with red tracers coming down out of a black sky against a few VC green tracers going back-up, no match! What a show! It was a solid line of red hellfire from the night sky that sounded like metal being ripped apart! It was the most impressive firepower show I'd ever seen.

It started to rain, and poured all night. In the morning, the trucks were quite late and finally picked us up just before noon, wet, tired and hungry.

Lt. Suydam
September 14 - Echo Company was positioned in a place of tall grass. Tall grass is everywhere in the backcountry of Vietnam. This place was rolling, small hills with only an occasional sparsely populated tree line and no civilian population. Our new commander was Captain Baker.   Of course, registering artillery and mortar points around your perimeter was textbook training for combat officers. Experience taught that there were consequences. The idea is to pick out some strategic spots around your position, have the mortars or artillery fire upon these targets and then register the coordinates. Registration is the term used by the Fire Direction Center (FDC), which has calculated the correct direction, angle and charge for the shells to reach the specific targets and this information is saved for future use. If during the night the position is attacked, fire can quickly be brought or adjusted from these spots.

It's good textbook tactics. Trouble is that it causes more trouble than it's worth. If you have acquired your position without being discovered by the enemy, registration will surely call attention to your presence. Then there is always the possibility that a short round or a Fire Direction Control Center (FDC) error will endanger your own troops.   Now, comes the next bad thing to result from registration. The first white phosphorus round which came into the tall grass set the grass afire.   Imagine if you will, a wall of fire spreading out toward your position from the flaming dry grass standing eight to eleven feet tall.   It was a mad dash without orders and without organization. It was every man for himself, as we picked up our belongings and chose the best path to evade the worst of the fire.

During the scramble, a small, blinded deer came into my path. No bigger than a medium-sized dog, he was burned on his hindquarters and other places on his legs. I captured it with little trouble, tied it to my belt and had some idea of an eventual feast. The deer was too heavy and feasting was not something that we had time or security to do. I let the critter go, knowing that it would soon die, for it had not the capacity to survive its burns and blindness.

Chris

September 15 - Just got back from Combined Action Patrol (CAP) area, manned by the ARVN. They were happy to see us, of course. Our Marine truck drivers live here. We have two mascots, "Damn-It", who goes in the field with us on daily patrols and "Sarge", who stays in camp, slums around, feeding off table scraps.

Three Echo Company guys were on Anderson Trail and received approximately 8 rounds, they returned 67 rounds. Good balance, Marines!

Picture above taken by Cpl MJ Coates, Combat Photographer

2nd Bn 1st Marines - Getting Feet Wet - RVN

Even though it is extremely difficult for anyone to explain what it is like during a firefight, Roger Goss shares his feeling as he describes the intense action in his article to follow.

Roger Goss reports emotions of firefight

(EDITOR'S NOTE: The following report comes from Roger Goss in South Vietnam.)

June 18

FEAR!

The scene is a fierce firefight.

Maybe you could compare it to coming down a long winding road from a steep hill with no brakes and a stuck accelerator.

I comes at you so fast. You can barely react to one situation before you're faced with another.

Your heart seems the size of a football and involved in a scramble for a fumble. Each beat seems a blow against the rib cage.

Your throat and lungs seem constricted. Each breath is an effort. It feels like you're going to cry and all your automonous nervous system is short-circuited. You can whisper and yell but a normal tone of voice is almost impossible.

+ + +

YOUR STOMACH is ulcerish, knotted and loose and queasy at the same time. Bile rises to your cottonish mouth. Y o u r whole body seems to weaken.

It takes an effort to perform the simplest movements. The instant or second it takes your mind to get your body to do what it's been told seems an eternity. You seem numb all over.

It's an assault of sounds, smells and sights.

The sounds converge into a concert that drowns itself into chaos. Yet each note makes you flinch.

The smell is acrid burned cordite and the sickly sweet presence of blood, lots of it.

The sights are anatomy lessons no body should have to learn.

It's the heavy weary loss felt at a wake; several combined at once.

It's a fear of finality. Your finality. You just "know" it's going to happen to you next. You're not afraid of dying, just of it happening.

You almost resign yourself to it. "All you can do is your best now..."

Somehow it's over. Somehow you survived, but you'll be in a mild state of shock for days. You might have nightmares about it for weeks.

98

GO NOI ISLAND

Go Noi Island, almost entirely encircled by water during the monsoon periods, was a VC stronghold. When Marines entered the area bells would toll and dogs would bark in the distance. Everyone knew we were coming.

We would do battle, that was for certain. How many would we lose? It was always on our minds.

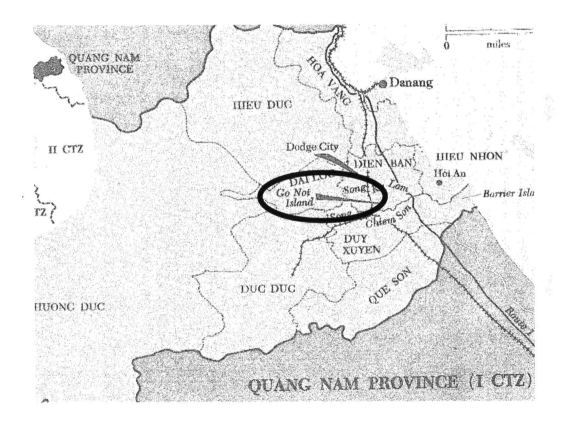

<u>Chris</u>

September 16 – Another sweep of Anderson Trail, East and West was completed. It's been raining all day and night. I'm told we are going on 6-10 day operation, going to the same place I caught those VC on Go Noi Island. We're expecting action. Everyone is checking out extra ammo, grenades and flares. I'm taking extra C-rats (C-rations) and a couple of canteens full of water. With the addition of all the extra ammo the load becomes incredibly heavy, but the load will lighten up a bit as we go along – we eat our C-rats, drink the water and fire our weapons. We learn to conserve each of these items, as we never know how long we'll be gone or when the next resupply chopper will be sent.

Doc Turner
September 16 – I just heard we are going back to Go Noi Island. I hate that place. We went there last summer, crossing the river to gain access to the island. It took two days to get onto the island. We marched all night long and they hit us about 0430-0500 in the morning, every hour on the hour. We climbed a mountain, looked over it and we could see the valley below. When you looked down the valley, you also saw that the adjacent mountain was very close to the mountain we were on. You could exit the valley at both ends, but you'd never be able to climb straight up and over the mountain. As always, it's gonna be a bitch. The island is covered with Viet Cong and their lookouts always know when we're coming.

Knobby
September 17 - We just finished digging a drainage ditch around our tent. It rains just about every day now.

Chris
September 17 – Now, our objective is someplace called Go Noi Island. It's not actually an island, but a place almost totally surrounded by water when the rains come.

Walking at night is very difficult. No one wants to make any sound, no matter how small, especially me, being one of the new guys. We are careful with each step, each branch that we come across. We want to go slowly, so that we are not detected by the enemy. We can't lose contact with the guys in front of us. It is so dark, which makes it so tough, walk slow, but don't lose sight of the guy in front of you. Shit, most of the time I can't even see him. The thought of getting separated from my squad is ever on my mind. If a sound is made by someone stepping on a branch or a cough, everyone freezes. Not a move. Not a sound, just listen and wait. Then, move forward, ever so carefully. It takes so long to walk short distances and you are so alert and ready to hit fire your weapon or to hit the ground. Every night. Every patrol. It doesn't change, unless you get ambushed or someone trips a mine.

Terry Halloran - Cincinnati, Ohio, Echo Co., 3rd Platoon
September 17 - Terry Fenenga carried a grease gun (a Thompson .45-automatic machine gun), not an M-16 rifle. The night of the river crossing, Terry and I were

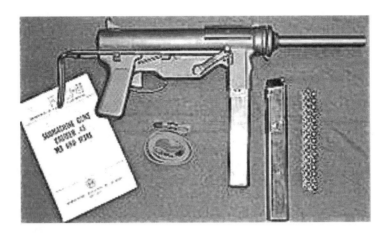

walking tail-end-Charlie (at the end of the squad) and we became separated from the rest of the platoon. We were also, at the rear of the Company. Terry was in front of me, so I was the last man. Terry usually just ditty-bopped or lollygagged slowly along and we got behind. I remembered when I had last seen someone and had a good idea of where we were going, so I took the point. We caught up to the rest of the squad at the river, just in time for us to cross. After crossing, I took the tail again. (You couldn't leave Terry alone; hard telling where you would find him). After the crossing, we settled in for the night. I stood the first two watches. Terry was beat and I was still keyed up from him getting us separated. I woke Robby Roberts up, to stand the last watch. I finally got a little sleep and it was right at dawn, not good daylight yet, when I woke to see a VC reaching for my M-16. I jumped up and got it, he took off running and I opened up on him about the same time everyone else saw him and opened up. We got him. Robby got a huge lump on the side of his head from the butt of my M-16 rifle. At that time, I really wanted to shoot him, but it passed.

I went with Lt. Suydam, to the company CP, stopping when we saw the Army of the Republic of Vietnam (ARVN) and I asked Lt. Suydam if there were supposed to be any friendlies in the area. I will always remember that ambush, the Marine behind him that got shot, had a sucking chest wound, the one of many that I had seen while over here. Without any hesitation the rest of the platoon came to our aid. I really wanted those C-rats. Terry had forgotten his C-rats (again), so I shared mine with him. We had been out since the day of the river crossing. That was just another day, that I was proud to be a member of Echo Company, 2nd Battalion, 1st Marines, 3rd herd (third platoon).

Chris
September 17 - Most Marines are carrying the standard 7.5 pound M-16 gas operated assault rifle, which fired most of the time, but not always. The rifle fires a .223 round that was packaged in 20-round magazines and a bandolier carried 10 magazines, meaning another substantial weight of 20-30 mags or 15-20 pounds of ammo. I also carried a three pound loaded .45 automatic pistol, with an extra magazine and my second favorite weapon was the lightweight, expandable M-72 LAW anti-tank rocket, which would take out a gathered enemy, a hooch or numerous other larger targets. Many of us carried the M-79 grenade launcher, my favorite. We've got a corpsman carrying a shotgun, a guy in my squad carries 2 .38 caliber pistols and the list goes on and on. My friend, Cpl. Chuck Estes, carried the PRC-25 squad radio, an absolute beast at 26 pounds. The rear command is passing the word for anyone carrying anything other than a Marine Corps issue weapon to turn it in immediately.

Lt. Suydam
September 18 - Terry Fenenga was thirty-two years old, half again as old as any of us boys. He spoke slowly and deeply and was not anywhere near the fastest boat in the fleet. Some called him the "old man" because of his age. Back in the states, he was a biker and he owned a Harley. He also owned and loved a "grease gun", which is a .45 caliber submachine gun. The grease gun is not to be confused with the beautifully sculpted .45 caliber Thompson submachine gun that G-men, like Elliott Ness carried on The Untouchables. No, the grease gun looked more like.........well, a grease gun. It was cheaply made and had one purpose. Tank crewmen, during World War II, carried it. If their tank should ever be put out of action and the crew had to come out among hostile troops, the grease gun was the weapon of choice. It could spray bullets and big bullets, very quickly. But, like all .45 caliber weapons I know of, it couldn't hit the broad side of a barn past twenty feet. A while back, we were on a shooting exercise. I positioned my pistol on top of a bunker. We used binoculars and 200 shells to hit an eight-inch mine sign in the mine field about 75 feet away. The .45 slug is just too big to go far with accuracy. The round is almost as big as a .50 caliber, but look at the difference in the shell casing between the two. The .50-caliber shell is five to six times bigger.

Before he joined the Marines, Terry would mount his grease gun to the handlebars of his Harley and ride down some deserted country road, shooting at beer cans. I can just imagine what kind of marksmanship he experienced with this crude and inaccurate relic.

When Terry shipped out for Vietnam, he disassembled his beloved grease gun and taped it to his legs with electrical tape. Consequently, he carried his beloved grease gun on patrols, instead of his issued weapon. We all learned to hate it when he would open up in the middle of the night, at some dark shadow he thought had moved. He never killed anything, but he sure did wake up the countryside.

Chris
September 18 – Last night all hell broke loose about ½ -1 mile away from us. It sounded like it was happening right next door. We grabbed our rifles and got ready for anything coming. Nothing…it was scary, as you anticipate it will all break out and be bad. The anticipation is amazing. No one got hurt. The word is tomorrow we're going out again for another operation.

The rains continue every day and night. We try to protect ourselves when we sleep, by lying down with our poncho, used as a water break against the ground, then folded over our body for some type of protection. When we awake for watch, we notice we've been sleeping in water. You just can't seem to keep it out. This is the way it is for everyone. No wonder we are always so cold.

When it's time for our watch at night, the rain disrupts the scary place we find ourselves in. The rain takes away the silence of the night. It disturbs the one true sense we count on - our hearing. If we are set in a brushy area or in the jungle itself, we can't see in front or to our sides more than a couple of yards. It would be quite easy for the enemy to crawl up on our position and lob a grenade in on our sleeping Marines. The night is very difficult on our nerves.

House
September 19 – We're back from six patrols in three days, covering about nine miles of bush. Heavy rains all day and night, with no moon. We spent time on mine sweeps on the dirt roads looking for tank/truck mines. We are also providing roadside security for men putting up poles and stringing wire all along Hwy. #1. These guys are real targets, up on the poles! For six hours at a time, we are standing in a rice paddy, or squatting behind a dike, then we move onto CAP #6, as a night blocking force. We have to slog through the flooded rice paddies to get set up, but this way we are able to bypass the booby traps that may have been waiting for us on the trail. The water is so cold and my glasses

103

keep fogging up from my sweat. The bamboo thickets that separate the paddies are very dense and some have heavy thorns that are very sharp. I made the mistake of grabbing onto one and get a couple of bad punctures, and now have oozing blood which the mosquitoes have an easy time tracking! If I squeeze repellent onto the wounds, it will burn like hell! Oh well, better than being bitten all night! Ooooow! It really burns deep….

We come under fire at CAP#6, bullets smacking the trees and paddy dikes, cracking off the brick buildings, smashing plaster and exploding in the dirt all around us, as we dive for whatever cover we can find. Pinned down for ten minutes we just hold fire and wait for them to run low on what small amount of ammo they are carrying. Then we all get up together on command and rip loose at once! Blasting away on-line, across the river, throwing a solid wall of lead their way! The FO (forward observer for artillery fire) calls in an artillery mission, and the explosions are big and loud. No more incoming rounds. We found a mine on the trail and blew it in place with C-4 plastic explosives. There are mines everywhere around us!

We take one casualty from 3rd platoon, who stepped into a punji-stake trap. It is a steel rod, sharpened with a hook on top and dipped in human crap, to make the infection really bad. The steel spike is set in a big tin can, filled with cement, buried in the ground. Then they wire it to a grenade, with the pin pulled in another can on its side, so when he pulled his foot out with the stake through his boot and foot, the wire would pull the grenade and blowup anyone else coming to help. Nice, huh? Spanky immediately stopped the guy that had stepped on the pungi-stick. He had spotted the attached wire. Spanky crawled down the slight embankment, where the scared Marine was standing. He was so afraid to move. Spanky, appearing quite clam, used his K-Bar knife to cut the boot off the Marine's foot, being careful to keep the boot from moving since it was attached to a mine. The hole through the trooper's foot was so nasty from the punji-stake. It has got to be so infected!

I was so hot and thirsty with all that was going on and my cuts were burning so bad with salt from my own sweat, I got cramps and almost passed out. The guys poured their canteens over me to cool me off and Doc Turner gave me some salt tabs and fixed up my cuts, in the shade.

Lt. Suydam
September 19 - The hammer and anvil is military terminology for a pincer movement by two units, where one is stationary (the anvil) and one is mobile (the

hammer). Echo Company, third platoon was assigned as an anvil for a company moving from our south. It was in the Phong Ngu area actually, on the southern border marked by a river with deep banks.

Rivers are dangerous. Border areas are dangerous. They are like the dividing lines between police jurisdictions. Sooner or later, the bad guys get the picture that the area isn't patrolled as often as other areas. The river with its steep banks provides cover. We set up and waited for the better part of an afternoon. We felt that the dangerous part of the mission was just getting there and getting back and we never really expected to see any action. But, then the third squad, about 300 meters to my left, called on the radio, to say that there were about twenty VC to their front. They asked for orders. I said, "shoot 'em!"

They blasted away for a while, scattering the VC. Neither the second, nor the first squad saw anything. We were too spread out? It was dusk and time to pull out. Did we kill anyone? I don't know.

Chris
September 19 - Our squad came to a halt, which was a normal procedure when walking down trails, if something was not in order. Caution always prevailed. The squad halted and went down on one knee. Spanky yelled at a Marine in front of me, about 2-3 guys away, not to move. Spanky removed his canteen and ammo belt, set his rifle down and slowly moved to the young Marine's position. As he approached him, Spanky began to sweat profusely. He stepped off the side of the trail up ahead and bent over, next to the Marine. One of the new guys had gotten off the trail and had stepped on some type of buried device, probably an explosive mine.

I couldn't, actually see Spanky. For all we knew he was directly in front of us about 10 yards and was attempting to help a young Marine in trouble. It was quite serious for both of them. It took a long time and the tension was thick. Everyone was quiet.

We were all waiting for something to blow up both of them. Finally, Spanky appeared. He was totally drained, exhausted from the tedious work of removing the boot, removing the mine and saving the Marine's life. We all congratulated him and told him we were going to put him up for a medal. He would have no talk of medals. That was it. We picked up our gear and continued down the trail, the event forgotten.

When I thought about this event later, I realized how prepared Spanky had been. Now only did he selflessly embark on a life-saving mission with the young Marine, but depended on the lessons we all had been taught - calmly and methodically, he used his combat knife to cut through the tough Marine Corps boot to release the young man's foot. Wonder if the knife hadn't been sharp? We were all quite proud of our squad leader.

Spanky just saved the private's life and now needed a smoke break.

House

September 20 - Da Nang TAOR (Tactical Area of Responsibility) - Cpl. D.J. Teebo, 1st Fire Team Leader says we will be going out on a search & destroy mission called Operation Shelbyville, against the 5th North Vietnam Regiment for about 6 to 10 days. We hear they are hardened veterans that fought the French Foreign Legion and killed lots of them. These guys stand and die!

The operation was to be in a place called Go Noi Island, 25 miles south of Da Nang, where rivers isolate a piece of land. It was a bleak, desperately hot place, which resembled a moonscape covered with tall elephant grass. It had a bad reputation and there were no permanent positions on it. Estes hated this place

Photo by Cpl MJ Coates

and rightfully so. It was inhabited by the Viet Cong and we got hurt every time we went there. Actually, we got our asses kicked each and every time.

Note: Companies E and F and the 2/1 command group participated in Operation Shelbyville, a search and destroy operation on Go No Island, from September 22 through September 28. ARVN troops and units from 3/5 and 1/3 also participated.

Echo 2/1 moved by truck to Cau Lau Bridge and foot marched to the battalion assembly area near My Hat. At first light the company was to follow in trace of Fox Company and establish a blocking force. Echo company had attachments of engineers, snipers and scouts and scout dogs and was supported by the battalion's 81mm mortar platoon and by B battery, 11th Marines (artillery).

House

September 21 - We have Combat Photographer Cpl. Michael J, Coates and ISO combat reporter Cpl. Steve Bernston assigned to our platoon. They string along with each squad. They're good company and promise to get us all in *Stars and Stripes* magazine and make us famous. Coates keeps a notebook and documents every photo with the name and the hometown of each guy he photographs.

We all load up onto tracked ARVN armored personal carriers (APC) that float and move across a wide river, about fifteen miles south of Da Nang.

The point where we cross is about 100 meters wide, but it looks like it narrows farther downstream. The ARVN troops running the APC's are nuts, revving the diesel like race car drivers. Their insignia is a big white racehorse, painted on the side in full gallop.

We find out we have just been deposited onto a nasty piece of real estate that Marines will have a tough time far into the future, called "Go Noi Island." It is not really an island, but a big area surrounded by rivers and streams. This place has a very bad reputation. To the south, is a big mountain range that is used by the NVA and VC to infiltrate from Laos. Almost all the young men around here are active VC. It has been a staging area for NVA units building up for attacks against Da Nang for years. It is covered with flooded rice paddies, high elephant grass, graveyards, and bamboo thickets.

We are wet all night and we try to settle in. I put a heat tab under my can of spaghetti and meatballs and two mortar rounds come in from behind a big bunch of grave headstones, explode, and the air lights up with green tracers! My good poncho, which I had strung up over me to keep myself and my food dry, had two bullet holes in it and the mortar concussion has blown mud all over me, including my food, but then it all just stops! Scrambling for my rifle, I knocked over my warrior statue and his hand and spear broke in three pieces, but I can fix it. Everyone is all nerves, sticking out everywhere. Nobody saw any of these guys and they were gone! We all stayed one-eye-open all night!

Chris

September 21 – Operation Shelbyville – 6x6 trucks carry Echo and Fox Company to the "Song Bien River" Bridge and a small village called My Hat, then turn east (to confuse the VC). We promptly took sniper fire! (they were supposed to think we would go west, I guess).

Cpl Mike Coates, Combat Photographer

As we moved along the road, there was a slowdown, and we crept past a horrible sight I will never forget. From what we could tell, in the usual gathering of curious and excited children crowded on the side of the road, somehow a little girl had been pushed or fell into the path of one of our trucks, and was crushed under the wheels. She was wearing the traditional Ao-Dai silk dress that was a soft pink, and her intestines, which were the same soft pink color had been popped out of her abdomen, and were thrown clear across the width of the road in a straight line, maybe fifteen feet long. They glistened in the sunlight, against the blacktop road, and I had a hard time realizing what I was seeing. They were so long and clean, as if someone had stretched them out, like a rope. It was such a shame to think that her mother had combed her hair, and dressed her so pretty and sent her off in the morning to school or play, and she was lost in an instant as roadkill, trying to catch some candy, from the generous Americans speeding by. As tragic as this was, it was part of callousness of the men, during this time.

The engineers find numerous booby-traps along the way, made from 155mm artillery shells, and blew them up. (We must shoot too many duds, or else, we leave a lot of artillery shells laying around). We took three mortar rounds close-by, but it was soft dirt, the explosion went underground and nobody was hit.

Lt. Suydam

September 22 - Highway 1 is the north-south artery that runs from the North Vietnamese capital of Hanoi in North Vietnam to Saigon, the South Vietnamese capital. The highway runs along the eastern side of Vietnam following the coastline. As you travel south along Route 1, you pass through Dien Ban, a French built city-market with walls and eventually cross the Song Cau Lau River. This great river is formed by the merger of the great Song Ky Lam and the lesser Song Chiem Sun. These two rivers run close together forming a landmass between them that we called Go Noi Island. In reality the place is not an island at all, but an area in which the low-lying areas were flooded so that access was usually only possible by boat. The island runs east and west for eighteen kilometers and is four kilometers at its widest point. Echo Company had been there before and there were many old stories circulating among the troops about the horrors to be found there. Abandoned by the civilian population, the area is filled with trench works and fortifications and had the signs of a battlefield. The Island is reportedly a VC regimental headquarters. Echo Company is to reach the island by stealth and in darkness and then root out the enemy.

We approached Go Noi Island from the south, sometime after midnight by wading across the Song Chiem Sun River. The water was cold and neck deep, but no current. Third platoon was last to cross. Echo turned left upon entering the island and formed a line along the river. We set up a listening post and patiently awaited the dawn.

Before dawn arrived my troops saw a man in a round basket boat paddling in circles in the area where we had just crossed the river. He stayed there for an hour, then vanished. As dawn came three VC walked into our perimeter and stepped on some of our sleeping troops. These VC were the first three casualties of our visit. Moments later, a VC opened a tunnel entrance in the middle of the company command post (CP). He was summarily dispatched. The four dead VC confirmed that we had successfully entered their midst, undiscovered and that we were waking up among them.

The company CP was about 300 meters to our west circled by the middle platoon. At some point, a chopper landed with mail and C-rations. I dispatched a fire team to walk the 300 meters down to the CP and return with our share. At the last minute, the company commander (CO) radioed for platoon commanders to assemble. So I got up and followed the fire team to the CP. I didn't think to take the radioman. It had been quiet for a long time and it was only 300 meters away. On our way down, we saw four ARVN troops (South Vietnamese Army) along a tree line with their colorful Boy Scout-like neckerchiefs. They gave us a friendly wave and we all waved back. Our comment at the time was, "I didn't know there were ARVN troops on this mission." We thought no more of it. ARVN troops among our own were a common situation. These men not only looked ARVN but also carried the typical U.S. issued WW II era weapons.

We had our meeting, we talked about the strange events of the first morning, and we were on our way back to our platoon perimeter. Suddenly, the world was shooting at us. We dropped the mail and C-rats in the trail and fell into a trench along the right side the trail. I pulled my .45 and aimed it forward. The lead man had jumped left off the trail, so I was the most forward one in the trench. My .45-caliber pistol was like a popgun compared to the opposing firepower, but it was the only thing I had.

There was clearly a Browning Automatic Rifle (BAR) booming down the trail and the mailbag danced a jig each time he opened up. The C-rats boxes were being perforated as peach juice and beans oozed out and ran down the sides. There was also an M-79 grenade launcher trying to find our range and several other automatic and semi-automatic small arms popping over our heads. I distinctly heard the chirping of a U.S. M1 carbine. Suddenly, the trooper behind me took a round in his left lung, high, near his collarbone. I looked forward and saw the side of the trench explode and knew they were firing down the trench. (At the time, I thought the round had come past me, but later we figured that a round had hit a log over the trench and ricocheted down into the trooper's lung). I took the wounded trooper's M-16 rifle and handed him my cocked 45-cal. pistol. Big Mistake! As he rotated left and collapsed in pain, he squeezed off three rounds into the side of the trench. It would have been me except for his twisting motion as he sunk down.

Had the trench been straighter, we would have perished there. At one point, still unconvinced that we were under hostile fire, I yelled out, "Cease fire, we're Marines." I didn't understand the Vietnamese answer I received but the tone of the enemy soldier's voice removed all doubt, but that we were destined for annihilation. We never saw anyone to shoot at and within seconds, troops from our perimeter came out to our rescue. We found a place to scoot out from the trench and retire to our perimeter lines. Meanwhile, an airborne Forward Observer (FO) who watched the whole thing from his small plane was bringing in artillery fire to disrupt the ambush and drive off the enemy. I know now that they were the four ARVN-looking troops we had seen earlier. As the ambushers departed, they scarfed up the mailbag and all the C-rats boxes they could carry.

One of our platoons M-60 machine gun crews.

Picture by Cpl MJ Coates - Combat Photographer

Were they regular ARVN soldiers that played both sides against the middle? Were they VC wearing captured clothing and equipment to deceive the enemy? Either way, it wasn't pleasant to think about.

I took the absolute worst ass chewing of my life from the captain for getting ambushed, getting ambushed and having wounded, getting ambushed and loosing the U.S. mail, for getting ambushed without a radio and for going anywhere without a radio. Oh, did I mention losing the mail? We all had to write our loved ones, admit this humiliating experience and urge them not to open any strange packages.

House
September 22 - We moved out at midnight, crossing a chest-deep river. We took a few sniper rounds, while crossing, and then Marines, guarding the bridge down-river thought we were enemy and opened up on us! They shot illumination canisters from their 81mm mortars and a couple of casings splashed down in the

river, where we could see and hear them – too close! Luckily, everyone was on their radios real fast and stopped the shooting, before anyone got hit.

In the morning, as we moved up the trail towards a village, our Chu-Hoi Scout, "Yung" found a "farmer" hiding in a hole and "questioned" him with his rifle-butt! After feeling the impact of the rifle butt, the Vietnamese guy told him two places where the VC were hiding!

Our squad moved over a couple of rice paddy dikes to a flat spot where there was a small temple or shrine that had been damaged. Part of the roof had been blown off.   There was a big drum suspended from the beams with ropes and many carved panels, wood grillwork and statues scattered around.   There were also old French coins and candles, and bowls of rice left as offerings.   The lieutenant told us to destroy the drum, so the VC could not use it as a signaling device. Easy! One grenade would do the trick!

I spotted a carved statue of an ancient warrior, about 18" tall standing in the far corner, all painted blue and gold (my high-school colors). He had carved armor and real hair, whiskers and sideburns and a huge spear with a dragon buckle on his fat belly – he was awesome!

The drum was made of a beautiful mahogany wood and had ebony wood pegs holding the skin drumheads. The drum had to go, but I did not intend to let that warrior statue be destroyed or be left behind!   (This was my first and only experience as a war looter!). I rolled him up inside my poncho and strapped him to the bottom outside of my pack. Now, I have to carry the extra weight and bulk with me the whole rest of the operation and explain him to any superior that asks and take my chances at being disciplined, but if I can send him home, what a trophy!

The ARVN were there by then, and those guys were NOT HAPPY to see me roll him up! They jabbered and pointed their little M-1 rifles at me, like I was robbing their church or something! (Maybe I was, but I did not care, I was saving the statue from destruction!) Speck pointed his M-79 right back at them and told them to move away, as he was going to blow up the building. He not only blew the drum and the building to pieces, he threw in a thermite grenade and set it all on fire! The candle wax and dry splintered wood went up like a match!

We dug-in and it rained all night. Our recently dug holes filled up with water and my legs began cramping, from the cold water. I was so cold and shivering, that I could not wait to piss myself, just to warm the frigid water I was sitting in, even for a short time for a little warmth. I kept the statue dry, and the ARVN troops moved down the line away from us.

The next morning, we set up around a small village and just hunkered down. Nothing much goes on for hours. No water for resupply, and we are all hot and thirsty. We fill canteens from a small creek, flowing into the rice paddies. It smells bad enough to put three Halazone tabs (water purification) into each canteen and shake'em up real good in a feeble, yet hopeful attempt to kill all the bad dysentery bugs. The hot muddy water burns all the way through your mouth and down your throat and then burns again when you burp it back up, but at least it is wet! The Halazone burns for an hour longer and I regret it!

September 23 - After crossing about ten rice paddies, by 0700 hours we are on a big 1,000 meter line-sweep with multiple companies. We found a large rusty painted-metal sign hanging on a barb-wire fence at the entrance to the next village we are about to enter. It reads, in rusting faded colors: "25,000 FRENCH COLONIAL BODIES ARE ROTTING HERE- GET OUT OF VIETNAM BEFORE YOURS JOINS THEM." Now, who do you think we might find in that next village - friend or foe?

Yung, our company Chieu Hoi, (VC turned U.S. "good-guy" interpreter) finds a tunnel close by. He just throws in two grenades. We do not get to do that sort of thing. His rules of engagement" are pretty loose, compared to ours! We need to get permission from the lieutenant and it goes on from there at times, as there could be civilians inside. The grenade Yung throws is followed by an explosion and then it starts a fire inside. Thirty seconds later, one hell big explosion! How did he know there was ammo hidden inside? (He didn't).

Doc Turner
September 23 - We were coming in from the sweep, at the far end of Goi Noi Island, when the three squads of 2nd platoon split up. I went with second squad, which ended up at a modern hooch, bomb shelter place. I was given a percussion grenade and told that when I threw it in the hole, I would only have 5 seconds before it would explode. I pulled the pin, threw it in and ran, only getting about 15 feet from the entrance of the bomb shelter, when it blew. Then it blew again, about 150 feet away from us. Explosions were going off all over the place. Captain Baker replied "you're blowing up the entire island". It turned out to be an underground explosives factory. Not bad for a "noncombatant's" first opportunity at some actual action.

I told Chris there was a double explosion, when I threw the grenade into the bunker, the second one greater than the first. I was blown past where I was supposed to land and received minute particles of shrapnel in my butt. Also, have a piece in one of my eyes. That is how I got my Purple Heart.

House
September 23 - Moving across open paddy dikes, we take AK-47 fire from a lone brick house on the far side, about 200 meters away. We all dive down into the filthy water and we hear "Corpsman up!". One of our guys has been shot through the jaw." One of the corpsmen – Doc Miller runs past us, on top of the dike, fully exposed to the fire, tracers flying around him and I see him flip his new 35mm Instamatic camera off his wrist, into the water where it disappears.

Speck is up and on it with the M-79. His eyes kind of glaze over and he just keeps advancing and firing, oblivious to the incoming fire and blows the house apart!

The corpsman has the trooper on his back, partially protected by a dike and partially shielded by his own body. The poor guy is thrashing around so hard. He has been hit, badly. As usual, Doc Miller does a great job and is able to stop the bleeding and after he gives him a shot of morphine, we carry him off the paddy dikes and back to a clearing for a medevac.

Chris
September 23 - Yung finds another dug-in bunker (this guy is like a bloodhound sniffing the dirt) with a teenage boy inside. Yung is positive he is VC and wants to beat him up too, but the lieutenant won't let him and Yung is pissed! He tells the Lt that he can get more VC information, if he can beat him, but no deal. We tie him up and sit him down, away from Yung! We turn him over to the ARVN, and watch as they beat and take him away!

Ahead of us, our Huey gun ships are working on dug-in VC for about three hours straight. It is like a light show in the sky. Flares are in the air all night over the area. We got a couple grenades thrown at us during the night, but nobody got close enough to hurt us. One of our guys got bitten by a bright red centipede that had to be 8 inches long, with big pincers. His arm swelled to three times normal size, like a balloon that was about to pop, and he got terribly sick. He was medevaced out to an aid station in about thirty minutes.

September 24 - We all just sat around and watched F-105 Thunder-Thud aircraft and helicopter gunships conduct air strikes on VC positions way out from us, it was too cool! We made water runs and resupply for ammo at 1300 hours, then were moved north 2,000 meters by truck.

Chris

September 24 – Sometimes we have engineers with us that take care of the detection and removal of mines. When they're not with us, it's our job to either turn around and walk the other way or dig it up ourselves. We make note of where we suspect a mine might be, so other Marines don't walk into trouble if we decide not to mess with it. Otherwise, someone has to step up with their K-Bar or better a bayonet, as it has a longer blade. The weapon is carefully pushed into the ground at a 45 degree angle, so when it meets something it's on the side of the mine, and not on the top part or the pressure plate, which would cause detonation. When a mine is found it can be removed or even better, blown in place. It's a terrible job, no matter what is going to be done. Nerves of steel! Quiet concentration. Only a few of the guys do this and only if they have to. Better yet, go around it and report it to command.

September 25 – We settled in during the late night. It was scary enough being on Go Noi Island, but we found ourselves sleeping in a cemetery. To have some protection, should we get in a firefight, a few of us slept on fresh graves. These were mass graves, with mounds built up 3' high, so they were larger than normal and provided more protection. They stunk so badly, we had a difficult time getting to sleep. It was probably sacrilegious to hide on fresh graves, but we needed to hide and get cover, until dawn. I couldn't sleep.

House

September 26 - Early morning, we had to cross this filthy, swamp/ garbage dump/ pond that smelled so bad, with mud and weeds so thick and rotting on top and crawling with ants, you had to push it out of the way with your rifle to make headway. Puke! We should have had 6-8 ropes at the far end, to scale out of the steep bank and to clear the water, but we only had two. No cover - what a screw-up! Bunched-up exposed, waiting in line in the water, just to get out, just like our guys during WW II going in at low tide at Tarawa and getting slaughtered! If the VC had been there, we would have been sitting ducks! Poor tactics and bad planning! Leadership? Walk, walk, walk some more, but don't plan enough to bring ropes! Guys were clawing their way up the bank to get out of the open, swearing blue streaks all the way up.

September 27 - Our last night on Go Noi Island. All the guys call it "Gonad Island" because you really have to have balls to stay here! The VC own this place and they want us to know they do not want us here! We get probed, sniped, grenades, and harassed every night! I threw my last grenade at one of them and heard the guy run well beyond range before it could go off! The VC here are seasoned fighters. They know what they are doing! They disappear so quickly it is like magic or they drop into holes in the ground we cannot find.

I now have the runs so bad I'm going in my pants every hour or so and stink to heaven! The bugs in that paddy water were a lot stronger than the Halazone purification tabs I used. I have got to see the corpsmen and get some chalk or something to stop this. It hurts, I cannot stand the smell of myself, and I cannot keep rinsing out my pants in the river!

Lt. Suydam
September 28 - Our biggest success from our raid on Go Noi Island was the discovery of a mine factory, which was being operated by the young women that did laundry and ran small stores around our battalion HQ in An Tu. These girls were keeping tabs on us for the VC and running mines up Highway 1 on their bikes. What a mess we were in Vietnam. These same sixteen-year old girls who sell Cokes by the roadside had been trying all the time to blow us up. The feeling of betrayal from this experience permeated the morale of every one of us. We had worked hard to gain respect and show friendship toward the civilian population around our battalion CP, only to find that our friends were, in actuality, our enemies

Chris
September 28 – One of the worst personal experiences happened earlier today. We were on a squad size patrol through one of the hamlets, when we received a couple of sniper rounds. We all hit the deck and tried to identify where the rounds were coming from. L/Cpl. Davis and Pvt. Spelling called out to me as they ran towards where they thought the round had been shot. I had been in country long enough to know to respond immediately when told to do something. I trailed them by about 30-40 yards and when I finally reached the place they had stopped, they had three Vietnamese villagers lined up. They had lined them up

One of our 81MM mortars in action!

Photo by Cpl Mike Coates - Combat

about 8 yards in front of where they were standing. Both of the guys turned their rifles at me and said, "We're going to kill these gooks and you better fire or we'll kill you." They immediately turned their rifles on the man, woman and young male and each fired their weapons, each emptying a full magazine from their M-16 rifles. It was just horrible. They were unarmed and had just been torn apart with 40 rounds of M-16 ammo. I just stood there, in shock. I couldn't fire. It was not an option. I had just witnessed my first murder of innocent people. Neither of them said anything, just turned and walked back to where we had come. I couldn't report what I had seen. There were two of them and only one of me. I felt so alone and if they could kill these guys, then they could kill me. I knew they would. It was a horrible feeling.

Later on, Davis was seen by others in the squad to carry out similar atrocities during his tour. No one seemed to know what to do. If an accusation was to be brought up, it would only take one night and the individual that reported the action would be killed.

September 29 - A guy named Cpl. Joe Keller tripped a mine while on patrol and died of wounds. Keller was good friends with Lavelle, who was killed earlier this month. Davis and Spelling probably took it worse than anyone. (They would later take their own personal revenge). Big firefight today, also.

Knobby
September 29 - We got in from Operation Shelby around 3 this morning. We'll be leaving on a short patrol pretty soon, but should be back in 2-3 days, which means we get paid as soon as we get in. I had been saving money each month to take on R&R by leaving it on the books. I think I'll send it home though and have my parents bring it with them to Hawaii. I don't want to be carrying too much cash on me.

Doc Turner
September 29 – I don't know why Lt. Swiss didn't say anything about Davis/ Spelling murder incident, as I do believe he knew about it, yet nothing was said. Maybe it was because we couldn't afford to lose any additional men. We'll probably never know. I believe the best way to say that would be, "I feel the lieutenant had his suspicions regarding the death of those probable North Vietnamese regulars, but it would be extremely hard to prove. Secondly, bringing those facts or suspicions to light would put him as an officer, his life, in jeopardy. The reason I say that is the two guys, by training, were proficient killers and I think they loved it. Mentally, it gave them a feeling of power in a situation they were unable to control. Like, I'm over here, I don't want to be, so I'm gonna do what I want.

 Note: Communists who killed civilians received commendations. The NVA death squads focused on leaders at the village level and on anyone who improved the lives of the peasants, such as medical personnel, social workers and schoolteachers.

House
September 29 - The captain passes the word that we will be walking all the way back to the rear area. There are no trucks available for us. They are in need, elsewhere. That's 9,000 meters for the troops.

We all have trench-foot or ringworm and I have blisters with strips of skin peeling off in raw chunks. The corpsmen are swamped with foot-care problems. If it was not raining, it was flooded, and we were always wet! I never had enough dry socks. I carried eight pairs and could not keep my feet dry.

Chris is really in bad shape. He is limping hard, but will not ask for help. He even carries others extra gear, if they need it. His feet are a bloody mess – shredded! The corpsman keeps patching him up and he keeps moving along, and does not complain. I know he has GOT to be hurting!

Getting off Go Noi Island is not quite as easy as the mobile ARVN APC (personnel carrier) trip across to get us there. Someone comes up with these big rubber boats and Fox Company goes down over the bank onto the sandy beach and starts loading up, like twenty guys to a boat, big boats. Everybody is happy to get off the lousy island! Outboards crank up and the boats move out into the channel. Then the VC open up with rifle-grenades and AK-47's to try to sink the boats midstream, loaded with Marines with no life jackets!

We are still on the sandy beach below the riverbank (in front of the high bank, actually with no cover) and all we can do is drop or run! Running on loose sand, with bullets flying around and no cover is pretty tough! I decided I have to get a clear shot from cover, so I turn my back and climb the loose sand bank. By the time I get to the top, everyone else up there had already opened-up on the tree line across the river and ripped it to shreds, and artillery came down on it big-time! It was gone! The trees had disappeared in that area due to so much fire power that had been concentrated on it in response. I did not get off a single shot.

One of the Golf Co. guys in a boat was hit in the back and one man on our side of the river was shot in the stomach. Two boats were damaged, almost sunk, and we lost a radio, five rifles and some ammo boxes, nothing more. Both Marines were medevaced in about twenty minutes and we heard they made it okay.

We marched for six hours straight. Every man was dead on his feet. About 2000 hours our point man – Keller, in 3rd squad, started to pull open a bamboo panel on a fence and set off a booby-trapped M-26 grenade. It lifted him straight up in the air and he landed on the barbed wire. That was the VC signal to open their ambush on us. Out of this bamboo thicket flies a stream of green-tracers machine gun fire! We are already on-line and flipped to full auto, with the M-60 gun crew up and ready. The corpsman was on the wounded point man. We opened up over the top of the two guys at the base of the fence into that bamboo thicket and blew it to hell! Speck kept putting M-79 rounds into it like shotgun shells and the M-60 tore it up!

About 30 meters to our right was a big strong-looking paddy dike, and as I was running for it, it was shot-up from another gun site the VC had as a cross fire. I kept running, looking for cover, and our corpsman, Doc Tuner ran past me even faster with his med-kit out, chasing Keller, who was wounded, but was now up and really hauling!

Doc Turner
September 29 - Anselman and I marched together for part of the day. He was a pretty good guy. He was from Wisconsin and he always talked about wanting to be a professional hockey player. That was almost all he talked about. He wanted to return to the states to play hockey - that was it. It had been a long day for both of us, with so much going on. It was good to get a short break and talk with him before the next shit hit the fan, as we both knew it would.

House
September 29 - The captain was directing M-60 machine guns and 60mm mortars into another tree-line where the Gunny had spotted VC about 25 meters further to the right. Then just as fast as it had all started, we hear this VC bugle and it all stopped. The VC disappeared into the trees.

Come to find out, Keller had been hit really bad and was running on pure adrenalin, pumping out all his blood! Doc Turner was running as hard as he could through all that fire to try to stop and treat him! By the time the medevac chopper came in, another man sat on a booby-trap and was hurt and it took an hour to get him and poor Keller out - It was too long! A black sergeant from weapons platoon found eight booby-trap grenades in the same fence line. He told us he could smell them!

After Fox Company secured the far side about 2100 hours, the rubber boat trip across to the other side started in the dark. We started the long slog back home. My pack had cut deep into my shoulders. I had heat rash on my back and my crotch, my feet were already killing me and I just ached all over! We had at least seven men badly wounded today and we all hate Go Noi Island!!!

Finally, at 0030 this morning, we got moving to cross a small river. I was so thirsty I drank straight from it and filled both canteens. It was so cold and good, and since I already had the runs I figured I had nothing to lose, as my guts HAD to be empty by now.

Here is Echo Company coming down off the bank from Go Noi Island to load into the rubber boats just before the shit hit the fan when they opened-up on us. It was a long run back up that hill with bullets coming at my back, but all these guys were ahead of me!

Photo by Cpl MJ Coates

The lieutenant then tells us our squad will have to guide this amphibious tractor called an Otter that is run by some Australians back to our area. Spanky is furious! This is making us sitting ducks! The machine has these little running lights, noisy tracks and diesel motor, but the lieutenant says "Sgt. Baldwin, yours is the best squad for the job!" We get to be the last troops in the whole battalion to walk-in at 0230 in the morning with this Otter following us! The racket is terrible and it made us a huge target, but nothing happened! Not a single sniper round!

We had free beer and soda waiting, hot chow, ice water, showers and my rain gear had finally arrived in the mail from home! Oh, man, how wonderful! I drank my soda, ate my chalk pills, gave my beers to Chris and Speck, took my mail and slept!

**Lance Corporal J. Keller, Newark, New Jersey
(panel 27E line 29 on The Wall)**

We got word Keller had died of his wounds on way to the aid station. Everyone went stone silent the rest of the day. It was so hard to believe. The guys were tight and had lost someone special. I did not ask any questions. I saw a deep hurt on all the guys' faces. I am too new to say anything and just kept quiet out of respect.

The lieutenant briefs us, saying we will be leaving this area soon, being relieved by 3/5, and will move north for a "more aggressive push", as President Johnson wants the Marines to be doing more. Our work here is described as more of a "civil action and pacification." All the guys look at each other and raise eyebrows? Huh? (no snickers or smiles). "We will be moving north as a unit - how far north we are not sure yet, but 2/1 will be moving up against some stronger stuff than we have seen around Da Nang."

Chris
September 29 - While everyone was breaking down weapons, two men approached. The guys immediately noticed that there were strap marks on their shoulders and backs, which told us they were VC. They asked for water and were given water and salt by the senior guys in the squad. Evidently they had done this before. They then put heat tabs under a poncho and gassed them when they asked for food. When the heat tabs were lit, they gave off a gas, which was poisonous. The squad was adamant about putting these guys through a few exercises before turning them over to command. It seemed to be the only way they could release the built-up anger and hatred they had stored from losing friends.

September 30 – It's been so bad lately. I got back from Operation Shelbyville at midnight on the 29th. It was not a good operation, as we didn't get many VC kills and we incurred some damage. We hadn't lost any guys until six hours before we returned. We just learned that a good friend of mine, named Keller, was injured and died of injuries caused by a tripped booby trap mine. Doc Turner ran through bullets raining down to get to Keller and help. Doc is probably the bravest man out here. No flash or boasting about anything, just calm, concerned professional, looks out for all of us. I don't know how he does it. After Keller got hurt, we immediately got into a firefight. An additional four men were hurt on a separate situation, also by a trip wired booby trap, including a San Antonio guy - I can't remember his name. Davis and Spelling really took Keller's death hard, as they were good buddies. It was really a fouled-up operation, with both the captain and the colonel new to 'Nam and I guess it showed. We walked 30-40 miles or more and it was rough. My feet were really hurtin' from being in wet rice-paddies constantly. I have a touch of ringworm on my feet, along with many open sores that bleed, but I'm trying real hard to keep them in good shape. We just received word that we are heading north, probably to replace 1st Battalion, 9th Marines at Con Thien. This is the place we have been so lucky to avoid since I've been in Vietnam. We hear of the NVA mass attacks against this base on the DMZ. Tens of thousands of NVA troops have tried to overrun the base and have gotten through the wire. Hand to hand combat is reported.

I do appreciate all the letters from Dad, you Mom, Bel and everyone. I am a team leader now, with three other men in my team and am second in command of the squad.

House

September 30 – The lieutenant tells us to start sorting out all non-essential goods, send home any non-issue gear or get rid of it, and burn all of our letters. We are moving our unit to Quang Tri, which is north of our current position. Only the bare essentials are to go. Welcome to hard times, Marines! I mailed home, the Billy the Warrior statue that I had acquired, and everything else, including my tape recorder and our baby's first tapes and all of Nancy's letters, my pictures, everything. Now we start over!

I watched as the supply lieutenant walks around with a camera and clipboard, documenting thousands of dollars worth of gear thrown in piles, getting rained-on and ruined. I take pictures of guys throwing stuff onto fires, TV's, radios, record players, clothes, personal stuff and USMC gear strewn all around.   The Vietnamese civilians are scooping up everything they can. Crates are out in the open with stuff throw-in, rained on and ruined like radios and with nobody in control, its crazy!

Some idiots even throw ammo into the fires, and bullets pop! We have to dig it all back out. We find one claymore mine, two M-26 grenades and 1000 rounds M-60 machine gun ammo in one pile!

Later, we heard a division-level Inspector General charge was made against Lt. Col. Van Winkle for not taking care of government property in the proper manner for our move.

As we were loading out on our trucks, there was a steady flow back and forth of troops from 3rd Battalion, 5th Marine Regiment with all their gear to take over our area. Those guys were getting the deal of the century, most of our stuff for free, because we had abandoned it all! Some fine turnover! What a waste!

We are told we will be going to Da Nang Airbase and load out onto KC-130 transport aircraft to fly to Dong Ha Airbase up north approximately 100 miles to a new command post on Hill #25, slightly southwest (about 4,000 meters) of the city of Quang Tri.

Note: The September Command Chronology for 2nd Battalion, 1st Marines indicates an increased amount of enemy activity and an increase in the size of the enemy units sighted. From September 22-28 the battalion command group plus companies E and F and company K from 3/1 participated in Operation Shelbyville on Go Noi Island. Twelve VC were confirmed killed with 8 probables and 3 captured. 2nd Battalion, 1st Marines casualties for September: 5 enlisted KIA and 46 enlisted WIA.

Runner's Job Not a Waltz

Written Written by Cpl Bernston, Combat

DA NANG—Although in recent years the radio has become the normal way of a company contacting its platoons, one man still remains very important in any field company group—the company runner.

The man designated "company runner" is generally a "jack of all trades" and is used for various jobs around a company office, whether in the battalion area or in the field on combat operations.

One such "runner" is LCpl. Clinton N. Davis, Hackensack, N.J., and "E" Co., 2nd Bn., First Marine Regiment, 1st Marine Division.

Davis, previously a 3.5-inch rocket team leader, has been company runner for the past two months.

"A runner's most important tasks occur when the company is in the field. Out there on an operation, I'm constantly with the captain. When he can't reach one of the platoons by radio, or if he can't repeat instructions over the radio net I deliver the m e s s a g e personally," said Davis.

When not on an operation, Davis' main duties are driving the company "mule," a small flat-bed vehicle used to shuttle supplies and gear around the area, carrying and delivering administrative papers, and just being the "Gunny's helper."

6

OPERATION MEDINA

Note: The 1st and 2nd battalions of the 1st Marine Regiment, 1st Marine Division were "chopped op-con" to the 3rd Marine Division to supplement the Marine battalions operating in Quang Tri Province. From October 11-19 the battalion participated in Operation Medina in the Hai Lang National Forest Preserve southwest of Quang Tri.

Operation Medina -
Hai Lang forest

Knobby

October 1 - The 1st Marines are being moved north to Quang Tri province (close to the DMZ). Our battalion will spearhead the move, which is scheduled in the next 3-5 days. I got most of my personal gear packed today. I had thought that I would have to send a lot of it home, but now I don't think I will. T and I sold the record player and most of the records. I m going to try to take my recorder and the 2 records I got from home. Everything else I can just about cram into my sea bag.

The DMZ has a lot of good points as well as bad. The enemy we'll be fighting up there can be defeated. The peasants and farmers (local VC) we've been fighting down here will never be defeated. They are small in number and their weapons are crude but they have been making fools out of us the past 5 years or so. They seem to believe in what they are doing and I think the locals will be harassing U.S. troops as long as we're over here. The NVA troops are different. They are massed mostly in and near the DMZ and greatly outnumber us up there. They will stand and fight as long as they are wiling to buck heads, we can beat them. They do have artillery support, but so do we. We also have air support which they don't have. We won't have to worry about mines and booby traps up there because the NVA doesn't use them as much as the local V.C. down here. The weather isn't quite so extreme at the DMZ as it is here either.

The next few days we'll be on working parties to get everything in the battalion packed and ready to go.

Chris

October 2 – We fly out tomorrow morning at 0700 from Da Nang to our new base, which is supposed to be 15-20 miles from the DMZ. (We are out of artillery range). We will be on Hill 25. Hill 22, a few miles away, will be our nearest support. We don't have a clue what that all means. Does that mean we have good support? How much support will we need? These thoughts are going through each of our heads. We talk about it amongst ourselves.

Another group of Marines just traveled through our camp and I got a chance to speak with a few of my buddies I recognized from the states. They are moving into the area we are leaving. I was able to put my hands on a newspaper from Portland, Oregon. The Oregonian Society Page listed eight different couples who were getting married. They had all been classmates I had met during my first two years at Grant High School.

House

October 2 – Spent a quiet night at Viem Tay outpost.

Chris

October 3 – I just received a letter from Dad. He put a lot of thought into it. I read it very carefully, as it bore a lot of meaning. It's hard to get time to write letters. Writing supplies are hard to come by. When we get rations, sometimes there are writing tables and the individual sheets of paper get distributed – officers first, then command post guys, then down to the platoons, the top ranks first, then to the squads and their guys. Everything is handed out this way. Everyone bitches, but no one really cares – that's the way it's going to be.

Yesterday, we went out to provide security for two other companies. We came back in, after a very long walk. We were beat, dead tired. We were in the area about an hour and were called back out to the same place. We got in late. Got word that we're heading out tonight at 2100 hours. Quang Tri City is supposed to be mortared tonight. Up tomorrow morning at 0430 and off on another operation. The NP-27 foot ointment for my feet arrived today from my parents. I am so hopeful that I can get my feet healed up. The sores just won't heal. They are so open and red. Also, I received lots of goodies from the folks - popcorn, Kool-Aid, cookies - an incredible list. Wow! Gotta go, as my candlelight is almost finished.

House

October 3 - We are at Da Nang Airbase, ready to get loaded with gear, chow, ammo and a weapons platoon, all on a KC-130 transport plane. It belongs to the Air Force and everything is very efficient. It is a big damn airplane with four huge propellers. The ramp in the back drops down and we all march up into a big empty hole with aluminum ribs and nylon webbing on the sides. You cannot even see the pilots; they are far forward and high above the nose. It's like two stories up!

Before they light-up the engines the crew chief gives us a safety briefing like what to do in case of an aircraft fire - yeah right. He smiles and disappears up front somewhere for a sandwich and a hot cup of coffee, I'll bet! The four engines are at least sixteen cylinder radials that make so much noise and vibration there is no hope of us communicating on this flight. And it is wide open, with pallets of stuff already strapped to the deck with chains, so there is no place to sit but on the deck! Gunny tells everyone to sit on their helmets. The reasoning was easily understood, as we would be flying over hostile territory and the likelihood of being fired upon was high.

As we approach our landing site, Gunny Webster steps up and has everybody sit back-to-back on the deck for support, he says when we get ready to land, lock arms and sit on as much of our gear as possible. Keep our flak jackets on and zipped-up, helmets on and clipped on, your weapons low. Hey, it's a hundred mile trip, how fast does this thing go anyway? It took us about thirty-five minutes to get us there, no sweat!

At final approach, the pilot comes on the P.A. system and announces that there is so much of the Marston matting shot away from enemy fire that the runway is a bit shorter that they would like, and they were declaring a "controlled crash landing! We bounced so hard some of the guys in the back were thrown up in the air and landed on others six to eight feet ahead of them, with gear and ammo boxes, too! They received cuts and bruises trying to hold onto their weapons. The plane slid sideways and we all slid around inside. As fast as that big ramp came down we were out of there!

They had trucks ready to deliver us to Hill #25 and now we live in a green rolling-hill desert, with no real trees, little scrub bushes only, no cover, on a hill too small for a whole battalion. So, we end up around Hill #25, outside our own wire! How damn stupid a tactical position is that?

Chris
October 3 - When we moved to Dong Ha in Quang Tri Province, we piled in large troop transport planes loaded with supplies. Gunny Weathers had us sitting on our helmets. We didn't quite understand. Then, it hit us. Yes, it might provide a bit of protection against a bullet coming through the airplane and maybe hitting you in the butt.

We landed in Dong Ha Airport and were transported by truck to the ridge, which was south of the Quang Tri City. We lived in shelter halves (pup tents) and foxholes in the ground for more than a month, stuck alone out on a ridge (close to gooks-1/2 mile away). The ground was hard and rocky so our holes weren't very deep. We figure if we were hit at night, it would be difficult to hold off too many of the enemy. Our support was a ways from us, so we made sure to stay vigilant all night. We ran patrols from there - basically isolated from the rest of the troops. We were very exposed on the ridge – no decent cover at all. It was ridiculous - living on the side of a hill, with no cover.

October 4 - We were now told to set up camp as we would staying on this hill for awhile. This place is bad. There was no cover, absolutely no cover. We each had a shelter half, which by putting up two of them, made us a tent for two guys. House and I put up a tent and then dug a trench around the tent so we wouldn't be flooded as the monsoons were here. We dug and dug, trying our best, but only engineered a 4-5 inch wide by 4 inch deep trench. It wasn't much, but it was finished. It would have to do. We were trying to dig into this damn rock-laden hill. It was tough. There was no way we could make a suitable foxhole, which made us totally exposed - no cover, sitting ducks!

We test fired and then cleaned our rifles today, as we try to do this every time we get back to a rear base or camp. My rifle continues to jam every time I am in the rear area. It never gets jammed when we are under attack, but seems to when we get back to the rear. I tried to get another rifle today, but was told to "clean it better, Marine". I'll try to exchange my rifle again later.

House

October 5 – Hill #25, Quang Tri. This is crap! Living in holes only covered with our own ponchos, given ten sandbags each to use for personal protection. We move to the edge of the hill and stand our security lines at night, living like moles! The sun has not come out since we landed at Dong Ha. It is now bitter cold and raining again! I am sleeping sitting up in a one-man fighting hole dug in hardpan. I need a field jacket, because it is so cold up here and my body aches. The sky looks black and mean.

We are just hanging out in the area, more digging in, trying to get some sort of perimeter and fighting positions, setting up fields of fire, mine fields, wire, etc... No patrols today.

I make a friend of Coby, a seventeen year-old Canadian supply clerk, by giving him a K-bar and some VC web gear! I have got to have a connection in the supply tent and this kid looks like he could use a friend! I met him in the mess tent, sitting all alone. He enlisted in the Marines, with his parents' permission, because there are no jobs available and he sends his combat pay home to them. He is a great kid and works like hell for a rotten supply sergeant who treats him like his own personal slave. He loves to hear war stories about what is going on out in the bush! My guys and I need stuff. I know it should work by official requisition or something, but friendships work better! I think I am going to be Coby's friend from now on and do whatever I can to keep our own supply line open. My guys get the gear they need out of the back of the tent at night, when they need it and when it first comes in.

Lt. Suydam

October 6 - Quang Tri is the capital city of the northern province of I Corps. When we arrived in the Quang Tri area, we set up a battalion perimeter in some low rolling hills and pitched tents. The ground was rocky and difficult to dig in. So most of our living/sleeping was above ground as we were unable to dig foxholes.

We were running patrols out of this place, sometimes for a day to three days. The troops like to give the heavy squad radio to the new men that come into country. It's all part of the hazing process. One new trooper had become so involved with the radio that he inadvertently left his rifle in the field following a break. The squad leader came to me at dusk, after we had returned to the battalion perimeter. He said that he didn't know quite how to break the news, but that a new private had left his weapon in a village hooch at the last break. Without a moment's thought, I took the private, the squad leader and one other in a Mighty Mite and we burst forth like gangbusters into the countryside in pursuit of the missing weapon.

The Mighty Mite was a small jeep-like product by American Motors but smaller. I doubt if a Mighty Mite could achieve a speed of 35 mph. Originally, designed to be dropped 15 feet from a moving helicopter, the Mighty Might had been a miserable failure for its original mission but evidently good enough for our Marine Corps. Leaving the perimeter that late in the day in haste was near suicidal. We could all have been killed and never heard from again. I wasn't concerned about that. I was concerned about what I would have to say to my company commander if we came back without the rifle.

We wheeled into the village to attempt to find the rifle and found the place the private remembered. We began flashing piasters (Vietnamese money) and Military Payment Certificates (MPC) and jabbering like crazy men for someone to come-up with a rifle. Finally, one old gentleman understood. He reached up into the grass roof of his hooch and withdrew an M-16 rifle. We gave him the money, thanked him profusely in our broken Vietnamese and got the hell out of there.

That evening when things were back to normal, the squad leader came to me to thank me. He also wanted me to know that the serial number on the rifle was not the same as on the rifle lost by the private. I told him that all was well that ended well and this would just have to be our little secret.

Ever since being ambushed on Go Noi Island and being armed only with a pistol, I sought and eventually obtained a bigger weapon. The Marines did not want their field officers carrying rifles. In the heat of battle, the officer is supposed to be engaged in all manner of leadership and communication roles and does not have time to fire upon the enemy. Consequently, officers are supposed to carry only their side arm for personal protection. Nevertheless, the "popgun" feeling had never left me and if I couldn't carry a rifle, then I wanted something with some oomph. Finally, I was allowed to draw a pump-action, twelve-gauge shotgun from the armory. It held about eight to ten rounds and had what I considered to be substantial stopping power.

Lt. Lee Suydam

Once we were on top of some mountain we had climbed from a stream below. A few of us ventured into the thick undergrowth, leaving the others to rest at the summit. We were several hundred meters from the main body reconnoitering the area when we heard noises. It sounded like a patrol of men working their way through the brush. Their path was going to cross ours about ten to fifteen meters away. Leaves and branches were rustling. Twigs were snapping.

We couldn't see a thing. We were very still. Could these be our own men? We waited.   If we shouted, would they fire back?   Why not just give them some double ought buckshot from the trench gun?   But then, I'd have to cock it; too much noise. Let's wait until we know for sure. Whatever it was, crossed our path without noticing us or being recognized and descended the ridge to our left.

I radioed an airborne forward observer to discuss the possibility of naval gunfire. This was the only kind of artillery support that could reach us. The FO heard me out and suggested that we may have happened on a rock ape. Yes, of course, it was some type of wildlife. Maybe even a rock ape. Right.

I still hadn't fired the shotgun, except on the firing range.

Chris

October 6 - We carried salt tabs and water purification labs, lighters with some type of macho saying imprinted, cigarettes, 1-2 canteens of water, a toothbrush, maybe, but probably not toothpaste., unless mom sent it from home. No such thing as having floss, deodorant, shaving cream or other such hygiene items. These items weren't good for our safety, as I've been told the gooks can smell you when you wear these items.

October 7 - We've been trying to dig foxholes and bunkers up to this point. The foxhole will provide us a more secure place to sleep and a fighting position, if we get attacked. Find a spot to sleep for the night, send out perimeter LP's, as soon as they could leave under the cover of night, silent and slow.   The rest of us would "man our foxholes." I don't think I've ever been so cold and hungry. With the season changing and being in a higher elevation, temperatures have really dropped. Realizing I hadn't eaten in a long time, I grabbed a can of something, didn't really matter if was beans or cheese and mac or something else. I was so tired, the cold can of something was all I had. Eat and sleep...

October 10 - We're up at our new home on Hill #25 outside of Quang Tri City For the rest of my tour, I will be living out of a hole, eating c-rats every day, etc. Heading out on an operation tomorrow and will be in the bush all the time. Operation Medina is supposed to be a big one. It is to be a 30-day operation. I've never been so cold (getting in the low 40's) and hungry, but I am in good spirits. What I wouldn't do for a field jacket or some rain gear.

Everyone is cold.

Cpl House has a rifle Starlight scope w/night vision capability.

House

October 10 - Quang Tri, Hill #25- Grid Coordinates – YD 334494 - Battalion briefing: Operation Medina starts tomorrow at 0800 hours. We go into the operation with 1/1, 2/1, 3/1 and two ARVN battalions against North Vietnamese infiltrators to "find 'em, fix 'em, and finish' em", in the Hai Lang National Forest, designated Combat Zone #101. It is held by the 9th NVA regiment and the 806th Main Force Bn. Intelligence says 11,000 VC and NVA regulars could occupy the area, with heavy dug-in bunkers, tunnels, artillery, hospitals, etc. Hell, that makes the odds pretty good, only five to one against us!

The plan is to fly 1/1 and 2/1 into Combat Zone #114 south of Area #101 in a helicopter assault landing, and then sweep into #101 about 4,000 meters, through dense jungle all the way! Battalion Landing Team, 1st Battalion 3rd Marines will be the blocking element. On completion, we will move to Hwy #1 for one week and act as security check points for the next election voting stations. Oh, sure!

On Hill #25 before we go out we are digging fighting positions to protect Battalion HQ, then ourselves. There are lots of sand bags for us, and big plastic covers

**The Claymore Mine is labeled on front with
"FRONT TOWARDS ENEMY"**

and iron stakes.   Next, was to set out the claymore mines out in front of our positions.

Cold, rain, and miserable! We all agree to make a good job of it together for our shelter and fighting positions, and work so hard our hands blistered and we are soaking wet, but we need a decent place to come back to at night.

Note: Operation Medina started October 11 and continued thru October 20, as 1/1, 2/1, 1/3 and two ARVN battalions moved into the Hai Lang Forest, about nine miles southwest of Quang Tri City. The search and destroy operation was against the well-honed North Vietnamese Army regulars and stretched from the Central Highlands westward to the Laotian Border. This operation, this battle, this war at its ugliest, took place in the deepest jungle battlefield of steep hills and mountains, with valley basins of bug-infested and steamy surroundings. It was quiet, it was dark, it was ready for the silent-watching NVA to spring their attack on us. Throughout the Hai Lang Forest, the NVA waited to open with bursts from their Communist-made AK-47 automatic weapons and grenades into the columns of Marines slowly moving along the narrow paths. They knew the jungle; we did not. The 9th NVA Regiment and the 806th Main Force Battalion were reported to be in Base Area 101 of the Hai Lang Forest, along with other forces.

Medina started with 1/1 and 2/1 making a helicopter assault into the forest. After the landing, we cleared the area around LZ Dove and then swept in a northeasterly direction. In the initial contact in Medina, the enemy more than held its own. One officer observed: "They were fast and agile and we were slow and clumsy. Terrain, vegetation, insufficient helo (helicopter) support had something to do with it". After offering resistance in a few heavy skirmishes during the first phase of the operation, the enemy forces eluded the Marines for the rest of the operation. This operation proved to be extremely difficult, as the terrain in the Hai Lang Forest was steep and its valley basins were dark and steamy bug-infected jungle. During the day, temperatures rose to 100+ degrees. At night it would cool to around 75 degrees. Physically, it proved to be one of the most difficult and demanding operations. Hacking our way through the jungles, climbing up slippery narrow mountain paths and exposing ourselves each time we crossed another waist or chest-high river or stream.

Chris
October 11 - We have been walking up/down the mountains, a lot. Short letter, as I only got one piece of paper on the last copter resupply. The jungles are so heavy with trees, vines and heavy thick leaves that block the sun in the day and turn it to coal black at night. The foliage canopy overhead does provide some relief from the constant rain. It also, muffles noise, whether it's us or them. The rains have been coming down heavily. I've never been so damn hungry before than I have been the last two days, with no food. We did finally get a meal resupply, took a bath (first one in 14 days). Feeling good. Well, at least I'm not at the DMZ. That's one good thing. We haven't had mail in a long time, either. Word is that the captain has been keeping our mail and the guys are about to frag him. (We were lucky not to have officers being fragged by subordinates, as was being done in other areas of Vietnam – to frag is to throw a grenade into the officer's foxhole at night and escape, unnoticed. Many blamed dumb moves in combat on their superiors and retaliated by fragging.

Lt. Suydam,
October 11 - The Medina Operation was to last a week or more. As usual, Echo was in the lead with my platoon, third platoon, on point. We had two guys that were natural born Indian fighters, Tilo Oesterreich and Dennis Knobloch. In the

jungle, there were two very dangerous places to be. One was on a bald mountaintop. From a bald, you could be seen for miles and be fired upon with rockets, mortars or artillery. The second dangerous place was in the deep ravines where water ran. These mountain streams of water were what the enemy used. They didn't have helicopters to bring water to the top, so it was likely that their base camps were down low.

We came upon a stream. We all got cautious. Suddenly, there was machine gun fire and return fire. I ran forward with others to find that Tilo and Knobby had stumbled onto an NVA hospital complex guarded by a single rear guard with a machine gun. They took him out in a few short minutes. Taking machine guns away from people is a ghastly business. But, we had no casualties. These empty hospitals were about 60 feet long, open air buildings with grass roofs and wooden floors. There were other living quarters and supply buildings. Echo Company followed us into this clearing and long after we left we could hear the crackle as the flames consumed this jungle facility.

We were in the jungle a long time, maybe several days. We were hungry. We had taken a sleeve of rice from the hospital complex. It was like a pant leg, filled with rice, tied off at each end with a rope that could be slung over the neck and shoulder. The rice was crude, unprocessed nodules of grain. If you know Uncle Ben's, you wouldn't recognize this material as rice. With a little C-4 explosive material or a heat tablet that we use for heating our meals, you could boil up a small hand full of rice, which gave quite a satisfying result.

Later, we came upon another clearing. The canopy was whole, but the underbrush was cut out. This place looked like a Boy Scout campground. There were worn places on the ground where hundreds of men had recently slept. We were moving cautiously, but rapidly. I didn't want to be caught in the middle of the clearing and I wanted to get to the other side quickly. I was about three fourths across when a machine gun barked to my left. I ran to my left, toward a little stream and a trail that went away from the clearing, backward and to the left about 45 degrees. It intersected with another trail that left the clearing at 90 degrees to the left. So, there was a little triangle of brush between the men on the short trail and the clearing where the main body was.

When I got to the men, there were three on the short trail and one dead (Terry Fenenga) in the intersection of the two trails. More machine-gun fire. We thought the fire was coming from the left. Then we heard a grenade sound, like a rock falling through the trees. Being close enough to throw grenades was not good news particularly when we did not know where the enemy was. The grenade landed in the triangle of brush not far from us. I was sitting down almost shoulder to shoulder with the others facing the grenade. I tried to lean backward in the brush, but it was not forgiving. So, I pulled my helmet over my face before the grenade went off. We were sprayed with shrapnel. A nickel-sized piece of shrapnel hit me on my third rib. My flak jacket was open. It cut a hole in my shirt and left a bloody spot, but did not penetrate. I felt that we were all dead men if we didn't find that machine gunner quickly.

Meanwhile, Tilo was in the main clearing. He had figured out that the machine gunner was in a hole in the triangle of brush. Since the bad guy was between the main body and us, none of us could have fired without hitting friendlies (our men). Tilo crawled into the thicket and located the enemy only after touching the top of his head. Tilo dispatched him immediately and we were saved. I wrote Tilo up for a Silver Star Medal.

Note: Lt. Suydam. Tilo's medal was never approved. After I got out of the Corps, I got correspondence from USMC about the event. Knobby had asked his Senator to look into the matter. I wrote him up again. Several years later, I wrote to Tilo's sister who said Tilo never got his medal. When I was forty-two years old, exactly twice as old as I was in Vietnam, the traveling Vietnam Memorial Wall was in Houston on Memorial Day. I took all my correspondence on Tilo and my Bronze Star and I presented them to Tilo, beneath his name on the wall. It was not big thing, except it made me feel a little better to know that even though the U.S. government would not give Tilo a medal, I could give him a medal and I did. He was a courageous warrior; a fine young man and he made a significant contribution to our country. He saved my life and I will never forget him.

Doc Turner
October 11 - This is one of those trips that was a waste of time and lives, and, due to ill planning, was a fiasco named Operation Medina. Not all of us got to prepare for this trip, it was just dropped on us. We woke up on a normal morning, ate our normal C-Ration breakfast and were told to saddle up. Shit happens. So, always plan ahead. We go walking to a large heliport about a mile from where we were trying to set up a compound up in Quang Tri Province. We had just shipped in there. Anyway, someone started mass rumors regarding a large movement of NVA a few miles west of us and that we were gonna get wiped out. Colonels going after a general's star, at the enlisted men's expense. However, great planning allowed for approximately 65 helicopters each carrying 12 to 13 men each trip and making about 4-5 trips each. We were dropped in a

20-30 acre opening in the jungle and kicked out of those choppers. Of course, with all the noise the multitude of choppers made, every living thing for miles around knew we were there - tigers, monkey, elephants, and Mr. Charles, (NVA). I and others in Echo Co. would always remember the night in which this fight took place. It was a night I and many others would like to forget.

We had hacked our way thru the jungle for four days. The morning after, in order to get back to the LZ, it took us about half a day. On the way back we found where the NVA had camped waiting for us to make a night return to the LZ. We were lucky we didn't try to do so.

Chris
October 11 - Heavy rains, but we were sheltered by the jungle canopy overhead - very hungry the last two days. I had a big meal, then took a shower in the rain, the first in 14 days. Two days without food has really drained me, and everyone else, I'm sure. When it rains and if we have soap and it's secure enough, we strip and have a shower. It doesn't happen very often. This was a good day. No matter how bad we think we have it, we know we're lucky not to be on the DMZ, so the complaining is kept at a minimum. Sorry, if I sounded a bit depressed last letter. I feel better now.

Climbing mountains thick with everything a jungle has to offer – slippery footing, leaves half the size of a man, weird sounds, snakes that will kill you before you have a chance to blink twice and on. We took turns using the machete, only hacking away for 5-10 minutes maximum. The extreme heat and the dense foliage only allowed for short duty, then the next guy's turn. The jungle was so thick you could not see any further than where you were cutting. The fear that you would actually expose yourself, as you wacked away, was high. If anyone was around, the noise, you and your machete were making, would bring them right to you. The vines were so thick, the humidity so high, exhaustion and constant fear of not being able to see anything in front of you caused a bit of anxiety. We crossed streams by holding on to a rope. We had to have some poor sucker swim across to the other side and anchor the rope to something on the other side. The current was taking some guys down. After establishing some type of foothold on the other bank, the rest of us would make it to the other side, making sure our weapons were kept out of the water and trying to keep our balance. Bad footing underneath and the strong current had their way with us.

After crossing, we put our gear down and removed the damn leeches from our arms, legs, and every conceivable spot. We normally used a cigarette lighter or better, some mosquito repellent, if you were lucky to have some. Spraying the repellant would cause the leeches to release their grip and fall off. Lighting the leeches would result in other problems.

Doc Turner

October 12 – We were constantly being sprayed by Agent Orange chemical on this operation while in the Hai Lang National Forest. Air Force C-123 aircraft were spraying the northern area of Vietnam to reduce the jungle canopy and hiding places the enemy was using. The chemical was a defoliant and was poison, not only to the brush, trees, jungle and grasslands, but to all of us. Sometimes, if a Marine was lucky enough to find some fruit still on a tree, they would wash it off in a puddle, before eating. I tried to tell them that they were just washing with Agent Orange and to stop it. No drinking, no washing fruit from puddles. I tried to reassure them that we would get water supply soon. I really had no idea when supply would come.

Note: October 12 - Charlie Company of 1/1 with 162 Marines fought the 9th NVA Regiment, calling for assistance from Delta Company as the day moved on. They fought for four uninterrupted hours. 42 Charlie Co. Marines were wounded. There were 44 NVA confirmed kills. Three quarters of the squad and fire team leaders were absent on the walk out of the jungle. Twenty-three Marines were nominated for individual decorations, including Corporal William T. Perkins, Jr. who received the Medal of Honor for his heroic action on the second night of the operation. As Charlie Company left Operation Medina, they immediately were assigned as the point company on another operation, which also began immediately.

Corporal William T. Perkins, Sepulveda, California
(panel 27E, line 97 on The Wall)

Chris

October 12 - The claymore mines we use often are anti-personnel mines which, when detonated, propelled 700 small steel balls in a 60 degree fan-shaped pattern to a maximum of 100 meters, the more effective range is 50 meters, with a kill rate of 30%. The 1/8 inch diameter steel balls were packed in epoxy and backed with C-4 explosive. The sound of the explosion is startling, as is its affect on the enemy at close range.

Doc Turner

October 12 - We are getting hit almost every night. Upon inspection in the morning of trip flares and claymores, which had been placed out in front of our positions, we found that one of the claymore mines was turned around on us. I don't understand why the gooks didn't cause some commotion and get us to fire the claymore, which had been turned around and would have fired directly at us, if we had activated the mine. So, we decided to place a grenade underneath the claymore, so if someone tried to lift the claymore again, it would blow-up right in their face. It turned out to be a great idea. All we found in the morning was a heart.

House

October 13 - We are on top of a very steep hill! I wish I had a damn map of this area! I do not know why they will not let us non-commissioned officers (NCOs) have more tactical info! We hardly know where the hell we are. Everything is treated as a big secret. I know maps, but I can't have one. We are out of food and everyone is hungry. We are low on water and the CO called for re-supply from Phu Bai according to our radio guy Chuck Estes.

There is such a thick jungle canopy here you cannot see up or down or through it. It has to be made of two hundred foot tall mahogany and teak forest that is really old. Without sunlight most of the day, it was perfect concealment for VC. Even smoke will not go up through the canopy. We move about 2,500 meters, hand-cutting our own trail with machetes while we move single file. Each man on point would hack at the jungle vines, thorns, branches, big leaves and bushes as long as his strength lasted. The guy behind him is carrying his gear and covering the field of fire in front of him. We do not dare use any of the existing VC trails here as they have them all covered with booby-traps and trip wires and punji traps, and they know their own warning signs of where they are hidden, we do not! On my turn up front, one of the vines I cut whipped right back and slashed straight across my face, slicing it open. I have this nasty bleeding cut across my nose, lips and cheek, looks and feels wicked! But it is because the stupid machete is so dull by now that it is not cutting anymore! It might as well be a club. We have no files or sharpening stones, so we just continue to hack away and beat the jungle down as best we can. Most of the guys get cuts across the face, hands and arms before we clear the thorn-vines. Everyone is bleeding, physically exhausted, sleep-deprived, hungry, thirsty, and miserable!

So far we have not had much enemy contact, but lost two men. One mortar man from weapons platoon fell to heat exhaustion. A big guy, he carried eight mortar rounds, plus his own gear. He turned bright red, then white as paper! The corpsmen threw him in a bomb crater filled with water to get his temperature down, but we heard later he went unconscious and died! The other guy fell off a cliff and hurt his back real bad but the medevac got him out okay.

Our spotter planes are keeping U.S. gunships over any NVA they can find and we hear air strikes off in the distance trying to keep them on the run and push them towards the flat lands where 1/3 is waiting for them, out of this cover. But, they are too smart for that! They know where to pick their fights and it isn't out in the open! They simply disappear into the jungle and go underground.

We finally have been issued some of that new Dow Silicone foot ointment we have been hearing so much about for our "trench foot". MDX-4-4056 with silicone for "investigational use only", two tubes for each man, really goopy stuff, like drilling lube! We all smear it on our feet, hoping it will be "the miracle cure".

We're on line doing night watch. Two Chi-Com grenades zip through the trees and explode, throwing fragments and dirt, but nobody gets hurt. We reply with about 10 grenades of our own. No more incoming. We came down off that hill in only two hours, and the captain said we sounded like a "thundering herd"! It took us two days to climb the damn thing!

We hear Charlie Co. 1/1 got into the three-hour firefight with the NVA and took a lot of casualties last night.

We set up an LZ perimeter for haul-out and the lieutenant let us go down to a big clear pool of water on this hillside with good cover to wash-up and shave. It was great! We got to wash our utilities and spread them in the sun to dry. We jumped in and splashed like kids, shaved and washed a layer of crud off. Even the captain joined us, and to see him smile after all this hard time was a real morale booster for all the troops! Choppers out at 1530 with C-rats all unloaded and passed out. We had nothing to eat for the past twenty-six hours and I would not be choosey, ham & lima beans (voted the worst of all c-rations) were okay by me. We could hear artillery and small arms, far off. Thank God!

Chris
October 13 – A couple of volunteers had been picked to swim across the stream and tie a rope to the other side. They were so exposed as they hurried across the swiftly running river. After they secured a rope on the other side of the river, we crossed by holding onto the rope with one hand, holding our rifle with our

other hand and trying so hard to hurry across. The river was quite swift and continued to push us around. My eyes scanned the riverbank the entire time, until I reached the slippery bank on the other side. We were still so exposed, but at least not in the river.

We haven't eaten in quite a while, but came across a barely visible garbage dump out in nowhere land. We scrounged and dug through the dirt and mess, salvaging some old c-rats. I felt like a buzzard going through the trash. The VC must have raided a supply truck or found some supplies that had been dropped from planes for Marine re-supply. Some the cans had not been damaged and we were so hungry, we easily justified our meal.

House
October 13 - I knew from the fence incident when Keller was killed that I did not want any of my guys pulling up booby traps themselves and I had Coby get the motor pool guys to weld-up a small grappling hook with about forty feet of rope. Coby "found" what he needed in supply, put it together and I made it part of my pack. It only added a few pounds but, we were the only squad that had one. We had to do a lot of river and stream crossings that had pretty strong currents, and it really worked well for helping us with difficult crossings.

We would throw it across first, let it hook-up, pull tight and everybody had a good handhold to get across. We crossed a lot of water on this operation. If we came across a log in our way or something that just doesn't look right, we throw the grapple hook out, hook it and drag it back a bit. If it goes off, we know we just saved one of our Marines by being smart.

House
October 13 - The morning sun is beautiful, but now the hill climbing is getting brutal. It is all vertical from here. I get stomach cramps. Doc Turner gives me chalk tabs and pills, tells me to go lie down and rest. But I do not want to sleep in the rain again tonight and need to help rebuild our shelter. The guys see I am hurting and let me rest more than help. We all have a good cover tonight, but it is still cold and we do not have much chow. The heavy rain makes it hard to get re-supply choppers to us. Hills and valleys – up and down forever.

Most of the guys' feet are in such bad shape now it is really getting to the corpsmen. They are tagging guys in my squad, including Gary Christensen, with immersion foot, and they are arguing with some officers that it is serious enough for a medevac, the same as if the guys were wounded. On Chris, it should be foot rot! His feet look like they could fall off. They have got to hurt so badly and he keeps going. He does not want to leave us. Anyway, we are losing Gary. The corpsmen have sent him back to our aid-station for treatment and recovery along with ten other guys, all because of their feet alone.

Chris

October 13 - Immersion foot got me and I find myself being medevaced out of the field and sent to the aid station outside Dong Ha. I'm lying on a cot, trying to heal my feet so I can walk again. My foot problem was caused by being in water constantly with sand and dirt rubbing so badly inside my boot that it caused blisters and bruises. I had ringworm and my feet were bleeding from my calves to the soles of my feet. I know it didn't help that I haven't been wearing socks, which would be nice if I could find some. The skin was just falling off my feet and my legs up to my calves. Eleven of us were taken out of the operation. They called in a copter and took us to a hospital down south. I really felt terrible leaving the guys, as it puts them one more guy short in our squad. We walked to an open area and the captain called in a medevac for us. I had no idea I was on a list to leave the operation. The squad leader came up to me and announced that I was leaving. That was it. The field perimeter was secured and the copter arrived in about 20 minutes.

The rest of the guys lying around me here at the hospital are here for much more serious wounds. I feel strange being here with such a minor injury among these guys that have really been banged up.

House

October 14 - Moving along higher ridge lines about 5,000 meters from our dug-in positions, one of our guys kicks a C-rat can off the trail in front of him, out rolls an M-26 grenade, he dives, but still gets lots of tiny pieces of hot, sharp steel in his soft pink body. We all sit and wait for forty-five minutes for a chopper and take a break, while he goes back to the aid station with a grin on his damn face! We have the luck to sleep out in the open rain again tonight. Geez, this poncho liner can really soak it up!

Quiet night, although Fox Company, which was about 400 meters away thought they had an infiltrator and threw a lot of grenades, but it turned out to be a false alarm. They just kept us awake all night. We are in reserve to hold the LZ, waiting to pick-up a hospital unit and extra ammo. Lenny Linares came back with full canteens of the last of the fresh water from our big water bag for everyone, nice guy.

145

If we start out of the jungle today it would take about four days to reach Highway #1. I wish I had the gloves I asked Nancy to send. Some of the thorn holes in my hand now have puss coming from them when I squeeze them. Doc Miller keeps pushing this ointment into the holes, and boy does that burn.

The lieutenant sends the squad to find a good water source at the bottom of the hill, but we only find a small fire. The air is dry and hot, the fire is spreading and it is hard to see the flames. One of our Marines, raised on a farm says, "I've seen grass fires spread like this before, and knew we better run. It's coming our way!" We run. When we need help during a firefight, we fire our mortars ahead of us and into the suspected enemy position. Our white phosphorous (WP) or illumination mortars probably started the fire last night. A mortar is a simple smoothbore, muzzle loading, high-angle-of-fire weapon, which is carried by a mortar team. A tube sits on the ground and a round is dropped in the top of the tube and allowed to slide down. When it hits the bottom of the tube, its firing pin discharges and the round is lobbed into the air towards the enemy. The weapon can also fire illumination rounds to light up the battlefield at night, and smoke rounds to provide concealment during the day.

Now, as the wind picks up and pushes the flames we figure we better get our gear out of the way (especially our plastic covers), because the grass is really crackling loud now. The flames are moving into our stacks of C-rats and ammo. We all grab cases of what we can carry and run while others beat at the flames with their ponchos. Three guys get burns serious enough for medevac. The Skipper is so happy, he says "Good job. You saved the command post (CP). Swim call at the pool". We got a second splash party in the hot sun, like a vacation in the jungle. The pool of water provided us a quick moment to forget the war and enjoy the fresh water. It probably helped clean us up. I know we were pretty ripe. The H&S guys had to stand security while the grunts got to play grab-ass and splash in the cool pool. This was a first for us, sort of a role reversal for someone else protecting us.

Doc Slater came around checking and doctoring all the troopers' feet. He collected everybody's outgoing letters. I got all my letters and sent them back with the medevac copter, along with two more guys with emersion-foot from 3rd platoon. I'm still doing okay with the new foot grease and extra dry socks. Doc Slater is such a mellow guy, he is always looking out for all us, but is not above giving you a good ass-chewing, if you are not taking care of yourself and following his instructions.

This jungle is so deep and so beautiful, quiet, with more colors in the daytime than I could ever imagine or believe. It is a magic place, so vibrant in the sunlight, with a million shades of green and some of the most beautiful flowers. It has a natural beauty that is simply beyond description, but it is a miserable place to navigate. At night we had white parachute flares with burning illumination dropping around us by the hundreds. They hang and swing crazily in the tree branches making shadows like monsters all over the forest floor, weird. But, what a sight. Every now and then some exotic birds will cut loose like those Martin Denny albums, like oooh-oooh-waa-waa-eee! Zoo-a-rama! Sounds sooo cool and everybody is quiet and digs it.

Knobby
October 14 - We're in the middle of an operation right now but they gave us some time to write letters. We're set in for the time being on a small hill. It hasn't rained for about 3 days which is fine with me. This afternoon though we could have used the rain. Our hill – mostly dry elephant grass – caught on fire and it took us just about all day to get it out. I think I made television because we have a camera man with us for the operation taking flicks for the newsreels. I also got in on one yesterday when we were moving down a jungle stream.

We don't have a battalion area anymore. They converted 2nd Battalion, 1st Marines into sort of a moving battalion, and everything is like one big happy operation. The Captain said they might decide to move us back to Hill 25 (hill names were designated according to their height in meters) in a couple of weeks, but nobody really knows for sure. I hope they get us a battalion area pretty soon because it would be nice to get mail and a hot meal every now and then.

I did all I could do about getting R&R in November for Hawaii. Now we'll just have to wait and see if a quota comes through. The 1st Sgt. said he thought I would be able to get it.

I was up for corporal this month but I seriously doubt I will make it. There are too many other guys in the company that have more time in than me.

Doc Turner
October 14 - House was with Lt. Reydel from 3rd platoon. They were positioned on a nearby hillside when House got shot at by one of our own snipers. I was with the captain when he said that you all weren't supposed to be up there, as you should have been in the valley. I looked through a scope and couldn't tell if

you were Marines or the enemy up there. It was later in the day, when I joined up with House and his squad.

We worked our way back to the compound when the captain ordered the lieutenant to change directions of travel. The lieutenant got mad and walked off the path in the direction the captain had ordered. I said to myself in a low breath that he was going to get his ass blown up…then the mine went off.

House
October 14 - The captain yelled for Lt. Reydel to change directions and we'd go out the same way the villagers had been traveling, as it would be safer. He had gone about 10-15 meters, as he turned towards us, then took another step when he stepped on a mine. BOOM! He steps on an old Z-10 French anti-personnel foot mine. A small cast-iron mine, like 20 years old, but still rips straight up the lieutenant's leg like a flash and he disappears in a cloud of dirt. Still standing, using his rifle like a crutch he hops and turns on his good leg, but falls backwards. Doc Turner is already there, helmet off, medical bag off his shoulders and open. He is like a rocket-man, no hesitation.

Doc Turner
October 14 - I ran to Lt. Reydel as fast as I could. I could tell he was bleeding pretty badly. I worked fast to stop the bleeding. He wanted me to assure him that he wasn't going to lose his leg. He kept pressing me to tell him his leg would be okay. I had to lie and tell him what he wanted to hear. Most of the calf of that leg was gone. I had to calm him down. I initially tried stopping the bleeding with a tourniquet. I continued to try to keep him lying down. I had to keep him away from looking down at his leg. If he had seen his injury, I'm sure he would have gone into trauma shock. I finally had to heat sear the wound in order to stop the bleeding.

After the lieutenant got back to the states and in New York, he wrote me a letter chewing me out for not telling him the truth about his leg. I wrote back telling him that he would have and/or could have died on me, if I had told him the truth. I told him I just wanted to get him out alive and safe from further harm. He would just have to forgive me for lying. I also told him his gun wasn't clean. (He always pounded at guys for ridiculous reasons. He was not at all popular with the troops). I did hear he died. He was about my age. I hope he had a good life.

Estes

October 14 – Lt. Reydel had stayed awake and alert, even with all the morphine in him. We shook his hand and wished him good luck and waved good-bye, as they loaded him on the copter, back to the real world. I was on the radio talking to the medevac corpsmen, as soon as the copter was in the air. I was asking condition status of the wounded Marine and Lt. Reydel answers, "tell them "I am in a highly agitated condition, that is my condition at the present time." We all cracked up! Doc took over the radio and described his foot and leg wound as serious, but stable. I think he might have lost his foot, I am not sure, but he was sent home.

Now, they were going to have to break in another new 2nd Lt., fresh from Officer Candidate School, how much more fun can a guy expect? WOW!

Note: It was learned later that Lt. Reydel did lose his left calf. Doc Turner heat-seared the wound to stop the bleeding, but couldn't keep him still, as his foul attitude had taken over.

Lt. Kirk

October 14 - When I arrived in Da Nang, I was dead tired. I had been awake a long time, waiting for the flight, then during the aborted flight, then more waiting, then another long flight. After we landed, I boarded a truck for a ride to the 1st Marine Division Headquarters. We drove on a dirt road through an area called Dogpatch. Everything was unfamiliar, noisy and chaotic, a disorienting kaleidoscope of tumbledown houses, mud, smoke, garbage, people with black teeth from chewing betel nut, half-naked kids, dogs, bicycles, motorcycles and old cars, accompanied by unpleasant smells and the sounds of artillery fire and the roar of jet fighters taking off. When we arrived at headquarters, I stowed my few civilian clothes and dress uniforms which, strangely, we were required to bring) in my sea bag and left it in a storage facility. I wondered if I would ever see my sea bag again. I wasn't thinking about being killed, just the chaos. Then I was ushered into the commanding general's office (Major General Donn J. Roberston, awarded the Navy Cross for his actions at Iwo Jima) and he gave me what must have been the standard pep talk. Afterwards, I looked up a lieutenant I had known at Kenyon College, Tate Egger, who was a big, strapping guy who was always lifting weights in college. He had been in country five months and was a company commander and 1st Lt. in the 11th Motor Transport battalion. Tate was running convoys up and down Rt. 1, the infamous Street Without Joy, the name of Bernard Fall's book. It struck me as ironic that big, strapping Tate

Lt. Jim Kirk
Platoon Commander

Egger had a job in motor transport while I was going to an infantry battalion. But I volunteered for it.

House

October 15 - Big resupply of food and ammo by helicopter today. We are covering an incredible amount of ground on rugged trails through heavy jungle with at least three layers of canopy cover over our heads. We happen to stop where there is an outcropping of rock heavily laced with beautiful quartz crystals that are the size of your fist. I pried a small piece out of the hillside with my bayonet for a souvenir. Some of the guys take big chunks, but they are heavy, and they soon abandon them on the trail. We see a couple of small deer dart off through the brush as we approach. All is quiet. I think we are too high up in the hills to expect much contact. The VC like to have room to run after they hit us, and there is not much flat country here. Soon we are going back down hill into dark bug-infested swamp that is going to be miserable to get through, but we must hold our line with the rest of the sweeping force.

Heading out on a night patrol, not 30 feet outside our lines, I was the third man back when the point-man stepped on a small VC homemade foot mine filled with glass and nails. It was just on the edge of his heel, and blew up the back of his legs into his butt. The blast hit his plastic canteens, and they burst open, throwing water up and behind him with great speed and force. It was like getting slapped with a wide board. The sudden noise of the explosion and dirt mixed with the water smashing into my face was an incredible shock. I could barely see in the darkness, and instantly thought I had been hit with his flesh and blood from the way he screamed in pain. I staggered back a couple steps into the man behind me, wiped the dirt out of my eyes and off my face, and stood there in shock. The number two man took some shrapnel in the legs and abdomen and his hand. The corpsmen had them both taken care of in short order, and they were medevaced out. I was lucky again, my ears were ringing and I was covered with mud, but no holes.

Doc Turner

October 15 - We marched for four days – that night when we settled in you could hear 1/1 getting hit. We were then directed to return to the copter drop area. As we re-traced our path, we noticed large matted down areas where the NVA had slept, as they followed us the previous few days. I do believe we escaped a battle.

Lt. Kirk

October 15 - I boarded a KC 130 transport plane and flew north to Dong Ha, 7 miles south of the DMZ. From there I went south to Quang Tri, the 1st Marine Regiment forward command post, on a truck convoy. Kids ran up to the trucks, yelling "Marines number one, VC number ten" and asked for C rations.

Chris

October 15 – I've been here at the hospital now for three days waiting for transportation back to battalion area for a copter ride back to the guys in the field. I have been eating hot meals and it's unbelievable how good it tastes – fresh eggs! I weighed in at 140 lbs. Not bad for a guy that was 172 lbs a short time ago, in August when I arrived in 'Nam.

Yesterday, I worked in the receiving area again. Our company had been hit pretty bad and the copters kept coming in with wounded, so anyone that could walk was told to get up from their beds and help with the wounded. We unloaded Marines by stretcher, took them inside and sometimes aided the docs wrapping up wounds, then lots of time in the operating room (OR), helping with surgeries. It was a terrible time. I'll never forget, but we all helped and got the job done. I found myself in the OR helping hold down a Marines' left leg, as his injury required amputation of his leg, just above the knee. It was tough to be a part of this type of procedure. I'm sure I'll never forget.

We continued unloading the wounded. It just continued for hours....lots of wounded, they just kept coming. It was such a strange feeling seeing so many guys suffering with terrible open wounds - the big red and black scars, still bleeding, it was so sad.

I met a couple of guys with the 26th Mariners here at the hospital. I learned that my best friend, Walt Pittman, whom I had formed such a close relationship, is now in Okinawa in the hospital. Walt has already received three Purple Hearts (PH). Walt got hit in both arms, both legs, had a head injury, and was shot in the groin. Their unit was stationed up at the DMZ and his outfit has continued to be hit hard for quite a long time. I've seen a lot of guys get hit by rifle-fire, grenades, artillery, etc. They're all so screwed up. The horror of battle wounds is so ugly. I don't let myself think about how bad he is probably hurt. Since Walt has three PHs (two serious), he will never have to return to Vietnam and maybe this brings me some comfort. I want to cry. I feel so alone and so scared for his safety.

Walt was my best friend in boot camp and long after that time. I met his girl friend, Kathy Reilly. Wow! What a looker. Kathy and his college friends – John Cruz and Frank Derdic, all from San Diego State University, were terrific people. The guys would drive up to the Camp Pendleton base in Frank's Volvo and pick up Walt and me for the weekend in San Diego. My mind wanders as I continue to think about where Walt and I might be if we had taken the Marine Corps offer to go to Officer Candidate School (OCS) instead of staying in the infantry as enlisted grunts. It's so hard to stop thinking about the pain my friend has gone through.

Someone here at the aid station gave me a State of Oregon flag. Not sure why they had it. I sent it back to the rear area for safe keeping, but will probably never see it again. No big deal.

Chris

October 15 - I returned to the squad today. The change is incredible. I went from a wet, mud hole in the forest to a warm hospital, with fresh bread and hot meals, and cots to sleep on, back to this dark, wet, muddy hole. I'm with the guys now and that feels right. The only real news we enjoy out here comes from the outside. The guys coming in from their Rest and Relaxation (R&R) bring great tales about their drunken week with the most beautiful girls on the island, (no, really, guys!). Sometimes married guys return, but their stories are no nowhere as much fun to listen to. The R&R guys tell "tall tales" and we love it. The married guys are boring, or at least to the majority single guys here. I was coming in from the outside and I too had stories. I told them as many of the events as I could - clean sheets, eating hot meals, seeing friends. Wow! I did have a great few of days. The squad seemed pleased that I had a few good days. I told them about raiding the bakery truck. A couple of us noticed that a truck which was backed up to the hospital loading dock had an incredibly pleasant smell. We decided to investigate further. No one seemed to be around, so we climbed up on the sides of the truck, lifted the heavy canvas tarps and exposed the "Fresh Bread". We were all over that truck and its contents, grabbing and eating the fresh loaves. Someone yelled at us and we were off the truck and out of there. We never heard another thing about the incident. We were heroes, taking the bread back to the others in the ward.

House
October 15 - Chris is back from the hospital, his feet all healed-up, but boy, he is skinny! They must not have fed him too well, or else he could not get to the chow hall on his own. We had one more man medevaced with malaria today. Lose two, get one back, sort of normal. We just seemed to get to full squad strength and something happens and we're below numbers, again.

Chris
October 16 - While on the Medina Op, we were moving across flat to hilly ground. A Marine private offered to help his friend climb out of a 4' ravine. The Marine leaned over and extended his rifle barrel to his waiting friend in the ravine. As his friend grabbed the rifle barrel to begin the climb out, his weight and the pull on the rifle exerted additional pressure on the trigger finger of the helping Marine. It was in the common place the trigger finger should be when walking through the jungle. It was positioned on the trigger, with the trigger finger ready, ready to pull and fire. A full magazine was immediately unloaded into the young man, ripping him apart…instantly killed, he fell back into the ravine. Word spread throughout the unit. We moved on. There is never any time to grieve for our lost Marines. Our minds must stay clear…be ready…always ready.

The loneliness that I felt after the Marine was killed by his buddy was terrible. The way in which he died was so gruesome. I'm sure his friend suffered in ways we will never know.

They say that for every grunt or infantry guy, there were nine guys in the rear, holding down some type of support position – truckers, office pogues, communication, artillery, medical, engineers, supply, graves registration, cooks, high command, etc.

We medevaced another one of our guys today. We seem to continue to lose men. It's hard to get a grip on this. We get hardened each day as the losses mount up. If a friend is shot, you are concerned, but normally it's for a small amount of time. A short time after the accident, we return to where we were. We spend our waking hours alert and aware. The losses disappear to make room for the next one.

House

October 16 - All up at 0600, standby until 0800 hours. Nothing left among us to even share to eat. Everyone is out of food, again. The gum from Nancy's last letter is even getting hard to chew. Next move is 3,000 meters away to hook-up with Fox Co at their LZ for re-supply.

My stomach feels like a knot doing flips, waiting for anything to come down inside. Copters finally arrive at 1400 and we get issued four C-rats meals for each of us, plus mail. Yeah! The mail is the best part. We had to carry a 60mm mortar (35 lbs), because the entire gun crew was medevaced with immersion foot and because of their use of that new Silicone Foot Ointment. Sand and dirt stuck to the ointment and acted like sandpaper to abrade and peel their skin raw and off their feet inside their boots. Those mortar crews carry a lot more weight than we do, because of the heavy ammo, plus all their own regular and personal stuff, and they really suffer on a long hump. We had to bring it along for the remaining crew. Plus, we had to carry all their extra 60mm ammo rounds at nine pounds each. But, we got to split them up, not carry ten each, like a mortar-man. They get treated like mules.

Lt. Kirk

October 16 - The 1st Marines command post was an old French fort, with observation towers, bunkers and shell holes in the walls of buildings. I was not yet able to distinguish incoming from outgoing and was therefore alarmed by both. We received a briefing from the intelligence officer and met the regimental commander.

October 17 - I went on to the 2nd battalion command post south of Quang Tri with nine other 2nd lieutenants, including Graffam (who would serve as Echo, 2nd Platoon commander), Burgess, Lang, Cummings, Donahue, Taylor, Flanagan and Paredes.

House

October 17 - Operation Medina is put us into the heavy triple canopy jungle. We had to go out about a hundred meters out from our lines, and found a spot in a bunch of bamboo to stand a listening post (LP) all night in the rain. The LP's were located forward of base camps and used to early identify any enemy movement prior to any action taking place. Basically, we were an early warning system. Bases camps always held the central command, support teams and the rest of the troops not on the lines. Their men didn't stand lines, which doesn't seem right to us.

It rained so hard today, coming down like I've never seen it. Everyone looked like prunes. Rain gear does not keep you dry, it just makes you a bit warmer by retaining your body heat, but you still get wet! Especially when you have to lay in a flooded fighting hole! My helmet floated alongside me as it was too heavy to keep on all night. When I pulled my poncho over my head the smell from my own body would get so bad it would be hard to breathe my own stink and I would have to surface for air to sleep, fifteen to twenty minutes at a time and stretch to keep my legs from cramping in the cold water filling the hole.

When we came in from the LP at dawn we popped a green flare to let them know, but the outpost got all stupid and fired a round over our heads in challenge! Cpl. Teebo jumped all over him and called the sergeant of the guard and jumped all over him, too! It was all humble pie from them! Teebo was hot stuff! He strutted all day after chewing out a sergeant and getting away with it! We found our "home" had been reduced to a pile of rubble, undermined by a small river of rain runoff - totally caved in! So we started all over again, in the rain, then got word to saddle-up for a company-size patrol before we could finish. BUMMER!

Oh, the rain gear I got from home felt so good last night. A VC mortar crew kept a steady pace of harassment fire, but did not get a bead on any of our positions. We are beginning to head east towards Hwy #1, but that may not mean much yet, as there is still a lot of jungle to get out of.

It started raining again at 0130 yesterday and did not stop until noon today. We ate our last meal on the trail of a VC camp before we dug-in after dark, then we moved about 500 meters uphill. It was a real struggle to climb the hill, with the tree roots grown over the trail and exposed 3-4". We slowly continued in the dark, with the muddy slope causing us to walk ever so slowly. Somebody had strung a rope out and attached it ahead of us. A few good strong steps were also cut into the pathway where we really needed them.

My watch was 0300 to 0500 hours, but I just sat, shivered and looked at Nancy's picture until 0800. I did not have the heart to wake my relief – Lance Corporal Anselment. He was so wet and cold, he was shivering, but he was sound asleep. I had to let him get some rest, if he could. I could not sleep.

We eat what we can and get word to "saddle-up". Out another 4,000 meters, I cross a big log and spilt the crotch of my pants wide-open. We are now using my grappling hook and rope on a routine basis to cross many small streams and creeks that are very swift flowing and easy to lose your footing and fall while crossing. I am not going to be a reserve swimmer with all this heavy gear on, and I know if one of our guys goes down, he is not going to get back on his own. One of the scariest things we have to do is cross streams and rivers on foot, because you have to send one or two men across first to secure the rope to the other side, and they are sitting ducks for any sniper or ambush the enemy may have waiting for you on the other side. We try to provide as much cover as possible from the bank, but the first men out know they are expendable, as they expose themselves in the open, and cannot move quickly to cover while in the water.

Chris

October 17 - During Operation Medina, our guys were covered by Agent Orange, which was constantly being dumped from our planes flying over the territory. Doc Turner told the captain to have everyone stop and wash that crap off our bodies. Doc took a lot of heat, especially being an E-4 in rank. The captain had to do what he was told in this situation. It was a medical situation and the senior corpsman had the call. The captain didn't want to stop and take the time. He was interested in moving on. Doc was interested in saving our lives from that damn chemical that had already killed the foliation all around us. We were lucky Doc Turner held his ground.

House

October 17 - We hear re-supply is delayed 24 hours due to rain. Erosion of copter blades has been so bad they need to be changed more often to allow them to lift as much as they are supposed to. The monsoon rain is powerful stuff. I thought it rained hard in Washington. It is nothing compared to Vietnam rain! Too bad these guys don't have good engineers to convert it to electricity and make some real power to help move these poor folks move forward in the world, rather than just let it flood them all the time and grow rice and vegetables.

Work parties are busy clearing another big LZ (landing zone) for re-supply. After about two to three hours of hard clearing, battalion says no, let's move somewhere else.

Three hours later, 3rd platoon walks right into the VC base camp we have been hunting for all this time! They surprise five VC squatting around a campfire having their lunch, killing one, and wounding the other four. They capture four heavy machine guns, lots of small arms, a big hospital unit compound, and massive amounts of stored ammo and supplies, all marked "FROM YOUR COMARADES IN RED CHINA".

We all go in to destroy the hooches built of bamboo with grass roofs above ground and have the small ARVN scouts that are attached to our company at this time go down the bunkers and tunnels to look for Intel. The Chu Hoi Scout guys get paid for stuff they find and they are good sniffers! A couple of them find this bunker entrance built into the hillside that slants down to about eight feet and runs about sixty feet in. It is a hospital. One bed is stained with blood. A big cavern about 20' x 20' is filled with supplies marked plasma from Japan, penicillin and medicines from China and different foods from "Hands Across the Sea", a program from the American people to the people of South Vietnam.

Makes you wonder sometimes, who is your friend and who is your enemy? People in U.S. send them food? Being good Marines, we put C-4 or satchel charges in everything and destroyed it in the most efficient way we knew how. We blew it to Hell with high explosive charges and set it on fire! To be safe, the captain pulled us back from the immediate area, and a Forward Artillery Observer (FO) called-in coordinates for high explosive with time delay explosives (HET) to hit our target. It collapsed the entire hillside.

We raided the NVA hospital, discovered USA plasma in volume and other supplies from Russia and China. We shot at those that were the last to leave the evacuation. The jungle hid the hospital and its supplies, beds, and people from the sky. The area was a main aid station and had many elevated beds and cots.

Chris
October 17 - It was difficult climbing this mountain, as the dense jungle did not allow one to see very far ahead. We were very quiet, and moved slowly. It

seemed so difficult climbing over the tree roots that were exposed across the path as we walked up this slippery narrow mountain path, deep in the jungle. Then we heard a couple of rounds fired up ahead of us. We had been spotted by the enemy, fired back and all hell broke loose. They were running away and we were doing our best to move fast enough to get as many fired rounds as possible. As we ran through the hospital area, we had to make sure to cover ourselves and not miss anyone or we would get a bullet in the back.

Evidently, our guys caught the last of the enemy retreating as we came up the path. The jungle was so thick, I didn't realize how close we were to their camp. We didn't spend much time searching the camp, as others ahead of us probably did that. We continued down the path in search of those that had been living there.

As we passed through the hospital, I noticed containers marked "PLASMA", from your friends at University of California, Berkeley." I can't believe it!

Doc Turner

October 17 - We found a large hospital. It was furnished with medical supplies donated by the communist sympathizers and traitors (in my opinion) of University of California Berkeley (UCB), by way of Japan. It had operating rooms with V Mueller instruments, which are made in Germany. Evidence was found that they were training their field medics, both male and female nurses. We captured 12-14 of those nurses and sent them back to a rear area. I don't know what happened to them.

Items were marked showing UCB students had sent them. Terry Savio found numerous OR instruments in the large cave, which was about the size of a gymnasium and contained approximately 150 beds. It was definitely a main area facility and a great find for us.

House

October 17 - The captain had an idea we should stay the night and set-up ambush sites around the hill in hopes the VC might come back to see what they could salvage, but no deal - too smart. All quiet - good sleep to jungle music from the birds and bugs only.

"The Big Leech"

Our squad position ends up where the VC had a flat area to bury three of their dead. They scrape a shoulder wide slot about two feet down, wrap them in a sheet, sprinkle the body with spice of perfume, (which they don't have much of in the jungle) then throw the loose dirt on top of the body and let nature take it from there. The grass grows over the area pretty quickly, the worms and vegetation take over, and you get pretty flowers in that spot for generations. But, when it is new---it really smells ripe; especially the stuff the rain is oozing out from the mud layer. The stench is god-awful! Once you smell rotting corpses you never forget the smell, and we have to stay next to them all night. My stomach is rolling, I'm going to puke. A gentle rain that smells real sweet starts to fall with a gentle breeze, it is like an answer to a prayer. There are some lemon-smelling trees over us dropping soft, fragrant leaves on the ground, so we keep shoving them over the graves to cover the smell! It works great.

About 0200, alone on my watch, a bright full moon, no rain, quiet, peaceful and still. I feel a "tingle" in my crotch and I know it isn't the kind of tingle because I miss Nancy so much. My rain gear crotch had been ripped wide open earlier and my utility trousers had popped buttons climbing over all the down trees and sharp branches, it was an easy reach straight into the "private zone" for the leeches. I grabbed onto a leach I imaged was the size of a summer sausage attached to my inner thigh and yanked him off in a wild panic. As I jerked him up to my face, I saw he was really not that big, only five or six inches, but that was big enough! That meant he had all of that blood, my blood, in his little black velvet smooth body. And, I was so mad, I somehow wanted it back. He had been there, God knows how long, feasting silently, warm and soft and slow, sharing my body heat, robbing me. Setting me up for infection and possible death in this far-away God forsaken country to die a dishonorable death? Hell, No! Not by a damn leach.

I squeezed his fat, blood-filled body as hard as I could, and he exploded between my fingers, spraying my own blood into my face and eyes, down my open mouth and onto my neck. It ran down my arm in the moonlight and tasted salty and stung my eyes. I shuddered and my eyes burned. I choked, spit and gagged, then, I puked, and continued to retch with the dry heaves.

Two of the guys jumped up thinking I had been hit with something, and was hurt. They tried to quiet me down from puking more, as we did not want to give away our position to the enemy, by making noise. Doc Slater kept looking for a wound and wiping the blood from my face and neck, to place a battle compress and I would bat his hand away and try to puke some more. They were choking me by covering my mouth and I was fighting them just to breathe. All from a little leech. He almost killed me by asphyxiation. When they found out what it was, they

were all pissed at me, but in the morning everybody had fat black leaches all over them. It was because of the heavy leaf debris we were sitting in. They were thick under it. We All Hate Leeches. Especially Me!

We did take a few grenades and some machine gun fire on our flanks, but no one got too close to lucky Echo Company. We made too much noise. I think we had about 300 effective troops out on line and had lots of heavy weapons backup. We were ready, but the other units were taking the heat of the enemy's wrath.

Estes

October 18 – I was in the middle of crossing a jungle stream when the ambush on Hotel Company occurred and we started taking lots of stray rounds from the fight. I was acting as the radio operator and remember some of what I heard. I remember being told, and still believe that an entire platoon of Hotel Company had been wiped out.

The platoon commander, a lieutenant, had been forward in the column and ran back to his platoon, which was caught in the killing zone. He picked up a backpack full of explosives that the NVA had thrown on the trail, to throw it back – only to have it blow up in his face.

The fight was all one-sided and took place after Hotel and Golf Companies had formed one column, Fox and Echo Companies formed another column. We were all walking single-file out of the jungle and back to a road where we were to meet trucks that would take us back to Quang Tri. It was supposed to be the last day of the operation. The NVA did a skillful and clever job of setting up an ambush on the trail leading out of the jungle. Golf Company had the lead (I talked to the kid walking point when we made it back to the battalion area), and Hotel Company brought up the rear. The ambush was sprung on the last 30 men in the column. The NVA had lain on the trail unseen while more than 200 Marines walked past them, no more than ten feet away.

To my knowledge, no NVA were killed. A platoon in Golf Company picked up the dead and put them on the medevac copters.

Of Hotel's dead, I remember the name Churchill. He was a machine gunner. His father, a first sergeant in the USMC Air Wing, had requested duty in Vietnam, so that his son would not have to stay there (according to the rule that said only one male from a family was to be in a combat zone at any one time. This rule was made following the Normandy Landings, when a group of U.S. soldiers went behind enemy lines to retrieve a paratrooper whose three brothers had already been killed in action. He was the last male survivor in his family). The father thought that someone in the air wing would have a better chance to survive that someone in the infantry, so he went to Vietnam, to replace his son and reported to his unit the day his son was killed.

Chris

October 18 - Sad day. Hotel Company was nearly wiped out. The NVA had laid in waiting for the company to pass by them. Patient and quiet, they stayed hidden until the last of the column of Marines from Hotel Company entered the killing zone and then opened up. Machine guns, automatic rifles and grenades all took their toll immediately. Within 45 minutes, the enemy had decimated Hotel Company. The company had been cut into three isolated pieces. Corpsmen were overwhelmed, radio communications were nil, everyone screamed over the Marines next to them - ammunition was needed, medical help was needed, support was lacking, M-60 machined gun ammo had been totally expended. The on-rushing enemy chanted "Marine, you die"!

At the time of the Hotel ambush, Echo Company readied to reinforce the deeply embedded Marines. We could hear the constant firing. It just continued, never seeming to end. It was horrible, knowing that they were having a terrible battle and that we weren't being sent to help them. No information on Hotel Company. So often it goes like this – we don't find out anything. Everyone felt the same, we should be there…helping.

Finally, as Marine reinforcements joined the battle, the NVA broke off contact and withdrew from the area. Word spread quickly to the rest of the battalion. We could, of course, hear the battle going on forever. Now word was being passed regarding their demise. It made me sick inside. It was a terrible feeling to hear the battle go on for such a long time. We continued to feel we would be called to reinforce Hotel. It actually scared the hell out of everyone, knowing what had happened to our fellow Marines, yet we wanted to help them. Then, the silence.

The horror of that night was very hard to stuff away. With all the battlefield action around us and of course with everything that Hotel Company had just endured, our senses were elevated to a higher level. The fact that we had lost so many causalities was almost unbelievable. It was a very difficult few days.

House

October 18 - We just heard more radio traffic (others than ourselves that were conducting a conversation and we just listened in). We learned that a large VC force had ambushed Hotel Company, which was assigned as the rear guard to cover our six (rear guard) on the way out of the jungle. They wanted revenge for the casualties we had inflicted on them during the operation. The firefight continued for 30-45 minutes, and it was a hell of a battle. Artillery was called in to cover Hotel Company. The VC hit and run and some were likely coming our way on the big trail, not knowing we would be there to block their escape, so we set-up for the kill!

Doc Mike Hill, Senior Corpsman, Hotel Co

October 18 – I recall the ambush, as Captain Barrett called for help from Golf Co, his clothes covered in blood from helping his Marines. It was bad. There were only four corpsmen for all the wounded in the company and it just wasn't enough.

Tony Galasso, Golf Co., southern New Jersey

October 18 – The NVA ambushed 2/1 battalion during Operation Medina on this day. Hotel Co took a lot of casualties - 11 KIA and 21 WIA.

Ray Hannon, Hotel Company

October 18 – Everyone was marching in line. Just like every day in the jungle. The battalion commanders kept a fast pace through the jungle, too fast as it turned out. We had made contact with the enemy two or three times over the previous couple of days, killing them and, also taking our loses. We already knew the NVA were around us and why we were chasing them, I don't know. We were going straight up the valley, following the enemy.

And, all of the sudden, the NVA were just all over the place. They were on those higher places on the hillside. Some of them came out of spider traps in the ground...they dropped everything on us...30 calibers, machine guns, satchel charges, everything. I was losing guys all around me. They hit us in the middle of the platoon, which was at the end of the battalion. It took 35-40 minutes for the battalion to get back to us. All three of our platoons were hit badly. We lost a lot of men.

I got up. I had an AK-47 Communist rifle in my hands and two chest pouches of ammo. I have no idea where I got them. I don't know where my M-16 rifle was. I never found it.

Holloran

October 18 - Terry Fenenga was killed on this Operation Medina. He took three rounds in his chest, was unconscious and bleeding badly. After Tilo reduced the enemy threat, we called in a medevac. Our corpsman stayed with Terry giving him mouth to mouth and CPR. We learned by radio that Terry was pronounced dead after take off. It really hit our platoon hard.

**Corporal Terry Fenegna, Iona, South Dakota
Panel 28E, Line 36**

Note: October 18 - Along the perimeter of the Hai Lang Forest, our sister company, Hotel of the 2nd Battalion, 1st Marines, took point for the battalion strike force as they entered the jungle with 160 Marines. The pace was slow and deliberate, as they worked their way through the jungle, slogging up the narrow slippery trails and stumbling down the other side. It continued all that day. The next evening, Hotel Company approached the top of a hill and from their position they could see the red and green tracer rounds from the battle 1/1 was fighting. Sapper squads (elite commando enemy forces armed with automatic weapons and explosive packages they throw) began to probe the top of the hill. In the morning, the march continued…right into an enemy supply base. An assault through the base continued, exposing an enormous enemy bunker complex, filled with food rations, ammunition, weapons and medical supplies. Hotel continued their march through the deep brush and thick canopy forest. As Hotel's last man entered the killing zone (which was the area within an ambush where everyone is either killed or wounded), the NVA opened up with automatic fire, which signaled to the rest of the concealed enemy that the main body of Marines was in front of them. In the first 45 minutes of battle the enemy decimated Hotel Company. The company had been cut into three pieces and each man fought desperately to save his life, no radio communication. Chants of "Marine You Die" were heard as the enemy assaulted. The Marines led a counter-attack into the face of the NVA, who broke contact and withdrew into the forest. According to the 1st Marines Command Chronology, 11 Marines were killed and 21 were wounded. Two NVA were confirmed KIA with 12 probables.

Lt. Suydam

October 18 - Operation Medina was a battalion-sized, search and destroy mission in the Hai Lang Forest. There was quite a bit of fighting during Medina, most of which Echo was not involved in. I'm told that Hotel Company was ambushed badly as the operation was coming to a close and that many casualties were taken. The place was a jungle. We usually worked with 1:25000 photo-picto maps with contour lines every 10 meters. With such maps, you could easily identify your spot on the ground using roads, tree lines, elevation and rivers. The maps were very accurate and you could call in artillery fire with confidence. When we moved into the Hai Lang Forest, we changed to a 1:50000 (details four times smaller) with a contour elevation every 20 meters. That's sixty feet, my friends, and that's not very helpful at all. There were no roads or villages in the jungle. The map was solid green. The only thing we had to go on was the contour lines, which were too far apart to be able to read the map with the limited visibility in the jungle. As a consequence, we stayed lost. Once, the battalion commander called in helicopters and fired starburst clusters through the canopy so that we could be located by air.

House

October 19 - Leaving "Uncle Ho's Woods" (reference to Ho Chi Minh, North Vietnam's leader), as we called Combat Zone #101, the "Hai-Lang National Forest of Vietnam." As we continued to chop and hack our way out of the jungle, due east for five solid hours, the same way we cut our way in, we found a wide trail, and could hear fighting off to our flank. The radios came alive with excited traffic and calls for help.

Heavy machine guns, rocket propelled grenade (RPG) rounds, mortars, AK-47 automatic weapons rattling and our M-60 machine guns were firing like crazy. Nothing gets the blood up like hearing your fellow Marines in a fight close by! The officers were pumped. We were pumped. We wanted to go to their aid, but were told to hold our current positions until the situation was better known.

We had to get across a small swamp, about four meters wide and found a primary VC ambush site. There were dug-in holes, along the trail and signs they had pulled-out and moved, not long before, as there were wet footprints all over the dirt. They obviously had moved to alternate ambush positions on Hotel Company, as we moved towards them and we now cut-off their alternate retreat route. We take over their ambush positions with good cover and wait for the VC to come flying back and take it from their own holes. Everything is silent, nothing moving, nobody makes a sound. You cannot even make spit. We watch the area parallel to the stream for little ripples, to see if they may be moving in the water now. An AK-47 opens on 3rd platoon first and we hear our guys being hit and their screams. Grenades explode, and more screams, and we all get down in our holes because we are all now in the direct line of fire behind 3rd Platoon.

We have to wait for the VC to get past or around 3rd Platoon to shoot at them. It is a lousy tactical position, but it is all we have at the time. Then we hear it, "Corpsman...get a corpsman over here now. Gunny's been hit!" All the shooting stops. The VC break-off the firefight and take-off in the opposite direction. The FO (Forward Observer) calls for artillery (located in the rear area) to fire and pursue their escape.

Leeches – Everybody has leaches on them now, you cannot help it. You cannot keep them off you. Anything you do is not enough. When you are in the water, the leaches find your body heat and slide inside your clothes, even through the eyelets of your boots. When we leave the rivers and streams and if the officers allow us to stop, we peel off our boots and drop trow and open shirts and utilities and check our crotches and each other's butts and backs and you look at your penis, under your armpits, and between your toes. Even on land in heavy jungle, they hang on the underside of the leaves and have heat sensors that can detect when you are walking underneath, and drop right onto you as you pass. They like warm spots to hide, and start real small, about a ½" long, with a round mouth the same size as their body, and no eyes. The larger leeches will be 5-6" long. You sweep your fingers over them first, and if they do not have a good hold yet, they drop right off. Everybody does it for everybody else, no shame. If they do have a good hold, a squirt of mosquito repellent or holding a lit cigarette close and down they go. If the thing is on a guys butt or by or even on his penis, the cigarette is best because the repellent stings! They always move to the warmest area – the most sensitive skin is usually the thinnest and they find it every time.

You cannot let them hang on and fill up because of the wound they make with their round mouth. They have a circular tooth that rasps the skin raw and injects an anti-coagulant that continues bleeding and allows infection to set in after they fill up with your blood and drop off. I scrape two off my ankles, do a quick check and move on, all okay.

Medevac helicopters were coming and going non-stop, and were taking heavy fire to get the wounded out.

We move over to a small hill, set-up a perimeter around the LZ, and help the wounded with their gear. We walk-up on three guys, with fresh grenade fragments in them, and they make it okay with a little help. Then we automatically start to dig-in.

The bad news is it is our Gunnery Sergeant Nathaniel Weathers, has been shot. He is the neatest guy you would ever want to serve under as a combat Marine. He is everything the Marine is supposed to be. Cool under fire, and wise as they get. It seems he has been everywhere, seen everything, knows everything. Officers come to him to learn what they need to know. We all admire and respect him so much, and now he has been shot in the head.

To our relief, we find out the bullet hit low in front of his helmet, pierced the steel and fiberglass liner, skinned across his forehead and went out the other side. It knocked him down and made him pretty wobbly, but it was only a flesh wound. And all he would say (as he was such a gentleman) was, "Good heavens, this is the worst headache I believe I have ever had. Man! We were all relieved we still had our Gunny. Alive and well. Too good a man to lose.

We had to stay on that hill all night and by 2000 hours (8pm), enemy snipers were on us again, with an occasional rifle grenade or mortar round fired toward us as well. All we could do was dig our holes deeper, into the soft dirt, dig deeper, keep your head down and pray they don't come straight down in your hole.

Lt. Suydam came around the line and ordered all positions to crawl down the hill, the length of a claymore wire and set the devices out, three each, in case of an enemy assault or the VC trying to crawl up on us within grenade range during the night. I thought what for? I can toss my grenades a lot further down the hill than they can up-hill. But, he is the officer, right? Crawling down in the dark, every shadow I saw I imagined was a VC. By the time I got back to my hole, I was shaking like a leaf and my knees were quivering. But, I sure felt a lot better with all those claymores surrounding the hill, between them and us. The night air is so quiet, except for the word passed between positions or an occasional cough. And then you hear the very distinctive sound of a Chi-Com grenade being thrown towards us. One of the enemy's homemade ones, with the friction-match in the long wood handle, which is pulled like a string and it goes kind of ziiiipppp! It is thrown overhead like a stick with a body of cast iron with black powder inside on top, so it tumbles through the air end over end, zoop-zoop-zoop-zoop, especially if they throw it through the bamboo or trees. You can kind of track its direction as it approaches, snapping twigs and moving the air. There are a lot of duds with these homemade grenades. Problems caused by the chemicals in the friction match in the handle of the grenade, just do not hold up to the moisture, and they frizzle out. But a lot of them do work and they are plenty strong enough to kill a man, if they get close. But most of the time it is a bad shrapnel wound, because

DEADLY CLOSE—GySgt. Nathaniel Webster points out the hole left by an enemy machinegun round during Operation Medina in mid-October. The round was deflected and just creased the sergeant's forehead. Webster is company gunnery sergeant for E Co., 2nd Bn., 1st Marine Reg., 1st Marine Div. (USMC photo)

the cast iron head bursts off in one direction, not a uniform disbursal like ours are grenades are designed to do. Anyway, it explodes alright, and the whole line on our side of the hill for sixty feet, on both sides open up with a full burst from our weapons.

We now know the VC are moving up the slope, within throwing distance. I squeeze the trigger device and my blow my claymore, sending thousands of BB's down upon the intruders. Then I throw one illumination grenade. I was trying to backlight any VC moving up-slope. The illumination grenade hit tall grass and started a fire, just enough to convince them to leave our side of the hill alone for the rest of the night. Our own artillery was being called in, around our positions and the other side of the hill, so close that stray shrapnel would sometimes whistle high through the air and we could hear it fly and fall. We had strict orders, from our officers, swearing at us, "Damn it, you had damn well better keep your damn helmets and flack jackets on, and keep your heads down in those holes. If I see one of your sorry damn faces looking up, I will personally kick it to the bottom of your damn hole!" (I don't think they wanted any of us to get hurt in a "friendly-fire" incident and have to write a letter home to our wife or momma, or explain it to the General). Man, it was cold down in those holes, but it was safe. Nobody was hit.

Lt. Kirk
October 19 - The battalion was engaged in an operation in the Hai Lang Forest (Operation Medina) and had taken quite a few casualties. The S-1 (adjutant) assigned us all to companies and we received a briefing from the S-2 (intelligence officer). Initially, I was assigned to H&S (Headquarters and Service) Company, which meant I would be a platoon leader for 81mm mortars or a 106 recoilless rifle platoon, which was disappointing. I wanted a rifle platoon.

Chris
October 19 – I remember our position last night, as we set-in the low standing bushes. We had an advantage, because we were on the upper side of the slightly slanted hillside. We knew that throwing grenades and shooting downhill was definitely a plus, especially if they decided to try to overrun us. The 2-3' low profile bushes offered us almost nothing to help us conceal ourselves, so we stayed as low as we could, just praying nothing would come close to us. Close meant we'd get hit. Geez, it was a long night, as no one could sleep. Intermittent probing of grenades continued.

House
October 19 - In the morning, we are moving up as a strong, determined, fighting force with a sense of purpose. We have a bunch of gunships (these are helicopters outfitted with machine guns and rockets) flying over and alongside us like guardian angels. We have protective cover right out of the jungle. They open fire with mini-guns, rockets, M-60's on anything they even think look like

enemy or ambush sites ahead of us or off to our flanks. It really felt safe with them there for us. They would peel off in pairs, refuel, re-arm and come back, hour after hour. That was good tactics. Drive the enemy out ahead of you. We finally broke-out into open rolling treeless hills about 1300 hours and marched to Hwy #1 where our battalion had arranged for lots of 6BY troop transport trucks. They were all waiting for us. They looked like Cadillac's to me after all that walking. It only took forty minutes to ride back to Hill #25 – our "home base".

We hear that headquarters considers the operation a huge success, and that we had mostly destroyed two full regiments of NVA, and stopped their plan to attack and occupy Quang Tri City, dead in its tracks. We had bloodied them pretty bad, but we lost a lot of our own in the process.

Note: During Operation Medina, in the nearly impenetrable jungle terrain, 2/1 uncovered enemy base camps and storage areas, with little signs of NVA and VC troops. After confiscating more than four tons of enemy rice and miscellaneous weapons and ammunition, the battalion continued with Operation Osceloa. In Operation Osceola, the 1st Marines with two battalions, 2/4 and 2/1, remained in the same objective area as they were in during Medina. 1st Marines also became responsible for the newly established Quang Tri base.

Night watch is first duty for marines in S. Vietnam

Article written by Cpl Roger Goss

(EDITOR'S NOTE: This is the third letter, received from Pfc. Roger Goss from Vietnam.)
2-April

Standing perimeter watch is one of the first duties a Marine draws in Vietnam.

He reports for duty about 5:30 in the evening. The duty N.C.O. calls roll then issues instructions for the night's watch.

"Tonight, men, we'll have three listening posts consisting of four men each leaving the compound. They will carry three signal flares. Red means they're in trouble; yellow is a special signal to the officer of the day and green simply means they're either moving to their alternate position or coming back in. If you see any of these signals report them immediately. We'll have two patrols of twenty men each leaving as soon as it gets dark. One will leave from Alpha sector, the other from Charlie. They should be coming in about dawn.

"We'll be on fifty per cent alert, two men to each position. How you divide up the watch is up to you. We're on 100 per cent alert til 2200. For you civilians at heart that's ten o'clock. No one sleeps till after ten!

"Anyone caught asleep on post had just better stand by 'cause if THEY don't get you, WE will!

"Need I remind you. . .there will be NO smoking after dark or radios playing. Do not fire your machine guns unless you have permission from your sector chief.

"There's no moon tonight so if you want to sit on top of your bunkers where it's cooler you may.

"The password tonight is 'Detroit Lions'. . . . ."

One Marine interrupts the sergeant's instructions with, "Yea, DE-troit!"

"The alternate, "Baltimore Bullets'— nobody here from Baltimore?"

The Marines chorus, "Detroit Lions— Baltimore Bullets."

"Get your gear and get out there," the Sergeant shouts.

Marines draw extra ammo, grenades and a Claymore mine for each position, then straggle out to their assigned places on the line.

Once in the bunkers they test the phones to the sector chief:

"Alpha one, this is Alpha two, how do you hear me? Over." The reply, "Loud and clear Alpha two, how me? Over."

"Hear you same, out."

Next they check their weapons then arrange all their gear in handy positions.

By this time the sun is sinking.

Two Marines watch the sunset over the barbed wire entanglements in front of their bunker. One remarks:

"This is really for real, ain't it?"

"Yeah, but it's funny. It looks so peaceful and serene out there."

"Well, let's have one more smoke 'fore it gets dark."

"Okay."

The two talk and alternately watch the terrain. They talk about home, sweethearts, cars and stories they've heard about the V.C. sneaking into the lines and cutting the throats of a sleeping guard. They decide it won't be hard to stay awake.

"Man, it's like pitch out there. How close do you think someone could get before we'd see 'em?"

"I don't know, ten yards? Ten feet?"

"Sure could use a smoke."

"Yeah."

They watch illumination flares in the distance and listen to occasional muffled machine gun bursts.

At ten o'clock one says to the other:

"Why don't you get some sleep?

"Alright."

The comfort of company is gone to the Marine on watch. His eyes strain. His ears ache from trying to listen. The night and his imagination play tricks on both senses. His nerves are taunt. He has butterflies in his stomach.

Suddenly he screams. It's a scream from out of his guts, a scream of sheer fear.

The other Marine is instantly awake and instictively takes his weapon off safe.

"Whatsamatter?"

"A rat, I guess. He jumped through the window on me. I thought I was done had. Must have been the size of a possum!

"Well, you scared me to death! You nervous or somethin'?"

"No. Hell no, just plain sacred.

"I wasn't sleeping anyway. I'll just stay up with you."

The night drags on. About one a.m. a sergeant brings coffee around, the coffee is black and strong and hot. Its heat and strength revitalizes the Marines' nummed altertness.

They continue watching and listening. Mostly listening.

Clank.

"Did you hear that?"

Clank. Clank.

"Yeah! Sounds like something in the wire."

The Marine gets on the phone

"Alpha one, this is Alpha two."

He is surprised at the casual nonchalance of his own voice.

"We think we got something down here. How about some light?"

"Comin' up, Alpha two."

A few seconds later the Marines hear the 'Whump' of a mortar sending up a flare, then a 'pop' as it lights up the position.

"There he is!"

They laugh. "He" is a cow.

"Remember though," one says, "sometimes they send cows through as decoys or to trip our flares ahead of them."

"What time is it?"

"Bout three-thirty."

Darkness continues.

7

MOVE NORTH TO QUANG TRI

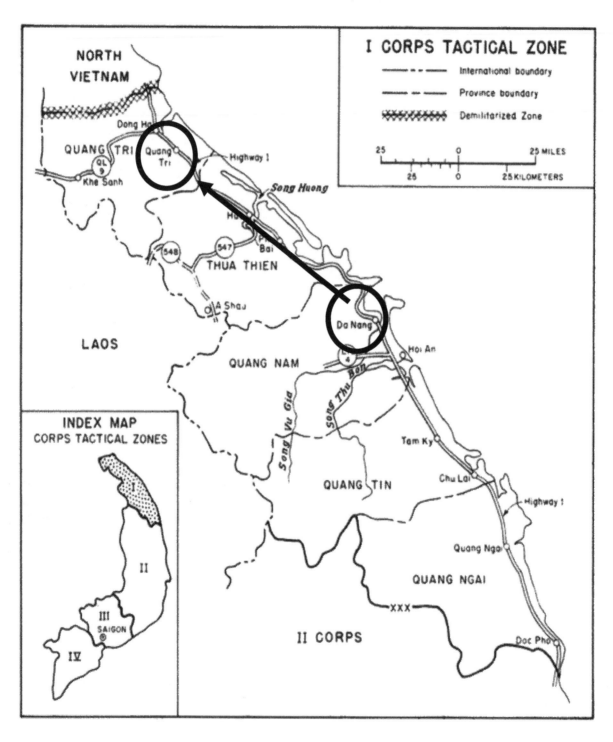

Out of artillery range from North Vietnam, the Quang Tri base served as a backup to the main logistic base at Dong Ha and provided a new air facility for the Marine forces in the north.

Cpl Chuck Estes, Dallas, TX, L/Cpl Larry Herfel, Madison, WI
Doc Turner, Wilmot, LA - Awaiting truck transport to Hill #25

House

October 21 - When we arrived back at our base camp near Quang Tri, we found some progress, but still no hardback tents for us grunts. They had built a fair size field mess tent, no hard floor or lights yet, and they still had the boiling water field stoves, like Korea, but at least we would get hot chow! We had fried chicken, mashed potatoes, vegetables and cold chocolate milk. After so long in the bush, you tend to forget that there really is real food out there somewhere.

They had all our mail, and Nancy sent my new rain gear, the best from Sears, along with spearmint leaves, gum, and Kool-Aid. Grandma Behning sent hip flasks of brandy, a hand-warmer and two pairs of gloves. My God, it was too good to be true. After eating C-rats for so long, we all got diarrhea from the hot chow. We all looked like we had been out in the bush too long and needed some serious clean-up. Everyone got shaves, showers and haircuts. I got to go to supply to check-out two sets of utilities and got two pair of new boots. I upsized my size of jungle boots to give my feet more room to swell-up when they get wet (per the wise Gunny's advice) and I feel like a new man. We got real cold milk and lots of it.

We fixed-up our individual tent shelters for a while, staking everything down real secure and stood by. Word passes down, saddle-up, draw fresh ammo and four C-rats apiece. We will be out on small patrols for foothill screening, overnight only. Sure, and who believes that?

The newly-acquired foot goop is working much better now, and the supply is increasing. Doc issues eight tubes per man. Healing our feet is so important. We are only getting a breakfast and a dinner for each day. We are told to expect that type of rationing until we move north in December. They say it is to be to Con Thien, right on the hill overlooking the DMZ (demilitarized zone between North & South Vietnam). We will be face-to face across the line with the commie bastards, looking them straight in the eye!

Operation Medina becomes Operation Osceola, then Operation Liberty II - Outpost at Vien Tay. We moved into positions after dark, as a blocking force for a "hammer and anvil" operation. Other outfits will sweep the enemy force in front of them and push them towards us. We ran a river patrol last night, catching sporadic sniper fire all night from opposite bank. They move, fire one shot, we never see a muzzle flash, do not know where to return fire, and we must stay alert and awake all night. No hope of accurate return fire. Heavy rain starts and we are sitting out in it, fully exposed. Sgt. Baldwin says, "The hell with this!" He had spotted a brick house down the trail, checked it out, and he moves the squad inside to set up a solid defensive perimeter for the night. I'm impressed. This is small-unit incentive command /control at its best. He has each of us stand one hour watches and lets the rest sleep. Bliss. It rains so hard and is so cold, but we are all under cover instead of out in the open on that riverbank, only that sniper does not know it. I hope he is out there in that cold rain. Yea.

October 22 - I woke-up at 0830, fixed hot cocoa, cookies, bread and pineapple jam for breakfast, so good. Everybody was in such a great mood, we wanted to recommend Spanky for a promotion. He would have none of that. We finished off the last of C-rats. We need re-supply but expect no lunch or dinner tonight.

Chris

October 22 - We just got a new lieutenant in the company today. When lieutenants get assigned the responsibility of a platoon, they become the senior ranking, yet the most inexperienced member of the team. He may have 6-10 months of schooling, but really doesn't know how a platoon operates, especially when engaging the enemy. And, he's the one that's supposed to lead the troops. It's a tough position for the new officers. If a lieutenant is lucky he gets assigned to a unit that has NCO's (enlisted non-commissioned officers) with 6, 8, 10 years experience.

Estes

October 22 - I got lost on this operation. It was the damnest thing. I was following the guy in front of me and then all the sudden he wasn't there. We were following a creek bed and the trail split. I went one way and the rest of the guys went the other way. Shit! Sure, I was scared, I was alone. I had the radio, so I knew I could probably communicate with platoon command. I got in touch with them and finally got back to where I was supposed to be. Wow, was I happy to see the guys!

Lt. Kirk

October 22 – The next day when the battalion and the battalion commander returned, I was assigned to Echo Company as a rifle platoon commander. I met my company commander, Captain Baker and my platoon sergeant, Staff Sergeant Valoria, a Mexican-Filipino, who was on his second tour in Vietnam. I took over as platoon commander, 1st platoon, Echo Company. I was fortunate to have Valoria to show me the ropes.

2/1 was chopped or operationally controlled (op-con) to the 3rd Marine Division at this time.

The U.S.M.C. (United States Marine Corps) table of organization says a rifle platoon is supposed to have 48 men: 3 squads of 14 men each, with a squad leader and three four man fire teams, plus a platoon commander, platoon sergeant, platoon guide, a radioman and two Navy medical corpsmen. Usually, the platoon would have a machine gun squad and a rocket squad (3.5" rocket launchers or LAAW's – light anti-tank weapons) attached and sometimes an 81mm mortar forward observer, a sniper team or a scout dog team, so theoretically a platoon could include a lot more men. However, because of casualties and illness, we were usually under-strength. The squad leaders were supposed to be sergeants and the fire team leaders corporals, but almost always the squad leaders were corporals.

Doc Turner setting up his tent on the rocky hillside at Quang Tri.

Chris

October 22 – 1045 hrs – We lost another guy. As our platoon was moving in company formation a guy stepped on another anti-personnel mine. Medevac was called in for 1 WIA and we continued on our way. 1150 hours medevac for 1 KIA, 1157 hrs another medevac for 2 WIA from fragmentation wounds. We're a bit on nerves these days.

House

October 23 - We are in a small village outside Quang Tri. Rolling hills and valleys are widely disbursed along small river valleys. We make long humps along ridge lines that make us good targets, so we try to stay on the side slopes. It makes for hard walks and one leg keeps getting shorter. Low valleys make good VC minefields and booby trap trails are everywhere.

Thirty minutes later one of our machine gunners steps on another one of these little VC Z-10 mines, but most of it goes right past his legs and a chunk of iron hits another man square center in his chest. We could hear the steel whiz through the air and thud into him when it hit. He just stood there looked down at the blood spot growing on his chest, sat down, put his M-60 machine gun down at his side and called out, "Hey corpsman, I'm hit." He was so calm about it, it was weird. Two corpsmen were on him now. The helicopter was already there and they loaded him aboard and he was gone in a flash. No idea what the result was, or who he was. Two more good men wounded and out of action. We had to stay for an extra two hours to send out search parties to find some of our men who had gotten separated and lost, and could not hook-up with the main force. Too scary to be left out there alone. Finally, we found everybody and marched out all together. "Semper Fi" (the Marine Corps motto - "Always Faithful").

Lt. Kirk
October 23 - My first patrol was with the whole company near Notre Dame of La Vang cathedral. It was an impressive structure and completely out of place in a rural environment, having few substantial buildings. The Pope visited here once before the war. On a boulevard in front of the cathedral were huge statues representing the Stations of the Cross. The Quang Tri area had a lot of Catholics who had fled from North Vietnam when the country was partitioned. A second squad member, a black Marine from Cleveland, walking in back of me was wounded by a mine just south of the cathedral.

Knobby
October 23 - The quotas for R&R came in last night and I got Hawaii for November 30. I thought I was pretty lucky! I should leave Da Nang and be in Hawaii sometime on the 30th (probably late evening). We're scheduled for an operation Nov. 15th I found out so there is a slight possibility I could be 1 or 2 days late. If we are in real heavy jungle they might night be able to get a chopper in to lift me out right away. I doubt very much that this will happen. They usually send R&R personnel to Da Nang a couple of days ahead of time so I should have some leeway there.

Got back from Operation Medina a few days ago. T, two other guys and myself got a beautiful Chinese Communist light machine gun. T and I get to keep it since it was just he and I that actually shot the enemy gunner. He killed one and injured two Marines before we could get to him. A CBS camera man with us at the time said he got a lot on film.

A reporter for the Stars and Stripes and The Sea Tiger got ahold of T and I afterward and had us give him the story. The reporter said they always send the stories to our hometown papers, but I imagine the Journal is too big to print anything like that.

Chris

October 24 - Mom, your letter says Dad got a big promotion and now is working directly for the governor as a management analyst and will be writing the Governor's speeches. It makes me feel so good to hear good news. Also, I am so proud of my sister. All the news from college sounds so good. I get numerous letters from her, and it reminds me of my days at Southern Oregon College (SOC). I continue to get letters from Rick Grabenhorst. He is sick of being in Korea with the Army. We're making lots of plans for when we get back to the "world." It's so good to make plans for the future. Mom said I have a 3.9 GPA - 2nd cousin attending school at SOC and she's a knockout! Well, while I was playing football and attending a few college functions, she must have been hitting the books. It's funny how people choose to spend their time, isn't it. Just got a terrific letter from Doc Schneider. I don't know if you knew it or not, but Doc offered me his 9mm Browning automatic pistol when I left for Vietnam. I had borrowed it many times at home when I was going out in the country for target shooting. I didn't accept the pistol, as I figured I'd get caught with an unauthorized weapon, or maybe I wouldn't be able to find ammo for it or maybe even lose it. Anyway, it was a real neat offer and much appreciated.

House

October 24 - I got into big trouble this morning, at first light. I tried to "commandeer" a rather large tarp for our departing squad. It would make a great tent to keep us dry. It was already covering a small vehicle called a "mule" and a bunch of its gear for a 106mm recoilless rifle crew. (Mules were, at times, armed with machine guns, or used for transport of supplies or as a litter for the wounded.

The tarp was pretty big for me to handle by myself, but I was all alone. Anyway, some 106mm recoilless rifle troops spotted me and called their first sergeant. He ran over and grabbed me with another sergeant, so I was had. They haul me over into their area in front of a lieutenant who started shouting about a court martial offense for "misappropriating government property". I stood there head down looking real guilty, and when they all quieted down and asked what I had to say, I explained my squad had been out on patrols all week, sleeping in rain gear and our tent leaked when we got back, and we were still sleeping wet. And, I just thought his mule was designed to sit outside, but I was sorry and would wait until supply got in some more and saluted. It took away all of his thunder! He saluted me and said, "Dismissed".

Mule

The squad got a good laugh out of it. They thought it was cool. I tried to steal the tarp from the other guys to help. Still, we just do not get the supplies we need.

We have a small depression below the hill we use for a firing range to get rid of all the dirty and corroded ammo we bring back from our operations, after it had been out in the rain, and mud. So, we are told to fire it off, or burn it or blow it up. We get to shoot everything until it gets boring. We make "daisy-chains" (A is wired to device B, which is wired to device C...) with old mortar rounds, rockets, M-60 assault packs, flares, C-4 bombs, claymores, cool. Big firework displays with dangerous explosives compliments of the USMC. We only take fresh ammo into the bush to meet and greet Charles (Charles, Charlie, VC, gooks, etc).

Trucks take us over to regimental HQ for cold showers. No heaters yet. It still felt pretty good. At the PX (Post Exchange), I bought a big tin pail for a wash tub for $1.00, two candles for $.70, a coke for $.050, but did not have time to get a haircut and make the truck back in time. Kendricks scored a big foxhole cover for us at night and now we have a tent cover, no more leaks.

Sgt. Baldwin is getting short and will be going on R&R, I will be senior and taking over the squad while he is gone. I hope I am up to it.

I have gotten fairly close to one guy here, the guy assigned to show me the ropes, our M-79 grenadier Richard Speck. He is from the inner city, Warren, Michigan (Detroit) and is kind of a hoodlum. He has a kind of cruel killer instinct that is scary, but he can teach me a lot and he is watching out for me. Even though he is a Lance Corporal, he sure is salty. "Kill them first and fast and let's go home, he says." He carries a pair of .38 revolvers in shoulder holsters under his armpits and his Dad sends him fresh ammo for them in his goodie packages. It is his "last resort" against capture. A good idea. I have no idea how he smuggled them over here as they are totally non-issue weapons. He is sharing his goody packages from home with me, so I share all of Nancy's, Mom's and Grandma's stuff with him. He loves it. I hope he does not get blown away here. He takes way too many chances by exposing himself to open fire to get a good shot. He already has shrapnel in his back with one Purple Heart, so two more wounds and he goes home.

Speck- The Business Man

Richard Speck is from Detroit – with the same name and home town as the guy who murdered eight nurses with a knife a few months ago. One day while we were on stand-down, I came around the corner of our tent and found a long line of guys waiting to get up to a table he had set-up with a Polaroid camera and a stack of film on it. He had money stuffed in every pocket and all the guys in line had fists full of more money to give to him. He had all the last twelve months of the centerfolds from *Playboy* magazine cutout and pasted to cardboard so they would stand-up on the table.   The guys could select any or all to have their picture taken with for $5 each, and some guys had all twelve. He would have them stand back and to the side of the cut-out so it appeared they were the same height in the frame, and the pictures turned out pretty good. He made a fortune. He told me his next step would be to get to the big PX in Da Nang where they sold Norataki China and Akai reel-to-reel tape players at deep discounts and no tax straight from Japan, and buy as much as he could. He would then ship them home for free (we didn't have to pay for postage going out of a combat zone) to his brother who owned a second-hand store and could sell them for a huge profit. He planned to be rich when he got home.

My participation in a daylight robbery!

Yesterday, we had a group of Vietnamese civilians from Quang Tri City walk-up next to the barbwire we have around our area, mostly women and kids. They are not supposed to be so close.   The adults all wear long heavy coats with big pockets sewn inside to hold contraband stuff for sale, like whiskey, coke, candles, drugs, etc. Speck says "Come on, House". Let's go see what they got. He gets three women to come up close to the wire, open their coats to show him all their wares, and agree to a price. He suddenly pulls both his pistols, yells at them to empty everything on the ground on our side of the wire and run and never come back or he will shoot them. And, they do run! We gather it all up as they are running and screaming off into the distance. Speck is laughing like a wild man proclaiming we have only liberated American goods they probably stole from our containers on the docks at China Beach (a R &R destination for wounded) that should have been delivered to us anyway. Let's go back to the squad tent and party. I was an accessory to armed robbery, but it was kind of fun. Speck is definitely CRAZY!

Doc Turner
October 25 – Operation Granite lasted from October 26 through the 30th. We were a blocking force for the 4th Marines. Bernie Bernston, our combat reporter, worked this operation along with me. The rest of you guys stayed attached to the main force of Echo Company.

Chris
October 25 - We have nine in our squad again. PFC Bitsuie has been added. Geez...he looks so young, young and scared. I think he's 18 years old. As I look at him, I try to visualize myself and ask the question,. Did I look as young and scared as Bitsuie? Probably so. We are so under strength, it's great to have another body with us.

We marched out to our objective - about 4,000 meters. We set up around a ville and blocked all exits. We then searched the ville, the people, the hooches, tree lines, and the outbuildings. We found a couple of grenades, booby traps, about nine VC suspects and three confirmed VC. We took them into custody and sent them to headquarters for interrogation.

Our platoon, which is a bit under 40 men, headed back to camp, ate a meal and then left again at night for another 3-5 day operation. We are supposed to eat about two meals a day when in the field and three meals a day when in the rear area. A lot of times, we don't even get two meals. On our last 10-day trip, we averaged 1.6 meals a day. I don't understand why we can't have better access to food. We get no answers from the brass. I believe the Corps doesn't have enough copters to run food and ammo to the troops, as medevac copters serve as the first need and we all know this.

Lt. Kirk
October 25 - The cordon & search operation at Nu Le was an unexpected success. The search teams captured a number of VC and killed a few more,

while the three Marine rifle companies were involved in cordoning off the village. It was an impressive coordination of ARVN, Regional Forces, Popular Forces and

Chris, Oncale, Mully, Bitsuie, Lenny, Speck & Dodd of second squad.

police, as well as Marine and Air Force air cover and Marine infantry units. My CP was in a schoolhouse on the edge of the ville, which was also the collecting point for the villagers, so it was quite a spectacle for me. We set in the cordon at 0430 hours. At 0530 a chopper dropped leaflets. At 0630 a loudspeaker instructed the villagers to assemble, concurrent with an ARVN & RF sweep of the ville; the RFs & police checked IDs, interrogated suspected VC & a cultural team did its propaganda thing. The lieutenant from Fox Co, 1st platoon, was killed by 20# of C-4 explosive on a bridge yesterday. Two enlisted men were wounded, also. Since 2/1 has come into the area, the local VC have been planting mines and booby traps more extensively. We're engaged in two wars up here, one against the NVA in the jungle highlands and the other against the local VC.

We were later told that during the cordon and search of this village, VC escaped across the Quang Tri River using an underwater bridge and using reeds for breathing tubes.

House

October 25 - The day patrol is an easy two mile hump to surround a no-name village. We meet a little kid with a switch herding a huge water buffalo down the path we have to travel. We back off and let him have the right-of-way. The ARVN have already swept the village and broadcast planes told the VC they know who they are, give up, they are trapped. We sat for two hours waiting for the ARVN commander to allow us to move up, and it started to rain. We were close to the buffalo kid's house, and his dad steps out and waves us inside. It is a family of five in a big brick farmhouse. Four big rooms and big stable out back for the buffalo, chickens and goats, and real clean, plus a separate work shop full of big stones. He is a stonemason, all kinds of carvings, mostly headstones, though, nice looking work. There are three girls about twelve to fifteen years old and a boy about eight or nine years old. We broke out phase-books and tried small talk, but Speck did best and had them laughing right away. The boy would laugh at me and correct my bad pronunciation, as long as I laughed and smiled back. He loved it when I got tongue-tied. We all got together for a picture from Linares' new Instamatic Camera, a small compact, point and shoot. It normally carried a roll of film of 12 or 20 pictures. It was easiest to sent the roll of film home and let our parents develop and keep the pictures for us. I gave them a couple cans of my C-rats - beef slices, potatoes and beef spiced with sauce as a gift and they decided that meant it was dinner. They broke-out their rice, fish, sauces and pots were boiling in no time flat with all foods combined and smelling good. I passed out all my C-rat cigarettes to Papa-San and the guys, and was pretty popular. Two of us had Kool-Aid and we mixed a couple of canteens full and poured a round for all to their delight as well.

The ARVN never did allow us to move into the village and our trucks came early for a change and got us back in time for hot chow, a solid nights sleep with no watches, no line duty, no patrols, just solid sleep, it was so good and too good to be true, but good.

October 26 - Speck and Dodd come over to my little hooch to share goodie packages from home - cocoa, cookies, Jiffy-pop Popcorn and Kool-Aid. We had a radio and two packages of Spearmint Leaves, Yum! Yum. Stuffed to the gills.

We went to the gook hooch Post Exchange (PX) for a haircut and bought a 4" x 6" green plastic picture album "Souvenir of Vietnam" for my pictures. Things are getting strict, we now have to put candles out at 2000 (8pm), wear regulation covers, no more Boonie Hats allowed, and carry our rifles at all times in the area, but no ammo. Worse yet, they have mess-gear inspections. Today, anyone with any grease on their plate or utensils had to go to the back of the line. Chicken-shit stuff. All of the mascot puppies had to be tied-up now, too. New officers crap! So, in semi-official protest, Sgt. Hogan, our guide, has adopted a "pet rock". He named him "Zebachcaneezer" and drags him around the area on a rope and whistles at it to piss-off the officers. So far they have ignored him. We'll see?

The M72 LAAW was a prepackaged round. It was a disposable lightweight bakooka, firing a 66mm warhead capable of penetrating 6-8" of steel, 2 feet of concrete or completely destroying an enemy bunker or hooch.

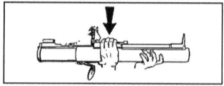

Figure 2-19. Firing the launcher.

Lt. Kirk

October 26 - One day, after we had completed a platoon size patrol, Staff Sergeant Valoria, suggested we walk through a nearby village on the south bank of the Quang Tri River. It wasn't part of our assigned route, but I agreed. Sergeant Valoria made a woman go in front of us as we walked down the main, east/west road along the Quang Tri River through the village. I had my doubts about the ethics and hearts and minds aspect of this, but I deferred to his greater experience. As we continued, we came near an intersection with a north/south road and spotted a VC with an AK-47 rifle running away from us through the hooches. We ran down the north/south road to cut him off. My Marines near the front fired and killed him as he ran down a rice paddy dike.

Lt. Suydam

October 27 - My last day as a platoon commander occurred in Quang Tri province under Captain Baker. We had been on a company sized sweep for several days and were making our way back to the battalion perimeter. It was getting toward dusk and we were trying to find a place to set in the company for the night. Third Platoon was on point as usual and there had been no contact during the entire patrol.

We passed a bombed out Cathedral. I was told it is called the Notre Dame de La Vang. The place was surreal. The Cathedral sat on a hill; no others for miles and there were pine trees around; none others in the country, as far as I know. The Cathedral itself was haunting and out of place. Nothing else was around, but typical agricultural countryside; rice paddies, bamboo tree lines and villages.

To our right was a big irrigation ditch. You would call it a bayou in Texas. I had to have a look into the ditch. It was the perfect place for the enemy to approach us with protection for escape. As the point squad passed a small trail over a culvert to our right, without thinking, I peeled off right to cross the culvert and head over about 20 meters to the right to look into the ditch. My radioman and one other rifleman instinctively followed me. Blam!

The mine, a Z-10 grenade-sized, with a pull friction fuse, was hidden under the culvert. The brick culvert, no doubt, absorbed most of the blast and probably saved my leg and foot. As it was, only the worst of the shrapnel escaped the brick to wound the three of us. My error in crossing this culvert was a classic boo-boo. Had I seen a trooper of mine attempting to do the same thing, I would have stopped him. We were in mine country and our battalion had already suffered enormous casualties. This was a trail and trails are terrible for mines. Worse, this was a narrow place in the trail. The wet places to either side of the culvert channeled the victim across the mine. Finally, this culvert was a wonderful place to hide explosives.

First, I smelled the black powder, then I heard the sound, and finally I saw the flash of light. It was all backward and all in slow motion. I tried to run, but my feet weren't working. When I hit the ground, I searched for my weapon thinking that we would be attacked instantly. We weren't. The two behind me seemed to be hurt worse than I was. I did some cussing for making such a stupid mistake. Others were taking charge, binding our wounds and calling in a medevac chopper.

As the chopper took off with us, the VC opened up on it. They were very close and they were in great numbers. Others that came in wounded to the Battalion Aide Station (BAS) told us that there was much fighting that night. The BAS in Quang Tri was a tent, just like you see on MASH.

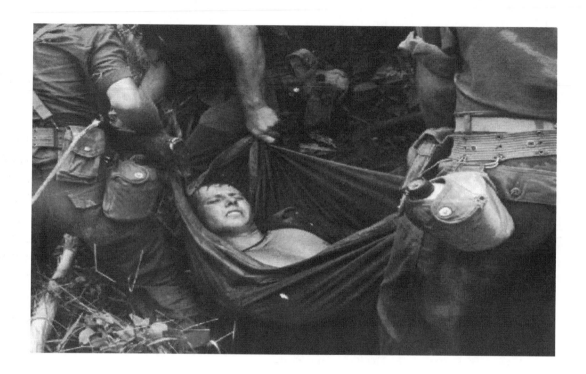

Doctors in the BAS were amused by my case. I took small wounds in my right forearm and right buttocks. I had much greater wounds in my left and right ankles. What amused them was the wound in my right ankle was just above the boot line. Marines don't tuck their trousers into their boots. They use a blousing band, a spring or elastic around the leg. The trousers are folded up and under. This method keeps out leeches, ticks and other critters. My choice was to use a metal spring. The shrapnel had driven the spring into my flesh and was now dangling out of my wound like TV rabbit ears.

Of course there was an audience. "Hey, come get a load of this." The doctor called for his camera, and then when ready for surgery, he called for the wire cutters from his tool chest. I think I had local anesthetic only because I was not totally out for the surgery. The doctor only removed visible shrapnel and did not do damage fishing around. He merely cleaned the wounds and sewed them up. There was enough meat and skin missing from my right leg that sewing up was like stringing a banjo.

I was sore beyond description. The next day, a chopper carried me to Cam Ranh Bay, which is an enormous U.S. military complex and hospital area in the south of the country on the coast. I started walking in four weeks with occasional strolls on the beach. The uneven ground helped me to regain my strength.

Lt. Kirk
October 27 - On another company size patrol, one of the other Echo Co. platoon commanders, Lt. Lee Suydam, 3rd platoon, stepped on a mine going over a little bridge near a hill covered with pine trees. Lee was sent to an in- country hospital.

The area around us was filled with pine trees, which were an anomaly, reminding me of home and offering some relief from the heat. We were attacked that night at 0300 hours with small arms fire and grenades. The Command Chronology says we had seven WIA. The noise was shocking, deafening and disorienting. I remember thinking about the expression that buttons are too thick when you're being shot at as I embraced the ground. Then I saw Sgt. Valoria, my platoon sergeant, moving around, talking to the men and directing their fire. That's what I'm supposed to be doing also, I remembered, and I did likewise. When the firefight was over I was too excited and anxious to sleep. I remember deciding to keep my right leg cocked when I laid down so I could get up quickly. I decide to get in the habit of going to sleep that way.

Chris
October 27 – I have malaria with a temperature of 105.9, very cold, shakes, and hot sweats. I was told to just lay on the ground, nothing to do, but to wait it out. They put blankets on me, as the shakes were taking their toll. I had been taking my malaria medicine every week, until I got sick, then not again. One less thing to contend with – the Wednesday pill and the nasty water to chase it down.

House
October 27 – We're on patrol outside Quang Tri - 0430 hrs. We stopped for an early breakfast of meatballs and beans with bread and cheese C-rat, a pound cake with cherry Kool-Aid, mmm…good! What I wouldn't give for one of Nancy's Sunday morning breakfast feasts of fried eggs over easy, extra crispy bacon, a big stack of large pancakes smothered in butter and maple syrup, cold milk and orange juice. Oh man. To kill for. God, I miss that woman! And, her cooking. And, her mother's greater cooking. (Do not tell her that.)

We had another change before getting here this morning. I had the lead team and my compass worked just fine, thank you. But the captain wanted to move off one way or the other (he is the captain, after all). And we end-up about 3000 meters out of our position, moving in a big semi-circle. Everybody is scratching their heads and ticked-off, and our poor 2nd Lt. is confused as hell, he has no clue why? He had only been in the Corps for six to eight months, knows nothing about the field, is going spastic trying to figure where we are on the map and plot a correct compass heading to our next point. We all suspect the captain is using this as a test of this new officer's navigation skills at our expense, but, we do not dare ask or say a word, or offer any help. No Way.

We stop at this big deep pool to fill canteens and the lieutenant is taking so long trying to brush away the leaves and debris on the surface, I just bend down and push his hand and canteen under it all the way to make the air bubbles push the junk out of the mouth and he looks up and says, "Thanks, corporal, pretty sharp trick." I say, "Yes sir. Welcome. This is one small thing you pick-up after being out here a while." Like a real veteran. All the guys standing back smiled like I just committed a crime talking to him. Poor guy. He is really okay, just like the rest of us, only he is an officer and there are higher expectations for officers.

I lost my sharpening stone for my K-Bar (combat knife carried by most Marines) when I was helping with the wounded guys. And I need to ask Nancy to get me a good replacement one from the Coast-to-Coast Hardware Store, 1 ½" x 4" Arkansas pocket size.

The lieutenant from 3rd platoon was wounded by a mine under a bridge today. He did not even step on it. The troop in front of him did and the whole blast went straight to the rear, only putting cuts and burns on the guy who stepped on it.

We are in a very old part of Vietnam that was quite rich and cultured in ancient time. Close by is the City of Hue. It was a kingdom capital with high castle walls all around the whole city. Quang Tri is kind of a suburb with big beautiful buildings, churches and temples. They are landscaped with rivers, bridges and flowering trees. Many are abandoned and grown over now though, so sad.

October 28 - Outside Quang Tri - Hill #34 - We are setup on a small hill, open positions all around, with open rice paddies all below us. Our squad is picked to be sent out to find a good ambush site. Speck and I are held behind to stand line for three hours each. Somehow, no word is passed as to when Speck is to wake-up Sgt. Baldwin (or maybe Spanky just fell asleep in the short-timers tent again, like he had been doing lately now). But, I stood my watch and went to sleep, expecting to be awakened again at 0100 hours for my next watch. I get shaken awake hard at 0230 hours by both the lieutenant and Spanky. Nobody had been awakened for the next watch by our radio guy, Estes, who never misses anything. Nobody was awakened of the eleven men who were scheduled. All should have been standing watch at least twice during the night. Estes never got the word he was to notify the watch list. This was a big time watch screw up, and heads must roll. It is dark, and angry voices were raised with nasty questions. All of us were in a circle, watch list out, flashlights on. Who messed up?

Down below us at the bridge we hear, "Marines coming in" loud and clear. We have a five man listening post at this side under the bridge abutment on shore. Then a machine gun opens up and bullets crack all around us and tracers fly by off to our left. We all stumble and dive into any hole we can find and bullets keep hitting close! Then four big explosions – grenades going off under the bridge and our guys yelling, "Mother! Mother! I'm hit! corpsman up!" Then a never-ending spray of rifle fire in return. Green tracers keep coming in steady from the other side of the river. Charlie is serious. He is set-up to kill us all tonight. I scramble for my gear, grab my helmet, grenade pouch and crawl back to my hole to look across the river to try and spot muzzle flashes through the trees. I do not know why I did not try to shoot back at the flash, but they tell us so many times not to give away your position at night, if you do not have to. I took off my helmet, pulled the pin on a grenade, stood up and threw it as hard and far as I possibly could, to try to get it to the other side of the river where I thought "they" were. It hit the opposite bank, but only put up a cloud of mud and big thud.

Illumination by 60mm mortars was up by then and a squad was down into our LP to help the wounded. But God, they kept screaming for a long time with those grenade wounds! White-hot steel slivers and chunks of shrapnel ripped their skin open and burned so deep. We pounded the opposite back for ten minutes with machine-guns, 60mm mortars, small arms and M-79 grenades, as they slipped away. We figure the VC swam across the river and came within about ten feet of our LP in an attempt to blow the bridge, not knowing our guys were under there. When they saw the Marines, they tossed their grenades into our position and swam back out. They killed one man, L/Cpl. Daniel Hopper, just back two days from R&R, and wounded the other four in the listening post. They will make it, but with lots of big scars, stitches and bad memories of that night. All with Purple Hearts from a grateful nation for the blood they have spilled in battle.

Lance Corporal Daniel Hopper, Ocala, Florida
(panel 28E line 91 on The Wall)

The VC, after sliding back and throwing their grenades, made their way to the other end of the bridge and up onto the trail running parallel to the river, throwing more grenades and firing long bursts from their AK's, wounding four more Marines on their way out, running and gunning.

That gave them a total of eight WIA plus one KIA on us, and we got zero on them, a clean get-away. It all happened so fast, most of our guys could not even react, or like me, did not get off a single clear shot in defense. Damn, those little gook bastards can be smart and brave fighters sometimes. Much better than us, when they decide when and where to hit. We all stayed at 100% alert from 0245 until 0800 hours with the medevacs and ran six patrols across the river at morning light trying to find the enemy's covers, hides and any bunkers. We found three bunkers and blew them all with C-4 explosives.

We moved across the valley to a big abandoned white church, with a bell tower about sixty to eighty feet tall. The captain figured the VC must be using the tower for observation of our movements and the bell to signal. We packed the tower with about ten or twelve one-pound blocks of C-4 explosive and fused them together for a ten-minute delayed detonation and we all backed off to watch the fireworks. Everyone with a camera had it out and ready. When the charges went off the roof tiles went straight up, the tower crumbled completely away, killing thousands of bats inside, and the bell shattered and shot-out the sides of the tower! (I think they put a charge directly inside the bell). The whole thing turned to red dust. Done. Mission accomplished - another successful destruction of a beautiful ancient structure.

It is a good feeling to have been under fire, in a few rough spots, with the unit now, because you feel so green, slow and clumsy at first. My fire team is accepting my authority and starting to trust my decisions. When I ask or direct they accept it as okay and so do the other teams in our squad. I get back-up from most of the guys now. I still get a lot of questions on fairness, like walking point, and standing watch, but that goes with the job of being a squad leader, you have to make and enforce the rules. Picking who is to walk point is the hardest to do, as so many of the guys consider it to be almost a death sentence. I have to be as fair as I can and keep rotating point-men, and taking "point" myself in turn, to spread the risk.

I am still hoping and praying my words with Lt. Col. Van Winkle will come true and he will transfer to me to Division Headquarters as a draftsman, to get me out of the field. Division G-3 Headquarters is where I want to be. For a guy with a beautiful wife, a new baby and a good apprenticeship in civil service waiting at home, I would love to add to my resume that I ran the Division drafting section. How cool would that look for my engineering degree!?

And when I get back home, we will move out of her folks' place and get our own apartment and a new Chevy SS 396 or 427 Mustang, and go see all our friends at the drags, at the airport. Or I could modify the '34 Ford as a B-Gas Dragster with small-block Chevy 327 or the new 350 motor, cool. All the apprentices that returned from military service to the shipyard got a nice pay increase and bought new cars. Why not me?

Chris

October 28 - I felt better today. My temperature was gone, my chills and my hot sweats were also gone, yet I still felt quite weak. Malaria zaps all the energy out of you. There was nothing to do except put on my gear and proceed to getting ready to hike out with the guys.

Note – The early morning reports from 3 LP's indicated movement to their north. The Marines in the LP's threw a few grenades and received automatic rifle fire and enemy grenades. They called in an artillery mission and the enemy broke contact. Additional contact was reported around the area. There was not much sleep time. Two bridges were blown in the area. Seven Marines were medevaced. We continued to call in reports of VC in the area as late as 2250 hrs.

House

October 29 – Quang Tri - We spent the day and night guarding "Alpha Battery" a 105mm artillery battery being set up and dug in. Helped string new "German Tape Razor Wire", wicked stuff. Not like barbwire. It has razor sharp barbs and razor edges stamped along the wire. You need special gloves to string it, or it will cut you bad, real quick.

October 30 - Quang Tri - Up at 0430 hours, we moved along the river sweeping three villages as we moved through, looking for moving groups of men. It was a long hard walk, through flooded rice paddies.   We were called back towards same area where 3rd platoon spotted two VC behind us.   So we stopped while the 3rd herd swept them towards us.   My team was up on high ground, and we set up in a good ambush site, but they did not come by us.   We had to move out at 0300 hours and I got real bad stomach cramps.   We got rides in amphibious vehicles and rode security for a couple hours with two other companies.   Nice ride.   It was dark when we reached the other side of the river and finally dug-in for the night.   "Happy Halloween"

The Friendly Fire Sniper Incident

0630 - The early morning sun is drying-out the tall grass after a heavy rain.   We are up and stretching from living in our holes like prairie dogs on their dirt mounds.   Some small black kid had the radio, he is still wearing his dark green rain gear with the hood up, and he walks over and extends the handset towards me and says the lieutenant wanted to speak to me.

Craaaack!   A sonic boom splits the air between our faces!   No mistake, it is a rifle bullet.   We are the target and have been missed by about six inches.   On the deck, we roll into our holes and scream for everyone to get down.   But they are already down and screaming for a corpsman, thinking we have been shot.   We call off the corpsman, so he does not come up into the field of fire needlessly.   The radio crackles again, "this is sniper Team #4, and we have a confirmed hit on Hill #22 Bravo.   I have the handset and scream back in poor radio protocol, "You dumb bastards, you missed."   This is echo-two-bravo-alpha and you just missed me and my radioman by inches and, this sure as hell isn't Hill #22 Bravo.   Total silence.   The lieutenant then yells into the radio, "Knock off all the chatter.   Get back to the CP."

That afternoon the lieutenant introduces me to Sniper Team #4 in the mess tent, at chow.   The shooters name is Rick Barnes.   We end up having a good laugh together when he explains how he was given a bad set of coordinates and poor intel on his target.   Their set-up was wrong and he apologized all over the place to us. He gave me his cold milk, a real sacrifice, as we only got one milk a day, if ever.   He offered to shake hands and asked if I would forgive his mistake because his dad taught him that was the right thing to do. I had to agree. I said sure you can shoot at me anytime you want to from now on as long as you keep missing.   He liked that.   He asked what it sounded like, a .308 round from a Remington 700 Bull Barrel from 1,700 meters away coming that close. I said it was like a giant clapping his hands next to my ear. I told him he probably needed a couple more shots to get centered on target from that distance, but he sure as hell scared us.   He really scared me when he said he had made kill shots on gooks from that distance multiple times before, and thought this may have been a wind drift problem or he sure would have hit one of the two of us, although he was aiming at the radioman in the "black pajamas". Again, God and His Angels and prayers from home must have been watching over me, keeping me safe.

This is a typical shot of the rice paddies and dikes we had to cross out in the open with no cover, and the bamboo thickets that provide cover for ambushes or snipers on both sides as we tried to cross. We always spread way out when up on the dikes. If they did fire at us we had to dive into the water to get down behind the dike for cover and prayed they had not planted punji-stakes just below the surface where you were jumping! We had lots of guys hurt this way. Nasty punctures!

Photo by Cpl MJ Coates, Combat Photographer

Lt. Kirk

October 29 - One night the company commander instructed me to take my platoon to a certain position south of our battalion base camp and set up an ambush.   There was no moon and it was pitch dark. I couldn't read my map without getting under a poncho with a flashlight, which I did occasionally. I could, however, read my compass, which had a luminous dial. I counted the steps I took in each direction. When I thought we had reached our objective, we set in and I radioed back to the company that we were in place.   The night was uneventful. In the morning light, I looked at the terrain and realized we were well short of our objective. So much for dead reckoning in the dark. With all the H&I (harass and interdict) fires our artillery put out, plus other patrols, not being where you are supposed to be, is dangerous. I resolved to get better. I learned, when unsure of my position, to call for two illumination rounds from artillery or mortars at two different coordinates, shoot a compass azimuth to them, then plot the back azimuths (the compass reading plus or minus 180 degrees) from the coordinates on my map. Where they intersected on the map was my position.

Chris

October 30 - <u>Free Postage, No Writing Paper</u>

One more thing to complain about is the lack of writing paper. It's not that we complain a lot, it's just something to do, something to entertain ourselves. It's great to be able to send our correspondence home "free" of any postage. But how often do we have something to write on? I tore this envelope open and wrote on the inside, then sealed and sent it. We use TP, C-ration cardboard and anything else we find to write our letters on.

Letters going home to Mom, Dad, sister, brother, girl friends, the next door neighbor and anyone else, always went FREE!

House

October 30 - The captain knows I am a trained topographical draftsman and now has me keeping his and all platoon commanders maps and overlays. I also update the gunny's and the platoon sergeants' maps as well and now have one of my very own. This is good. Sgt. Baldwin goes to regiment this week, then on to R&R. I take over the squad in his absence as senior corporal.

We had a nice memorial service, not only for the Echo Company guys lost in September and October, but all the battalion KIA in the past sixty days. It was sad, but good closure for all, but God, it was a lot of names! Twenty-three KIA, fifteen of them were from Hotel Co. on "Operation Medina" alone. After the services, we all got two free cans of cold beer and soda, ice cold. It helped to have the downtime to talk it out and made things better to help say good-bye to some of our friends. It is so hard to get to be buddies with a guy and then have him get killed. It's almost better to avoid making friends and stay emotionally separated to protect yourself from such a great sense of loss and grief. Some guys can, and they become so hard and quiet and detached it is like they lose their humanity and become numb. The 1,000 yard stare. (Known among all that have been in battle, as the eyes become lifeless, staring straight ahead without emotion. The mind is also without thought).

Lt. Jerry Graffam,
2nd Plt Commander
Maine

Lt. Graffam is giving a platoon briefing and I need to draw C-rats, ammo, grenades, trip flares, laws rockets, C-4 explosive, all the gear the squad needs and check-out their personal needs too, like a good squad leader is supposed to do and know.

The October Command Chronology for 2nd Battalion, 1st Marines notes that the battalion moved north to assume responsibility in the Quang Tri TAOR and participated in Operation Medina from October 11-19 in the Hai Lang National Forest Reserve. Contact progressed from light to moderate and mining activity grew from light to heavy. The battalion reported 11 enemy confirmed KIA with 16 probables and 1 captured. 2nd Battalion, 1st Marines casualties for October: 2 officers and 16 enlisted KIA, 4 officers and 60 enlisted WIA.

House

November 1 - The Mine Field, at Night! - I was trying to get the squad out to a small security outpost on a hilltop about 100 meters from the rest of the company, when I realized we had walked into a mine-field by mistake! It was my fault. I missed seeing a small yellow triangle warning sign that marked the edge of this area. The wire was broken at the point where I turned into the field, instead of turning away from the field, had I remembered the map layout correctly. One of the squad spotted a warning marker after we were inside the minefield. We had to call the company engineers, who followed our path with mine detection equipment and found five tomato-can mines off the side of our path. Wow! Again, the Lord had been walking close by me, I believe! We all backed-out single-file okay. I felt I really let my guys down hard. It shook me hard, but nobody got hurt or mad at me. Echo Company then returned by Otter armored personnel carrier to CP (Command Post). The Otter looks like a tank without the turret extending out, just an armored box on tracks to haul personnel around.

Chris
November 1 - I sat on a hill this morning and ate my breakfast of chopped ham and eggs C-rations. It wasn't good, nor was it bad. The eggs were a yellow-green and tasted like that. Just something to eat. Also, had some crackers and peanut butter and a cup of instant coffee.

House gathers the squad and lets everyone know that as the senior corporal, he is now our squad leader. Spanky has gone to the rear and will be leaving for home soon, his tour is over. House lays out a few thoughts, nothing crazy, just lets us know what he expects. Everyone will be expected to participate in all squad duties, such as walking point. House says he will also walk point when his turn comes. He expects us to do what he says and promises to do his best job for the squad. He seems confident and everyone follows along. This seemed like a very smooth transition. Everyone nods and a change of the guard has been smooth.

We walked into a minefield today, which scared the heck out of all of us, especially our squad leader. He missed a sign and had trouble forgetting about the situation, feeling that he had really let us down. What House didn't realize was the fact that everyone believed so much in his ability to be our leader, that as soon as we were out of trouble, we all forgot about it. House did not. He learned a bit more about his job and I'm sure became better for it.

We had nine guys in our squad, at the start of this operation. Spanky, our squad leader, left, as his tour was over, and another guy went on R&R. My old team leader stayed back with bad feet. One guy had asthma. One guy left on a chopper an hour ago on emergency leave. I am now the team leader, House is squad leader, and we have three additional guys. I think we're management heavy. Cards are out for a game. Bye.

Lt. Kirk
November 1 - At first, we slept in pup tents in the battalion rear. This was actually a treat as we would usually spend 2-3 days in the bush sleeping, to the extent we could, in the open, usually in the rain, as it was monsoon season. Later we got GP (general purpose) tents for the troops and I and the other lieutenants in the company shared an accordion tent, where we had cots. Usually, only one of us lieutenants was back in the rear with the gear at a time. When we were back in the rear we had to man the perimeter. The troops would often fall asleep as they were exhausted from being out in the bush and felt pretty safe back at battalion headquarters. It was hard to motivate them back there. We had no showers at first, but we are told eventually the engineers would rig up some, which would be great. We are also told a mess tent would be coming.

November 2 - In the battalion rear south of Quang Tri, I went into a GP tent to talk to one of my squad leaders. While I was talking, a Marine accidentally discharged a .45 caliber pistol through the top of the tent a couple of feet from where I and some other Marines were standing. An accidental discharge is considered a serious offense. I decided to give him a break. I walked out of the tent without saying a word about it.

Chris
November 2 – Vice President Hubert Humphrey visited Vietnam today and presented the 1st Marine Division with the Presidential Unit Citation Medal. I never heard anyone say anything about the award. There wasn't one person I ever met that cared about receiving medals of any kind. The only thought was to make it thru the day and ultimately, get home.

We're running out of water, again. I can only carry two canteens, as the weight takes its toll. I try to remember to always drop the purification tabs in the canteens when I fill them, because normally it's water that's not coming from a good source, like some slimy green pond, a creek or river maybe, but one that has dead animals or worse lying in it. It's whatever we can get at the time. Drop the tabs in and forget about where it came from. The tabs make the water taste bad, but it's wet and we need to continually hydrate ourselves. Sometimes I would mix in some Kool-Aid Mom sent from home, which makes the water tolerable. We are always fighting dysentery. You wonder why.

I still probably carry more ammunition than the rest of the guys, but it's something I choose to do. I carry extra M-16 rifle ammo, .45 pistol ammo, grenades and ammo for the M-79 rocket launcher, if I am carrying it at the time. I also like to carry 1-2 LAAW (Light Anti-Tank Weapon) rockets, which are lightweight and disposable weapon after one shot. Some of the guys do just the opposite, carrying less ammo, as it's heavy. It's nice to have the option. The thought of running low or running out of ammo is something I just can't bear thinking about.

House

November 2 - About 1500 hours, we start back to the command post (CP), all riding on the Otter. Bumping along, free and easy, big targets, but lots of fire power. We pass through a big village grove of ripe banana trees on both sides of the road and Lt. Graffam says "House, why don't you get us some fresh fruit"? I grab my K-Bar knife, the driver pulls over to the tree and I cut down a couple bunches of bananas and pass them out. They are small and green, but they are something different from C-rations. The lieutenant. says, "Okay, Good! Now, if you get caught with that bunch of bananas by the captain, I never saw you do it!" We all cracked up. He is pretty cool, twenty-two years old, from Maine and he hates the "Crotch"! (Marine Corps) Pretty loose officer, we like him.

We arrive back at the company position at 0530, get some hot chow, and are told to be ready to go back out at 0900 to set-up ambushes and a blocking force. We are expecting a large VC (Viet Cong) force to be coming our way. They have been hitting small villages and outposts around Quang Tri and have been rocketing and mortaring the Dong Ha Airbase regularly. We can see the smoke from eleven miles away.

This part of the operation is the 2nd part of "Operation Lancaster". We are in the "Cam Lo Valley", just 10,000 meters (6 miles) south of the DMZ. We walk that far in one day! Needless to say, full helmets, flak jackets and we dig deep holes, I am squad leader full time now. Sgt. Baldwin is out of the field as a "short-timer.'

November 4 - Near the DMZ, Cam Lo Valley, west of Dong Ha - We had a three hour ride by truck north on Highway #1, then due west on Highway #9, straight towards Laos, and some really big mountains. Dong Ha is a big city, really spread-out. We hear a typhoon is bearing down on us and could rally to hamper this operation to say the least. My squad is now the smallest in the whole company with only five men. Estes is on R&R, Dodd and Kendricks are on light duty with immersion foot problems, so we are a bit shorthanded. Therefore, we get picked for dirty little jobs, like LP (listening posts) and ambush site details.

We were sent out of our overnight camp to place trip flares and claymore mines in front of our position. We made a trail back up to our sleeping/fighting holes in case we have to fall back to secondary positions. I had planned to go down this dry stream bed to get to the position and set-up, but the captain would not let us. He wanted us to go through the brush. I told him it would be too much noise, but he says, "Take it slow and easy, and it will not". Wow. We start at 2000 hours moving slowly, in the rain, and dark, and with me on point. I lost the trail and ended-up in thick, noisy brush, and a grenade goes off twenty feet from us. The radio reports it was "incoming". Then 3rd platoon radio says they are being probed with rocks, and tin cans. We are about twenty meters outside of our own lines and still had 80 meters to go to reach our ambush site. It's going too slow. I had to find the trail again. We finally got some illumination and I found the trail, with sweat pouring off me. We would move ten feet and stop and listen. It took two hours to move 200 feet. After setting up and reporting hearing incoming movement, we called, asking permission to throw grenades and the captain replied, "No, wait until they get closer!" Wow! I could not believe it. We may as well have just waited to use our damn bayonets. Radio calls and says a full squad is coming down the dry stream bed, do not shoot - our guys.

I am thinking, why send a squad down the stream bed now - reinforcements? A couple minutes later, and two guys walk down the stream bed and past us in the dark. Then radio says, no, there will be no squad reinforcements.

Chris and I went out to set up claymore mines around a forward LP about 200 feet in front of the company lines. We set-down in heavy brush and high grass just feet off a well-used trail across from a dry stream bed. We had VC probing all around us, but we were refused permission to throw grenades, and radio communications by the Captain told us one of our squads was on the way past us.

It was raining so hard we could hardly hear anything and I questioned the radio again if they were sending us reinforcements. Waiting for a response, two men moved past us within a few feet, hard to distinguish through the brush and foliage, and the dark rain that night.   They passed closest to Chris, maybe bayonet distance. He could have easily shot them, but I waited for the answer on the radio, and the rest of our friendly squad to follow. The radio response came back a minute or so later, no, no squad will be coming past us or to reinforce. That meant they were VC or NVA! When I went to retrieve two trip flares I had set across the trail, they had been disconnected! We had let them walk past thinking they were our guys. It made me physically sick I let them get by us! We could have blown them away so easy. I was just sick. It rained so hard all night, my hands were so numb. I could not have pulled a grenade pin, if I had to. The claymores were intact.

I told the lieutenant about what happened and he said it was his fault. It really was not, it was the captain's fault, but that's the kind of guy Lt. Graffam is. He is cool.

Last night during our normal briefing, we got an emergency request for ambulance security due to an accident at the 81mm mortar section. We were told a round had gone off in the tube and all five men in the crew were hurt. We later found out that was not the case, as some idiot took what he thought was a dud round into their tent and hit it with a hammer trying to remove the fuse, and blew off one of his hands and another guys whole arm. All five guys in the tent were emergency evacs with major wounds. Damn, we keep doing it to ourselves. Five more lost.

Big rainstorm lasted four straight hours. The lieutenant cut us slack and only asked us to stay out forty-five minutes and come back to sack-out. Last night at 0030 hours, we sat and talked for an hour before we work back home. It was nice.

This morning our 3rd squad leader, Cpl. Hill, accidentally shot himself in the foot, when a branch caught his trigger and caused an accidental discharge, when the muzzle was pointed at his foot. (Yea, right! A "go-home" million-dollar accident.) Then, a half hour later, a guy from 1st platoon got one of his grenades snagged on a branch and came off his belt, pin out and blew up his back, put steel in his legs and butt. Like I said, we do it to ourselves.

We moved off the hill early and Operation Lancaster is back on again. And, we are now on another hill, 1,000 meters further north within sight of the city of Cam Lo to our south watching B-52 bombers pounding around the hill at Con Thien and the hills to the west. It is a wild sight at night. We are digging some real deep holes right now. Rumors are we will be jumping beyond Con Thien to sweep into the DMZ and try to destroy NVA artillery batteries they have moved there. I just came back from a small recon patrol out in front of our lines and now the colonel wants all troops in our holes. Buttoned up and waiting. We are to just stand-by, until they make a plan. I hope it's a good one.

November 6 - Operation Lancaster, Cam-Lo - Still standing-by. Relaxing and watching the big air show. Artillery and air strikes, B52 arc-light-strikes and Rolling Thunder on the Cam Lo Valley complex (lots of VC and regular NVA troops reported in the hills and valley). We can feel the concussion pressure on your eardrums and chest when the clouds get low in the sky. We are miles away and can feel the impacts. It must be hell on the ground. There are tens of thousands of bombs and shells falling there. It is ripping down hills and clearing away jungle to bare ground or making it look like the craters of the moon. We could literally hear the gooks screaming after our artillery lifted last night, they must have caught a bunch of them out in the open.

One of my squad, Larry Herfel, just got word he is going home on emergency leave. They won't tell him why, but it must be bad. But, in one way I am glad for him, it will get him out of here for a little while. So now, I am down to a four-man squad and do not even rate a radioman anymore.

We got a good re-supply today. Four C-rats, SP (Special Pack has extra items like writing paper, cold milk and orange juice). Must be a new supply officer ahead of the game, taking good care of his troopers on this OP (operation).

Chris
November 7 - Larry Herfel has been relieved of duty and is headed to the rear area and then directly home to Madison, Wisconsin. There is some type of emergency or they wouldn't be pulling him out of the field. This is the first time we've had this happen. Larry has been one of our closest friends. He's a quiet guy. Larry doesn't get much mail from home. We all try to share our packages of food and snacks. His sister writes once in awhile, but not often. I don't know if he gets anything from his parents. He doesn't talk about life at home, so we don't ask either. I will miss him and his smile. He is also very reliable and thus another reason we hate to see him go. If he is able to stay in the states, good for him. He and I came in together. He's seen a lot.

House
November 7 - Had LP last night. (An LP or listening post is a small group that quietly sneaks into position to watch for any enemy walking around at night). We are in a free-fire zone, so we don't have to ask permission to fire. If someone is out there, they get hit with everything we have. Everything was all quiet. No action for us. 1st platoon had three wounded by booby traps set by our own engineers. It took 1-½ hours for the medevac to show up. The entire time was

well illuminated and kept that way by the constant firing from our artillery and mortars. What a mess!

This morning we had to go to a platoon size patrol and go to another CP, to get twelve radio batteries and the captain insisted on full camouflage.

We painted our faces, and camouflaged ourselves like the VC with sticks and branches. We made painfully slow movement in broad daylight. It looked like a creeping brush forest. It sure seemed stupid just to pick-up batteries. Lt. Graffam was pissed. And then, a 3rd platoon guy trips a grenade booby trap and wounds two more. We have to stay here again tonight. We are in bad positions tonight, if we are hit. Warm today.

Chris

November 7 - We got another new guy in our squad today, Private Falcon. Another young-looking scared, quiet guy with a rifle. At least we are finally starting to get reinforcements. He seems to be okay. He's quiet, just like the rest of us were when we checked in. He looks so young, as I continue to look over at him.

We ran into another firefight today with some NVA, while out on a patrol and our new-guy Falcon got hit. Well, we lost another one. He was medevac'd and we returned to camp.

Lt. Kirk

Nov 7 - My platoon was on patrol about a mile and a half north of the battalion. I spotted an NVA soldier through my binoculars. I had the FO call in artillery. The company commander had the FAC (forward air controller) call in an air strike. Based on the intelligence we gathered, our battalion FAC called in the biggest air strike of his career – napalm, rockets and 250 and 500 lb. bombs. The Air Observer spotted fortified positions on the hill, which were uncovered by the air strike and a lot of NVA making their hat to the north. This is our third night on this same hill and we're expecting the gooks to hit us with mortars and recoilless rifles tonight and possibly try to overrun our position. They'll play hell getting 1st platoon, though. We've got holes so deep you can stand up in them, Claymores, trip flares, two second delay booby trapped frag grenades and even punji stakes out in front of us. I lost two more men today due to booby traps so I'm operating with a three man squad, a five man squad & a six man squad. But the captain relies on 1st platoon. He's always got us on the point, gives us the toughest patrols and gives us the toughest position to defend in the lines. After we finish in this area, we'll be sweeping north to Con Thien and coming back, so we'll probably spend the Marine Corps Birthday in the field. We heard they've got showers and beer back at 2/1 area in Quang Tri now, so things will be decent when we get back there.

Knobby
November 8 - I'm on Operation Lancaster right now, which is being conducted 5-6 miles below the DMZ. Our battalion is set in as a blocking force and we've had it pretty easy so far. I think either the 3rd or 9th Marines have control of the operation.

House
November 8 - Threw grenades at phantoms all night, nothing in response or found in the morning. I'm so tired, it is really hard to stay awake at night, during my night watch times. I just want a full night sleep.

November 10 - The Marine Corps Birthday - A real traditional celebration day and we had nothing. No chow, no mail. It was pretty bleak. But, this place is harsh. Three Bird-Dog planes with loud speakers flew over wishing U.S. Marines, Happy Birthday and Best Wishes from General Green and President Johnson. You should have heard some of the responses, not nice.

As we are moving up the road, I look over at a bunch of Marines digging in to provide security to our flanks, and who do I spot, but our old houseguest from 1/27 in Hawaii, Corporal Bill Andrews with a big smile as always. It was a short but happy reunion since we were moving. He had already lost a number of buddies. He said Shirley and Applegate were both wounded and back in the states within three months, with three Purple Hearts each. Bill already has one purple heart. Cpl. Frazier is their platoon sergeant and has a Purple Heart, too.

We now start Operation Kentucky - This is just a continuation of Operation Lancaster, and it is the longest the battalion had ever been out, fourteen days straight in the bush. We will all be smelly, hairy, cruddy animals when we come back in, yuck.

Chris
November 10 - Sure we grumbled, but we always did our job. At times, we would move without emotion or feeling of any kind. We would just drudge ahead, one more step, each time feeling the encumbrance of weight of the helmet, flak jacket, frag grenades, bandoliers, trip flares, of extra M-16 ammo, more M-60

machine gun ammo, C-4 plastic explosive, claymore mines, a couple of canteens of water, C-rats, M-72 LAAW's rockets, a butt pack (which lays across our butt and supported my suspenders and as waist belt) or backpack filled with stuff and lots more. One more step...

We normally knew that we would be stopping before nightfall, and traveling with a lot of weight is not done without the casualty of noise. We carried very few personal items, like letters from girl friends, or pictures from home or anything that wasn't vital to our mission. It all weighed something. Some of the guys carried cameras, most did not. There didn't seem to be anything I wanted a picture of, most of it would probably stay in my mind much longer than I wanted.

On the 10th, we were north of Con Thien (in the DMZ) making sweeps, as intel told us that enemy troops were assembling and the Con Thien Marine Combat Base might be overrun. Since Con Thien was the closest base to North Vietnam, it was considered a strategic combat outpost. We crossed the Trace and advanced towards the DMZ. As we prepared for the evening, the wind was coming up, so many of us gathered the dry grass and made a bed. We gathered more of the grass to cover ourselves from the cold wind. As dusk was setting in, one of the new guys spotted movement in the distance. The NVA were well camo'd with trees and branches covering themselves. A few gathered to look, got House and someone else, who finally got the lieutenant, then the captain.

As this was going on, Cpl. Jay Chappel, our tunnel rat, a small E-4 squad leader from the 3rd herd (platoon), and a tough SOB, found some enemy spider holes (spider holes were normally well camouflaged enemy entry holes to hiding/living areas underground) and believed a tunnel system to be directly below us. He ventured down a few tunnels, with his .45 automatic in one hand and a flashlight in the other. I knew he didn't like to go down in the tunnels, but he was definitely the smallest in the company. As an NCO, he was elected. He dropped a few grenades down the holes after he snooped and pooped around. We started discovering that there were quite a few tunnels in the area.

When the captain arrived, to view the field movement in the distance, an AO (aerial observer) in a small plane was flying overhead of us. A radio call to him confirmed a battalion-sized, semi-circle of thousands of NVA troops were bearing down on us. The AO said it looked like a moving forest. The enemy was closing very quickly and so the captain called-in to fire directly on "our present position." Fire for effect. We ran like hell back across the Trace, at a very weak company strength.

The rounds sailed directly overhead. You could hear the whistling of the artillery rounds and hitting right behind us. It was an eerie feeling, with the rounds so close, not only overhead, but exploding right behind us. We ran across the Trace, yelling like we were John Wayne. We never looked back, as our mission was to run like hell. Our intel was correct - the NVA was massing considerable strength for an assault on the Marine base.

The weather was the worst. I've never been so cold and hungry at night. No chow again for a couple of days, which didn't go over very well with the guys. Our mail has been held for the past two weeks. Some colonel decided we didn't need it. It put a big dent in our attitude. You should have heard the talk. Nope, you shouldn't have.

Lt. Kirk

November 10 - At one point during this operation the battalion crossed the Trace. This was an area, bulldozed of trees, about 1/3 of a mile wide, running eight miles between Con Thien and Geo Linh to the east, The Trace was part of McNamara's wall, Defense Secretary Robert McNamara's plan to curtail infiltration from North Vietnam with outposts and electronic surveillance gear. The official name for McNamara's wall was the Strong Point Obstacle System (SPOS), code named Dye-marker. It involved construction of combat outposts and fire support bases along the DMZ, clearing of the Trace between Gio Linh and Con Thien and construction of bunkers. As we set in for the night we took some mortar fire and saw movement to our front. Every once in a while it seemed like a bush or small tree moved. Soon we saw what looked like an entire line of small trees moving towards us. The mortar fire increased. The battalion commander ordered us to saddle up and move back across the Trace. As we retreated, we took more mortar fire. We ran back across the Trace in the dark. I never thought I would see an entire Marine battalion turn tail and run. I suspect that battalion commander believed we were hopelessly outnumbered. As we reached our position for the night, the company commander called the platoon commanders to his position for a meeting. When I returned I found my men had dug foxholes for themselves, without being told, and one for me.

House

November 11 - We can now look across the DMZ (Demilitarized Zone). Yea, that is a joke, everybody in there is armed to the teeth and full blown battles are constantly going on. We have a view straight into North Vietnam. There is a road sign in Dong Ha that gives directions from Highway #1 to Highway #9 to

Saigon, 1157 km South, 581km to Hanoi. I sure wish I had snapped a picture of that one, maybe I can get one on the way back.

It is now a constant cold pouring, thunderous rain, all day and all night that does not ever seem to want to stop, it will drive you mad. I am even starting to like the taste of the instant coffee in the C-rats, I used to throw it away, but now I will take anything hot.

November 11 – 0745 hours - Observation Post, northeast of Con Thien - I just finished a fine breakfast of meatballs and beans, bread and jam. This is a wild place. We missed two meals yesterday; resupply up here is sporadic at best. Battalion tells us they have lost some of our mail in combat, when re-supply helicopters were shot down and burned. It is really hard to walk on the roads here, as it is so wet and heavy mud is churned-up by the tracked vehicles.

They are building a support artillery base below the hill, about three miles south of the Con Thien outpost. The new road is real long and goes straight up the hill at Con Thien, which is about 160 meters high. I was talking to one of the engineers who said he has been on his dozer working on the road a solid fourteen hours a day, every day, rain or shine for three months. The road-bed is built-up from about three feet of big rocks, then about a foot of smaller crushed rock on top of that and gravel and oil on top of that. It has to hold up to the monsoon rains that would come down that hill and attempt to wash it away. The engineers lost a lot of guys just to get that road built up the hill. If the road does not hold there would be no way to get enough re-supply once we occupy it. The NVA and VC could then attack, overrun us and wipe us out. They want that hill as bad as we do and we are told there are three full regiments of NVA regulars up in front of us, ready to attack at any time (that's about 12,000 enemy). We have maybe 2,500 on the hill, but we have considerable back-up from artillery, air, and naval gunfire, if needed.

The amount of utter destruction of the earth was unbelievable, as we moved further northwest and up into the foothills. The land was transformed from green to brown. From trees, to grass to mud and holes and dead branches with shattered tree trunks, standing like black armless skeletons, everywhere along the way. There are thousands of bomb craters, big enough to hold an entire company around their perimeter as far as you could see. They are filled with water and have dirt berms three to four feet high, all around them from the earth ejected by the bombs. It looks as though the earth has been converted to look like the moon.

November 12 - Operation Kentucky – We pulled back to Artillery Hill, north of the Cam Lo area. My God, the strain on the unit from these op's. Operation Lancaster I & II, & Operation Kentucky I & II are exhausting us to our physical and mental minimums. We have been out pushing hard with 1-½ meals per day, no mail, with solid rain. We covered lots of ground with seven battalions and only light enemy contact. The big problem has been the mud, so thick, cold and deep. The mud is always covering you and sticking and building like lead weights on your boots, hands, rifle, and in your hair, face and food.

At night, the bitter cold wind of the monsoon whips stinging rain in your face and standing watch is so hard. My hands and feet would go numb and I had no feeling in them or in my face for hours and could only cry from the terrible ache, because there was NO RELIEF. The rain was driven by the wind so hard sometimes it would blow me backwards and it would find any small opening through my rain suit and poncho. Every morning I found myself lying in a puddle of water, inside my rain gear, warmed by my own body heat and pee, but as soon as I got up, I would be freezing again. Now I know what combat fatigue really means.

I found out Bill Thornton is up around here with Kilo Company, 3rd Battalion, 3rd Marines, but I do not have a map with their position. Sure wish I could find him. I know the chance of that is very slim.

Every time my pack starts to cut in too deep or the rain cuts my face or I fall in the mud, I look down at my gold wedding band and remember my beautiful wife and son waiting for me, and I find the strength to get up and keep going. I give it a tender kiss, as tender as I have ever kissed Nancy and that muddy ring never tasted better.

We got re-supplied with a "feast" from Con Thien with seven meals each, four to carry for two days and three to eat in one day, because we were owed two for the day before. Linares found a grapefruit tree and Speck found tangerine trees with some shriveled fruit still on them. We had watched a group of planes fly over the day before, spraying chemicals to kill the leaves on the trees to keep the vegetation back, and so we washed the fruit in the mud puddles and chowed down. The fruit tasted a little different than what we are used to, but we were so hungry, it was a real treat. I even took some good pictures of the planes spraying in formation, as they flew over us. We later found out it was called "Agent Orange", a toxic chemical called "Dioxin" that does not wash-off food!!! I was so hungry, I ate cold ham & lima beans C-rats, along with the fruit, while the others were cooking theirs. The grapefruit were as big as soccer-balls. We kept a nice little fire going, from all the shattered wood in the fruit groves, by digging a deep pit, and the hot coals dried out all our wet gear, giving us lots of warm, dry socks. It felt so good to sleep warm and dry.

Chris
November 13 - No mail since the second food resupply. Freezing cold now, no let up in rain, it is really bad. Everything socked-in and mud, mud, mud, all mud and rain. So cold up here and now, rats, too! God, I hate rats! We all suffer together.

Lt. Kirk
November 13 - Lancaster I is over, and yesterday we completed Kentucky I. Tomorrow we start on Kentucky II. We're in an assembly area about 500 yards south of Con Thien right now.   We completed a sweep around Con Thien yesterday and are waiting to sweep down the supply route back to Dong Ha. We've been in the field for 11 straight days now and we're wet, tired and dirty as hell. I'm down to two three-man and one five-man squad and I've got to use my rocket squad to stand lines at night. Even the corpsmen are packing rifles and standing watch. Word came down from division that our battalion (2/1) will be prepared to relieve the battalion at Con Thien in December. It's exhilarating to be in the hot spots, but it's disconcerting too. The NVA are good soldiers and it's a little rougher than chasing local VC around the rice paddies near Quang Tri.

During Operation Kentucky a bad guy threw a concussion grenade, which went off near me. It made one Marine deaf. I couldn't hear out of one ear the rest of the day.

I observed two instances of self-inflicted wounds on this operation. Checking lines one night I came up in back of a Marine just as he shot himself in the hand with his pistol. On another occasion, as we set in for the night, I saw one of my troops pacing off a distance, going back and forth. I wondered what he was doing and watched him curiously. He then dropped a grenade over his shoulder and kept walking. The grenade exploded – the back of his legs and his back were sprayed with shrapnel.

Chris
November 14 - Back in the hospital, but nothing bad – I got a case of malaria, with a 105 degree temperature. Temp down, but still own a very large headache, feeling weak, but am told I will get some rest (sleep) soon. I weighed in at the

hospital at 132 lbs. In the past 3-1/2 months, I have lost 40 lbs. – from the high temperatures (120 degrees) in the summer months to the recent time in the bush and only 1-2 meals a day and a tremendous amount of physical work has brought everyone down to skinny. We all look the same.

Major General Hochmuth, who was in command of MCRD Boot Camp in San Diego, when I entered the Marine Corps, and was our 1st Marine Division Commander in Vietnam, was killed today when his helicopter was shot down outside Hue City today, along with the five others in the chopper. General Hockmuth awarded me a "silver engraved bracelet" in the states, which I never picked up in Oceanside, California. It was given to me for achieving the highest physical fitness score in the battalion, before I left Camp Pendleton for overseas.

Note: November 15 - Fox Company, which did not participate in Operations Lancaster and Kentucky but remained at Quang Tri, captured six children carrying grenades and 5.56mm rifle rounds. Ages were 10-13.

Lt. Kirk
November 16 - My company, Echo, along with Company Golf, was operationally committed to our sister battalion, 1/1, in a large search & destroy operation called Lancaster I, up around Con Thien from November 4-17. There was lots of exhausting humping. I had dysentery and was very weak. We moved out north from Cam Lo, which is four miles south of Con Thien.

Chris
November 17– We're just back from our little excursion up north, the country up by the big DMZ. We pulled off three operations and tonight I'm feeling them all – in my feet, my back, my head and every place in my body. We're all so tired. We left November 3rd, on Operation Lancaster. Before we returned to the Quang Tri area, we also participated in Operation Kentucky and Kentucky II. We traveled *en masse* – about 14 companies. I am now a fire team leader in charge of a team of four. Three of these teams make up a full squad, including a radioman and the squad leader. We haven't had a full strength squad for a long time.

It has been terrific, as meals and our mail are available. Mom's latest packages were probably the best of any of the guys. I get cookies, fudge, frosted flakes, graham crackers, tuna fish, pretzels, and popcorn. I don't boast, or I'll lose all I have. We share amongst a few, mostly with House, Herfel and Estes. Herfel is from Madison, Wisconsin. He's really a nice guy that never gets mail or packages from home, so of course, he gets some from all of us. He is one of the guys that everyone likes. He is not close to family, other than his sister and receives very little mail. Sad.

Mom just wrote that my friend, Eric Brown, from South Salem HS, Class of 1965, just died in a car wreck. I said a prayer for him. He was a fun and well appreciated guy, always seen with a smile on his face. It seemed so sad that while we lose guys all the time here that we should have to lose our friends at home, also. Tough to understand. As always, we eat, then clean our rifles and other gear. We need to be ready to move on a moment's notice.

We now have a new battalion commander and with him comes the order of theday – no beer and soda, no mail in the field, anymore. I can't believe he is doing this and the troops are about to rebel. Mail is what keeps us going in the field. It's that part of the "World" (the "World" is a term that we all use when talking about home) that we need in order to keep up our morale.

Chris
November 17 – Lt. Col. Parker takes over for Lt. Col. Archie Van Winkle as CO of 2nd Battalion, 1st Marines. It was too bad, as Van Winkle had proven to his men his leadership in the field, now someone new was in charge. We had lost our Medal of Honor winner, our Marines' "Marine".

I remember Lt. Col. Van Winkle passing us one day as we were climbing a hill during a recent operation. Climbing up the mountain three meters from our left side, the colonel gave a big "How's it going, troops?", as he acknowledged us and kept his quick pace in passing us. He had a strong face filled with confidence and carried a larger pack on operations than anyone I had ever seen in 'Nam. He liked to sleep in a tent, so he carried one. He was a true inspiration to all the troops. His positive comments and quick gait gave us all a lift, as we ascended the hill.

We had a new leader and Major Chuck Daugherty came in as the S-3 Officer. Many other changes seemed to occur on a regular basis. No one ever understood why the higher command had such a high turnover.

House
November 17 - 1000 hours - We trucked back from Artillery Hill to the regiment headquarters at Quang Tri for the treat of hot showers and hot chow! Hot chow tastes so good, but it really messes with our guts, after eating only c-rations, we all get the runs for a couple days afterwards. We each scrubbed off pounds and

layers of muck. I found waiting for me eight care packages and twenty-two letters. It was heaven.

Lt. Kirk

November 17 - After I had been here about one month, Staff Sergeant Valoria was wounded. I was now much more on my own without his help.

My first battalion commander was Lt. Col. Archie Van Winkle, a Medal of Honor winner in Korea. He was relieved of command. The rumor was that it was because two Starlight scopes (night vision scopes, costing thousands of dollars) were lost on the move to Quang Tri.

Note: Staff Sergeant Valoria later received a battlefield commission and retired as a major.

Note: I later learned that Major Joy, the executive officer, was in charge of moving the gear to Quang Tri, that only the cases for the Starlight scopes were lost and that Lt. Col. Van Winkle's relief had something to do with a spat between Major Joy and the commander of the battalion that relieved 2/1 south of Da Nang.

Our new battalion commander, Lt. Col. Parker chewed out the officers and staff NCOs in front of his tent: "We're going into the valley of the shadow of death and this battalion is not ready." I remember the blood vessels in his neck standing and seeming to throb as he chewed us out.

Chris

November 17 - Everyone has the word now. We are going to Con Thien for 30 days. We have heard about this place since we've been in Vietnam and now it's our turn. It's our "Turn in the Barrel" they say. Shit. There's nothing anyone can do about it. Con Thien is the closest U.S. base to North Vietnam and the dreaded DMZ. This is where the NVA crosses into South Vietnam. There are tens of thousands of enemy all around the area. We've heard too much bad stuff about this lone Marine base - the constant shelling, the isolation, the mass attacks of NVA Regulars and on and on. I try to forget about it, as it's not going to happen for a while and there's so much more to be thinking about. Am I scared? Yes, along with everyone else.

House

November 17 - We now have a new battalion CO, XO and S-3 officer. What a change. We got word now: we will be going into Con Thien for one month, December 20th to January 20th. Looks like we get shelled for Christmas! And, we get to live in the mud, hiding in bunkers like rats during World War I. This will not be good, being human targets for the commie artillery.

Captain Baker and 1st platoon all got transferred to 1st Battalion, 1st Marines at Con Thien today. So, we will be getting a whole new platoon to take their place. They put us under Captain Black, from H&S Company. He has us moving our hooches across the hill. I got a new air mattress from Coby, the supply guy, I've recently met. He also gave me a new pack and set of utilities. He sure takes good care of me.

Lt. Kirk

November 18 - There was an incident in 1/1 in which a platoon of Marines shot up some civilians – the platoon is under investigation and has been withdrawn from the field. As a result, Echo 2/1 was split up and part of us went to 1/1 while the rest of us stayed here. One squad was taken from each platoon in E 2/1 and sent to Bravo 1/1. I'm staying and taking over the third platoon. We're back at the battalion area at Quang Tri now with Operation Lancaster I, Kentucky I & Kentucky II completed. What we did, in brief, was to sweep north from Dong Ha, around McNamara's trace and Con Thien, and then sweep back down the other side and down the supply route back to Dong Ha. Other than a few minor firefights, there was little contact. Have to spend the night guarding an Arty Battery.

My platoon was sent north to Quang Tri to guard an artillery battery (Alpha Battery, 1st Battalion, 11th Marines) one night at an old French fort. This was easy duty. I slept on an air mattress out in the open. That night it rained hard. The next morning I found myself floating in a shell crater.

PFC Williams kept begging me to promote him to lance corporal. He said he had a girlfriend, the mother of his baby. He said he needed a raise so he could send more money to his girlfriend. "Lieutenant, the baby needs shoes, the baby needs milk" he would say. Eventually, I did promote him to Lance Corporal. He said his mother was very proud of him because she thought that's as high as you could go.

**Cpl House ready to apply camo and begin
evening patrol deep into the jungle.**

House

November 19 – Captain Robert A. Black was appointed CO of Echo. We don't know where Captain Baker went. Normally, we don't know when an officer leaves. There were a lot of changes in the management.

Lt. Kirk

November 19 – *letter home*: We do not know one day from the next. My watch keeps me informed of the date, but I only know when Wednesday rolls around, because that's the day we take malaria pills. I grew a mustache on Operation Lancaster – it's my pride and joy – will send a picture home. The M-16 is a darn fine weapon. I've carried it on most of the operations and we haven't had a stoppage yet. It's simply a matter of cleaning it. As I told you in my last letter home, 2/1 will be relieving 1/1 at Con Thien about December 19th. It did this company a world of good to operate up there last week – it's been made into quite a legend by the press – actually, it looks like any other outpost and it's well fortified with wire, minefields and bunkers. The NVA couldn't overrun it with a division.

House

November 20 - The squad pulled guard duty on the 105mm artillery Battery last night. My God, it gets loud, when they shoot a fire mission or just start blasting away on H&I (harassment and interdiction).

It is malaria pill day, that means it's Wednesday. The corpsmen are passing them out and they stand there and verify you swallow them. It's not the malaria pills that are so bad, it's the darn water we have to swallow – water that has probably been treated with our purification tablets. The water tastes so bad.

November 22 - Overnight patrol. We are moving south along the river looking for places for troops and vehicle crossings points and plotting them on our maps for future ops. The lieutenant gave us a "well done!" It went smooth and very efficient, and he was impressed with my map work. We moved 2,000 meters west to Hill #40, with a FO (forward artillery observer) to plot concentration fire zones along our routes.

Note: Doc Turner - November 22 - I felt like an old man by combat standards – 24 years old. Most of the guys were 18. To me, Chris was the most terrific kid in our company. He wasn't gullible and he was sharp and wanting to survive, with no pretense of being superman.

Knobby

November 20 - We finally got in from the field. It was the longest I had gone without mail in a long time. I had 26 letters and 12 packages waiting for me! I think I legally come out of the field on the 27th and fly to Da Nang on the 28th, then Hawaii on the 30th. If we go on any big operations after the 24th, I plan on developing a fast case of immersion foot. That way I won't have to worry about being able to get a chopper to take me out of the jungle.

T and I are in the process of devouring some frankfurters and pumpernickel right now. His parents went back to Germany to celebrate their 25th wedding anniversary and they sent him a package from there.

Lt. Kirk

November 22 - During the time at Quang Tri I was assigned to be the prosecuting attorney for a special court martial. The defense counsel was an attorney. The Marine Corps used non-attorney officers as prosecutors and defense counsel at that time. The only rule was that if the prosecutor was an attorney, the defense counsel had to be an attorney also. I thought my assignment was ridiculous, as I was spending several days in the field for every day back at the battalion rear. I wondered why this couldn't be assigned to one of the pogue officers in the rear. I kept putting it off. When I was back in the rear we were busy surveying gear, cleaning weapons and trying to get some sleep between periods of guarding the perimeter. Finally, I could put it off no longer and the court martial went forward. My only guidance was a manual, which I studied as much as I could before the court martial and referred to during the trial. I remember that the Marine was found guilty, but I can't remember the charge.

House

November 22 - 2,000 meters West of Hill #40 - We have two new men in my squad, and soon to get a third, I am told. It would sure be good to have a full squad or at least more strength. That gives me eight men now. We are out on open rolling hills in a platoon size patrol, and one of the new guys, Oncale, spotted a suspected VC at about 1500 meters or more. We had a real good view of the whole area down in the valley below us. I call to the FO (forward artillery observer in the field who works with a radio and helps direct fire with his guys in the rear area) with his huge glasses and he spots four more suspected VC out on the flank of the first guy. I take a compass reading, plot their position on my map, and radio the FO team.   By then, behind the five guys on the valley floor are about fifteen more, all carrying gear with what looks like a small rear security element. All are dressed in black pajama uniforms!

Lt. Graffam asks the captain for clearance to fire. Granted. The FO gets a full battery of nine 4.2 inch mortars and nine 81 mm mortars, seventeen guns in all to shoot this mission. It took about 10 minutes to get it set-up before the first WP. Grid coordinates 353460.   A white phosphorous spotter round hits near the enemy and then, holy cow! 6 WP (Willy-Peter) & 72 HE (high explosive) rounds found their mark. It blew the area all apart.

Air burst, ground explosions, trees flying through the air! Smoke, shrapnel, dirt, dust, logs, everything flying. Then, as we moved down off the hill to check the area out with our squad on point, the Skipper (the name given to the commander in charge) held us back and called for Huey (UHIE) Helicopter Gunships with 36 rocket rods and 3000 round M-60 machine gun mounts each to strafe the area along the tree line we had to enter.

The gunships send two of them over our heads, rockets slamming into the smoking ruins and their guns blazing. They ripped the brush and trees to pieces.

Talk about massive fire power. Having expended all their ammo they turned and went back to Dong Ha, duty done.

We went in on-line searching for bodies and weapons, looking for the supplies we saw them carrying. We only found (2) grenades, a magazine pouch, a magazine for a .30 carbine rifle and lots of bundles of wood and joy sticks for carrying over both shoulders.

We did find blood pools and trails, but nothing we could follow for any distance as a trail. They carry off their dead and wounded very fast.

Lt. Graffam figures it was a platoon of VC trying to get back to their village after a patrol, and by carrying the wood, which they need for cooking anyway, they were trying to look "normal" like farmers or wood cutters gathering firewood. They had their weapons and gear hidden in the bundles of wood. The mistake was moving in a military formation as we spotted them from a safe distance away. Well, we got some of them as probables anyway.

Mr. Hill and Grandma sent me some clever wet-suit rubber covers for the straps on my pack and a pad to go under my pack to cushion my spine. Oh, Man. It works great and is so soft. What a gift! All the guys want them. I could make a fortune selling these.

We are still scheduled to go to Con Thien on 20 December. We are supposed to have a big inspection before we go to The Hill by our new battalion commander, Lt. Col. Parker. He succeeded Lt. Col. Van Winkle after Parker was blamed for the loss of $30,000 worth of gear destroyed by rain! Hell, it was not his fault! It was all due to the lousy supply system we have and a typhoon! The engineers recorded 12-15 inches of rain a day!

November 23 – Departed CP at 2302 hrs – at 0330 hrs – Echo emergency medevac for three WIA's with frag wounds on back and both legs. The last man in our squad detonated an unknown type of mine.

Chris
November 23 – We are back to our tent living. When we are in a rear area campsite, we have the luxury of food being prepared and getting in a chow line – one cold pancake, two cold eggs, one piece of bread and jam, bacon and potatoes. This is really something that we didn't realize we would wish for later, when it would all be a distant memory, as the C-rats returned.

At about 0700, we got our gear on, I made sure the other members of my team were gear-ready. We now have nine men total. When ready, we marched out in single file towards our objective, which was a small village about 4,000 meters away. We set-up around the village and blocked off all the exits. We proceeded to search the entire area, the people, the hooches, tree lines, etc. We found a couple of grenades, a booby trap, and nine suspected VC and three confirmed. Our platoon, of about 40 men then headed back for camp at about 1800 hours. We ate chow and then headed back into the field at 2100 for a 3-5 day operation. We normally get two meals a day while we're in the field, but on the last operation we averaged 1.5 meals day. Other times we don't get that much. It's not a lot.

House

November 24 - Lt. Col. Archie Van Winkle Calls - I am told by Lt. Graffam to report to S-3. Major Todd and Gunny are there and tell me our old battalion commander personally called from 1st Marine Division headquarters in Da Nang requesting that I be transferred to become his G-3 draftsman. Wow, Wow, Wow! What a turn of events. He gets relieved of his combat command, because of rain and I get out of combat because he gets to headquarters and remembers me. Yea!

The Gunny asked me all kinds of questions and then asked if I would extend for six more months in Vietnam to get the job. I looked him square in the eye and said, "No, Sir" and he asked for three more months, I said yes, I would if I got the job first. He offered me a sergeant's stripe for a six month extension with Echo Co. He said he will work on this because we are short handed now and the transfer may take some time.

I do not know which way this is going to go. The major and the colonel were not happy to know Lt. Col. Van Winkle is trying to raid men from their unit. I may be screwed.

Last night, I had to take my squad and an M-60 machine gun crew to a hill overlooking the river. The lieutenant and I went to the armory and had a new Starlight Scope worth $3,100 installed on my M-16. It is a night sniper scope that gathers and intensifies light from any surrounding source like the moon or stars or night sky reflection. It glows a funny, green color and it makes a lit cigarette looks like a flashlight. The thing is amazing, and it really works, but it is big and heavy.

We ran two man watches with the scope for two hours each. At 1100, Chris spots three gooks coming down-river in a long dugout canoe, loaded with a pig, their gear, and rifles. It is pitch-black dark. Nobody can see them without the scope. We have to wait until they come by us within range and I have to fire tracer rounds only to show everyone else where they have to fire into the dark to hit their target.

Or we could illuminate them with flares, as soon as possible, but that would blind the scope as it would be so intense. As they came by, I opened-up with the tracers walking in closer. The M-60 got off about 30 rounds and jammed solid, hitting close, but did not hit the boat. They tipped over the boat and the pig squealed and screamed. I think we shot the pig, but I do not know for sure if we killed them or not. But wow! To be able to see them at night. Awesome!

We lost three more men in the past two nights to mines. Graves lost his left hand and Klingman had his right foot blown off, and Scott got a big chunk of iron in his shoulder.

Both Speck and Sgt. Mills got office hours discipline today for sending contraband home, I guess FPO San Francisco is now opening the packages we are sending back to the states, because of the drugs guys are buying here. I think they sent home military gear, also. Now, Speck won't get his promotion. He has been busted back before but wow, he had been a PFC for 13 months. Now, too bad, no stripe or raise for him, but he really does not care.

Thanksgiving dinner was really great. The cooks went all out to make it special and we did feast. The chaplains' service was pretty special, too. I sure miss home, but the USMC really did try to make it special. We even found some whiskey and all shared a drink to each other.

November 25 - Running small patrols lately. I talked to the gunny and he says G-3 at Headquarters, Da Nang, must cut and send my orders. It is their responsibility to do it by the book, if they want to transfer me and he does not know how long it will take, could be days, week or months, be patient. He does not think it will be blocked by battalion staff.

Chris got some lemon and vanilla pudding from his Mom in big 303 size cans and instant oatmeal. Oh, wow! Talk about great shares! That guy is too good to me. But, he loves Nancy's chocolate chip and snicker-doodle cookies too, so we try to keep it even.

Lt. Kirk

November 27 - We cordoned and searched another village between Phu Bai and Hue. A 101st Airborne unit was on my right. When we started taking fire, we were ordered to advance. The Marines attacked in a frontal assault: "high diddle diddle right up the middle." The adjacent 101st Airborne unit sat back and called in a long mortar barrage before moving in – a lot more efficient in terms of friendly lives, but destructive of property, civilians and more expensive.

Chris

November 28 - We get to spend all day in camp. We really need it. It hasn't happened in a long time that we can actually rest! I'm going to get some sleep, as I had none last night. I got my picture in the *Sea Tiger*, a Navy newspaper which is sent to the troops throughout 'Nam. Mass was held out in the field - up north towards the DMZ. I have just completed 4-1/2 months down the drain and I mean down the drain.

With the downtime today, comes thinking, mostly about coming home. I have 8-1/2 months to go. It seems so far away. I'm 20 yrs old and have so many things I want to do. Getting home ranks pretty high on the list, seeing my family, being safe. We all think about it, but it just doesn't seem real. I think about R&R a lot. Another way to get out of here. We can go to many different countries for our seven day rest. Australia seems to be a great place to go, or Hawaii. I don't have any desire to visit the other countries, as they are oriental and I just don't think it would be the same.

The guy I live with is from Bremerton, WA. His name is Mike House, married and trained to be a draftsman. He is an E-4 Corporal and my squad leader. He's very sharp and we are very lucky to have him as our leader. We have a good time at night when we are able - cooking our goodies, working our crossword puzzles. He really has a lot on the ball.

Lt. Kirk

November 29 – I had a feeling of exhilaration one day on patrol. We were armed to the teeth, seemingly masters of all we surveyed and my platoon was moving and responding just the way I wanted. I felt powerful.

House

November 29 - 2100 hours - A four hour hump on 29th and we surround a village on the river. I carry the Starlight Scope again and spot two VC trying to get away across the river in a long dugout canoe. We all open-up with red tracers flying hard and fast, and get them both this time! I could see them go down and their bodies float away using the scope.

Coming back in the morning our entire 60mm mortar crew of four guys were wounded by one big mine. We later heard that it was a buried 105 artillery shell, and two of them were sent back to the States with nerve damage too bad to fix in the hospitals in Japan. Our whole squad walked past it about 30 feet away, just a few minutes before. When it went off it was so close it scared us near to death.

I was the third guy to reach them and ran for splints for their legs and arms. Their wounds were long gashes opening the flesh on their legs down to the bone. The muscles were open and exposed, and blood was pouring all over.   Their wounds were filled with dirt, but everyone was awake and alert, but starting to go into shock. Dealing with all that blood and hurt in a guy's eyes and trying to calm him down is pretty hard to do. I could never be a corpsman - those guys have seen too much suffering not to be affected forever. I know it sure gets to me. I have nightmares almost every night for weeks after, hearing the screams and cries from all those guys you see hurt so badly.

A bunch of ARVN, with a propaganda team from the U.S. Army, came into the area along with a team of U.S. news reporters plus two American women. The women had flak jackets on and short-cut hair, but no chests or hips. Dang. They looked like guys the way they were dressed.   Round eyes, but what a disappointment. They did not give us much to look at.

We had to go over to Alpha Battery to stand security for the big 105 mm guns again. I have now been awake for 36 hours straight, and I am really tired. It is so hard to keep awake on watch. With the rain so cold and miserable you just want to curl up and get warm and sleep, but no deal.

When we got back our job was to fill 400 sand bags and build a bunker out on the point of the hill where we will be posting our watch. Then we had to dig bigger fighting holes behind our shelters.

I have come down with ringworm on my feet and my knee is killing me. I rub oil of wintergreen on it and keep it wrapped up and it helps, but man, does it ache.

Lenny has burned the Jiffy-pop, so no popcorn for us tonight, but he eats it burned, anyways.

Chris

November 29 - We surrounded a village late tonight and spotted a couple of guys trying to escape by using a dugout canoe. House spots them with his starlight scope and fires some tracer rounds, which the rest of us can then aim in on and blast them away. House confirms they are killed. The starlight scope is one of the best pieces of equipment we have. House continues to carry the scope, even though it adds quite a bit of weight. He also carries the rope and grapple hook. We are very lucky to him as our squad leader. He doesn't assign any task that he himself would not do.

Normally, we are unable to positively count a kill because the enemy drags their guys away from the action area. It wears on us, as the only way we can feel anything good about this place and the war is to know that we are doing damage to the enemy, also. We see our guys being medevaced too often, either being sent to the hospital for wounds or to the morgue. It's war. Nothing prepares us for what we are going through. It's done. It all starts over again in the morning.

Lt. Kirk

November 30 - I've never done anything more satisfying than what I'm doing now. 3rd platoon is well-oiled and efficient in the field and in the rear area here. Some of the guys from my old platoon are at Con Thien now – received two letters from them today – they've taken no casualties yet, although the NVA pump 100 rounds of artillery in on them each day. They eat 3 C-rats a day now and get SP (special packs) (cigarettes, candy, soap and more) every three days. They run platoon-sized patrols outside the perimeter. Biggest problem is rats – one man was medevaced for a rat bite. He was my radio operator. I saw him on his way to the rear (Da Nang) and he says the shots for rabies aren't bad at all. They work all day improving their positions and stand lines at night. From what I saw on Operation Lancaster, Con Thien is an impregnable fortress. The ABII [pi]s at U. of Illinois have adopted Echo and send us cookies, etc. Also, write the troops personally. I am writing to a real doll at home. Moustache is in full bloom now. I'm extremely vain about it.

The November Command Chronology for 2nd Battalion, 1st Marines noted that enemy contact was light to moderate but mining activity increased substantially. From November 4-17 Companies E and G joined 1/1 in Operation Lancaster near Con Thien. 2nd Battalion, 1st Marines casualties for November: 1 officer and 2 enlisted KIA, 1 officer and 26 enlisted WIA.

House

December 1 - 2100 hours - Chris just woke me up coming in from his night compass training in the driving rain. Captain Black is a nut job. He keeps our guys going like this until they drop. We all need rest so badly! Everybody is worn-out and dragging.

I could not go out in the field. Doc Turner says I have some kind of flu with a fever. We worked again in the rain all day digging holes deeper, building heavier sand bag bunkers and stringing barb wire. All the guys just shiver whenever they stop moving and a lot of us do not have any dry utilities to swap into at the end of work. I almost expect it to snow, it feels so cold.

Our tent is full of leaks now and it is tough to keep it closed in the high winds. My candle is almost gone. There were none at the gook PX (the local Vietnamese bring trading items to the wire fence) today.

We were told maybe we won't be going to Con Thien on the 20th, but maybe south to Camp Evans by Phu Bai. They have nice Quonset huts there with stoves in them and you can dry your gear. Impossible, because it sounds too good to be true.

The psy-ops guys have been dropping thousands of leaflets to show the villagers a reward program in which we pay Vietnamese piasters (piasters are the local paper currency) to any civilians who bring us weapons or ammo or mines or booby-traps. Mostly it is the younger kids who find all kinds of stuff as they run around the trails and woods, and a few of them get hurt when they trip the booby-traps by accident. If the kids' dads are PF's (popular forces) or ARVN soldiers, they get ammo from them, bring it to us to collect a reward, and we turn around and issue it back to the dad the next day or so because he's probably a South Vietnamese soldier (at least by day). What a racket.

Still no sign of my transfer order to division G-3.

Lt. Kirk

December 2 - I went out on patrol today with my platoon. We came to a rice paddy we had to cross. I set my 1st squad in on the near side to cover the crossing, then sent my 2nd squad across, which set up on the far side. Then my 3rd squad crossed and the finally the 1st. One squad screwed up. I was so mad and distracted that I got in front of my troops. I walked up on three VC reading a map. I threw myself to the ground and pulled out my .45 caliber pistol.

Unfortunately, it was in a WP (waterproof plastic) bag I'd put it in after cleaning. Fortunately, the VC were more scared than me and "de-deed" (left quickly).

December 3 - Standing security at Alpha Battery (artillery base) tonight.

House

December 4 - We were standing security last night at Alpha Battery, and we figured we would drown and freeze to death like we did last time we were there, so we took big plastic covers with us and built our own shelter, snug, dry and warm. So, then it does not rain, which is ok, but we were all disappointed we did not get to cheat the Viet Nam Monsoon Rain Gods.

The 105mm artillery guns shot over our heads all night long. The cigarette filters we use for earplugs were barely effective even if you jammed them in your ears real deep. I don't know if my head hurts so badly from the concussion of the artillery or the pressure of the earplugs. The sun is shining bright and it feels good to be warm and dry again.

We are at a small village called Nu-Lei, on a riverbank, running a "med-cap" (Medical Civic Action Platoon), giving out band-aids to the locals. The corpsmen are treating sores and coughs and baby colds, and passing aspirin, while we also run patrols and provide the village with some sense of security. The ARVN (Army of Republic of Vietnam) are here as well as the PSY-OPS (psychological operations) guys. The ARVN guys are pretty lax. I would hate to have to travel with them.

The whole squad went for a swim in the river and Chris took a picture of me, all soaped up while there was an airstrike going on right across the river from us. I think the rising smoke from the explosion will be in the background of my soapy body.

The 3rd platoon found a VC with a .30 Cal M-1 carbine rifle when they went for water at the river edge. Good catch. We have a good ambush site picked out for tonight. Hope it does not rain.

We moved into the site with the lieutenant deciding to come along, just to get the practice. It was very unusual, but cool. It took us about one hour to move about 600 meters down a very dark trail to the spot we had scoped-out during the day. It was a big concrete grave mound outside the tree line of the village, so we had good protective cover and could see the approaches on both sides of our position.   Open rice paddies were on one side and the main trail around the outside of the village on the other, which provided a very likely path for the VC if they wanted to come in and mix it up with us tonight.

Doc Turner
December 5 - We are staying in the schoolhouse tonight, after a cool dip in the river. It stopped raining last night after six straight days. It will be nice staying indoors tonight because we will be able to keep dry. The schoolhouse is made of concrete – 4 rooms, break, then 6 rooms, at a right angle, along the river.

Since we relieved Hotel Co, we've been hit almost every night. Last night the claymore mine that was put out in front of our position had been turned around on us. We found out the next day when we went out to retrieve it. Then we re-positioned it and put a hand grenade underneath the claymore mine, just in case a VC decided to mess with it again.   Later that evening, the silence was interrupted when the mine was picked up by a VC. Upon our morning inspection, all we found was a heart.

House
December 5 - About 0145 hours, maybe 15-20 VC slipped in from the other side of the village and open-up on the School House with rifle grenades, automatic weapons fire and RPG rockets! We are still in our LP position. We can hear and see the flashes, but are on the outside of the tree line and cannot move to help. The rockets blast big holes in the building walls, and the Gunny gets wounded in the head- again! Our Top Sergeant was hit in the hand, eight other guys were hurt, one killed.

They tried to take our M-60 machine gun and wounded all four of the gun crew in the fight, but did not get it. One Marine killed a gook and dragged him and his new Russian AK-47 into the machine gun position with him.

The VC broke off and they all scattered, and we hear on our radio, "Ambush site! They are coming your way!"

We are guns up and ready, and see them running straight at us in the light of illumination flares and they run straight into our opening bursts.   Dodd shoots another M-79 flare, but it is a dud.   Pitch black darkness, no illumination, we scramble for pop-up flares as we can hear them crashing through the brush and bamboo and we fire full magazines as we follow their sound and we get their full magazines right back at us.   But, they shoot high.   Green tracers from their

AK-47 automatics are overhead at least ten feet in the air. We shoot low, bounce 'em off the ground and get 'em with the ricochet and dirt and rocks. They were running and shooting to cover their retreat, with no fire discipline, just spraying the general area to make us keep our heads down.

Then, our position starts to receive well-aimed fire from the hills behind us and beyond the rice paddies. It must have been a back-up team or a couple of extra guys that spilt-off the main attack force. Bullets were flying all around us, but we all just moved to the other side of the concrete grave wall and let them fly over. No sweat.

Searching at first light we found an AK-47, two empty magazines, a couple of their Chinese first aid packets and lots of brass, but no bodies. Only one bloody battle dressing was found and a couple of blood trails, so we know we hit more than the one guy we saw go down. Major Brooks from S-3 classified our ambush action as two probable kills. Then another squad finds a VC body. We are not sure if it is the guy we hit or not.

December 5 - We are in a reserve position with the squad at the School House standing radio watch only. Suddenly, three rifle grenades landed on the roof. Big chunks of tile and brick and dust rain down around us with splinters off the big wood beams. We all dove outside and into our holes.

Positions close by were throwing illumination and hand grenades toward our position. Everyone was real jumpy and our line opened up on our own listening post team, as they were coming back through the wire, killing one of our own and wounding two others!

The new guy that was killed had just joined the company the day yesterday and it was his first night in the bush. I was so sick, I almost cried. We helped carry his body in from the trees with bullets flying all around us. We set him down in the aid station tent. The three of us were soaked in his blood. The corpsmen worked so hard to save him, but he was hit too bad in the throat and died right there in front of us.

I got hit by a small piece of shrapnel in my arm from something fragmenting as I ran back, but it was nothing a band-aid will not cover and certainly not worth asking for a Purple Heart after what I have seen guys suffer here. I would be ashamed. Battalion policy says 5 stitches minimum for a Purple Heart Medal, but

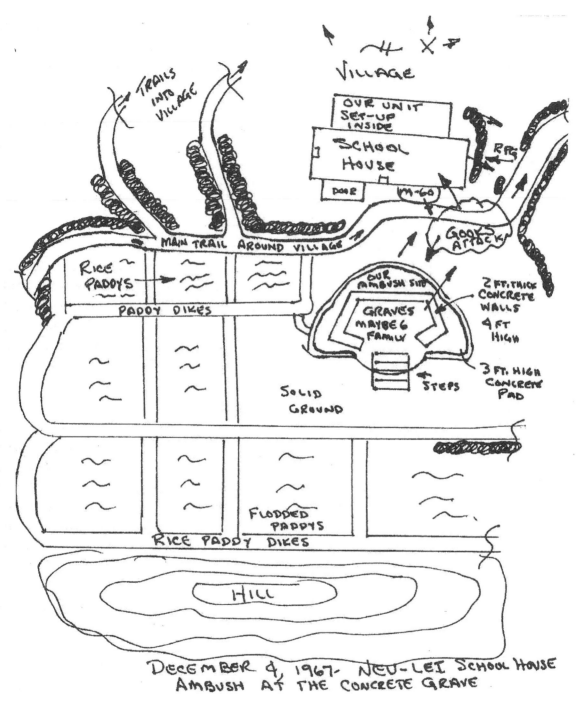

Labels within figure:

VILLAGE

TRAILS INTO VILLAGE

OUR UNIT SET-UP INSIDE

SCHOOL HOUSE

RPG

DOOR

M-60

GOOK ATTACK

MAIN TRAIL AROUND VILLAGE

RICE PADDYS

PADDY DIKES

OUR AMBUSH SITE

GRAVES MAYBE 6 FAMILY

2 FT. THICK CONCRETE WALLS

4 FT HIGH

3 FT. HIGH CONCRETE PAD

STEPS

SOLID GROUND

FLODDED PADDYS

RICE PADDY DIKES

HILL

DECEMBER 4, 1967- NEU-LEI SCHOOL HOUSE AMBUSH AT THE CONCRETE GRAVE

December 67 The Battle at the Nu-Lei School

I do not think it is enforced the same for all. I have seen guys get Purple Hearts for cuts from c-rat can lids they got cut by diving for cover during a mortar attack.

The next day while digging through my pack, I found a can of ham and lima beans that had been punctured, and inside it had stopped a pretty good sized chunk of shrapnel that would have gone into my back. Luck or God's grace was with me again.

We go back to pick up chow, mail, ammo and new maps. These are cool colored aerial photomaps that are easy to see and read and have 1,000 meter grid coordinates laid out on them that makes compass orientation a breeze.

We got an interpreter assigned to our company, which is a big help trying to talk to the locals.

There are all kinds of American news reporters here trying to interview troops. It is plain stupid to talk to those bastards, as they only look for bad news and bad apples with bad attitudes that want to cry to mommy and their senators and congressmen back home. We all stay far away from them. They cannot be trusted, and will twist anything you say to fit their own agenda, which is against the war and us being here. CBS is the worst. They are all a bunch of commie traitors that hate America as far as I am concerned.

We got back out to the company late in the afternoon and the skipper had decided to move to a hill outside the village since the VC knew all our positions around the school house. He had us set up an ambush for the expected VC night patrol, but we missed them and nearly froze to death waiting in a foot of water in a ditch next to a likely trail. It was a nasty night and they chose another trail or stayed at home all cozy. My legs cramped up so bad I could hardly stand up, and then it was murder walking for the first half-hour. My knee is getting better.

We got back up on the hill, the sun came out and dried us nice and warm, and it sure felt good. Like a lizard on a hot rock, soak it up.

Captain Black took our squad and the interpreter, ARVN Sgt. Hoaen, and we went back to the school house where they talked with the owners about the battle damage to the building because we were there. He paid them about $100.00 for the repairs. He also paid the lady $10.00 for a pouch and water urn that a grenade blew away and $2.00 for two ducks that were killed, but let her keep them to eat.

An old man brought his cow around to show us it had been hit in the flank by shrapnel, but it was really OK. Doc Miller slapped a big gob of zinc ointment on the wound and the cow tried to kick him. We all cracked up! I wish I had my camera with me.

Then Lt. Graffam found a backpack with almost $15,000 worth of North Vietnamese money with Ho-Chi-Minh's picture on it and a local pay roster for all the VC in the area. It was an outstanding intelligence find. Apparently they dropped it during the fight for our M-60, and could not get it back. The ARVN were delighted, and went out after all the bad guys on the list right away with the help of some locals that hate the VC.

Lt. Kirk

Dec. 5 - E Company went into a village (the same one where we shot the fleeing VC earlier) late one afternoon to relieve another company. The other company had been in the same position, around a schoolhouse in the eastern end of the village, for a couple of days. This was foolish. Spending more than one night in the same place gives the bad guys an opportunity to reconnoiter your position. One of the platoon commanders from the other company told me they had been hit the previous night and he had detonated a Claymore. He opened his poncho and showed me little bits of flesh he had picked up, all that remained of the VC. What a sicko!

During the night, we were hit by B-40 rockets (RPG's), grenades and small arms fire. Part of the schoolhouse roof fell in. I crawled out and down the stairs to take command of my platoon. We had a vicious firefight. I remember the incredible noise and the blinding muzzle flashes. When it was over, we found dead VC on our perimeter and blood trails. My company commander told me to create an LZ for our wounded to our southeast. Of course, this was outside our perimeter and we might very well encounter more bad guys. I think we were all scared. I know I was. But we went.

As we moved out, I saw one of my Marines cowering behind some barbed wire next to the schoolhouse wall. I reached through the barbed wire, grabbed him by the shirt, shook him and told him to fall in with his squad. He did. Later this evening, we went on patrol and at dusk I looked back and saw, silhouetted against the moonlight, my platoon sergeant beating the tar out of this Marine.

Note: This same platoon commander was later killed at Con Thien, out in front of his platoon leading a charge with a pistol.

228

House

December 6 - VC probes continued all night. Light contacts. We threw hand grenades at each other in pitch-black darkness all night, but they were not strong enough or bold enough to get close.

Gary "Chris"Christensen showed me a trick he had for keeping the noise of our grenades from giving away our position. He would hold the grenade tight to his chest, pull the pin, roll over on top of it, and let the spoon go between his chest and the ground to conceal the loud "ping" of the spoon flying and the fuse train spring snapping closed, then roll back up and toss it through the trees. We had to be able to trust those fuses giving us a full five seconds until detonation!

Chris

December 6 - We've had all the action we need lately. We went out on an ambush tonight. It has been friggin' nasty. We sat in a pretty good ambush position, well focused on the trail ahead of us and allowing good visual towards our sides and to the rear. Everyone feels good and we sat in, placing grenades, canteens and ammo close to the position we are individually responsible. There is no reason to keep all our gear on, as we are to fire directly on any enemy coming towards us and no reason to be uncomfortable. We will be here until morning light. A couple of guys verve their rifles toward the sides and make sure nothing disturbs us from those directions. Their gear is also lying in front of them and ready. A couple of the other guys keep their attention to covering the area to our rear. House and I cover the front, which I believe is the most apt direction we will see action tonight. If we are out for a short patrol or ambush, we all stay awake, waiting for that first shot. Our ambush patrol is sometimes a full squad with a machine gun crew, giving us 12-14 guys and sometimes a mere 4-5 men. Either situation is basically the same - make contact! Tonight there only eight of us.

If we are able to take two hour shifts, normally it's going to be just one guy awake. It's damn lonely if you're the guy staying awake at midnight or "zero dark thirty", as it's called. It's probably black dark, quiet and far from help. After an hour by yourself, it can get very difficult to stay awake for that second hour to pass. We all are constantly sleep deprived. We get an average of four hours of sleep each night. Guys find all sorts of things to do to stay awake - taking off your boots, then your socks, then wring the water out of your socks and hang them on a branch next to you. You are really gambling that all shit doesn't break out and there you are with no socks, no boots. It's a gamble. Sometimes you can nibble on some c-rats or take a drink of crappy water, or clean your glasses. Not much else. You must stay as still as possible.

If you hear something or think you heard something while you are on watch, you have a couple of alternatives - wake everyone immediately. If the enemy is coming, you did a good job. If no one comes and it was maybe your imagination, the guys are not pleased. They were finally able to sleep until you woke them. If there is no action or the action didn't amount to anyone getting killed or seriously wounded, the morning light seemed to bring something extra. Just having the morning come up, makes it a good morning. When the sun breaks through it starts to warm up and a bit less tension is felt by all. It doesn't mean everything is going to be okay, it just means we made it through the night. With the sun we get our vision back.

We then did a very careful search of the whole area, but found nothing more than a bunch of NVA propaganda leaflets and a small amount of money and some batteries in a haystack. We stood lines in three man positions again tonight, and had extra trip flares and pop-ups set-out, but nothing disturbed us except the cold rain.

House
December 8 - The ringworm is getting worse on my feet. It really looks bad, smells worse, and hurts.

I am thinking about the Gunny's offer to extend three months, and plan on going to him and agreeing to his conditions today. We lost one man in the company today who stepped on a small foot mine filled with nails.

We got word from the CP that two little boys bringing in ammo for rewards were killed when one of the 60mm mortar rounds they had, exploded.

The ladies from Lincoln Ave. Bible Church sent me a nice package today of cookies, fudge, divinity, gum, peppermint, candy, pop-corn and two books on Christianity and a tiny Bible. It was very nice of them, and they included a personal note - "I hope you will like this". Maybe I will find a few answers to my questions between me and J.C. in their books.

Some of the guys in Golf Co. had to kill a big water buffalo that charged them on a trail. The noise from the M-60 machine gun really set us all on edge, and the buffalo bellowed in pain for a while until they finished it off. I wonder what we have to pay for one of those monsters?

December 9 – One of the guys in our platoon tripped a small homemade mine, another WIA.

Knobby
December 9 - I arrived back in Da Nang around 4:00 on the afternoon of the seventh. I'm in the USO right now at China Beach. They have clocks on the wall here that give the times to different places in the U.S. Here, it is 1105 hours and in Chicago it is 1005 hours on December 8th. I guess that puts us 13 hours ahead of you.

I stopped at the PX yesterday and found out about buying a car over here. I would have to pay cash, which would mean getting a loan through a bank. I can get a Corvette with accessories for $4,101, which is around $1,000 less than it would cost me in the States.

I'm gong back to battalion tomorrow if I can get a plane.

Lt. Kirk
December 9 - My radioman, Peterson, a big red-haired guy, with a big smile, with whom I was very close, (we were together night and day) stepped on a punji stick. It went through the bottom of his boot and out the top. We medevaced him and I never saw him again.

House
December 10 - We had to move 500 meters up the hill next to the 4.2" mortar positions. It took all day and it rained and rained and rained some more while we moved. The tent we built is so drafty and it leaks like a sieve. We are all soaked cold, tired, hungry, miserable and pissed. I found three centipedes under my gear and a mouse in my pack. He had a cozy place already built for himself.

Captain Robert A. Black, Echo Co. commander
December 10 – Echo's Mad Moment – We were south of the 2/1 base in training prep for the trip to Con Thien. As we built up to final protection fires, Drs. Lee and Geha jumped out of their skins and rushed into the BAS (Battalion Aid Station) to prepare for mass causalities. No one had told them. Echo would be doing a night defensive position fire exercise. Oh.......

Chris

December 10 – The sergeant said I should be able to get my college cut. This would mean that I would be able to be released from the Marine Corps about 90 days early, if I can prove that I have been accepted to a college. I asked Dad to do some work for me re: the acceptance to college. This will allow me to get out of here, early. Guys are getting these early "outs", so I'm hoping. The dream of leaving 'Nam is so unbelievable…actually I don't allow myself to think about it much.

Lt. Kirk

December 11 - An ARVN (Army of the Republic of Vietnam) colonel's wife, children and parents lived in the biggest hooch or house, in Nhu Le, the now familiar village west of the La Vang cathedral and on the south bank of the Quang Tri River. The house was at the intersection of two main trails through the village. She invited my platoon sergeant and me for supper one night. We ate rice and fish sauce (nouc mam). The whole family, mother, children and grandparents, slept in one bed. Their house was the biggest and nicest house in the village, but still it had a dirt floor. This village was located, west of the La Vang cathedral and on the south bank of the Quang Tri River.

House

December 12 - Moving to my watch position in the darkness last night, I fell in a big hole, and lost my only pair of glasses, crushed in the gravel. I have got to go down to Da Nang to get a couple of new pairs made, maybe 2-3 days turnaround to get back. Crap!

I "found" a kerosene stove and lantern in supply and set it up in the squad tent, making points with the guys. Our tent was hot as an oven when they came back from patrol in the rain. Boy, did they appreciate that. Everything gets to dry out.

S-1 lost my orders to Da Nang and I need new ones to get my glasses, and now the VC have blown down the big bridge between here and Dong Ha airbase. So, there will be further delays getting to the airbase for a ride 100 miles south to Da Nang, which is the only place where they can make eye glasses.

I plan on visiting a couple of buddies in the hospital while I am there and going up to the big P.X. in the sky at Freedom Hill to send something cool back to Nancy. I borrowed $10.00 from Lenny, just in case.

If I can find Lt. Col. Van Winkle at Headquarters, I am going to try to see him personally about my transfer as well. He told me to come and talk to him anytime I wanted to. I'll take him up on that, like a job interview, only better. It would mean an instant promotion out of the bush if all goes right.

The word had just been officially passed, we will be moving onto the hill at Con Thien on Dec. 20, and I am sure it will be a beautiful Christmas there for ECHO 2/1. We will be there for 30 days minimum, probably longer the way the Marine Corps works.

Our son will be four months old on Christmas Day 1967. Dinner at the famous Space Needle in Seattle next year - all together to celebrate his birthday.

Lt. Kirk
December 14 - In the TAOR (tactical area of operations) just to the south of us operated a unit of the ROK (Republic of Korea) Marines. They had a reputation of being very tough with captured Viet Cong and civilians harboring bad guys. As a result, they reportedly had more success with pacification than we did. We were saddled with restrictions on our behavior towards prisoners and civilians. One day a sniper team attached to my platoon insisted they had some Viet Cong in their sights and wanted to shoot. I checked with higher headquarters and discovered they were ROK Marines.

Chris
December 14 - I was lying in my rack and the lieutenant walked in and told me that me and my gear would be ready in two hours. They needed to send someone to Radar School and I was the chosen person. I waited for a truck to transport me to Ground Radar Observation School. Our company is moving to Con Thien for 30 days. While we're up there, I'll be with the radar unit guys. Because of bad weather at Con Thien this time of year, we are told that not many patrols are run in the field. We are finally getting "Our Turn in the Barrel". We have heard stories about the DMZ and the base called Con Thien ever since we've been in Vietnam. The stories about "The Hill" and the thousands of NVA troops that continue to attempt to overrun the base are legendary. Now, it's our turn. We are supposed to be there by Christmas.

December 14 – Our platoon received incoming small arms fire. We called in an arty mission. All quiet.

Lt. Kirk

December 15 - The company commander, Captain Black, assigned my platoon a mission to move south on what we called the woodcutters' trail, secure a hill and return in the morning. It was well known that the trail was mined and booby trapped. I argued that we ought to stay off the trail. Captain Black insisted. So, we went down the trail, carefully probing for booby traps and mines. But we set off a mine and took casualties. We couldn't get a medevac helicopter. We all knew that many helicopters had been grounded at this time for mechanical reasons. It was now dark. We carried the wounded back to camp in ponchos. We had to shimmy across the I-beams of a destroyed bridge (the deck was gone, but the I-beams were still in place), pulling the wounded behind us. Captain Black came out with a patrol, including a jeep and a mechanical mule, to retrieve our wounded, meeting us near the cathedral. To my surprise and chagrin, Captain Black sent us back out in the dark over the same mined trail that had caused us so much trouble in the daylight. Our point man was on his hands and knees the whole way out to our objective, feeling for trip wires and probing the ground with a K-Bar knife. He found several booby traps and disarmed them. What courage that took, knowing what would happen if you missed one. As we reached our objective, I used what became my normal procedure for confusing the bad guys, dropping off a squad, then setting the remaining two squads in another place, then infiltrating back to the first squad. In spite of that, the VC probed us just before dawn. We drove them off. We took casualties, but again we could not get a medevac helicopter and had to carry our wounded back once again.

House

December 15 – I'm sitting at the Da Nang 11th motor pool battalion waiting to get on the flight manifest to Dong Ha at 0730 hours tomorrow morning. As the sergeant called out names for spaces available, another Marine answered to "House," and I met a distant cousin, David House. David is a PFC from Morgantown, Kentucky and is my step dad's uncle's son. Small world huh? I also got my new glasses, with a stronger prescription. This is good, I can see so much clearer now.

I hitched a ride to the Freedom Hill USO/PX at Hill 327, 1st Marine Division. They give out free writing paper and envelopes to anyone that wants to write home, and lots of nice folks and a bunch of cute Red Cross "donut dollies" there provide all kinds of services to help all servicemen. Their big snack-bar provided me with three cheeseburgers, a chocolate shake and a large order of French fries for $2.00. Almost like the Dairy Queen back home. I was stuffed and feeling pretty good.

I hitched a ride further up the road to 1st Marine Division Headquarters, and walked into Lt. Col. Van Winkle's office, asking his orderly to speak to him personally. He remembered me and took my name again, said his draftsman would be gone in two weeks and would do what he could to get those orders cut. He even thanked me for coming in to see him. I told him how much I appreciated the opportunity, and would not let him down. It was a good conversation. He treated me with respect, and did not talk down to me like so many other officers do. It is probably because he was a mustang officer - he came up through the enlisted ranks himself, and understands what it is like to be an enlisted trooper. I like the guy.

December 17 - Still stuck in Da Nang. I'm supposed to go out on a chopper this morning, but it was loaded with Christmas mail and they would not allow passengers. They have added a tremendous administrative staff just for all the volume of Christmas packages. Only America fights a war like this. I know I am stuck here for at least another day like this. Sgt. Garcia, in charge of the transit motor facility, is a great guy and will try to get you anywhere you need to go - anywhere, just not back to Quang Tri, yet. Too much mail. Truck loads full of Christmas presents and goodie-boxes just keep coming in for the troops. Mountains of the stuff are piled up here.

December 18 - Finally back. I left Da Nang at 0830 hours this morning for a 23 minute flight. It was the smoothest flight I ever had. Got an ambulance ride to regiment and a jeep to battalion. I walked into the company office, plunked down my medical records and orders and nobody said a word. No questions asked. I was ready. Nobody gave me any crap about being two days late.

I report back to Lt. Graffam, he says "Welcome back, Cpl. House. Nice glasses".

We now are scheduled to move to Con Thien or, as it is known as the A-4 Strongpoint, on December 22. Sgt. Baldwin and Sgt. Mills will not be going with us as they are too short, ("short" means you are almost ready to go home) and will stay behind in the battalion rear area until their flight back home. Con Thien was named by Catholic missionaries. It means "Hill of Angels" in Vietnamese.

Note: Lt. Kirk - Captain David A. Quinlan replaced Captain Robert A. Black as CO of Echo Co on December 19. Captain Black, a Naval Academy grad, later commanded Bravo Company, 1/1 and distinguished himself in the battle for Hue. He was a very competent officer.

Chris
December 19 - Dong Ha - Radar School. Radar is sound waves.

Just received the pipes and the numerous types of pipe tobacco from home, also some magazines. It's very strange to read material from back home. It all seems so far away, so unrealistic. It has nothing to do with our day to day life.

We're going to the DMZ soon and I'll be involved with the ground radar unit. It will keep me off the lines and off the constant drill of going into the bush every other night, which will really be great. I guess it means I get to sleep, every night. Doesn't seem fair, with the guys going out and setting up ambushes and me back here sleeping. I sure hope nothing happens to them. With me gone, they are one man down.

Mom just wrote and told me Dad is sick. I didn't get too much info, so he must be bad.

We now know that our greatest fears will be realized. We're heading to the DMZ and specifically Con Thien. It is located 14 miles inland from the South China Sea and two miles south of the DMZ and North Vietnam. In the previous months of September, October, November, "The Hill", as Con Thien is sometimes called, had experienced not only the heaviest shelling of the war, but were attacked in force by the NVA trying to penetrate the defenses and enter the wire surrounding the compound. The Marines were able to turn back the major attack to the perimeter. The 2/4 Marines suffered heavy losses, as they were reduced from 952 to about 300 men by the end of October. The NVA had suffered losses of approximately 1800 dead or wounded. Monsoons then hit and brought on its difficulties. Now it was our "Turn in the Barrel". We had avoided this area for a long time.

House
December 20 – The sun is shining bright and clear! We are all packed up and standing by, scheduled to move out to Yankee Station by truck the morning of December 22, Yankee Station is supposed to be about one mile south of Con Thien.

Knobby

December 20 - I got a package today from my parents with rain gear and shake-a-puddings. I had a pretty good stack of mail waiting when we got back from patrol this morning.

We've finally gotten a little break in the weather. It has stopped raining (knock on wood) and isn't quite as cold as it was when I first got back. I managed to pick up a pretty good cold during all the bad weather we had – I should be able to get rid of it now that the sun is shining again.

We've been real busy around here getting ready for our move to Con Thien on the 22nd. The last time I was up there (Operation Lancaster) the place was one big mud hole and I hear it hasn't changed much. The mud is actually waist deep in some places. The rats are pretty bad too, but T is going to take his 25 caliber pistol so we'll probably be baiting them in our bunker to give us some target practice.

Chris

December 20 – I'm still at my ten day radar school. It's a few days 'til Christmas Eve. Easy living, good hot chow, good sleep. Seems strange, with all the guys living in the mud, and I'm dry here at the school. Also, I heard about the possibility of going to Vietnamese Language School in Okinawa. I think I would do well at this school, plus it would get me out of here for awhile. All I can do is put my name in and wait. I say prayers for dad every day and hope he is recovering.

Note: Lt. Kirk - Dec 21 - My platoon ran seven patrols or ambushes from December 1 through December 21 (we went to Con Thien on the 22nd). This is in addition to company size patrols.

By: Sgt. Steve Bernston

CON THIEN—Sitting in a 15-foot observation tower equipped with a pair of binoculars, a compass, a map and three radios, an artillery forward observer at Con Thien is a deadly threat to enemy troops.

One is Cpl. Keith D. Frutchey (Lindon, Mich.), Frutchey is an AO for elements of the First Marine Regiment.

He stands a daily watch at observation post 3.

The view from OP-3 allows the observer to watch most of the area around the perimeter of the outpost.

"The main purpose for the OP is to call in artillery on anything that moves in the demilitarized zone and North Vietnam," Frutchey said. "Also, we man the post to call counter-fire on the enemy when they fire on us."

At Frutchey's use are a vast array of artillery pieces. All he needs to do is to call on the radios and they are at his command.

"We average about 25 fire missions a day from this OP. There are also two other OPs and they average about the same. But there have been occasions where this OP has fired as many as 100 missions in a two-day period," said Frutchey who is presently serving on a six-month extension in Vietnam.

Some of the fire missions from OP-3 are fired into suspected enemy strongholds and possible mortar sites. Others are fired at confirmed enemy movement in the DMZ and farther north.

A position 15 feet high in Con Thien doesn't go unnoticed and the tower has been the target of several enemy rounds.

"It does get quite hairy sitting up here when the rounds start coming in," admits Frutchey.

"The dangerous job as a forward observer in a tower provides some personal satisfaction," explained Frutchey.

"It's a test to see how fast and accurately we can fire back into their positions," he explains. "It puts me on a more personal basis with the enemy. It's me calling in 'arty' against an enemy forward observer."

8

THE DMZ - CON THIEN

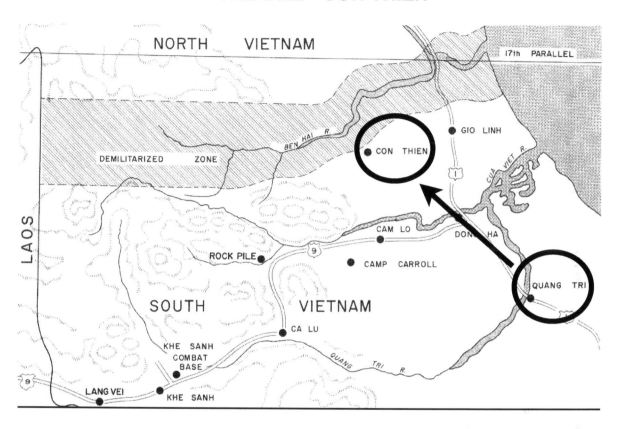

A series of fortified strong points were built along the southern edge of the DMZ separating North from South Vietnam. These fortified positions south of the DMZ began at Gio Linh in the east and proceeded west to include Con Thien, Cam Lo, Camp Carroll, The Rockpile, Ca Lu, and ending at Khe Sanh, on the far northwestern corner and next to Laos.

All of the strong points were important in denying North Vietnam easy access to the two northern provinces of South Vietnam. This line of bases prevented the movement of men and supplies to the south and also provided protection for our left or western flank. By mid-January of 1968 enemy (NVA regulars, Viet Cong main force, and hard-core guerrillas) strength was estimated to be between 75,000 and 90,000. Of all the Marine fortified positions along the DMZ, the closest to the DMZ was Con Thien. The enemy could fire artillery, rockets, and mortars from safe areas in the DMZ. It was policy not to allow U.S. Marines to go after the enemy and into areas outside of South Vietnam. Thus, the Marines at

Con Thien, for the most part, had to stay in a defensive position and withstand the thousands of shells that came their way.

Known as the "The Hill of Angels" to the Vietnamese, the Marines called Con Thien the Meatgrinder and referred to time there as "Our Turn in the Barrel". It was a grim place. The constant danger of artillery, rocket, mortar fire, massed infantry assaults and the depressing drizzle and mud from which there was no escape, combined to make Con Thien miserable for Marines there. Neuropsychiatric or shell shock casualties, relatively unheard of elsewhere in South Vietnam, were not unusual.

Note: Under Lt. Col. Evan Parker 2/1moved to Con Thien on December 22. Since Con Thien was such a difficult place to endure, the policy was to rotate battalions every 30 days. This proved not to be the case for 2nd Battalion, 1st Marines. Our stay lasted for 77 days. We endured 2760 rounds of incoming artillery, mortar and recoilless rifle rounds. Instead of fighting the lightly armed and elusive VC guerrillas in the south, we are now up against a different type of enemy, NVA soldiers who often stand their ground, supported by heavy machine guns, mortars, and artillery. During the Christmas truce period, everyone worked hard building up the existing bunkers and building new ones and strengthening the fighting positions.

House

December 22 - The 2nd Battalion, 1st Marines (2/1) is finally moving in a large convoy of 6X6 trucks along the road towards Con Thien. All the traffic causes some excitement for the villages along the route, and little Vietnamese kids line the sides of the narrow roads calling out at us as we passed for candy and cigarettes. They would all hold up their hands and flinch or turn their backs in a defensive move as each truck passed. All the guys are standing at the truck rails, some gently lobbing gum or cans of c-rats as we go. I realized why the flinch, when I saw one of the new troopers in the truck raise his hand high above his head, and pitch a heavy can of ham and lima beans directly into the crowd of young kids. It hit one little guy with such force I could hear the impact on his body, and he cried out in pain. I watched as another kid beside him scooped the can up and ran away. The Marine laughed at what he had done and some of the other troops smiled in quiet agreement. I was outraged and white anger blinded my senses, and I tore into him swearing at the top of my lungs. I called him a F---ing coward, and I was so mad it was all I could do not to punch him out, but as a squad leader, I could not strike a subordinate. After I chewed him out, everyone else in the truck quickly lost the smiles. They all knew it was wrong. I kept him burning "shitters" (55 gallon cans were cut in half, a board with a hole cut out was placed across the can for sitting on. The cans were filled with kerosene and lit when they became full). I kept him on this assignment for two weeks and he stayed mad at me for a long time, but he knew it was wrong too.

Captain Black got relieved of duty and we got a new CO. He was too harsh and a real hard-ass. We are all glad he is gone.

Gary Christensen is back from his radar school just in time to ship out to the hill with us. We loaded-up on Army trucks about 1100 hours, and after four hours we reached Yankee Station, about 600 yards south of Con Thien.

Speck did not have his helmet on and Colonel Parker spotted him as we unloaded. Man, did the shit hit the fan. He jumped all over him and then rolled right onto me as his squad leader. He ripped us a big hole. We all must have our helmets and flak jackets on and properly secured FROM NOW ON! Everyone got the message loud and clear.

We then formed up in column of twos and humped up the hill, single file both sides of the nice new road called the MSR (Main Supply Route), and right through the big gate. It was as easy as you please. We kept expecting to get shelled at any moment, but not of single round of incoming. We are replacing Bravo Company, 1st Battalion, 1st Marines.

All the vegetation was gone for about 200 yards on both sides of the road due to it being bulldozed after it was all killed by Agent Orange defoliant. No close cover available for the bad guys, but we know they are out there, just taking their time, until it is right to hit us.

I now have a full squad of 14 men. I can hardly keep track of them all. They tell us we will have to hump up the road the final mile carrying all our gear, all we will need for the next 30 days. How crazy it that? Why not drive it all in trucks? Because...Marines march. They do not want to give the enemy the big target of a convoy of trucks all lined up on a road like sitting ducks.

They told us each bunker sleeps four men each and we all pitched-in to buy a couple of small kerosene stoves for heat. (No USMC issue). I am sure it will get a lot colder up here. Rumor is we will not be getting any mail once we occupy the ground, only NVA artillery.

After our 30 days in the meat-grinder at Con Thien, we are supposed to be rotated out to Camp Evans, south of here near Phu Bai, where they will have our gear waiting for us and a little in-country R&R. I hope I am in Da Nang in Division G-3 by then.

Chris

December 22 - We move *en masse* to Con Thien (CT) by truck. We all know how badly hit this Marine Corps Base has been recently. CT came under mass infantry assaults lasting over a period of several days, along with artillery bombardment. It was now our "Turn in the Barrel" at the northern-most outpost in South Vietnam, less than one mile south of the DMZ - 2/1 would defend the A-4 Strong Point. Con Thien, as well as Gio Linh, had been French forts, which indicated that both sites were recognized positions as key strategic terrain. We would set a record for staying at Con Thien, longer than any other unit had endured. I arrived with Herfel, Dodd, Lenny, Speck, Estes, House, Reidinger, Falcon, Mullineaux, Hendricks and couple other new guys.

We learned we would not be engaged in an offensive action, rather the opposite. The emphasis would be on good defensive positions - deep trenches and sleeping quarters underground. The sleeping bunkers would be built with numerous layers of sandbags (called a "burster layer", which included airfield steel matting "to burst delayed fuse rounds") in the roof above us. We used everything we could get our hands on for protection from the, soon to come, 2760 artillery, rocket and mortar rounds, that would be raining down on us during the next 77 days. Our positions on the line had one hundred yards of clear ground in front of us, then concertina wire, 40 additional yards of clear ground, more concentina wire, new razor-sharp German-type barbed wire, claymore mines, elevated ground, and then our firing positions. That made up our defensive position. It didn't seem like much of a clear area out in front of the bunkers. The mental visualization of thousands of yelling and screaming NVA soldiers running at us, firing automatic machine guns and throwing satchel charges was a terrible thought, which I quickly erased. The isolation of this bare hill, far from away from everything, was a real awakening. This was it. It wasn't gonna change.

This was the place we all thought we had been so lucky to have avoided. Con Thien is called the "graveyard" by the grunts and called "The Hill of Angels" by the Vietnamese. The hill had been on the receiving end of lots of artillery, mortar, rocket and recoilless rifle rounds. In September, the base received an average of 342 rounds a day. Live vegetation was virtually non-existent and gave us an immediate gut-check feeling that we were entering a devastated place, a truly grim war zone. The red-brown mud blanketed the hill where we were soon to live.

One part of the vast minefield in front of our position is basically void of live mines, as the vast number of incoming mortars and artillery had taken them out. This place was bad. No one felt good about being here. It was very exposed. It brought a chill as we realized we were here in a defensive position.

Nui Con Thien - Con Thien – The Hill – The Hill of Angels - The McNamara Line – the DMZ - It is all the same. It's the area which separates North from South Vietnam. Con Thien is about two miles south of the DMZ and about five miles east of the Laotian border. Con Thien had been a constant target of enemy artillery attacks since the Marines set up the base early in the war. It was a strategic position overlooking the DMZ and providing a 180 degree view of North Vietnam from its elevated position.

The Hill was connected by a series of sandbagged bunkers and waist-to-chest high trenches connecting fighting positions and situated as a defensive perimeter line. We were protecting the artillery guns, the command posts, the aid station, the ammo areas and everything else in the interior part of the base. The only thing in front of the fighting positions was concertina wire and mine fields. When the enemy came and they would, they would barge through the minefields and wire and were then right in front of you. They strapped drugs to their arms and would release the drug into themselves when shot or injured, allowing them to continue their mission to overrun the base. In a drug-crazed rage they had stormed Con Thien with troops in October-November. They would come again and we knew it. Our job was to be as prepared as possible. It seemed like we dug everyday – dug holes to hide in, dug to fill sandbags to fortify our positions.

Immediately, as we move into the base, we are assigned to positions on the line. We have been positioned on part of the perimeter line, facing outward, with our rifles, machine guns, mortars, tanks and everything else pointed toward the south-southwest. This is an incredible day. The feeling is eery. We have one position. That's it. There's the trench line, just like in WWII. The enemy will come from in front of you. Next, we are assigned our bunker, which is directed in back of our fighting position. That's the place where four of us will sleep, right in back of the trench line. We will be living and eating our meals in the red-brown mud and underground bunkers and holes. And with this brought on the rats scrounging for bits of food. Our predecessors had lived like pigs. Cleaning out the four-man living bunker was going to be a chore. Tomorrow, we will start by throwing out all the garbage and cleaning out our bunker. Ours is a mess - with paper wrappers, c-rat cans, old clothes - all left by our predecessors. We had lots to do before this was going to be comfortable.

Lt. Kirk
December 22 - As we disembarked from the trucks near Con Thien, we found ourselves in knee-deep mud. As we were struggling through the mud, a Lt. Colonel I didn't know chewed me out because some of my troops didn't have flak jackets zipped and buttoned. The troops didn't like to zip their flak jackets for fear a bullet or shrapnel would jam the zipper and the corpsmen would have trouble getting their flak jacket off and tending to them.

I was ordered to sweep outside the perimeter at Yankee Station the day we arrived. I had my troops on line for most of the patrol, so we could see every inch of ground, but the terrain got too thick and I went to a column with fire teams out on either side for flank security. We encountered sniper fire, without result.

Lt. Suydam
December 23 - When I was released from the U.S. Hospital in Cam Ranh Bay, I rejoined 2nd Battalion, 1st Marines at Con Thien as the XO. I had been in rehab for six weeks after my injury. This place consisted of three gently rising and interlocking hilltops overlooking the Song (river) Bien Hai, about 12 kilometers away. The Song Bien Hai River divides South from North Vietnam. Con Thien was in the middle of Robert MacNamarra's Demilitarized Zone (DMZ) and was a prominent terrain feature about mid-way from the South China Sea coast and Laos.

I came by vehicle over what was a river of mud. Large crushed stone had been laid over the road to try to create a passable roadway. The stones sank quickly and had to be replaced. Inside the perimeter, there was an Amphibious Tractor (Am Trac) three quarters buried off the roadway. As time went along, the Am Trac sank and eventually disappeared beneath the sticky goo of Con Thien during the monsoon.

At Con Thien, there were tremendous living bunkers sunk into the ground by bulldozer and made of heavy timbers. We called them Dye Marker Bunkers. (Dye Marker was the code name for Defense Secretary McNamara's Strong Point Obstacle System (SPOS) which included establishment of combat bases along the DMZ, clearing of the Trace and construction of bunkers.) These were

CON THIEN

covered with massive mounds of dirt. Other fighting and living bunkers were located closer to the wire. Although, I must say that everything was located close to the wire at Con Thien. The position of the base left it subject to enemy tank fire, recoilless rifle fire, mortar fire and the relentless artillery fire. The NVA used 152 mm shells, as big as any we used. The biggest gun the US had in Vietnam was the 155 mm howitzer. When a barrage of 152's come in, you know you have been shelled. There is a boom, boom, boom way off in the distance, then, about four seconds, later a whistling zip and deafening crash. A 152 mm shell can explode through eight feet of dirt and break open a Dye Marker Bunker with sides of 2X6 lumber.

When I got to Con Thien, it was still monsoon season and the ground was very wet and mushy. Bunkers were ridiculously above ground. As time progressed and the earth dried out a ditch digging machine showed up and trenches were reestablished.

Later work produced bunkers with concealed fronts, low profiles and mud camo to hide the bags. Much safer.

Lt. Kirk

December 23 - The troops in Fox and Golf Company are positioned on the northern part of Con Thien and would probably take most of the incoming, which included 152 mm artillery rounds from North Vietnam. In September, another battalion averaged 342 rounds of incoming during a 9 day period.

House

December 24 - Christmas Eve at Con Thien

As I awoke, the sun was shining and the mud was pretty well packed down. Not as bad looking as I thought it would. But it is a kind of end of the road place. The bunkers we are in may sleep four easily, but we have five, so it is a bit crowded. The mud is everywhere. It is a fine red-clay type that turns to a powdery dust when dry (if ever), so it floats in the air too. Everything here is pretty much covered with it. It is called red laterite clay. Everyone and everything takes on a fine hue of red, our hands and faces, our weapons, and even our food.

We slept with rats running all around and a mildew/rot-damp basement stink inside the bunker on our first night. The air was stale. The fresh air outside was much better.

In the morning we ripped hell out of the place, pulled down the whole inside, dug the floor down another foot for some more headroom and got the wet mud out. We hauled out any garbage the rats might like, lined the inside walls with plastic sheeting and really squared the place away to make it more livable.

We went over to the artillery battery and carried back about 50 empty wooden shell boxes and built racks all the way around the inside walls for storage above our heads. It was wasted space otherwise, and we found it really worth the effort. We filled the rest of the crates with dirt and stacked them around the walls of the bunker to give us some added protection from shrapnel. There are a couple of 55 gallon barrels outside the entrance, and they have been shredded by incoming shrapnel. You should see the size of the chunks of steel, with razor-sharp ragged edges, that we pull out of the dirt filling these drums.

The weather has been warm and bright, with light rain at night, and sunny all day. After dark we put out listening posts from each platoon.

North and South Vietnam have negotiated a truce for Christmas that is to last from December 25 to December 30. NO SHOOTING! Yea, right.

December 25 - Christmas Day - Last night, just before the official 1600 (4pm) cease fire time, we took some sniper fire from the south tree line and responded with .50 caliber machine guns and a small artillery barrage. We are no longer a fighting force, we are simply TARGETS.

We have to wear our helmets and flak jackets to be outside our bunkers, and it is a $20.00 fine if we are caught without them. They do get heavy and I always get a headache wearing my helmet after a few hours, but it beats getting pierced by hot flying steel.

We filled 200 sandbags and put them all around and on top of our bunker today as an added layer of protection against a direct hit, as well as another layer of plastic sheeting to keep us dry. Maybe it will help keep the rats out as well. We also, built our own out-house close to our bunker from old ammo boxes so we do not have to go so far in the dark. And it shows real initiative to reuse valuable government equipment (like wooden ammo boxes) for new and exciting projects like outhouses, (but we still have to burn shitters). I carved the seat with my bayonet, and finished with my new pocket knife. I made sure it was real smooth, and it feels nice on the tush! NO SLIVERS. Some of the other positions just have two loose boards across the top edge of the oil drum, so ours is really DELUXE.

We started digging our trench lines between fighting positions and the bunkers, and have been digging like dogs ever since. Lots of earth moving and hand-tool engineering going on here. Where is the heavy equipment when you need it?

Tomorrow we start on a deep bunker - at least 8 feet underground. Real protection. We have some heavy fire power here with us. Our three squad bunkers have around them: a M-48 tank on one side, a 40mm anti-tank/anti-aircraft "Duster" on the other, a .50 caliber machine gun and a M-60 machine gun. Each bunker has a full case of grenades, 1,000 rounds of rifle ammo per man, cases of Claymore mines and M-79 LAAW's 66mm anti-tank rockets.

We are issued four C-ration packs per man, per day - lots of chow. We have extra food and choices now where we used to have little or none out in the bush. A whole case twelve C-rats is called a B-1A unit.

As I walked the perimeter, I noticed the support equipment we have on the Hill. It makes me feel a bit better, as I view the "Whole Team".

Complying with the order "Always wear your helmet" (even during bath time). Yes, Sir!

There are 2-105 mm Howitzer Gun batteries here - 12 guns total
  8 - quad .50 caliber machine guns on tracks
  2 - 81 mm mortar batteries
  2 - 4.2" mortar batteries
  8 - 60 mm mortar batteries
12 - M-48 tanks
12 - "Dusters"- 40mm anti-aircraft guns on tracks
12 - 106 mm recoilless rifle "ONTOS" tank- killers with 6 rifles each
20 - .50 caliber machine guns on tripods
60 - M-60 machine guns

This is just my count from a quick walk around the south side of the hill. We have 22 artillery batteries within range if and when we need them.

The Hill has already been surrounded by a minefield placed by our engineers with 146,000 land mines, plus eight strands of barb-wire barriers, including the new "German Razor – Wire-Tape. It is a fortress!

Our purpose here is to hold this piece of real estate no matter what they throw at us. We will have to take a pounding like sitting ducks, but we are also capable of giving it right back with counter-fire measures and heavy artillery as back-up, but we have heard the NVA have their real heavy guns back inside caves in the hills of Laos, and we are not allowed to shoot across the border. What's with that?

We all keep asking ourselves why would any military force want to lock into a fixed position as targets for enemy artillery instead of taking the offensive and attacking and destroying the guns right across the DMZ and the Laotian border that are killing us every day? This is sheer madness. We are not allowed to attack because of politics decided in Washington DC by President Lyndon B Johnson and Secretary of Defense Robert McNamara, not the generals here that can see how insane this is. This is war, and Marines should attack, not defend. The gooks will sure have a hard time trying to get through to us with all this, but I remember stories from my Uncle Ron about his fighting the Chinese and Koreans at the Chosen Reservoir and how they overpowered the Marine defenses with human waves. If the NVA wants it bad enough, they will get Chinese tanks and planes and artillery and APC's (armored personnel carriers) and fight a real hardware war for this hill!

Our Christmas Spirit is GREAT! We are all inside our cozy bunker now listening to Christmas carols and writing letters. A Christmas and New Years truce had been negotiated - how civilized. No firing, so we should get some good sleep.

A CBS News crew was here all day, and just took off. One of them was John Lawrence from the TV evening news and his cameraman, Keith Kay. They were OK, didn't ask anything too stupid. I did not talk to them and neither did anyone in our squad. We didn't see the point.

Our new captain is a hoot. He just gave us the password for the night: "pig-leg." The reply is "canned-dandruff." How do you remember that and not get shot? Both Captain Quinlan and Lieutenant Colonel Parker are walking all around the outpost together through the area greeting each of the troops by name and wishing us a Merry Christmas.

We all washed and shaved and had C-rats for breakfast. Seems like we have been eating forever. We added another layer of sand bags to the top of our fighting bunker and then a work party took away most of my squad for a large chopper re-supply - 1,000 cases of C-rats and big stainless containers full of hot chow for Christmas dinner.

Dinner was roast beef, mashed potatos, thick gravy, peaches, pears, candy, cold milk and ice-cream, the whole works. It was wonderful. We all sat and talked about Christmas at home and our families and it felt so warm and normal. We all got lots of mail too - that was great.

Chris
December 25 - The U.S. Army, with its large inventory of helicopters, brought in a **hot meal** to their troops in the field every day we are told. The U.S. Marine Corps re-supply was only able to bring C-rations into the field for us every 4-5 days, if we were lucky. That was only with enough food for 2-3 days. We ate 1.5 meals per day when in the bush. I can't figure out why the discrepancy.

The U.S. Marine Corps surprised everyone on Christmas Day by bringing in a hot meal. The morale was was so high, it was incredible. We had never considered the idea of a hot meal at Con Thien. It wasn't expected, but truly appreciated. We had a full helping of food, today. It was truly a feast.

House
December 25 - I went outside and thanked God and his Angels for taking such good care of me and that they might continue to get me home safely to my wife, son and loving family. Happy Birthday, Jesus!

The war starts again in 40 minutes, I looked at my watch and the "Truce" is over at 1800 hours. Weird huh? I hope it stays as quiet as the past three days have been. Chaplains services were pretty brief, no more than 20 men allowed to gather together as a rule. And, no helmets off.

U.S. Army General Westmoreland flew up to the outpost in his shiny new Huey helicopter to greet all the U.S. Army guys here too; I snapped a picture of his chopper, but could not get one of him - Darn.

As soon as the truce ended, our entire 105 battery and the Dusters twin 40 millimeter guns cut loose. We did not get back a single incoming round. It is 2000 hours and the lines are popping illumination and red and green pop-up

Echo 2/1 67-68 - Christmas 1967

flares in celebration and shouting "Merry Christmas" and guys are slapping each other on the back. The whole sky is lit up around the outpost. A quarter mile over at Yankee Station it is the same thing. Beautiful.

We are really having our own great celebration. The lieutenant just came in to share his own bottle of booze with us and wish us all Merry Christmas and asked that we do not shoot any more pop-ups, because the captain was mad we were wasting them. Screw the captain. - Drink. Cheers, Lt Graffam. (It is his bottle after all.)

On my watch "Puff", the Air Force AC-47 gunship worked a hill about 4,000 meters to the west, ending with a big air-strike of napalm. The lieutenant reported to us in the morning that a 4th Marines patrol found 67 VC and NVA bodies out there. WOW!

Chris
December 25 – One of the most incredible sites we will ever see occurred again tonight. "Puff" the Magic Dragon is a C-47 cargo aircraft with 200,000 candle power flares to light up the night and three mini-guns each able to spit out 6,000

rounds per minute. Every fourth round a red tracer so it looks like a stream of fire is emanating from the aircraft. It has its own weird sound, like nothing I have ever heard. It is so devastating to the enemy and so up-lifting to us. The firepower is incredible. We watch the aircraft absolutely destroying an area in the distance. We cheer. The incredible show is overwhelming. For a brief moment we are winning. For a brief moment we aren't scared.

Lt. Kirk

Dec 25 - First platoon was detached from Echo Company and we were attached to Hotel Company, which was responsible for an outpost called Yankee Station, 600 yards south of the hill at Con Thien. The most notable landmark was a wrecked helicopter just off the MSR (Main Supply Route). The Echo company commander told me I had the best platoon and he was confident I would do him proud and that the other platoons needed close supervision.

Guys from Echo - 1st Platoon

Yankee station was on low ground and not as well defended as Con Thien itself in terms of bunkers and trench lines and wire and obstacles. On the other hand, most of the artillery rounds were directed at the hill.

Lt. Suydam
December 25 - We are spending the Christmas of 1967 at Con Thien. A truck convoy bought us hot food. It was a glorious hiatus from the tedium of C-rations. We expect to be here for the Vietnamese holiday of Tet (Vietnamese New Year), in January. Weeks before this our battalion CO was asking for a "gung-ho" lieutenant to lead some volunteers into North Vietnam and "snatch" an enemy soldier and bring him back alive. I politely said, "No" when I was asked. This group of six was practicing their craft out east of Con Thien when a superior enemy force pinned them down. What they observed was thousands of NVA regulars, trucks and tanks streaming by and heading south. Meanwhile back at Con Thien, we were amazed to hear hundreds of artillery pieces firing. This time the shells did not land on us, but cut through the air over our heads for southern targets.

Cpl Chuck Estes

Estes
December 26 - We call the barrier between Gio Linh and Con Thien "the Trace". It is the cleared area facing the DMZ. The Army unit was called "Charlie Sound". We run patrols with them, checking out cut wires leading to their listening devices that are imbedded along the DMZ. These were the guys at Christmas that sent up all the pop-ups and pissed off the battalion commander. They'll probably do it again on New Years Eve.

Yankee Station is outside the wire at Con Thien, just to the left of our bunkers. Coming down the road from C-2, it is on the left hand side of the road where it makes a 90 degree turn into Con Thien. It was a company size plus position. Hotel is stationed there plus our 3rd platoon. We had to be careful about shooting to our left because we would have fired into their positions. The Washout is down the road just before we get to C-2. There is a bridge there, where we took the only bath I had at Con Thien. We ran a mine sweep down the road with two tanks, took a bath before we returned to Con Thien. It was a real treat to get clean.

Chris
December 26 - Rats are everywhere at night. You hear them as soon as you blow out your candle and start to sleep. We've got to clean this place out tomorrow and figure out how to get rid of those damn rats. I'm so tired, not even the rats will keep me awake. Last night I had one rat jump on my chest. It absolutely scared the crap out of me. I hate rats. The guys that were here before us were a bunch of pigs. There's food crumbs and paper all around, not too sanitary.

Bernie
December 26 – There were many holiday highlights for the Leathernecks of the 2nd Battalion, 1st Marine Regiment as they manned the northern Marine outpost at Con Thien. There were visits by commanding officers and commanding generals. There was a welcomed hot meal for Christmas (the only hot one in 77 days) and there was the always-appreciated mail call.

One of the bigger events dealt with the enemy. It was the discovery of a large North Vietnamese flag flying in the middle of the demilitarized zone in front of the Marines perimeter. The flag, red with a pale-colored star in the middle was first spotted by a U.S. forward observer. It seemed to appear around 1400 hours, four hours prior to the end of the ceasefire and was taken down at 1800 hours. It fluttered in the breeze atop a rather crude support.

House
December 26 - I had a good nights sleep, but I'm still tired. We continue digging our trench lines between positions and filling 200 sand bags per day per man. We are almost finished reinforcing and putting raised edges around the bunker roof. One side is real strong. We even added a bench on top. It is looking pretty decent, for a bunker. Listening posts went out at 1700 and came back in at 0600 hours.

Lt. Kirk
December 27 - When we first arrived, we used C4 to knock down trees and break up rocks so we could dig bunkers. The engineers arrived with a trench digging machine and a small bulldozer and that helped a lot. I slept in a bunker

with my platoon sergeant and radioman. We had Marston matting (steel airport runway matting) on the roof, covered with sandbags. Inside we put Marston matting on top of sandbags for beds. We then put our air mattresses on top of the matting. We covered up with our poncho liners. The floor, of course, was dirt. We burned candles at night for light. It also produced a bit of heat.

Chris

December 28 - Field jackets were issued before we moved north to the DMZ. Still we wrapped up in our ponchos. Temperatures dipped into the low 30's. Sometimes we were issued socks but sometimes we had no socks. Some had underwear but most of us didn't bother. We wore either a t-shirt or a standard dark green fatigue shirt with pockets.

House

December 28 - 0500 hours - Just off watch. Filled 300 sandbags today and put a new roof on Cpl. Teebo's bunker by hauling steel "mars matting" up from the LZ to use for the new bigger bunkers we are going to build. The mars matting is corrugated metal used on landing fields for aircraft and helo pads - very tough stuff.

The Company got six new guys in (none for my squad), plus a new Staff Sergeant Page as our new platoon sergeant. He is right off the drill field at MCRD San Diego (volunteered or screw up?) He is a real loser- numbskull-lifer pain-in-the-ass. We immediately do not like him at all! Day one, S/Sgt. Page mouths off about our squad taking a break. I tell him they really need it, and he backs off. Speck picks up a sand bag and starts tossing it around with the guys like a big medicine ball, trying to knock each other down. We all turn our backs to S/Sgt. Page and continue with the grab-ass to spite him. S/Sgt. Page stomps off, pissed because we are ignoring him. He won't last long with us.

We made a trip back down the road to "Yankee Station to check out their set-up. Our 3rd platoon is there, and they have all new bunkers, dug deep by bulldozers, and a machine that automatically fills sandbags and wires them closed and spits them out by the hundreds. All their barriers are the new German razor tape wire - wicked stuff!

This morning our squad will go down the Main Supply Route (MSR) with the mine-sweeping team and two tanks for security. Sometimes we get to take a bath when we reach the big stream at the bottom of the hill to turn around at 3,000 meters – it takes about three hours total, an everyday event. The captain

Cpl. House with his normal smile of confidence on the left. Cpl. Estes, next to his table, with peanuts from home, a candle for reading and rifle always ready.

tries to get all squads to rotate turns. We call it "the washout", because it does wash out when it floods, which is often. The engineers built a steel bridge over it, and I wonder why the NVA artillery has not taken it out. The weather has been beautiful, such a relief from the rain.

Rats! Big ugly rats in the bunker! Supply got us a big rat trap and we put it on the deck last night. This morning it is gone! We should have wired it down. They get in-between the plastic sheeting we have hung on the dirt walls. The guys try to catch them in there, but we cannot afford to puncture the plastic because the rain will get through. It is especially tempting to bayonet them while they are in the plastic right above you in the ceiling layer, but you can't because it would leak on you all night! We have got to control our C-rats that get dropped on the floor or left outside and wire-down the traps and kill these commy rats! I am afraid they may carry us off at night if we don't give them some offerings. I know- we will build a small rat temple outside and make offerings with ham and limas beans as a rat tribute.

Chris
December 29 - I got lots of packages and mail from friends and folks at home for Christmas - Harris', Lovelace, Grace, Bel & Hal, Williams, Schneider's, my folks and others. It means so much to receive mail from our friends at home. It's quite the morale booster. Having extra food is a big break, also. It's nice to have

something special in your pack when food supply doesn't come.

Since we came up north we have orders to wear our 6½ pound flak jackets and 5 pound helmets. Down south, we could go without either of the encumbrances. It made for easier and quieter walking, especially at night. Now, it was helmets and flak jackets every time you were out of your bunker. Many wore them religiously, even when in bunkers.

House
December 29 – It started to rain at 2000 hours last night, continued steadily all day. We were sweating one day and now we are wet and shivering cold again.

We went down the road again today to Artillery Hill with the mine-sweep team and two army tanks and got our bath in the stream. All trench work had pretty much stopped with this heavy rain. We get a lot of sleep. I stand watch on a .50 cal. machine gun inside a nice cover next to our hooch.

We now have field jackets with hoods, new rain gear, gloves and helmets liners, which help a lot, but we still get cold. The mud just keeps getting worse. Every time a vehicle goes over the mud or you even step on it, it gets deeper and stickier. The road along the back of the bunkers around the perimeter is the worst.. It's highly traveled by everyone. The tracked vehicles just churn it deeper on every pass. It is so deep in places it will pull you down. You can sink to your knees, like quicksand. We have to mark it off and throw wooden pallets on it to keep guys from getting trapped, especially at night. The sky is nasty looking. Black, angry, clouds that crash thunder and lightning that cracks and slashes at you like a storm from hell!

Our bunker has developed a leak. Fortunately, it is right by the door where is does not affect anybody when they are in their sleep/sitting positions. The rats are getting bolder every day. They like to come in to get warm and check out what we might have dropped on the floor or left out to munch on later, and they will take it. We try to throw our bayonets at them, but they are sly and quick.

We have had to dig a small garbage hole (that keeps getting bigger) and it is too much of an attractant to them. The officers are going to have a dozer or tank with a blade dig us a big hole farther away with steep sides, so when they fall in they can't get back out! (I mean the rats, not the officers, although some of the officers deserve it).

257

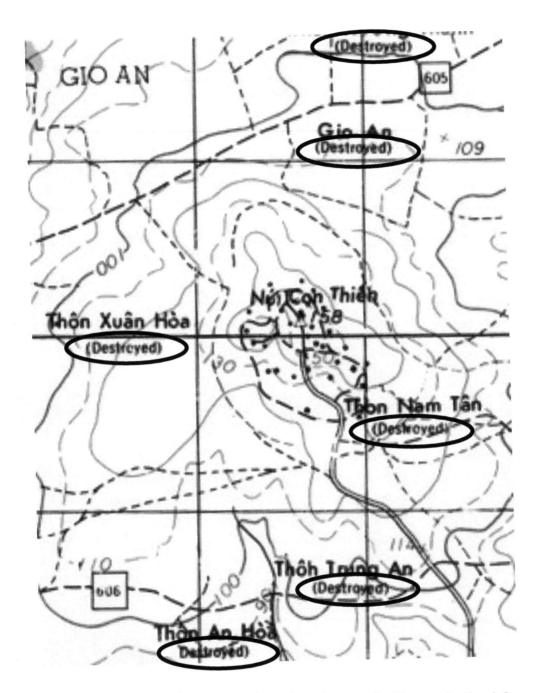

Note: Map above shows previous locations of villages in the I Corps area, which since have been destroyed. When we arrived there were 3,500 villages, when we left, there were 11.

Chris

December 29 – The weather is improving. I'm getting a little more sun, so the ground is getting less difficult to walk on. My radar unit broke so now I just stand lines, off and on, with one other guy. We sleep 'til noon and then work all night. I understand I'm going back on the lines with House, Estes and the squad. It'll be good to be back with the guys. It feels strange to be somewhat close to where my squad is located, but not to be actually with them. During the Xmas truce period, everyone worked hard building-up the existing bunkers and building new ones, strengthening the fighting positions. We are expecting to be hit quite hard as soon as the truce ends.

December 30 - Con Thien does not experience much of a truce. The harassing fire, with artillery and mortars, continues. It is difficult to patrol at night, as the weather is lousy. The winter monsoon season is a time of maximum misery and danger. Pneumonia, jungle rot, cold and ambushes are commonplace. We know the enemy's arms, troops and equipment continue to flow over the DMZ, especially coming over from the northwest along the Ho Chi Minh Trail. It is a main ingress to South Vietnam for NVA troops and supplies. The enemy stockpiles supplies north of the border, waits for weather breaks and, then, whether it's on bicycles, trucks or walking, the flow begins again. We are able to view part of one of their trails from our bunker position.

Lt. Kirk

December 30 - I found that the doctrine we had been trained in at Quantico about formations just wouldn't work in thick terrain. The only way you could move in dense terrain was in column, with a fire team out on each side for flank security.

Chris

December 31 - We receive in-coming artillery and mortar rounds every night. We seek out the deepest and nearest hole or bunker to dive into. Not much chatter from the guys until the shelling really starts, then a little talk, a little swearing. The anticipation of getting the next round in your hole keeps all of us on edge – no matter who you are. There is nothing we can do…just wait until it's over and get out of our hole…casualties so far are light and morale is high. We should be moving to Camp Evans near Phu Bai around January 20th, which is great, as any place is going to be better than here. We are so isolated, we have no hot chow. We always have to stay close to a hole or bunker - something to dive into when the artillery starts hitting, like it does every damn day.

After the shelling stops, we always get out of our bunkers and take a quick look

SGT Steve (Bernie) Berntson (left) -1stMarDiv ISO combat correspondent CPL John (Mac) McDonell (right) – from East Patterson, NJ – radioman 2nd Platoon Echo 2/1 – Con Thien on the DMZ – Christmas 1967

around at the destruction around us. We walk to the fighting holes/bunkers that are close to us and talk with everyone to insure ourselves that our guys are okay. The feeling we have knowing our friends are well and alive is enormous. A weak smile might be present for a short time. We now had a job to do. Bunkers had to be rebuilt, fighting holes inspected and trenches viewed. We needed to make sure everything was accounted for, repaired and ready for the next attack - whether they were going to come at us by ground through the perimeter wire or through the air with the mortars and artillery.

We had actually made it through another attack. By the grace of God, we were alive.

Total U.S. military personnel in Vietnam reaches 485,600. So far in the war, 16,021 U.S. troops have been killed. 3461 Marines have been killed with 25,525 wounded.

The December Command Chronology for 2nd Battalion, 1st Marines records the battalion's move from south of Quang Tri to Con Thien on December 22-23. The 90th NVA regiment operates in the area. Enemy artillery and mortar attacks dropped off considerably from the previous weeks, in part due to the holiday truce period. 19 enemy are confirmed KIA, with 18 probables and 1 captured. 2nd Battalion, 1st Marines casualties for December: 3 enlisted KIA, 26 enlisted WIA.

The new year starts with a cease-fire. Even though we held true to the cease-fire, the enemy did not. We cleaned our rifles, our bunkers and our gear during this time. The NVA used this time to move men and supplies into more strategic positions.

The cease-fire was cancelled as probing action was initiated by an enemy squad close to the base, with sniping incidents and small sized ambushes along the MSR (Main Supply Route) leading out of Con Thien. The enemy's offensive intentions and a marked build-up of enemy troops in the near area put the base on alert. Aerial electronic and infra-red detection devices disclosed considerable enemy movement within a few hundred meters of the perimeter of the base.

Target acquisition for this time period was largely the role of the three observation posts located on the three dominant terrain features at Con Thien. Several cuts in the defensive wire were found on the northern side of the perimeter and considerable enemy activity was detected in the U.S. minefield near the wire breaches at Con Thien.

House

January 1 - Happy New Year! - We are all working on the bunkers, more reinforcements, more sandbags, and more digging. I am standing my watch about an hour after sun-down and we have an army tank with a big Xenon-Light dug-in deep next to us with only his turret exposed to the south above the berm. These guys can button-up and be nice and warm inside and the corporal tank commander invites me inside for a look. It is cozy and warm with a radio, refer, and TV set!

We get a round of incoming 57mm recoilless rifle from the tree line about 1500 meters to the south. It is way out there and it hits the top of the hill! Only one round. We all stay quiet, must be H&I fire only? Waitfor orders.

The Command Post asks the tank commander if he can see the VC recoilless rifle. Says he could try if he could have permission to fire-up the big Xenon light.

This will make us a big target with the tank sitting right next to our bunker. I'm thinking this may not be too good for us.

The CP grants permission! I duck into the trench line and get ready for the tank to catch a round of incoming in the turret. But this solid white-hot-ray-beam of light 3 feet x 3 feet suddenly shoots out of the front of the tank along with a flaming stream of .50 cal. bullets and a 90mm HE round directly where the incoming round came from, plus it shreds about 100 meters both sides of it. The burst of gunfire blew the tree line back 10 feet. The whole area lit up like the sun with white-hot light so solid you could almost walk on it. When it snapped-off it still glowed a bit but the crew had a cover for it right away and we were dark again. It ruined our night vision for ten minutes.

Ten minutes later and 100 meters to the west, Boom! Here comes another 57mm round. The VC were shootin' and scootin'. Trying to get a hit, they would run and setup again. Their 57 recoilless is a lot smaller than our 106mm rifles

and easy for a 3-4 man crew to set-up and move fast. After 3-4 times of this, the CP gave orders for all heavy guns on the south side of the hill to open on the tree line on the next incoming round. Wow, what return fire it was! Every gun locked and loaded, ready to train and fire as soon as they saw the blast. It was a sight to see the outgoing so flat and fierce. About midnight, everything is real quiet. Soft air, mild breeze, no rain.

We hear noises out in the minefield and wire barriers to the south, where the recoilless rifle rounds came from. Our M-79 40mm grenade launchers each fire about 3-4 rounds which go out about 200 meters. All goes quiet, and we hear nothing. Are there enemy trying to crawl through the minefield and probing? Suddenly, the tank's Xenon is snapped back on and there is a body up on the wire about 100 meters out, caught on the wire, standing struggling. Sappers! About 4 or 5 machine guns open up and the tank fires a 90mm HE (high-explosive) round. It blows a huge hole right where the guy is standing, and that sets off three mines in the dirt from the concussion. It goes quiet. No more enemy sapper.

In the morning, big binoculars confirm it was not a VC, or even a human. It was a kind of monkey or small gorilla called a rock ape who probably smelled our garbage dump and was just trying to visit to get some chow. Pieces of its body were hanging out on that wire for a week.

2nd Platoon, 2nd Squad - Estes & Lenny sitting down on left, Speck standing, Lt. Jerry Graffam sitting on bunker reading a letter, Dodd standing in the middle, Teebo &

January 2 - About 1900 hours, about dusk, I am outside watching the tanks move into position for the night, and trying to get some alone time. The squad is all inside our big bunker listening to the Armed Forces Radio Station Hit Tunes Special from 1967.

The area around the opening to our bunker is slippery with that damn red mud, so thick from the rain, and everyone complains about tracking it around from the hole that has developed there. I decide I can fix things, if I can find a couple of those heavy steel pallets the choppers bring ammo in on their slings at the supply drop down by the south gate. I hike myself down and by golly, there is a nice pile of them, but they are bloody heavy. Must be about 100 pounds. But hey, I figure we can sure use a few of these to ease walking on a nice clean surface. I throw one up onto my shoulder and start back to the bunker, maybe 100 yards away. The ground is treacherous with ridges of hard and soft mud

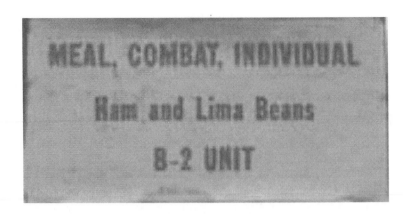

A supplement pack, shown below, was included with each meal - salt, creamer, coffee, sugar, TP, gum, matches, cigs and a spoon. Those that didn't smoke would trade for better meals.

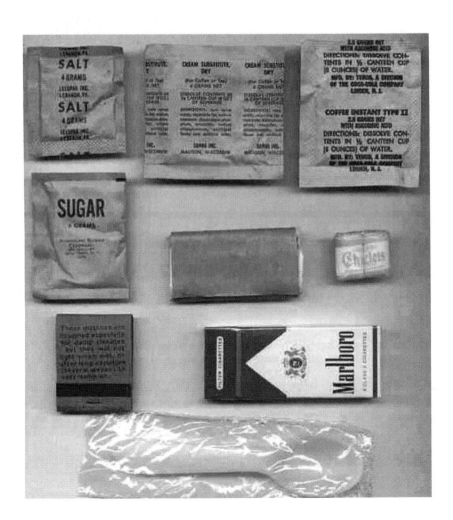

from the big tracks of the tanks, dozers and amtracs (amphibious personnel tractor). It is really hard to find sure footing and the extra weight on one side throws off my balance even more. I get about 20 yards away from home and make a mis-step into a deep mud hole, lose my footing and twist around, stabbing my loose foot into the thick muck past my boot tops. The pallet weight is now off balance and it pushes me sideways. With my ankles locked in the mud, my legs buckled and twisted under me as I continued to fall. As I go over to my right, I hear my ankle and knee POP! YEOW! Then I feel a sharp pain as my other ankle pulls against my stuck boot and snaps with a loud crack. I fall hard on my back and right side, struck my head and the pallet crashes down on top of me. It is too heavy to throw off and I am stuck to the ground, unable to push it away as my wrist is pinned under its full weight.

My legs, knees and ankles seared in pain and I was afraid I had been badly hurt, but when I looked and felt there were no holes and no blood!. Talk about luck. I was still whole and no leaks. The sharp edges of the pallet didn't get me, but I could not see my lower legs below the mud, and I could not pull free, no matter how hard I tried.

A corpsman and a bunch of the guys tried to pull me free, but my boots were stuck in the sticky mud, and I screamed in pain as it stretched my ankles. They had to dig my legs out with their bare hands and helmets. They carried me on a stretcher so carefully, but my leg kept cramping up and my knee would pop. Just as we were almost to the aid station, one guy at the head of my stretcher stepped into one of the deep mud holes and he sank past his knees. But he still held me up level with his free hand. It took three more guys to help me and two more to get him out of the mud. Poor guy.

Once we were inside the aid station bunker, the corpsman cut my boots off and slit my trousers past my knees. When he cut my socks off, I could see both my ankles had already swollen to about twice normal and were really throbbing. My legs became very stiff and ached so deeply from the muscles being pulled so far. I just knew my ankles were broken, and probably my leg as well. How damn stupid and clumsy could I be. I felt so embarrassed and like such a burden to others who should be taking care of the wounded.

Chris

January 2 - Mike House is WIA (so to speak), so we lose another one. House was a great squad leader, always looking out for his guys. He and I became good friends. He is going back to school when he gets out of the corps. He has

265

lots to do. He is very smart and always has a great attitude. He was just as miserable as the rest of us, but knew he had to continue to lead. He'll probably head to 1st Marine Division headquarters for reassignment as an engineer/map maker. He will be working with the general's staff in preparing mapping intel after his rehab. I really hated to see him leave.

Estes
January 2 – I took over as the squad leader on this day. The second squad has changed quite a bit in the past months. Chris is second in command, followed by Dodd, Speck, Hendricks, Anselment, Herfel, Oncale, Mullineaux, Falcon, Bitsuie and Ridinger. Lt. Jerry Graffam is our platoon commander.

There is a black guy who hasn't been with us very long and who always falls asleep on watch. Now that I am squad leader, I am almost ready to turn him in for sleeping on watch. He's gonna get someone killed, maybe all of us.

Chris
January 2 - Rations or C-rats were really the basic minimum, not only in flavor, selection, but probably nutrition, also. There were 12 meals in a case: ham and lima beans (or ham and mothers), meatballs and beans, spaghetti and meatballs, boned chicken, chicken and noodles,ham and eggs, maybe crackers, cheese spread, fruitcake, peaches, cocoa, coffee, etc. Each meal was canned and sitting on the shelves for who knows how long before we got 'em - 1200 calories per meal, normally 1.4 meals a day in the field. I will never understand why we didn't have more food. We got so hungry. Guys were always trading meals, but if you got the ham and mothers, you owned 'em - there was no one to trade with.

House
January 2 - They kept me doped-up with morphine in the battalion aid station overnight, taped me up nice and tight and then medevaced me out by copter the next morning. I gave away all my goodies to the squad and waved good-bye to them as they were pulling out in a 6X6 truck for a patrol. I did not know it, but that was the last time I would see them. I snapped a picture with my 35mm camera and bundled up for the long cold ride to Dong Ha.

When they got me into triage at Delta Med the x-rays showed a hairline fracture in the ankle only; no breaks. They shot me up with morphine, wrapped me up tight with ace bandages on both ankles and knees and put me to bed with warm blankets and soft pillows to sleep the day away in clean pajamas. My whole body felt like I had been beaten with a club.

I almost felt guilty because I was surrounded by wounded Marines, all bandaged and bloody. One guy had a severe case of malaria and was sweating gallons, as the corpsmen and nurses were pumping fluids right
back into him. He was shivering so hard, and the sweat was rolling off his body, literally dripping off the table.   I was cold and needed another blanket.   The corpsmen and nurses were so good and kind and caring.

The triage area looked like absolute chaos.   The wounded are brought in from the choppers and the doctors and nurses are covered with blood, going over each litter to see who gets priority. They are quickly stripped naked, slung up on a black plastic table, flipped over and over, IV's are pushed in and surgery starts in seconds.

The floor is covered 2-3 inches deep around and under the tables with clothing, boots, battle dressings, paper covers, packaging, sheets, needles, tubing and IV bags. Blood is all over the floor, and the doctors, corpsman, orderlies, and young nurses slip and slide in it as they work on each man. An orderly would throw a bucket of water on the floor and push the pile of stuff out of their way with a push-broom as fast as he could between each table as they were unloaded for the next man. It was both fascinating and frightening to see, but I could not watch for long. I was embarrassed to be hurt so little.

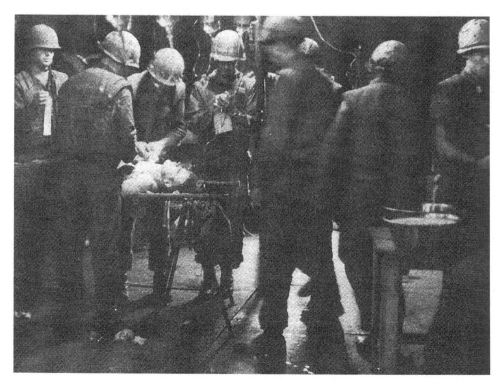

I don't know how long I will have to stay here. It's sure cold and lonely. It's been 18 days since I spoke with Lt. Col. Van Winkle. I wonder if this will make it easier or harder for Lt. Col. Parker to release me now.

It is still freezing cold at night in the hospital tent, and I can't walk on my ankle, yet. I only get one crutch to stay by my cot. I wish I had my rain gear and my M-16 is locked up in the armory, I feel naked without it.

January 3 - I opened a letter I have been carrying from Cpl. Archie Haas, from our old unit 1/27 in Hawaii. He was wounded with 2nd battalion, 4th Marines and sent home. His letter says Jim Smith was killed and Rozzi was badly wounded in September at Con Thien. Damn! Too many good guys we served with have been killed or hurt.

Chris

January 3 – The nights are cold. I spent all day trying to patch up holes in my bunker. I now live up on top of a knoll with three other guys, Jim, the other radar guy, and two snipers. One of my men spotted a red flashing light, off in the   -

distance, must have been some kind of signaling device, last night. The lieutenant said to drop some mortars out there, so I called in a mortar attack. It was exciting. I don't have any idea if I did any damage, but I'm sure I scared the hell out of anyone in the vicinity.

The mud up here is unbelievable. In some places it is three feet deep. In most places it's only about 6-12 inches, because the sun has allowed it to dry and harden. I just got a *Playboy* magazine from Geoff Grabenhorst, for a Christmas present. He is going through Navy Seal Team school now. It sure means a lot to get mail from my friends at home, especially from such a good friend like Geoff.

We are one of the main observation points on the lines (perimeter). The mud is bad. In some places, it's a mess, but the sun does dry it up sometimes. Then, again, comes the rain and mud.. Hopefully, it will get warmer. I've been in Quang Tri and Dong Ha, lately. There isn't a good place over here. If you're a front line combat Marine, it's all bad. The camaraderie is the glue. The guy next you is your brother. He looks out for you every day and night. You know that and it allows you to get your 3-4 hours of sleep every night and it gives you strength when you feel low and the odds are stacked against you. Each man depends on the Marine next to him today, tomorrow and the day after that. Being a Marine is tough and it was tough in boot camp – now I know why. Semper Fi (Always

Bringing out our dead from Con Thien. This was especially hard to look at as some of them could have been your buddies and you always wondered if you would be next. During the heavy rains the mud was so deep an amtrack or tank was the only way to reach the wounded or dead all around the hill.

Faithful). Time to hit the rack. It's been lonely lately and I"m probably feeling a bit low. Better tomorrow.

I hadn't thought about it, but just realized Doc Turner had not come up to Con Thien with us. We have been so busy trying to get our fighting positions and living areas set up, I had forgotten about Doc. It was at this point that I really knew how much we were going to miss him. He not only did his job of patching us up, he forced the captain to let us wash the Agent Orange off our bodies when we were out in the field, he hounded us about taking our malaria pills, taking care of our feet and the list goes on and on. He was always so concerned about our welfare. Doc was on his way to R & R (Rest and Relaxation) when our trip to this hill started and he had earned the time off. I don't how we let two corpsmen leave the company at the same time, but Doc Slater, also left on R & R.

House
January 4 - I get my orders to report to 1st Marine Division Headquarters, Da Nang G-3! This is the Big Time. I am in the walking-wounded ward tent, 0800 hours, in walks a clerk and says, "Cpl. House? You are directed to have all your gear turned in and be ready to go to division G-3 by tomorrow afternoon. Transport is being arranged for you."   Just like that he hands me my signed orders from Lt. Col. Parker.   YEA!!!   I knelt down and thanked God for his blessing. I have 157 days left in my enlistment in the Corps. I am so glad I did not sign that extension for the Gunny now, but it may be waiting for me at G-3.

Got paid $176, kept $10, sent rest home to Nancy. Miss her so much.

My legs are getting so stiff and my knees are really locked up. The ankle throbs deep all day and night, and I have no more meds from the corpsman, so I am on my own now. Bad headaches now, but I got lots of aspirin from a cute nurse-aid gal. Popping them like candy to keep the pain down and so I can function.

Chris
January 4 - I discovered a tracked vehicle with my radar system last night. I called the captain, according to procedure, and gave my report, with grid coordinates, placing the movement directly south of our Echo Company position. He called me back, still questioning me, as there haven't been any tracked vehicles reported in our area, ever. Then, after a few minutes, the colonel calls and questions my finding and my ability, when I say, "Look, you sent me to school and this is what I have on radar". I was very much matter of fact in what I had discovered and wasn't going to back down, which is probably what he was expecting. He settled down. He said he would send some troops out there in the morning and try to see if there were any signs of track vehicles.

I think we only have 20 days left on the Hill. It can't come too soon.

Lt. Suydam
January 4 – C-Rations came packaged in boxes of twelve Meals, Individual Rations. Now, a reasonable person with a command of the language would

simply say twelve individual meals.   But, military language will not conform to reason.

I don't remember the combinations now, but each meal had a number, like B-2. Eventually, you'd learn which meals you could tolerate and which you'd rather do without.   Don't get me wrong, the food packed in C-Ration cans was not bad tasting food, it's just that if you have only twelve choices for your food for 13 months, you grow tired of the selection.

I survived C-Rations by having my family mail me ketchup. You can eat anything with enough ketchup. I used to make a casserole using one of the large cans. I cut a layer of bread, which came in its own can, spoon in some ham and eggs, a squeeze of ketchup and then repeat the process filling the can. The casserole cooks in 5-8 seconds with a golf-ball size portion of C-4 plastic explosive (This was a common way to heat food). Don't worry, it can't explode without a blasting cap but it burns with such sputtering intensity you'll think the can will melt.

One of the meals comes with a small tin of peanut butter. If you squirt mosquito repellant on its surface to light it, the peanut butter will burn making a nice flambeau.   I never had to use it, but could have, to mark landing zones in the dark.

Packed in every case of C-rats were several P-38's, which were used for opening the cans.   That's what we called them, although I've heard many other nicknames for these small folding can openers.

So now let me tell you about LRP (Long Range Patrol) rations, referred to as lurp rations.   Unlike C-Rations, which is food packed in cans, ham and Lima beans, cheese and crackers, chocolate, etc., LRP rations are a modern field food of the type that you would find in a hiking store. It is dehydrated stuff in a plastic pouch. You just add water, stir and "poof" your chicken tetrazzini comes to life.   LRP rations were the food to die for and we had none.   On the other hand, Army troops were well supplied with all kinds of nice foodstuffs and equipment. They had so much and we had so little. It only made since that when we came into contact with Army troops that we should enrich ourselves from the largess of the U.S. taxpayer. And, there were many a dark night when Marines performed the midnight requisition while the Army slept.

Chris
January 5 - I just received a report from Lt. Graffam. He told me the colonel had

done as he told me and sent troops out to the site where I reported a track vehicle. Yep! They found just what I told them. Did the colonel call me and say "good job" Marine! Not a word. That's okay. I got satisfaction knowing I had accomplished what I was sent to do.

NVA gunners mortared Con Thien in groups of three to five round bursts between 0945 and 1015 hours. A total of 37 rounds, including five 120mm shells, fell on our positions, with a direct hit on the battalion command post. This resulted in one Marine KIA, and eight WIA, including Lt. Col. Parker, the battalion commander.

Estes

January 5 - Falcon rejoined us after getting wounded on his first patrol back in Quang Tri. It's great to get him back. He's a real nice young, quiet, white kid... 1st Class and a damn good Marine. Falcon is the only guy that will sleep with the one guy in our squad that falls asleep on watch. No one else will trust the guy. Falcon somehow makes it work.

Note: Doc Turner - Agent Orange is a herbicide containing dioxin which was sprayed from airplanes as a defoliant to clear extensive areas of jungle to prevent the enemy from concealing his operations. The drums containing this chemical were marked with orange bands, thus the name. It contains a 50/50 combination of two artificial plant hormones and an acutely toxic and potent carcinogen.

Lt. Suydam

January 5 - We were on a Company size patrol to the west of Con Thien. Suddenly, a CH-46 helicopter landed in our midst. I looked into the back to see that the cargo area was full of beer cases. I went to the front and took the telephone hand set by the co-pilot's seat. He said, "Where is Con Thien?" I held up my map to the glass, showed him our position and the location of Con Thien, then I pointed real big in that direction so he and the pilot could get the idea.

Lt. Kirk

January 5 - We figured if a serious ground attack were launched, it would come against Yankee Station first. It was on lower ground and protected the southern side of Con Thien. It was itself on lower ground than the northern side, which contained the LZ. We were probed a lot at Yankee Station, but only had one memorable ground attack. We had a furious exchange of fire that lasted a long time. As with other firefights, the noise was stunning. I went back and forth, in and out of the trench line, encouraging my troops and bringing extra ammo. I had only one casualty, who was shot in the arm as he was running beside me carrying ammo. He was very cheerful at first, as he had received a million dollar wound and a ticket home, but the pain increased as the minutes passed and pretty soon he was screaming in agony.

House 1st Marine Division, G-3, Da Nang

January 6 - I caught a flight from Dong-Ha and a Navy captain in a jeep spotted me with my cane and bandaged ankle and gave me a ride all the way from the Air Base to headquarters. He kept asking about what it was like at Con Thien. The office/admin staff guys in the rear are very envious of the guys out on the lines and want to hear anything they can about what is going on in the field. They want to see combat (or so they think!) They would forget that crap if they had seen what I have.

It's 0730 hours and I'm sitting in my new office. Pretty quiet here, only one clerk in this morning so far. Everyone else is at the chow hall for breakfast. I found my orders had been delayed for two weeks after being signed. Lt. Col. Van Winkle had them in on the 18th, but they got sent back by mistake.

I share a comfortable and clean hard-back hooch with three other guys. It has screens and a tin roof and a real bed with a mattress and a light. There is even a Vietnamese house-boy name Le-Cong who cleans, polishes boots and shoes, picks up laundry and sewing and runs errands for you, for a fee. We all chip in to pay for his services and he keeps the place spotless, as well as looks after our stuff.

I can throw a rock and hit our enlisted men's club from our front door. They sell cold beer, soda, peanuts, and popcorn and have movies every night. They even have pretty Vietnamese bar girls working there, if you like looking at slant-eyes. The world here has been turned upside down for me in one week.

This is so unfair to all the mud-Marines I have just left behind and I have such mixed emotions inside. I am struggling to find myself and get squared away for this job. I feel so guilty, like I am abandoning my squad, but I do not want to go back to that hell hole of Con Thien to be killed by some NVA shell or rocket while hiding in a bunker or out in a trench. It was bad and it will only get worse. Those guys are in for a pounding if the North Vietnamese move up more heavy artillery that will shoot bigger stuff across the border. I pray to God to keep the guys safe and give them my protection, wrap them with the wings of his special angels and guard them from harm. PLEASE!!! I do miss them, but I do not ever want to go back. It is a meat-grinder for humans and holds nothing, but death.

But I owe it to Lt. Col. Van Winkle to do him 110% more than my best, with no complaints. Extra volunteer time, anything more I can do to take any load off him or make him look good for helping me out.

The draftsman I am replacing is a Sgt. Levine, (nice, mellow guy). He leaves on the 12th. He is really a technical illustrator, not a map maker, and he is very good. He was with Fox Company, 2/1 for a short time as combat illustrator and was sent here as a topographical draftsman because he was so good at drawing things. Typical USMC, the guy's in the wrong billet, but he is doing the job the best he can. His drawings are beautiful. But his map work is really basic. I think I can punch it up to really make some improvements for the colonel. Levine left a two foot long charcoal sketch of a reclining nude Vietnamese woman over his rack for me when he left. It was a real nice piece of art work. I traded it to a clerk for an end table, which worked better for me.

I put in for R&R on the HQ G-3 roster for late Feb. How great is that?

Chris
January 8 - Today was a beer day. It sure doesn't happen often, like never. The story goes that Army General Rosen visited Con Thien and asked one of the officers for a beer and was told we didn't have any. A few days later 80 cases of Korean beer were delivered to the hill. It was rationed out at one beer per man, starting with the privates and working upward.   Now, that was sure a change. Normally, any extras flowed the opposite direction, starting with the command officers and worked its way down the line and sometime later on, finally to the "grunts".

House 1st Marine Division G-3, Da Nang
January 8 – Man, I sure learned how the news and politics works, starting at the bottom. I was told by the colonel that the general did not like the way my charts for his briefings showed our losses in big, bold bar graphs. He ordered me to rework them overnight to show them as small as possible (without lying) and make the bars on enemy losses bigger (without lying) to make them appear much larger! Also, the amount of captured weapons and enemy equipment was to be left blank on my charts as it was "in flux" and the general would fill it in with

his "updated information at the correct time". Boy! What a snow job coming up! Division staff snows CMC (Commandant of the Marine Corps), he snows the JCS (Joint Chiefs of Staff) and they snow the president (who wants to be snowed). And President Johnson gets to lie to all of America with a straight face that he has the best of all facts straight from the source in Vietnam.   Everything is distorted or twisted in some way to make it look better than it really is.

Note: Captain Eagen – (Echo Co Commander from February through August 1968) I was the XO he refers to as being on leave. His report includes the so-called official history of Union 1 and includes his sentiments which I share about the deceit and deception practiced by field grade officers, especially beyond the battalion level which created an enormous riff between the company grade officers and the field grades outside of the battalion level: the USMC equivalent of the contemporaneous belief of "Don't trust anyone over 30". As a brief aside, in the autumn of 1968, I was selected to go see the CMC along with a half dozen other infantry Lt's and Captains.   The CMC was purportedly concerned over "rumors" that company grade officers had "disconnected" from their seniors and he supposedly wanted the truth. I told him basically what Bill Wood says: false reporting, exaggerated body counts, severe criticism and too often disciplinary action taken against Lt's and Capt's who got into deep doo-doo, taking heavy casualties BECAUSE of idiot orders from senior commanders who had not one damned clue about what was really going on so they "doctored" the records and blamed the Marines whom they shoved into shit. Lying was so routine that we quit commenting on it. My interview with the CMC was terminated abruptly and I had my ass chewed by some Lt General whose name I do not recall, and several HQMC colonels whom I thought did a fine job proving my point. They, and that incident, cemented for me the view that there were (probably always have been) two Marine Corps: "Corporate" USMC, and the fighting, real Marine Corps.

House Note: *(written in 2009, after reading a statement by our old captain) This really confirms what I saw and heard in division HQ after I was there for a while. Our captain was 100% right – the officers in regiment and division just made shit up and added stuff to all reports to make us look or themselves look good.*

The lieutenants and captains liked to make the numbers look good, so "probables" become "confirmed" as the enemy dead reports go up the line. The pattern continued all the way to the generals and then back to the USA and ultimately to the President, etc. "Probables" were changed to "confirmed body counts" before my eyes, and I had my ass chewed by lieutenant colonels for

A couple of NFG's digging their bunker at Con Thien.

**Tank support directly to the left of 2nd squad,
bunker of House ,Estes and Chris.**

accurately recording data on my reports, graphs, charts and maps that I presented for the general's briefings by the G-3 officers.

The officers from my G-3 Unit were only majors and they had almost all come in from the field after being infantry captains, and they knew what was going on, but were told to shut-up if they wanted to make a career and retire.

Chris

January 9 – Lt. Col. B.R. "Billy" Duncan replaced Parker as battalion CO. Until the end of the month, there were several small actions, but no major attempt of the North Vietnamese units to penetrate in strength the Marine defenses. The holiday truce offered the NVA an opportunity to bring-up supplies and new troops, plus continue the harassing fire and pressure on our outpost. We used this time to re-build bunkers, etc. No one liked the cease-fire. It was dumb.

Estes

January 9 - I finally had it with one of the guys in my squad. He continues to fall asleep and he's going to get someone killed. I reported him to Lt. Graffam. We are short men in our platoon, so he may not get sent out of here. At least he knows where I stand. Some of the guys tell him he's gonna get fragged (grenade thrown on him when he is sleeping). Nothing is worse out here. Trust has been totally lost with this Marine. The senior command did nothing….we were so short handed. Falcon is the only guy who will stand watch with him. Falcon told me he would take care of things. I like this guy, he's helping us all. He came over around November '67 and if he lives, he will rotate out in December '68.

Note: House - On January 10, 1968, (8 days after I was medevaced), an official Marine engineering Dye marker (barrier) team visited the site to inspect the bunkers. According to the 2nd Battalion, 1st Marines Command Chronology, "None of the bunkers could be considered complete. Maximum effort was later directed at bunker completion in keeping with the tactical situation." In other words, they were not built properly to protect us from the size and type of artillery used to hit us.

Knobby

January 9 - They brought us in a hot meal today. We had sauerkraut, potatoes, spare ribs, apricots and coffee.

**Second squad - Bottom row, Hendricks, Spanky, Dodd, Chris
Top row, Estes, Herfel, Linares, Speck, House**

The weather here is still rainy and cold, not as cold as home though. My cold is all cleared up now.

Lt. Kirk
January 10 - One of our defensive efforts was to construct what we called fugasse (I think this was a misspelling of a French word). We planted a 55 gallon drum in the ground pointing up at a 45 degree angle, filled it with shell casings, scrap metal and plastic explosive, and connected a piece of detonation cord to a fuse and then to a fuse lighter. We set these off from time to time for entertainment and to perfect our skills, but I don't ever recall using them against the bad guys.

Chris
January 10 - We got hit late last night. Mortars were hitting and hitting often. I grabbed my helmet and quickly ducked by head outside to see if the enemy was

coming over the wire. My helmet was actually sitting on my head at a slant, covering the left side of my head and immediately a piece of shrapnel hit my helmet, knocking me backwards. After the shelling, and as the sun began to come up, I ventured outside and found lying at my feet – a sharp, irregular piece of metal that had hit my helmet. God was here today! Wow.

January 11 – Echo Company, 2nd platoon entered a minefield and received 1 KIA and 2 WIA. We found an underground bunker and destroyed it with C-4 explosive.

Mike Pipkin, Corpsman, Fox Co., Snohomish, WA
January 11 – Fox Company was leaving the compound area after dark and walked into a mine field where three Marines were WIA. Corpsman Loy went in to help and while carrying a badly wounded Marine out, he stepped on another mine, and was KIA. Corpsman Loy was awarded the Silver Star.

**HN James R. Loy, USN
(panel 34E, line 30 on The Wall).**

Chris
January 12 - Judge and I were sitting down and talking about home. He has become a really great friend. He's in another squad, same platoon, but we still see each other often. He doesn't have a girl to write back home, so I tell him about my sister, Sherri, who's attending the University of Oregon. He is excited and says yes, he'd like to write someone, especially a pretty blonde girl.

Dave Dillberg, Golf Co., 1st Platoon, squad leader
January 12 - The damnest thing happened and I saw it all, as if in slow motion. It was an 82mm recoilless round. It landed right in front of my feet and blew up. It knocked me out and when I woke up I was numb from my rib cage down. I thought I was blown away, so I didn't to look down toward my feet. I felt with my hands first and I was all there. I had a piece of shrapnel in my helmet and a big piece in my flak jacket, but none in me. Then I heard God say to me "Get up, the next one's going to land right where you are laying". I believed Him and I heard the guy shoot again, since I couldn't use my legs, I just rolled over into a mortar pit, just as the round landed right where I had been laying.

Lt. Suydam

January 12 - Corporal Melendez, squad leader, was a natural born leader and a hell of a nice person. He and others had been guarding truck convoys, which we

Lt Lee Suydam
Montgomery, AL

sent south every morning to fetch sandbags, which were filled by Vietnamese laborers at some southern point. On the way home one evening, Melendez was on the last truck with three others of his squad. When they loaded the truck, they sort of built a fort of sandbags. Then they laid down for a nap. Their truck was hit by an RPG-7 rocket, which knocked off a front wheel, sending the truck into a ditch. Four NVA soldiers got up blasting away, closing in to finish off the driver. It was the last day of their lives. Melendez and crew popped up out of the sandbags and returned the favor.

Chris

January 13 - We located a break in the perimeter wire at Con Thien, which gives access from the minefield directly to our fighting positions in camp. We found an enemy boot with a part of a foot in it. We received incoming rounds, which got two Marines WIA. Every day, something is happening to the guys. The rain continues to come down on us. The ground turns to mud, the mud turns really bad and thickens to about 1-1/2' thick, that's 18"! It is very difficult to move around in, especially if you're taking a path that is frequently used by others.

Lt. Suydam
January 14 - Our ammunition pit was hit. Mortars, shells, flares and bullets exploded for twenty-four hours. The fire would die down and then start popping again. My photograph of the aftermath shows spent and burned ammunition of all kinds scattered over the ground of Con Thien for about 300 meters in all directions. I'm sure that cost the taxpayers several million dollars.

Dave Dillberg, Golf Co., 1st platoon, squad leader
January 14 – Time at Con Thien was tough for all of us. We got hit real bad when OP 1 was inside the circle group patterns of the NVA 152mm artillery barrages of 6 to 8 at a time. We were inside calling in our 155's on the NVA and the firebase said they can't shoot into the DMZ. They denied us support right when we were getting blown up just because of a visiting dignitary from Congress was present. Another political move that cost lives.

Chris
January 14 - We are hit again and we are in our bunkers. Charlie was walking his barrage right in on us. (When looking to hit a target, rounds were fired, then adjusted, fried again, then adjusted and finally you had the distance and windage correct. The command "fire for effect" was given). The second blast erupted 50 meters away and right in front of our bunker. No one spoke, no one moved. There was absolutely no where to go. We were hunkered down in our hole. It was too late. The next artillery round had already been sent our direction. We just waited. It was all about "How lucky are you gonna be today?" Then the blast, geez, any closer it would have been in our hole. The concussion and sound are deadening. Two, three more rounds, oh, they're close…wait.

When it's finally over, we quickly moved outside to assess the damage. Did our squad fare ok today or did we lose more men, again? A direct hit would level and scatter a bunker and all the materials it had taken to build it. A desperate search by everyone began immediately, trying to find and administer aid to the wounded Marines. We called for a corpsman's help or quickly carried the wounded Marines to the aid station. As soon as the wounded were given first aid, wounds cleansed of the mud and debris and hemorrhaging stopped, they would then be rushed to the aid station. The aid station at Con Thien was a deep, well-fortified bunker about 400-500 meters away from our frontline position. If the wounds were serious enough they would be medevaced by helicopter, although sometimes the helicopters couldn't land due to incoming or bad weather. It was a terrible feeling to know that your friends couldn't get to the regional hospital in Phu Bai.

January 15 - Still no R&R, lots of maybe's... and maybe soon,...if not now, then it is supposed to be in the March-April period. For the most part, the 2nd Battalion, 1st Marines at Con Thien (A-4) bore the brunt of whatever enemy activity there was, largely continuing mortar and artillery bombardment. Having already lost one commander to enemy mortars, the 2nd Battalion earlier had hopes that in Operation Checkers, it would leave Con Thien and rejoin our parent regiment, the 1st Marines. Because of the continuing threat in the area, the relief at Con Thien was postponed until after Tet. The small hill, only 160 meters high, but less than two miles south of the Demilitarized Zone, remained a key terrain feature for the Marines and a favorite target for the North Vietnamese gunners and small infantry probes.

Lt. Kirk
Jan 15 - Occasionally, I would be called to meetings with the E company commander. I had to sprint across the open ground between Yankee Station and Con Thien, often with artillery fire coming in. More often than not, these meetings were in the late afternoon and I had to get back to Yankee Station in the dark. Even though I alerted the lines at both Con Thien and Yankee Station, I was still in danger of being mistaken for the enemy.

Chris
January 16 – One of the bunkers close to me has 18 rats to their name. They pin them up on a large piece of cardboard, which they display outside their bunker. This is a sick thing. I think we need some entertainment. More rockets today, as every day. Some of the rockets are freight-train-sounding, scare the hell out of you. It will just plain flatten you out, you're huggin' the ground, I mean your lips are as far into the soil as you can get 'em.

Estes
January 18 – We lost another guy in our squad today. Hendricks was shot in the neck. He was immediately medevaced.

Chris
January 18 - Tucker is going home. Our country boy from Kentucky was carrying a case of C-Rat meals, with his K-Bar combat knife lying on top of the case of chow. The knife slipped off and dropped directly down and into his boot, right through to the foot. He went to the rear area to get shots and recuperate and they checked his medical file. This man, with two purple hearts, was the best tracker of the company, best shot, etc.. He was found to have a heart murmur

and he should never have been sent to Vietnam. Good-bye, Tucker. We lost another one. I really liked Tucker, a good Marine and someone you would trust with your life. He was so good in the "bush" - quiet..methodical...a true shot...

Lt. Kirk
January 20 - Over the main entrance to Con Thien, on the south side where the road (MSR or main supply route) entered the base, there was a sign that said "Second Battalion, First Marines. Through this portal walk the world's finest fighting men." Corny and exaggerated as that was, it made me feel good.

Estes
January 20 – We relieved 1/1 on December 22, 1967 and they went back to Quang Tri and we were supposed to be relieved 30 days later. Word is that there is so much activity in the area, no one is moving out. It looks like we are going to serve additional time here because intelligence reports indicate that something big is about to happen to one of the "A" positions on the DMZ.

Note: January 21 - During the first part of 1968, the NVA were believed to have had two divisions in the area around Khe Sanh. On January 21, at 0530 hours, the base received a hail of 160 incoming rockets and mortars. The initial attack brought a round directly into the ammo dump, which contained 11,000 rounds of ordnance. It began to burn, causing rounds to detonate and fire into the base and its inhabitants, CS tear gas was ignited, hot artillery and recoilless rifle rounds started blowing up, as well as plastic explosives, C-4 and other ordnance. The runway was destroyed, as were living quarters. Eighteen Marines are killed, with 40 wounded.

It soon became apparent that the NVA intended to lay siege to Khe Sanh Combat Base and the Marine positions on surrounding hills, namely, 861, 881, 558 and 950. (A siege is a military operation in which enemy forces surround a town, building or an outpost, cutting off essential supplies, with the aim of compelling the surrender of those inside.) Supported by massive artillery and air bombardments, including B-52 strikes, the 6,000 man garrison would hold out for 77 days. The base took on the look of a slum.

Lt. Kirk
January 22 -We sometimes had trouble getting helicopters in for med-evac or resupply. The bad guys would rain down mortars, artillery and rockets on any approaching aircraft and the weather was sometimes a factor. We had a few tense days when we worried about running out of food, water and ammunition.

The MSR was usually open to convoys from Cam Lo and Dong Ha, but subject to occasional ambushes.

Estes

January 22 - On this day, Byars' 60mm mortar team was trying to set up and shell a suspected NVA artillery-spotter position. Gunny Weathers was helping them when a 152 mm round landed almost on top of their mortar position. It killed two and wounded the others. A guy in my squad, Christensen, carried the Gunny in his arms to the battalion aid station in Death Valley, a short distance away. Chris told me the Gunny was blown almost completely in two, suffering a huge wound in his stomach. Chris really liked the Gunny and he took it very hard. The Gunny was black, 30ish, a wife, two kids and a first-class guy. Byers was KIA by the same round that hit Gunny. Byers had just come back from R&R the day before. The 152mm artillery round gave off a very distinct whistle sound. Gunny read the bible every night. I'll never forget him. He really was a part of all of us 0311's. He truly cared.

House

January 22, 1968 - My Gunnery Sergeant , Nathaniel Weathers, 0369, was killed at Con Thien by enemy artillery fire. He was 32 years old, from Cleveland, Ohio.

The same day, a fellow squad leader in second platoon, Corporal Richard Byars was also killed by enemy artillery fire. He was 21 years old.

Gunnery Sergeant Nathaniel Weathers Cleveland, Ohio
\(panel 35E, line 12)

Corporal Richard Byars, Rye, Colorado
(panel 35E, line 10)

Lt. Suydam

January 22 - Our company first sergeant, Gunnery Sergeant Weathers was killed by artillery. Weathers was a decent man many of us regarded as a father figure. He and Captain Quinlan were running for a bunker. A shell struck the corner of the bunker they were running for. Weathers body was blown back into Captain Quinlan who was bruised from head to toe and had ruptured eardrums. All of a sudden, I was acting Company Commander.

**Cpl Chuck Estes, Radioman/
Squad Ldr**

Note: Captain Quinlan, a Naval Academy graduate, retired as a colonel.

Chris

January 22 - This was a terrible day. The shock of losing Gunny has really hit me hard. I remember looking toward the wooden rack that held Gunny, with doctors working on him frantically. I was in disbelief that something so terrible could happen to Gunny. Then I was being told that he was dead. I was so shocked. I moved over to the aid station bunker entrance, sat in a corner and cried. It was the only time I remember crying in my entire 13-month tour. Gunny meant so much to all of us. Evidently, he meant a lot to me. Sgt. Mike Gordon came up to me and we both exited the aid station, leaving Gunny behind. I had done all I could and it wasn't enough.

Doc Turner
January 22 - Gunny was supposed to be shipping out to go home a day or two after he was KIA. I loved and respected that man as much or more than most of the other non-coms. He smoked a pipe and read his bible and prayed every night. He was always honest and fair to all the men.

Note: January 22 - Shortly after noon, the enemy bombarded Con Thien with 100 rounds of 82mm mortar fire followed by 130 rounds of 152mm shells from guns within North Vietnam. The battalion sustained two men killed and 16 wounded. One day later about 1,000 meters north of the base companies F and G encountered a North Vietnamese infantry company. The Marines sustained two men KIA and eight WIA. The following night the enemy hit the base again, with 40 82mm mortar rounds, 20 60mm mortar rounds and 10 rounds of 152mm artillery shells. Six Marines were wounded.

Note: In his book Con Thien: Hill of Angels, James P. Coan said "…elite assault troops are neither trained nor accustomed to huddling in one place, taking a pounding day after day."

Estes
January 23 - Fox Company got the shit shot out of them today out on the Trace. (In early 1967, Marines were ordered to bulldoze a strip from Gio Linh westward to Con Thien. This became known by the Marines as "The Trace". It was cleared to at least 500 meters wide). The story I heard was Fox Company found a communication wire, which had been laid out as part of a listening post and started tracing it backwards. When the fog lifted, everyone was totally exposed to the enemy. The NVA caught them out in the open and hit them with mortars and artillery fire. Fox took a tremendous amount of casualties in a very few minutes. The number 46 sticks in my mind. I believe Golf Company went to help them, which put Echo in reserve. We saddled up and started to go help them, but were told to stand down and wait.

King was just back from R & R and had walked past us and grinned when we asked about the girls. He was dead 30 minutes later.

A red headed white-faced engineer I had never seen before - nor had I since - ran into our bunker during the shelling and asked if he could wait it out there. We passed the time lying face down on the bunker floor shaking in our boots, as the stuff hit all around us. Suddenly, this engineer said, "Now, I know what it is – it's a knee". He had seen a body part outside our bunker as he ran through the doorway and he had just figured it out. I think that was all that was left of King.

Chris

January 22 – I found myself back with my friend Judge (radioman) after leaving the aid station and Gunny's body. We lay on the ground, looking out at the terrain in front of us. Judge felt the same as everyone else regarding the Gunny. We didn't talk about his death much. Judge was constantly listening to the radio traffic, as all radio guys did. They needed to be vigilant with their jobs, but also they learned a lot about what we doing, where we might be going. At this time he turned to me and commented. "They're going to put you up for the Bronze Star for your action with the Gunny." I commented "Oh". I didn't bring it up again with anyone. It just didn't seem important.

Note: Chris - It's interesting as I reflect back on my time in 'Nam that no one cared about medals or achieving rank or position. It all meant so little in the scheme of things. We fought to stay alive. That was the prize.

Note: Lt. Kirk - We used the flash bang method to determine how far away the enemy artillery pieces were: count the seconds between seeing the flash of the gun and heard the sound and divide by five to get the distance to the enemy artillery in miles. We would then relay the estimated distance, a compass azimuth and our grid coordinates to our artillery battery. We would also analyze craters to determine the direction from which a round came.

Bob Dunbar, Echo Co.

January 25 – I just got to 'Nam when Tet kicked off and was sent up to Con Thien on this day. I was assigned to Echo Co, as an A-Gunner in 1st herd (platoon), to replace a short timer called Lucky who was to rotate back to "the world" the second week of February. The gunner's name was Zack and he left a few weeks after Lucky did, which made me the gunner. My fighting hole was to the left of the Army Listening Post (facing SW) and about the second to last bunker in the trench line, before it curved around the large dirt mound, which was behind me. My sleeping hole was about the safest place you could be on Con Thien because of its location in relation to Co Roc Mountain where most of the incoming rounds came from.

'Gunny' Epitomized SNCO Duties

By Sgt. Steve Berntson

CON THIEN — In a Marine rifle company there is one man who deals with and influences every Leatherneck at some time. He is a man who everyone listens to and knows as the company gunnery sergeant. As Gunny he is the important middle-man for the company commander and the troops.

The death of GySgt. Nathaniel Weathers (Cleveland, Ohio), found Marines later reflecting commemorative comments — epitomizing both the man and the continuing position. Weathers, the "gunny" for "E" Co. (2/1), was killed by an enemy artillery blast while the unit manned Con Thien.

A few days after his death, four Marines taking a smoke break from their job of filling sandbags sat talking.

"You know," said a young Marine, "Gunny was what I will always picture as a real Marine. He was always doing his job and helping others with theirs. He never got excited over anything and he could control any situation."

"I remember the time one of our platoons got ambushed," recollected a second Leatherneck. "A couple of the point men got hit bad, the corpsman and the gunny took off running towards them. Gunny took a bullet through the helmet and it knocked him down, but he got back up, wiped the blood out of his eyes and ran over to help 'Doc' with the wounded. He was a real tough one."

"It just seemed that there wasn't a question in the world that the Gunny couldn't answer or find out the answer for," remarked a skinny, bespectacled Marine. "And in a firefight, there he was running back and forth telling us where to fire and warning us about some hidden sniper. He was always keeping an eye on the new guys and helping them out."

"The old Gunny was a Marines' Marine," continued the fourth man. "He was like a friend, a father, and an Ann Landers—but most of all he was 'our Gunny.'"

Gunny Weathers had been with "E" Co. for more than 11 months. In between welcoming and bidding farewell to all company Marines, he was their "Gunny."

SEA TIGER 5

Chris

January 26 - We got hit late at night. Mortars were hitting and hitting often. I grabbed my helmet and quickly ducked by head outside to see if the NVA were coming over the wire. My helmet was actually sitting on my head at a slant, covering the left side of my head and as soon as I looked out the opening of the bunker, immediately a piece of shrapnel hit the left side of my helmet, knocking me back and down. If I had had my helmet on straight, I would have received a large piece of metal shrapnel to the side of my head, which would have killed me . I am absolutely being watched over, God has a plan for me. I know I will be hurt while in Vietnam. This I am certain. I also strongly believe that I will make it home.   Constant probing of the lines at night kept us awake.   We knew the enemy knew our lines. The Marines had been here for a long time. There were portions of the lines that had long ago been destroyed. These breaks in the wire and the minefield areas that had been destroyed made it easy to sneak in and get closer to our fighting positions.   We knew this and it wore on all the guys every night during watch.

Lt. Kirk

January 26 - My first radioman, Thomas, was killed, a couple of days after I fired him as my radioman and assigned him to a squad.   He was killed by his own M-16, going over a paddy dike.   His rifle safety was off and a round in the chamber, against standing orders. He extended the stock of his rifle to the guy in back of him to pull him up.   The guy's hand slipped and hit the trigger, putting several rounds through Thomas's flak jacket. We had to carry Thomas' body for a couple of days.

Note: Januray 26 - Major General Rathvon Tompkins, Commanding General, 3rd Marine Division, winner of the Navy Cross in World War II, said "It was believed at this time that the NVA will aim a major effort to overrun Camp Carroll, Thon Son Lam (the Rockpile area), and Ca Lu."

Chris

January 28 - Two new young guys, Ridinger and Oncale came in together and joined us at Con Thien. Ridinger seemed pretty squared away and proved to be an asset for our squad.

Doc Turner

January 29 - I left for R&R today.   I was so glad to be leaving for awhile. Everyone on the plane was is in an incredibly good mood. While on the plane, instructions were given to turn around and head back to Da Nang Airbase. The medical center was being overrun at this time. The helo port was being attacked by VC throwing satchel-charges.   The corpsmen at the medical facility had hidden rifles, which they used to hold off the attack by the NVA. Meanwhile, the plane I'm on also, includes an Admiral.   He gives direct orders to continue the plane to their R&R destination. Cheers for Big Guy!

House

January 29 - Tet is the lunar new year here, like Christmas and New-Year together back home.   It is supposed to be a time of celebration and family get-togethers, and honoring your ancestors. It was also supposed to be a time of cease fire negotiated with the North Vietnamese commies. That did not happen. Instead, the NVA and VC used it as cover, and launched an offensive with rocket attacks on Da Nang using 122mm Russian and 152mm Chinese-made rockets to terrorize the city. They carried them down the Ho Chi Minh trail in Laos and set them up using two long boards nailed together to form a "V" shape trough as a launching guide. Explosions went off all over the city. They are firing them over the mountain range that surrounds Da Nang, and are pretty effective as they have spotters in the city directing them.

Lt. Kirk

Jan 29 - A helicopter was shot down east of Con Thien. My company was ordered to rescue the crew and we went running out there in the late afternoon with no time to get food or replenish our water. I hadn't eaten since mid-day. We found the helicopter and crew and set in a perimeter, as it got dark. We were out for about 24 hours. I spent the night with a scout dog and his handler a few feet away. The dog would growl every time anybody moved. The next day we were ordered to do a patrol rather than returning immediately to base. I had an intense headache from the heat, lack of water and food and the weight of my helmet. We came across some abandoned bunkers, found a trash pit and went through the garbage looking for uneaten C rations. We found a few cans of crackers and cookies.

Chris

January 29 – We are starting to hear about guys who want off the Hill so badly they are inflicting wounds on themselves. In the past, if a rat bit you, (the sign was two puncture wounds next to each other), you would be sent to the rear area for rehab and daily shots in the stomach. No escape now, as every man is needed too badly. The stomach shots, I was told, were very painful, yet there were those that chose to put two puncture holes in their skin and fake a rat bite. Corpsmen were pretty good at spotting these fake attempts to get off "The Hill" and to the rear area. The corpsmen would not transfer them and would instead give them the shots themselves. The corpsmen swing a big stick, as far as health issues are concerned. Their word was "law" and was to be observed. Many times the corpsman take a stand for the welfare of the troops and actually force the captain to abide by their decision.

Note: January 30 – On the Tet holiday, 84,000 NVA/Vietcong units stormed into more than100 towns throughout Vietnam, including 36 of the 44 provincial capitals. The surge was immediate and forceful. By the end of the Tet offensive,

The famous AK-47 automatic rifle.

17,000 enemy were dead as were 4,954 ARVN troops and 4,124 Americans and other allied troops (South Korea, Australia, New Zealand) While a military disaster for the NVA and VC, the Tet offensive was shocking to the American public.

Chris

January 30 - Rockets, mortars and ground assaults hit Da Nang as the massive Tet offensive started today. Chuck Estes went on in-country R&R. He was sent back to Phu Bai, as China Beach, where many of the guys checked in, was being hit hard and being overrun. I'm concerned about him, as any R&R in-country is ridiculous. What do you do, take your rifle to the beach?

Knobby

January 30 - Our mail is pretty screwed up. I got 2 letters from Peoria today which is the first I have received from there in quite awhile. T and I are going on R&R to Penang (?), Malaysia, on February 7th. We leave for Da Nang on the 3rd (we leave 2 days earlier than we normally would because we're at Con Thien). I'll get paid around $200 February 1st and I'm going to borrow another $100 so I should be set financially.

We've been getting a taste of coming summer heat the last couple of days. We're digging more trenches and improving our fighting holes. I got a pretty good burn today. I'll take the sun to the rain any day.

We have a short platoon-sized patrol tomorrow. I doubt we'll be out more than half a day.

Lt. Kirk
January 31 - I took a tank and engineer team and my platoon and swept the road down to C-2, a firebase a few miles south. I ran into Mike Jackson, who had been in OCS and Basic School with me at Quantico. I shared a hotel room in San Francisco on the way over to Vietnam. Mike arranged to get my platoon fed. This was our first hot meal in a long time. The cook apologized, saying "Sorry, sir, all we have is steak and eggs." We also bathed in a dammed up stream. What I great day!

Cpl. Dennis Knobby

Note: Lt. Kirk - Or rather, what a great morning. The Command Chronology indicates we left the CP at 8:13 a.m. and returned by 11:18 a.m. so we packed a lot of living into three hours. I didn't see Mike again until the mid-1980s walking across E. 9th St. in Cleveland. Mike had become a very successful lawyer. At our Basic School reunion in 2008 Mike said he has a picture of me and my troops, naked in the stream. The Command Chronology indicates I did this road sweep again on February 11, completing that sweep in an hour and a half.

House

January 31 - As I am driving through Da Nang to deliver overlays this morning, the MP's have about 30 VC bodies piled up at the end of the bridge that goes to China Beach. There was a big firefight to stop them last night. The VC were also at the NSA hospital here in Da Nang, and 7th Marines Headquarters at An Hoa, where they over-ran a couple of positions for a while before the Marines were able to re-take the ground. They also set the fuel depot on fire!

Note: The three observation posts at Con Thien engaged some 1,027 targets with artillery, expending 17,374 rounds. There were also thousands of rounds fired as part of harassment and interdiction. The 81mm mortar platoon shot 30,256 rounds for the month, 122 rounds per day for each of the eight mortar tubes. That's 122 rounds per day for each of the 8 tubes. Mortar rounds cost $35 each, so that's over $1 million dollars worth.

Night patrols continued in order to keep the enemy away from the base. Normally, fire-team or squad sized groups would venture out of Con Thien and patrol up to 2,000 meters away from the base. Ambush sites were set-up for the evening in the free-fire zone area. The enemy was sometimes came close to the perimeter, within a few hundred meters. Lieutenant Colonel Duncan later recalled that the North Vietnamese artillery destroyed much of the northwest minefield protecting the Marine outpost, "...as well as the forward trenches and bunkers in that area." Casualties were mounting. The hospital bunkers exceeded capacity with wounded on stretchers." The battalion commander remembered that one of the chaplains "...broke under stress and attempted suicide" and had to be sent back to the states."

Incoming rounds destroyed 15 Marine bunkers.

There were 660 incoming rounds during the month. Several cuts in the defensive wire were found on the northern side of the perimeter and considerable enemy activity in the U.S. minefield near the breaks. Aerial observers, artillery

Supplies for the Con Thien outpost

forward observers and electronic and infra-red equipment detected a high level of enemy activity in the area. 26 confirmed enemy KIA are reported, along with 90 probables.

2nd Battalion, 1st Marines casualties for January: 9 enlisted KIA, 5 officers and 27 enlisted WIA.

The VC and NVA killed 2,800 civilians in Hue City after capturing parts of the ancient Imperial capital. It took three weeks of house-to-house and street-to-street fighting to re-take the city, causing enormous destruction.

Note:February 1, Captain Tom Eagen assumed command of Echo Company.

Lathan Williams, Echo Co, 1st platoon

February 2 – Since the Tet Offensive started we had a lot more incoming. They were planning to overrun us, they had us sealed off – no convoys could get through and very few copters. They were just waiting to take Hue and then come back and knock us out. They have over 20,000 NVA in the area and we only have about 2,000 at Con Thien.

Chris

February 3 - We were supposed to move out of here in January, but it looks like it's going to be February. There is too much trouble everywhere around to leave. The Marine Corps had been rotating battalions in and out of Con Thien every thirty days. The constant shelling and the threat of an NVA assault took a psychological toll on the Marines. We would stay.

The NVA has really increased its presence in the area. Oh, great! Now, they say February 20th will be the departure date. I guess we can handle it a little longer. No choice. As more guys leave, like House, and others are wounded, the composition of the squad changes. Many times the new guys don't get much support, other than in combat. It's difficult to make new friends, as we know they may be gone the same day you meet them. After they've made it for a while, they seem to get accepted and you have another friend. It's strange and very difficult to explain. It's got to be tough for the new guys, having to learn everything on their own, 'til finally someone steps up and starts talking to them. If they're smart, they stay quiet, observe, try to be helpful.

February 4 – Daily Action - Almost daily, the earth-shaking thunder of the daily rain of rockets and artillery fire is felt. The ground would bend and fold, as the rounds continued to fall all around us. For awhile, it was at 1500 hours in the middle of the afternoon that the show would start. We would find ourselves prepared for an emotionally controlled, hunker-down time in our bunkers, as the artillery rounds would soon begin falling. They would fall and we would wait. The small talk amongst your buddies normally consisted of "shit...that was close" or "damn, now they're firing the big stuff". Everyone knew - if you got hit, it was your time and nothing anyone could do about it. This thought was somewhat comforting, if that's correct to say. You didn't fear "fear." You feared the damn "hit'". The explosion would most definitely kill everyone in your bunker. We helped each other by staying calm.

House

February 4 – My protection of the U.S. Air Force" incident

Lately, I have been transporting two colonels to and from their meetings around the airbase. With my maps, my M-16, a .45 auto pistol, and a bandolier of ammo in the jeep, I pull to a stop and pick up the two colonels, as I am providing transportation to their meetings at the far side of the airbase. This should take 20 minutes tops! I found a flak jacket and a helmet and have them on full time. I find out the colonels have left and I am on my own to deliver the maps and overlays to each command and get their information back, and without my assistant, Rennison, to ride shotgun.

I have Gunny Laura's jeep. Several days ago, I took this same road I've been traveling and passed a pile of about 30 VC killed while they attempted to enter the China Beach area. The VC were also at the hospital, where they had overrun a couple of positions. I drive two colonels to their meeting at different places in the city. There are still lots of VC roaming around and firefights are occurring everywhere. As I swing around the north end by the Air Force maintenance sheds and barracks, all hell breaks loose on the far side of the run way.

About 100 yards away, a plane inside a protective revetment blows sky high. Aviation fuel is on fire and running in the rivers across the runway, parts are flying into the air and more explosions. Then the next plane explodes, and more explosions occur all along the revetment. I notice 30-40 Air Force guys are running for and jumping down into a big culvert next to their work area/barracks ahead of me. I roll the jeep over next to them, grab my M-16 and the bandolier of spare ammo and dive into the culvert, stumbling and losing my helmet.

The guard towers are now firing their M-60 machine guns at the VC who just destroyed the million dollar airplanes, and we are in direct line of fire and in the direction the bad guys are running! I got my helmet on as fast as possible and tried to look like a Marine ready to defend his position.

An Air Force sergeant looked at me as I stumbled to my feet and said Hey, the Marines are here". All the Air Force guys let out a yell - "Yea, the Marines are here". I said "Sir, the Marine is here. I am all alone. Do you know how to use this 45 auto"? He replies that he is qualified, so I gave him the 45 and two extra magazines. I asked him where their weapons were and he replied "Locked in the armory and no one has a key".

By the time I could see through the smoke and fuel fire, I realized one of the M-60 gun towers had been blown down and the people on the runway were

Refreshing Shower Disrupted By Incoming Enemy Rounds

By Sgt. Steve Bernston

DA NANG—This is the true story of three Marines who "barely" escaped an enemy barrage.

The afternoon of Feb. 1 seemed like a good time to start another month at Con Thien with real luxury — a refreshing shower. For four days the enemy had been dropping in a few artillery rounds only in the early morning and late evening. Three Leathernecks of an element of the First Marine Regiment headed for the shower stall near the end of the compound.

"I had just finished taking my shower and was drying off," recalled 2nd. Lt. Lee Suydam (Montgomery, Ala.), a company commander. "I had just said to the other two with me, 'Wouldn't it be something if they dropped in a couple of rounds now?!'"

"In fact," he continued, "we were thinking up newspaper headlines such as Marines Seen Running Bare in Attack or Assault Led By Marines in the Nude when we heard that sickening, screaming whistle of incoming."

Suydam and his companions, Sgt. Peter G. Walsh (Hamilton, Ontario), and Cpl. John Mac Donnell (East Patterson, N.J.), wasted no time taking cover behind a big rock as the first rounds came in.

"Just for a second we debated whether or not to put on our clothes and then run or just put on our helmets and flak jackets," said Walsh. "Then the second rounds hit and the decision was unanimous. It was helmets and flak jackets and run like blazes."

Suydam and Mac Donnell donned their armor and took off for a bunker while Walsh ran for shelter in another direction.

"I was running like the devil for the bunker," said Walsh, "hopping and skipping over the rocks on my bare feet, when I heard the voices of Marines cheering me on. I looked and saw a group of guys standing in the doorway of the bunker chanting. 'Don't stop! Don't stop! You've almost made it! Come on, don't worry about your feet—keep running!'"

Rushing into the bunker, Walsh was greeted by a round of applause and congratulations from the cheering section.

"I was standing there naked as a jaybird," he recalled.

Meanwhile, Suydam and Mac Donnell had arrived at a bunker. It was the first one in their path of flight and they jumped in with enemy rounds exploding.

The men in the bunker had mixed expressions of shock and amusement as they saw their commanding officer arrive dressed in only his helmet and flak jacket.

"They didn't seem to have any questions," said Suydam, "and I guess there wasn't much use for an explanation at the moment."

Mac Donnell took the whole thing pretty well, but admitted, "Despite the rounds and all, the hardest part of the whole episode as far as I was concerned was standing in the bunker trying to hide behind a bar of soap."

Marines. The VC had been cut down before they were half way across the runway.

I find out later that the sergeant had written down my name and the events of the day, which had been passed on to my division HQ. That resulted in my being awarded the "V" (for Valor In Combat) device to be worn on my Navy Achievement Medal. Nice guy!

Note: Anyone who knew House knew he would do anything, at anytime for his fellow man. He was truly an example of a leadership Marine. If he could help, he was there. Whether he was needed in a support role or that of leadership, he was always accountable and at his best.

Lt. Suydam

February 4 - Melendez was setting in night listening posts to the west of Con Thien. One of his men, he thought, the radio operator, had left his post and was squatting in the open moonlight. Melendez went over, squatted in front of the man's face and proceeded to whisper "a piece of his mind" when he suddenly realized that the radio operator was not his but theirs. The two reached this conclusion at the same time. So, Melendez just slugged the guy and ran off. Melendez lay low throughout the night as enemy troops poked and probed through the bushes looking for him. Melendez was lovable and lucky.

Chris

February 5 - We've been at Con Thien now for 45 days, more than any other Marine unit. We've run more patrols, also. We are so sick of the rain and mud and more rain and deeper mud. It's hard to walk or run in. Sleeping in the rain in our ponchos is just damn cold. Temperatures drop into the low 30's at night. The cold seems to give away to the need for sleep. We average four hours of sleep each night. Death seems even sadder in the mud. The dead, lying in their muddy ponchos waiting to be lifted out of the battlefield by helicopter. The dead somehow stand for the Vietnam War at its ugliest.

It's times like this when your buddies are there for your and you for them. The bond is incredible, honest and always there.

Judge and I spend a lot of time talking. He's going on R&R soon. He is so ready to go, as is everyone when the time finally comes – Hong Kong, Hawaii, Kuala Lumpur, Japan, Australia or Thailand. It didn't really matter where we get to go, just somewhere out of here. We're all pleased when one of our guys gets to go on R & R. We're happy for them. Sure, we're one guy down, but not a problem, we'll be fine.

Judge always has a good attitude and is liked by everyone. He's a squad radioman for one of the other squads in the platoon. He's from Louisiana and has the accent to prove it.

House

February 5 - (From Headquarters, Da Nang) Word from Con Thien - That Damn Muddy Rat Hole!

Word has reached the rear area that my old "Gunny," Nathaniel Weathers, was killed by an 82mm mortar round and Captain Quinlan was badly wounded with him, and is now at NSA hospital. My old CO, Captain Baker, was down and told me 2/1 has been extended for another 30 days on the Con Thien hill - Ugly! That is too long for those guys to sit and take a bloody pounding. Poor guys. Why no rotation? What a shame. The Gunny was such a Marines' Marine. We will all remember him the most. God just got another good Marine to guard the pearly gates. I later find out that Gary Christensen carried his body to the aid station. That had to be pretty tough on Gary. He thought a lot of the Gunny.

Chris

February 5 - We were awakened early this morning, probably about 0100-0200 hours. I didn't notice the time because everyone was running around in such a damn frantic hurry. Shit! The word was passed that we are leaving immediately. The 2/4 battalion, situated between Go Linh and C2 outpost, was under attack and close to be overrun and probably annihilated. We were the closest support troops to them. If we didn't get to them quickly, they wouldn't make it. We were given orders to draw ammo and stand by. We stood ready to go, helmets, flak jackets, ammo, grenades, water, more ammo...We were quiet. We were quiet because we were listening to the battle, especially the distinctive sound of the enemy's AK-47 rifles. We knew that 2/4 was really having a difficult time. It went on for hours. The emotion that build up inside us was unbelievable. We were told Echo Company would be point for the battalion, which meant we would lead the rest of the battalion into the on-going battle. Would the NVA be waiting for us with an ambush. Probably. Would we run at them? Would we sneak up on them, with the sky lit up with flares, so we could see them - face to face? The anticipation of going to a place that was getting destroyed, getting the crap beat out of it. It was bad. I carried more ammo than ever - scared to death. We would soon encounter the NVA troops at night. It would be the worst. I was standing next to Estes, who only had one month left in Vietnam. He was just as scared as I was, probably more, as he carried the platoon radio and was listening to the communication between 2/4 and our command group. He knew we were getting ready.

We were about to go on possibly the worst engagement we had so far in our tour. Word spread. We stood down in the early morning. We would not be going. We were all totally exhausted. The anticipation was the worst. We waited all night to relieve 2/4 - one of the worst nights I ever have ever had. It wasn't the battle that occurred, we didn't have one, it was hearing the terribly long fire fight in the distance, knowing the enemy was inflicting pain on our buddies and we would be there soon, very soon. Did we want to go? Did we see ourselves kicking the NVA out of the area and killing them all? No, were we damn scared, but to support our Marines, sure we'd go.   Now, we were not going.   We slowly dispersed and moved back to the safety of our bunkers, exhausted.

Note: February 5 - Silver Star Medal.
My close friend Lt. Jeff Bodenweiser (Salem, Oregon) was with Echo Company, 26th Marines at the Khe Sanh Combat Base on this day.   While defending Hill 861-A, a reinforced North Vietnamese battalion launched an aggressive and determined ground assault, nearly overrunning their position.   Lt. Bodenweiser immediately seized the initiative and effectively consolidated the 2nd and the 3rd platoons. Lt. Bodenweiser tactically deployed his Marines at the point of heaviest contact, sealing the breach and cutting off the enemy's retreat.   While consolidating his position, Lt. Bodenweiser immediately recognized a unique opportunity. He boldly seized the initiative by quickly and effectively ordering his Marines to fix bayonets, which was a first in Vietnam. Leading a counter-attack armed only with a .45 caliber pistol, the lieutenant effectively led his Marines in close combat.   Despite the danger to himself, he called for "danger close" fire support that bracketed the enemy as his ferocious bayonet charge overran them. The cool, level headed decisions and positive, aggressive actions under intense pressure made by him were instrumental in successfully repelling the enemy attack with a minimum of Marine casualties.   Company E sustained seven Marines killed and 25 wounded while repelling an enemy force that was vastly superior in numbers. 109 North Vietnamese Army soldiers were killed inside the perimeter and many others were carried away by their compatriots.

Chris
February 5 - Still on Tet alert and blackout, which means there are to be no lights on anywhere. If you are lucky enough to have a candle to read with, it better not show any light to the outside.   Everybody says a big attack is coming tonight. We never know how the word is being spread. Is it coming from the lieutenant or one of the radio guys reading something into a conversation they may have heard. It's bad around here and then when the word gets passed that something really bad is coming, it brings in a whole new dimension in fear.   Normally, the guys don't dwell on it with others, but it's there.

February 6 - The placement of our own 105mm artillery position is 40 yards directly behind our trench position here at Con Thien. It's bad enough that the NVA artillery and mortars constantly bombard our position, but we also contend with the constant firing from behind us. The noise is deafening, every single day.

Marine sniper, spotter and Lt. Jeff Bodenweiser, Salem, Oregon on Hill 861A, with the 2nd Battalion, 26th Marines

Capt. Thomas Eagen, Echo Company Commander
February 6 - I just got back to Con Thien and learned about the tragic death of Gunny Weathers last week. I was stuck in Da Nang because there were no flights going north. I went over to Nui Kim Sanh, a ville in the Marble Mountain area, which is just below the chopper strip at Da Nang East. Tet started that night when the NVA came to visit. I was lucky to get out the next day and flew into Phu Bai and ran into Colonel Archie Van Winkle, who was assistant operations officer for Task Force X-ray. He put me to work in Hue and then I escaped back to Con Thien.

Note: February 7- The Special Forces camp at Lang Vei, just seven kilometers southwest of Khe Sanh, was overrun, heightening the alarm over the fate of the Khe Sanh Combat Base.

It came as a shock to the Special Forces troopers at Lang Vei when twelve tanks attacked their camp. The Soviet-built PT-76 amphibious tanks churned over the defenses, followed by an infantry assault. The ground troops had been specially equipped for the attack with satchel charges, tear gas, and flame throwers. Although the camp's main defenses were overrun in only 13 minutes, the fighting lasted several hours, during which the Special Forces men and the local Montagnard tribe managed to knock out at least five of the tanks.

Those holding down the KSCB (Khe Sanh Combat Base) did not come to the rescue of the Special Forces (SF) Camp, as Colonel Lownds, the Commanding Officer of the 26th Marines, feared a relief force would be ambushed.

Chris

February 8 - Things got fouled up again. My name was left off the R & R roster, so I did not get a seat on the plane. I'm waiting for another flight tomorrow. I'll probably go back to the unit in a couple of days, if I don't get a flight. Rick Grabenhorst had his 21st birthday on the 10th. He was also promoted to E-4 in Korea. I'm so glad he's not here. He's not real excited about Korea, either, so his letters say.

February 11 - Oh, geez...the shelling started again. I was inside the Army tank, which was in the very next position to our fighting hole. The tank commander immediately called for his crew to get underway. I was further away from a large and much safer underground bunker and that's where I was headed as fast as I could go. As I approached the bunker, I ducked my head and headed downward into the 12' x 20' underground living area. We were getting hit so badly, like every day, the shells going off everywhere, exploding everywhere... I ran as fast as I could and my first or second step inside missed a step or the step was set back in slightly. I stumbled head over heels and somersaulted, landing halfway down the staircase and landing on my lower back. There I stopped. I was unable to move. A corpsman was called. I didn't have any feeling in my legs or arms. I was numb. I was moved to the underground aid-station and there I laid until someone was available to help me. I was not shot, I was taken care of by a corpsman who placed me on a table and injected my arm with a small capsular of morphine and placed a headset over my ears, playing a hit song from the Mama's and Papa's. I faded off into space as the morphine entered my system. Both of these efforts took the pain away and they had their way with me.

The USA blanket rose overhead and formed a tent. The docs and other people appeared to be having a party, laughing and dancing. I dozed off. I am now lying down and will be for awhile. That morphine is quite a drug.

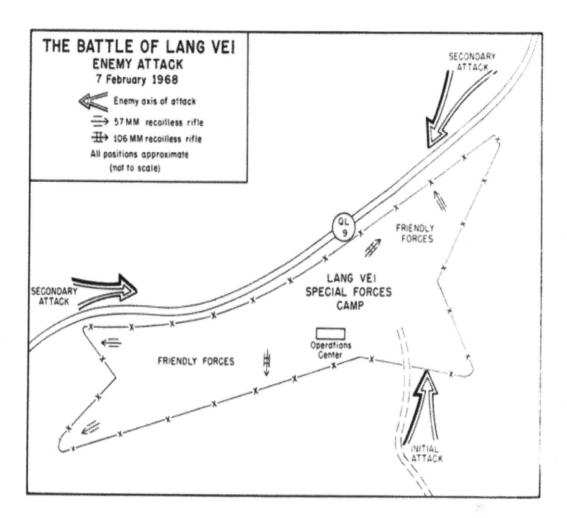

I don't remember much of the days to follow. We were getting way too much incoming artillery and rocket fire for me to be medevaced to a hospital, so I was drugged and put away. It was scary to lie in a dark space underground and not know if I would walk again. Within a week or so, I was released and back to my squad, where I was presented a walking cane by the guys. I walked a bit crunched over for a while and the back pain continued, but back on the lines – locked and loaded.

Lt. Kirk

February 12 - I ran a number of night ambushes around Con Thien. I used an L shaped formation with a listening post to the rear. We carried a rope with knots in it and each man took his position adjacent to his knot. I planted microphones in the kill zone with wires running back to a headset (later we had microphones that transmitted sound without wires). We used Starlight scopes to monitor the kill zone. We set in well away from the killing zone. We never got the action we had hoped for.

Chris

February 13 - Khe Sanh seems to be grabbing all the trouble at the present. The NVA now have tanks that are being used in the battle, 530 pound warhead rockets carried on tracked vehicles, have also been reported. Word is that North Vietnam is getting equipment from the Russians and the Chinese. We do find rifles and equipment quite often when we sweep through battlefields, especially the famous AK-47. It's a great automatic rifle. It can get wet and muddy while crossing streams and will fire when called on and keep on firing.

Chinese rifles, grenades and supplies are found all the time.

Our rifles are not as reliable as the weapons the NVA has. We have many issues with our rifles. They jam, cartridges don't extract all the time. We are told to clean them better.

 Note: Years later we learn about the gun powder that is used in the cartridges contributed to the breakdown of our M-16 rifles.

Our battalion rear area is down south at Phu Bai. They have been in the middle of some pretty bad fighting, but we understand things are starting to settle down and come under control now.

Dave Dillberg

February 13 – A delayed 152mm arty round went in the ground right in front of OP1 and proceeded down on an angle under it was right under us. When it blew up, it picked up the bunker about four feet in the air. I remember the floor of the bunker hitting me in the face as we were hiding on the floor in a hands over the head position waiting to be killed. After the floor hit me in the face, I looked up and saw the sunlight shining in between the sandbags as they all came back down loosely. The round went down far enough into the ground before exploding so that the bunker was still intact.

 Note: Numerous Marines were sent to Hue City, as they returned from the hospital, R&R or somewhere else in transit. The attack was so severe, all extra

Everyone had the same issue - staying dry, keeping your fighting hole dry

Marines were sent to help. Our senior corpsman Doc Turner, Sgt. "Bernie" Bernston, our combat correspondent and Captain Eagen all saw time in Hue.

The following article includes a discussion of how Sgt. Bernston was wounded in Hue. He was awarded a Bronze Star for bravery and two Purple Hearts.

Al Webb, *UPI Writer (in Hue Imperial City)*
February 18 - Hue straddled the ill-named Perfume River in the northern quarter of South Vietnam, and somehow it had remained a haven of sanity well into the war, a city of Oriental beauty, culture and education, of history and old tombs of old emperors centered in its walled Citadel, copied after the Imperial City in Peking, China.

Hue City had largely escaped the bullets and bombs of the war. Many westerners, including American correspondents, would call time out from the war to rest and relax at its pleasant little restaurants and bistros, or read a book, or just a night of rest aboard one of the scores of small boats on the Perfume River, watching the flashes of combat in the distance.

But then was then, and now was now. By the time I arrived in my muddy uniform from diving for protection behind a low, gray wall across from the besieged U.S. military compound, the city war being overrun. I was south of the river. The 20th century warfare had horrifically transformed the city of the Nguyen emperors and their Palace of Perfect Peace. Perhaps forever, I thought.

The emblem was plain enough - the yellow-starred flag of the National Liberation Front, guerrilla Viet Cong, that waved over the fortress gate of the Citadel, on the north side of the Perfume River. It would flutter there for the next 25 days as the longest and bloodiest single ground action of the Tet Offensive waxed and waned in its shadow.

For the next 10 days, Frank and Poncho and Kenny and the scores of other Marines who became my mates in combat battled door to door, in fighting the likes of which Corps veterans had not experienced since Seoul, Korea, in another war more than 15 years earlier.

I watched helplessly as one by one, Pancho and Frank and Kenny were killed, as the Marines fought to recapture what was left of the city's south. The university, with its classrooms bullet-ridden and incinerated books was in shambles. The pool tables were makeshift morgue slabs, drenched with the blackened blood of Marine bodies.

Finally, Col. Cheatham's troops raised the Stars and Stripes over the province headquarters - itself a risky job as North Vietnamese soldiers popped from human mole holes to open fire, until exasperated Marines silenced them with grenades dropped into their crude lairs.

But the job was only half-done. Across the river, inside the Citadel itself, other Marines were battling their way down the walls, capturing perhaps 100 yards in a day, only to have to fall back 50 yards after nightfall, when the NVA struck back.

At one point along the northeast wall, the Marines hoisted an American flag on a slender tree they had uprooted, and supported it with a wooden kitchen chair. They had to take it down that night, but they put it back up again the next day, *and the day after, until one day it stayed. To the Americans, it was one small sign that they were, at last, winning.*

And there was a Marine I had struck up a friendship with, one the truck ride along Highway 1 into Hue south. He had just returned from a week's leave with his children in Hawaii. Eight days later he lay a few feet from me, his stomach ripped out by two bullets.

On February 19th, a sniper's deadly fire had pinned me and Marine Sergeant Steve Bernston, beneath a wall behind a house. Across a street about 20 yards to our left, one of the sniper's bullets tore off a third of the skull of another Marine. His screams lasted for about 90 seconds that seemed an hour before he, too, became another of the American dead in Vietnam.

**Sgt. "Bernie" Bernston, on right, Combat Correspondant,
is seen helping carry out a wounded Marine in Hue City.
Bernie received 2 Purple Hearts and 1 Bronze Star
for his action during this time.**

Minutes later, about five feet from me, a Marine sergeant took a bullet through his throat. Bernston and I dragged him out of the line of fire, back to what we thought was relative safety, as we looked for something to use as a stretcher. My part in the Battle of Hue ended a few seconds after that, in the blast of a B-40 anti-tank rocket that effectively was the death blow for the sergeant we were trying to rescue, crippling Bernston for life, wounding fellow journalist David Greenway and sending me to a hospital with shrapnel injuries.

The battle lasted another five days, until the Viet Cong flag was finally torn down from atop the fortress gate.

<u>Chris</u>
February 19 - I had a new sniper guy delivered to me this afternoon, to join our group. I was standing on top of our bunker in conversation with others in my squad when the new guy was delivered. Our position looked out to the southwest and it was slightly elevated, with concertina wire, claymores and tin cans stretched in front of us and the minefield and more concertina were in front of that. I told the new guy to lie down on the sandbags and point his rifle and scope towards the northwest and try to pick up the Ho Chi Minh trail used by the enemy to bring their equipment into South Vietnam. I then turned back to continue my conversation with the other guys of my squad. The new guy just stood there without doing what I asked, so I told him again what I wanted him to do. He just stood there. I'm not sure exactly what happened next, but... he went flying over my back and down the incline of our position. None of us could figure out what his problem was. Anyway, we continued to talk and noticed a short while later that a medevac copter was lifting off from below and flew right past us. We continued to talk.

After a short while, the lieutenant came for me and announced that the battalion commander wanted to see me at the command bunker. I didn't even know where the command bunker was, but the lieutenant was instructed to accompany me. When I reported to the colonel he asked me to explain what happened to the new guy who flew over and down the bunker side (possibly, with some additional help from me). The colonel was a no-nonsense guy. I explained my story. I told him I had expected the Marine to do what he was told to do instead of complain or get sassy. Maybe I shouldn't be in a command position. He thought about what I had told him and then looked me in the eye and said "okay", slapped me on the back and said "dismissed". Weird.

Lt. Kirk

Feb 19 - The same lieutenant who showed me the VC body parts in a poncho led his platoon in a patrol north of Con Thien. He was killed leading his men in an assault with a .45 caliber pistol. He said he was a stunt man in the movies before joining the Marines.

Feb 20 - The battalion commander, a couple of other officers and I took a helicopter and did a reconnaissance of the DMZ. We had a great view of the Ben Hai River and into North Vietnam. It was interesting to see the area from the air and spooky to look down into North Vietnam.

Knobby

February 21 - I'm pretty busy right now as I will be for the next few days learning the job of platoon radio man. I have to copy the names and medevac numbers of everyone in the platoon and also the different frequencies and call signs that the battalion uses. Once I get everything down it will be a pretty skating job. I only go out when the Lieutenant does (platoon-sized patrols or larger), which means I won't have any squad patrols or ambushes. I'll be moving into the CP (command post) bunker with the Lieutenant, platoon sergeant, night guide and the two Navy corpsmen.

We just got some incoming artillery rounds. I think it was 152 mm. It sounded like it came from the mountains to the west. They only shot 4 rounds though and all of them fell about 50 meters short of the barbed wire; no one was hurt.

T still hasn't gotten up from the rear. They may just keep him back since he gets out of the field anyway March 15th. A man in his squad was killed a couple of days ago. We had a memorial service for him this morning.

Chris

February 22 - We had formation today, which was pretty strange, as we don't have that type of gathering unless we're leaving for a march. The captain was giving a few guys promotions - I made Corporal, E-4. I know the colonel could have thrown me in the brig for what I had done with the new sniper. Instead I got promoted. I haven't heard anything about getting another sniper assigned to me. Oh, well.

Note: February 23 – Over 1,300 artillery rounds hit Khe Sanh and its outposts, more than any other previous day of attacks. Bunkers continued to be rebuilt and built up to withstand larger rounds from the enemy. The guns firing the enemy rounds were so well hidden in the hills surrounding the base that it was extremely difficult to destroy them. The guns would fire and retreat back into the mountain on their tracks, undiscovered and unseen.

February 23 - Things are definitely happening around here, now. The gooks are on the offensive now. We are going out tomorrow to assault some NVA bunkers that are supposed to be quite well hidden and continuing to fire and inflict harm. We have quite a few new guys, but they seem OK. I guess we'll find out tomorrow. It's got to be really tough for the new guys, but nothing like a few rounds of fire coming your direction to tell the story of what's going on. Most of the guys do great. They hit the ground immediately, which is the most important move a guy can make...then take a peek around and see what the rest of your squad is doing and do the same. It works. It's on the job training at its best.

The DMZ area out in front of Con Thien was continuously sprayed by U.S. aircraft flying overhead dumping the chemical Agent Orange, during our tour of the war. It had been determined that the area needed to be kept clear, so any traffic crossing the DMZ could be easily spotted. Hopefully, it would keep out some of the enemy troops coming across and into South Vietnam. This action forced the NVA to supply troops, ammo and food through the borders of Laos and Cambodia, where U.S. troops were not allowed to venture. They would enter into South Vietnam from its western border.

Note: Chris: Agent Orange! The U.S. approved it, without knowing the ill-effects it would have on the men fighting on the ground. It destroys the foliage - the brush, trees, grass and anything else in its way. The problem was it got in our water, it got in our food, we breathed it, we slept in it and some took it home. The physical issues caused by this chemical were so numerous and broad-reaching, both to the Marines, but also their families and their children.

Chris
February 24 – Doc Turner returned from R&R today. He had been working in Hue City during the attack on that city and also had an extended stay at the hospital due to a puss pocket on his face resulting from an infection from something caught during field time. It is so good to get him back. Everyone has such great respect for him and his ability to help those wounded. He is a very smart guy and truly a great friend.

February 25 – Our base here at Con Thien has just gone through another long mortar attack, who knows how many rounds. We took a tremendous amount of damage to the area today and have a lot of work to do to the damaged bunkers and firing positions. We were unable to get troops out in medevac copters, as mortars continued to fall on the copter pad when they were attempting to land. We are so exposed.

The NVA can easily see an approaching copter. We're all lucky not to be a group of babbling idiots from all the incoming shelling.

We had to send a guy back to the States today, as he absolutely couldn't handle the constant explosions, the fear of battle and all that went with it. It was one thing to lose a guy in combat, but to lose a guy for this type of thing, hurt. We needed everyone so badly.

L/Cpl Larry Herfel

Yesterday a rifleman in my squad and my good friend Larry Herfel was killed by enemy artillery fire. He was 19 years old. Larry and Lenny were watching an air strike as they stood on a bunker. Lenny was WIA from the same round, a 152mm artillery round that exploded and Larry got hit in the eye. Larry was one of the few men I got close to. He was a very nice guy from Madison, Wisconsin. He hardly ever got mail, if he did it would be from his sister, not his parents. We all shared our packages from home with him, as he did not have the constant comfort of mail, from friends and family at home. He never complained. I know that he felt the same about the guys in our squad, as we felt about him. It was quite a sober day. Larry, Lenny, House, Estes and I stayed close throughout our tours. Now, we had lost Larry.

**Lance Corporal Larry Herfel, Madison, Wisconsin
(panel 41E, line 014 on The Wall)**

Lathan Williams

February 25 - We stayed here at Con Thien and have started running patrols again. Hopefully, the threat of being overrun has diminished. The Tet Offensive really put us on alert. We knew the enemy was massing its troops outside our base.

Note: February 25 - 1st Battalion 5th Marines seize The Citadel, a "castle" in the Imperial City of Hue. 452 ARVN and 216 U.S. troops (147 Marines) are killed in the battle. Estimates of NVA/VC dead range from 2400 to 8113. The beautiful ancient castle complex was destroyed.

Sgt. Mike Gordon (from Portland, Oregon), formerly of Echo Company, received a battlefield commission to 2nd Lieutenant this month.

Corpsman Mike Champagne received the Bronze Star for defending a small civilian hospital in Hue City. Regimental headquarters sent troops (Hue City was 8 miles from Phu Bai) to Hue City and Mike and others in the rear area were a part of that. Doc Turner, away from Con Thien, got pulled into the battle of Hue also, as he was in transit coming back from R&R. Also, Sergeant "Bernie" Bernston, our combat correspondent, was sent to Hue while in transit. The battle was so intense and the enemy had so many troops that all transit personnel were sent to help.

Chris

February 26 – Mom, I just received your letter about Grandma's death. She was such a great person. I will keep her in my prayers, as she meant so very much to all of us. No one person had so much good in them. I know she is with God now and still looking over me.

Note: On February 27, 1968, CBS news anchor Walter Cronkite concluded a special report by saying, "It seems now more certain than ever that the bloody experience of Vietnam is to end in a stalemate." After hearing the statement, President Johnson commented that "If I've lost Walter Cronkite, I've lost Mr. Average Citizen."

Chris

February 27 - Since we have been here at Con Thien, we have continued to strengthen the fighting positions by increasing the sandbags to the bunkers to help withstand the impact of the artillery which falls on us daily. Ammo boxes filled with sand, extra tarmac steel normally used on airfields and anything else we could find was ultimately used to fortify our positions. We were always trying to make them better bunkers.

Before and during our time at Con Thien, there were thousands of enemy soldiers in our neighborhood. During February it was estimated that we faced two regiments plus a battalion of infantry and two artillery regiments. The previous troops had to battle the on-coming enemy in droves and with morphine in their system. The enemy had morphine strapped to their arms, with an easily accessible strap to pull and thus begin the flow of the drugs into their bodies. The drugs allowed them to fight through pain and suffering if they were shot or wounded, continuing to try to over-run the American defensive front at our isolated base. They all knew this was the base which divided the North Communist country from its neighbors in the south.

The mental impact of being told that there were thousands of NVA troops surrounding us was incredible. We assembled all the weapons and ammo we could get our hands on. I was scared and so was everyone around me. It was fairly quiet most of the night. If you were talking, then you weren't listening....listening for the one sound that might save your life. Everyone on the hill was alert the entire night. When morning came we were all so relieved. No attack, no buddies killed, nothing. I can't imagine that we could have stopped such a large mass of enemy from overrunning our base. I thanked God, again. I seem to be doing that often.

Capt. Thomas Eagan
February 27 - Our new Gunny is Gunnery Sergeant Louis J. Lambert, ...with the many tattoos and "golden" shotgun.

Dave Dillberg, Golf Company, 2/1
February 27 - Con Thien was surrounded by thousands of NVA during Tet 68. We were told they were going to overrun us and to fight, until we died, to make every round count and never give up. We stocked up on grenades, ammunition and claymore mines. They didn't attack, but it was very traumatic being in the impact zone and seeing that many enemy moving past us... with nobody to help us. I always thought since we didn't get overrun it wasn't too bad, but being stuck in the impact zone and not being able to fight back was traumatic enough to make us think about it for the rest of our lives. We received almost 3000 rounds of 152mm arty inside our perimeter in 76 days.

Note: Quang Tri Province was subjected to the heaviest bombing campaign in the history of the World, more than in all of Europe during WWII - documented by Landmines Vietnam.

Note: General Westmoreland requests an additional 206,000 troops.

Chris

February 28 – I just received orders to go visit the morgue in Da Nang and identify some of the KIA Marines in our company that we have lost lately. I am one of the senior men in the platoon and therefore, know most of the guys. This is a very difficult situation. I've never had to do something like this. So, I go as just another mission, something required to do. I'll be back with the guys soon. So, armed with my .45 automatic pistol and K-Bar knife, I prepared for the journey. Since Highway 1 is temporarily being held by the gooks, I was able to catch a chopper to an aircraft carrier, way out in the ocean somewhere.

When the chopper landed on the deck of the U.S. Navy aircraft carrier, which was floating somewhere off the coast of Vietnam, I was rushed inside and asked if I wanted something to eat as chow was being served. That was funny. Of course, I would. As soon as I said yes, I was immediately ushered through a hatch, down a passageway and into the mess hall. I was led into the line, handed a tray and began to gather a fabulous hot lunch. Then I sat down to eat. The type of meal they were talking about was, well, a full meal. It was cafeteria-style, with everything and more - salad, meat, potatoes, jello, deserts, milk, and so much more!

I was directed to a place at one of the tables by one of the sailors in front of me in line. As I sat down and began to eat, I must have had a dozen sailor guys crowd around and ask me about the war. They were all so interested in what I did and how bad it was. I tried to explain what our company did, where we lived and what I did. I'm sure they noticed I had on a worn t-shirt, dirty pants and not looking too good. They asked if there was anything they could do for me. I told them I hadn't had a pair of socks in a long time. They brought two pair of socks and two t-shirts immediately. I threw my t-shirt away, as mine was pretty old, cruddy and tired, as was my whole body. I asked if I could get seconds on the chocolate cake and two guys jumped to retrieve an additional piece. While we ate, one person cleaned my pistol, the clips, and the ammo. They continued to ask questions, they wanted stories – what was going on, tell me more. How bad was it really? I probably looked as if I had crawled underground all the way to their ship. I was treated so well. As quick as I had gotten there, I was to leave. I was summoned and left immediately on the waiting copter for the trip to Da Nang. I carried that visit with me and shared it with all the guys when I returned. Oh, did I mention, I got two pieces of chocolate cake?

The copter landed at Da Nang Air Base and I exited the craft and asked where the morgue was located. I was directed toward a nondescript building, which was located close to the airstrip. The temperature was well over 110 degrees outside, as I slowly walked toward the morgue. It was easy to find the mortuary. Everyone knew where it was - too bad. It was a visit I hoped I would only have to take once, but I'm sure I would remember for the rest of my life.

After entering the facility, I gave my list of names to a person that appeared from behind a closed door. All business, no chit-chat. I was asked to follow him into a room, which was cool and clean. I entered the vault and they opened a stainless steel door on the left side of the room, the second drawer from the floor. They slid the drawer out. The bag was unzipped, exposing the lifeless remains of a fallen Marine. The face is non-descript. There is no soul. Questions are then asked regarding identification and the dark bag is closed up and on then we went on to the next body. I don't know how those morgue guys did their job. The graves (morgue worker) man pulled open the next drawer, unzipped the body bag, and we continued. I looked at each of the lifeless, cold faces of the Marines I had fought next to. The name would be read, the toe-tag checked and dog tags. I nodded or mumbled something and the drawer would be closed. The next name, the next drawer…

The February Command Chronology for 2nd Battalion, 1st Marines reports that ground contact was light but shelling increased, with almost 2000 rounds of incoming, much of it 152mm artillery rounds. Aerial observers noted heavy enemy activity to the north and west, often as close as 900 meters. Observation posts spotted many lights and vehicles, believed to be engaged in establishing artillery positions. The perimeter wire was breached and the minefield probed. Patrol activity increased to include longer company size patrols and more night patrols and ambushes. Almost 28,000 rounds of artillery were fired in support of the battalion and the 81mm mortar platoon fired 23,887 rounds. A mortar position was hit by incoming artillery which destroyed two mortar tubes and 700 rounds of mortar ammunition. 21 enemy were confirmed KIA, with 48 probables. 2nd Battalion, 1st Marines casualties for February: 4 enlisted KIA, 16 enlisted WIA.

Knobby

March 1 - I moved back into my old bunker with Willie, Buzz and Holland today. Willie and Buzz are the two black guys. Our old platoon radio man came back so I'm Bravo squad leader again. I'm glad to be back with the squad again and away from that crazy CP. 55 days left in the field.

Chris

March 2 - I leave for Dong Ha soon. I'll be going by truck convoy, then catch a chopper to Phu Bai, which is our battalion headquarters rear area. I have been told I will pick up my orders for R&R and then fly to Da Nang by transport C130 Air Force fixed wing plane or by chopper. Finally, I will head to Hong Kong for R&R (Rest & Relaxation). I finally get my day. I've waited for over seven months, which is way longer than most, but no complaints. Our battalion has lost so many guys, it's been hard to allow anyone to go on R&R. I understand.

Note: On March 2, General Tolson, commander of the Army's 1st Air Cavalry Division, got the green light to relieve Khe Sanh. Operation Pegasus had a mission to destroy the enemy forces within the region, open Highway 9 from Ca Lu to Khe Sanh, and relieve the Khe Sanh Combat Base. The 1st Marine Regiment would participate in this operation.

Lt. Kirk

March 2 - My platoon went on patrol with a platoon from H Company under Lt. Pete Flanagan, the H Co. XO. We went a long way to the west of Con Thien, further than I had ever been. I made the fire plan. We called in H&I (harassing and interdicting) fire when we turned around to cover our rear. Although we had no contact, it was exhilarating to be out patrolling so far from base rather than sitting still getting shot at.

Chris

March 3 - We sent one of the guys in our squad home, as it became too difficult for him, with the constant firing, artillery explosions, anticipation of injury, others around us being hauled off to the aid station or in a body bag. It all contributed. He was really a nice, shy guy, but it was easy to see early on, that he was just too young to be where we were. We wished well and continued, one man short.

Capt. Thomas Eagan

March 5 – For my money, Con Thien was the most dangerous place I'd been in, although the booby traps in the 3/1 area south of Marble Mountain probably killed and wounded more Marines consistently in dribs and drabs patrolling the mortar/ rocket belt. And Con Thien was a shit hole to live in. I told Lt. Col. Billy Duncan once that Con Thien should have stayed a recon team site and the battalions should have stayed outside the wire doing dirt to the NVA. All we were on Con Thien was one very large TARGET. He thought I was wrong to question the wisdom of the Elders, but he learned. On that occasion I ask him to reverse roles a minute: would we prefer for the NVA to dig in and defend strong points rather than wander around Leatherneck Square deciding when and where to hit us? Seemed obvious to me that we were the chumps, sitting in the V ring for their artillery.

Note: Captain Eagen couldn't have been more on target. Later on, Major General Ray Davis, Medal of Honor winner in Korea, took over the 3d Marine Division after working as deputy with the Army 23d Provisional Corps where he'd watched the way the Army 101st and 1st Air Cav operated. One of his first moves was to get Marines out of those damned bunkers along the McNamara Line and go after the enemy. He relieved colonels and lieutenant colonels who couldn't or wouldn't fight. He changed the world for the 3d Marine Division.

Note: Finally, after an extended tour at Con Thien, the 2nd Battalion, 1st Marines, left the hill that had held them captive for the past 77 days. Bunkers had been rebuilt to withstand the tremendous burden of daily artillery. The trenches had been rebuilt to be able to hold off the massive ground attacks that had occurred during the last quarter of 1967. The Hil" was much a much better defensive position now.

Chris

March 8 - Our unit served the longest period - 77 days, of any detachment at the Con Thien outpost, the Marine's northernmost outpost closest to the DMZ, guarded by a 225,000 mine field. We received almost 3,000 incoming rounds of artillery, mortars, rockets and recoilless rifle rounds during our time period. That's a lot to absorb.

My unit, Echo Company, held positions on the south side of the Hill. We suffered the terror of thousands of rounds of enemy shell fire during that time. Eleven of the fourteen men in my squad were either killed or wounded there. Estes, House and I escaped.

By the grace of God, I was able to leave that hell-hole alive. I totally recognize this fact and feel good about whatever lays in front of me in the future. The faces of the guys we lost will also stay with me. I continue to think about Herfel, Gunny Weathers and the others. Thoughts of the seemingly never-ending artillery barrages will also stay with me, I'm sure.

Note: Chris - In addition to artillery, rockets and mortars, we often received sniper fire. On more than one occasion, the Command Chronology records the sighting and destruction of enemy tanks north of the base by 8" guns and artillery. Aerial observers frequently saw heavy enemy activity north and northwest of the base, often as close as 900 yards. The bad guys frequently probed our perimeter, cut our barbed wire and even built fighting holes right in our wire.

Note: Lt. Kirk - There were several artillery observation posts on the north side of the hill. They were heavily sandbagged, small wooden towers. The enemy had them zeroed in and would take them out frequently. There were a lot of casualties among the FO's (forward observers). I don't know how the FO's had the guts to go up into those towers.

According to the Command Chronology, my platoon ran 6 patrols or night ambushes at Con Thien from December 23 - December 31, 22 in January, 15 in February and 9 from March 1 -March 8, when we left Con Thien. These were in addition to company size operations.

Note: The Command Chronology reports that Con Thien received about 2000 rounds of incoming artillery, mortar and recoilless rifle fire during February, or about 69 rounds per day.

The Place is called Con Thien (draft for newspaper publication)
by Roger Goss

The first impression of the place belies the brutality of survival there. Everything is either underground or heavily fortified. There are extra support units attached to the Marines there that giver the place an aura of unnecessary impregnability and unbelievable firepower. It appears to be an acne afflicted red scar on the face of an already haggard landscape. The acne scars are artillery craters and there lies the brutality of survival on "The Hill."

Life there is misery. If the monsoon rains are falling, the place is miasma of mud and you're wet and cold. If the weather is clear the med turns to chalking dust and the sun sizzles. There's no place to bathe or wash clothes. The diet is steady c-rations. The mail is late.

An artillery barrage is a whistling thundering hell on earth. And, it kills. It's like being in an earthquake inside a kettle drum. The air sings with falling projectiles and whines with flying shrapnel. The earth pitches and shakes with the shock of the hugh explosions. Your roof on your bunker leaks dirt and sandbags fall out of place. Trenches cave in, equipment is damaged, fires are started. The sounds and scenes are almost too much for the psyche. Some men shake; others just "go numb." And the worst part for the individual is you can't shoot back. You wait and hope and pray and curse.

After a barrage, there's work to do - clear out trenches, fill sand bags, repair broken communication wires, string barb wire and get ready for the next barrage. At night, it's 100% alert...no one sleeps, all eyes and ears on the perimeter, guarding against ground attacks.

Con Thien is also a state of mind. It's fear and loneliness. It's the depression accompanying death. The horror of mutilation. It's sick humor and short tempers. But, most of all, it's a humble heroism and a hope. A hope for one more tomorrow.

9

C-2 FIREBASE

On March 9th, the Battalion was relieved at Con Thien by the 1st Battalion, 4th Marines and moved to an artillery base three miles south of Con Thien called C-2.

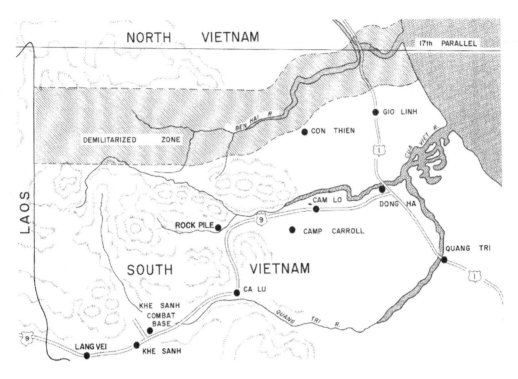

Lt. Kirk
March 9 - The battalion left Con Thien today. Fox and Golf Company, which had been positioned on the north side of the hill, received the brunt of the incoming artillery attacks. By the time we left, a lot of them were really freaked out or, as we said, squirrelly. I admired their courage and endurance tremendously.

We went south to an artillery firebase called C-2 and nearby location called C-2A, which guarded a bridge over a creek and was also known as the washout. C-2 was about three miles south of Con Thien and C-2A was about 1-½ miles south of Con Thien, both straddling the MSR.

Dave Dillberg, Golf Company, 1st Squad Leader
March 9 – We are now a few miles south of the hill at C-2 where all the big guns are. I just learned that 1st Battalion, 4th Marines have taken our place at Con Thien.

More assaults continue on Da Nang - VC sappers attacked the airbase and headquarters of the 1st Marine Division.

Bob Dunbar, Echo Co.
March 9 - I have been placed in a area called C-2, a water control point just south of Con Thien. It sounds like we will receive about the same amount of rockets, mortars and artillery as The Hill, which is what the guys call Con Thien.

Chris
March 9 – Well, I am out of Con Thien and finally in Da Nang, safe and sound. It is so unbelievable. I've waited so long. I went to the club and had a couple of beers, met a few guys headed back home. I met a tailor from Hong Kong at the club. He was selling suits. I told him I was going to Hong Kong in a couple of days. He asked me to deliver a package for him to his main office. For doing this favor for him I will receive free clothes - suit, sweater and shirts. FREE! I was to come by his store, as soon as I received my orders to a flight.

March 10 - My name was left off the flight list. No R&R. Again. I saw a bunch of guys I knew from the states, while waiting for my turn and spent time talking with them. Everybody talking about the **BIG PX** (USA), girl friends, new cars and lots of other cool stuff. My time will come, I'm sure of it. I've always felt I would return home, I would be injured, but I would be one of the lucky ones and be able to go home.

I will return to rear area headquarters, check in and return to the front. It was during this time that Corpsman Don Wilkens went crazy at Con Thien, from all the constant, daily shelling of rockets and other artillery rounds. He had to be sent back to the rear area and we lost track of him. Well, bad news – I probably won't get my college cut. Something was left off the papers. It was good to be in Da Nang for a while and relax, a bit.

Knobby
March 13 - We moved from Con Thien to C-2, which is an artillery battery a couple miles south of Con Thien. Our living conditions are 100% better than they were at Con Thien. C-2 is sort of a show piece as far as defensive positions.

Consequently, when we aren't out in the field there are always brass walking around pestering us with inspections and the like. We also go out in the field a lot more here than we did at Con Thien, especially squad and platoon-sized patrols.

We just got a call on the radio that the colonel is on his way to our area, so I had better get ready. 42 days in the field.

Chris

March 13 - While in the Phu Bai rear area and waiting for a flight to go on R& R, I was talking to one of my friends who works in the company rear office. He said they need another office worker in our company office, as one of the guys was rotating home. He wanted to know if I was interested. I said sure and he said he would put in my name. We both laughed about it. It would be too strange to be pulled out of a combat position and placed in an office. Not going to happen. I put some money in my 10% saving account. The weather is heating up. It will probably be in the 100's soon.

March 14 – Highway 1, which has been closed for quite awhile, opened up today. The number of NVA around Khe Sanh has decreased, or so we're told. So, where have they gone?

Khe Sanh continues to have difficulty getting supplies - food, ammo, first aid, clothes into the combat base. As helicopters and C-130 planes approach the runways, the NVA shelling is devastating, destroying the aircraft. In order in receive supplies the commander of the base has employed a couple of new means of receiving food, ammunition and medical supplies we are told.

Low Altitude Parachute Extraction System (LAPES) is used to unload C-130 freight cargo pallets, which never actually land on the runway. The resupply aircraft approaches the KSCB runway about six feet off the ground, the pilot automatically deploys a parachute attached to the cargo pallet, which is on rollers. The chute jerks the cargo pallet out of the rear door and it slides to a halt after it hits the runway. The pilot guns the aircraft in an accelerated climb to avoid enemy ground fire. As this is happening, the base personnel run out to retrieve the badly needed supplies before the enemy has an opportunity to bring their deeply-hidden artillery guns out of the mountain and fire on the runway.

A second method is to drop supplies by parachute. This is also difficult to retrieve the supplies, as they are scattered about the base and actually beyond the perimeter at times.

Note: March 16 - My Lai Massacre – A unit of the Army's Americal Division massacred as many as 500 civilians after receiving instructions from Captain Ernest Medina that anyone remaining in the village on market day was an enemy. The slaughter ended when a helicopter pilot, Warrant Officer Hugh Thompson, and his crew chief landed between the Americans and the Vietnamese. It was truly an American disgrace. Lieutenant Calley was the only one to serve a sentence for his crimes. Initially sentenced to life in prison, his sentence was reduced and he served only 3½ years of "house arrest" at Fort Benning, Georgia.

Note: Lt. Kirk - We took 15 rounds of incoming artillery/mortar fire one day since we left Con Thien, but there was no incoming the other 14 days we were there (2/1 Command Chronology). Unfortunately, there was no hot chow. Mike Jackson's battalion had a mess hall during its time there, but 2/1 did not. We continued to eat C-rations.

Note: The funny thing is that the 2/1 Command Chronology makes the statement almost every month that morale is good, in part due to the mess hall serving hot chow. The only mess hall for most of these months was in the battalion rear, at Phu Bai. This comment appears to be required boilerplate.

Chris

March 19 – The captain said he would send me anywhere I wanted to go for R&R next month. We all believe in Capt Eagen, so once again, I take his word. I'm supposed to get out of the field August 3rd, go through processing and then, home. Not being able to go on R&R is not good, but I understand I'm needed now. I am back in the company rear area trying to recuperate from my second back injury.

March 20 – It seems one of the men in the company office is getting ready to rotate back to the world. I guess my office worker friend that I spoke to a while ago spoke to Top (the top sergeant in the company, usually a first sergeant, who ran the rear area operations). Evidently, they checked my jacket (personnel file) and found I had been to college and could type (22 wpm). I would soon be given a "transfer to the rear area". You can't understand how incredible this made me feel. For every Marine in combat, there are 10 men in the rear area to support his activity in the field – truck drivers, artillery men, supply people, communications specialists, operational staff, cooks, medical personnel, etc. I was going to be one of them! I was going to be safe, (relatively). The feeling is overwhelming.

I figured I had seen enough of the war, lost too many good friends, been on operations from Da Nang to the DMZ, ran from and after gooks, NVA, the Viet Cong, and the Chinese. I've served my time in the bush and was given an opportunity to get out, so I took it. I will miss not being with the guys in the field, but my chances to get home again, will improve immensely. So now, I am in Phu Bai at our company rear headquarters. I've got lots to do, as the person I have taken over for in the office left numerous items uncompleted, disorganized and in a mess. Bad for him, good for me. I need to get this place organized, so I can stay in the rear area. I'm going to make myself valuable. I don't carry a weapon with me. I keep my rifle handy, but not attached to my body. It's a strange feeling as I'm still pretty sensitive to noises, especially at night.

Chris
March 21 – I'm here in the rear area. Lots to do. The books, assignment sheets, files, logs, daily reports, etc. are in bad shape. It's very hard not to be in the bush. I do feel safe, almost, as if I shouldn't. I'm starting to work out again. I need to get back in shape and gain some weight. After Operation Medina, I was down to 132 lbs, down from 172 lbs, when I achieved the highest physical fitness score in the battalion in the states. Now, I'm up to 154 pounds. Eating three meals a day seems to be helping. Getting late – I must "make my hat" – (leave). We do receive incoming every once in awhile. It keeps the new guys hopp'in. This life is so different. 99% of the guys here don't have a clue what being in the bush is all about. It's probably good. At least they won't take the nasty dreams home.

Lt. Kirk
Mar 21 - I led my platoon out of C-2 on patrol and dropped off a reinforced squad from the 1st platoon that included a scout dog and a sniper team.

Mar 22 - The squad we inserted on the 21st was ambushed by 20-30 NVA. The company commander led my platoon and another platoon out to rescue them. A lot of the men had little water when we started out and the going was rough. We ran all the way, guided by an AO (aerial observer) aircraft. Eventually, we came into a clearing and saw two NVA on our right. There were two men ahead of me on point. We fired, killing the two bad guys. They had stars for belt buckles, indicating they were NVA rather than VC. One guy had holes in him from a burning white phosphorous grenade he had been carrying.

Lt Jim Kirk

A short time later we made contact with the squad and the remaining NVA hit the trail. A medevac chopper came in. The dog handler pleaded with me to get himself and his wounded scout dog on the chopper, before wounded Marines. I said no. Holding the dog in his arms, he ran to the chopper and boarded. Wounded Marines had to wait for the next chopper. I was furious. I learned later that the dog died. We took 25 rounds of 60mm mortar fire on our return to C-2.

Life was simple. Your possessions were few and you carried them all in your knapsack. Everything you consumed was provided, with little effort on your part. There was a certain liberation and happiness about it. My platoon, in addition to company size patrols, ran five platoon size patrols from March 10 through March 22.

10

OPERATION PEGASUS - LIFTING THE SEIGE

Massive search and destroy sweeps are launched into the jungle around Khe Sanh near the Laotian border. Called Operation Pegasus, this was a large Army/ Marine/ARVN effort to reopen Route 9, allow supplies to again be brought into the base and lift the siege.

Lathan Williams, Echo Co, 1st Platoon
March 23 -We went to provide security to where a new air field was being built at LZ Stud on Highway 9 just east of the Rock Pile. We had the Montagnards (the mountain people) clearing fields of fire for us. The runway was being built to support our assault to relieve the poor Marit Khe Sanh.

Lt. Kirk
March 23 - We moved from C-2 by truck convoy to Dong Ha and then by helicopter to LZ Stud (Camp Vandergrift) near Ca Lu. Vandergrift was a staging area. It is located in a narrow valley, with steep cliffs, especially on the west side. There was a dammed up stream in the valley that created a little pool. We took baths in the pool, a great treat. Another great treat was the long range rations (freeze dried food) that the Army used for long range reconnaissance patrols. I sent a couple of my men to sneak under the tent flaps of an Army supply tent and steal some of these rations. An Army sergeant caught them and said "You can have all you want, we don't eat this crap." The Army had hot chow. Even in the midst of an operation, unless they were in contact with the enemy, the sky would get black with helicopters to bring them hot chow. We were always envious of the Army's new gear, hot chow and abundance of trucks, jeeps and helicopters. I recall watching an Army truck convoy run down Rt. 9 full of gear. A while later a Marine truck convoy came by – the beds of the trucks had a few 55 gallon barrels and some shovels. The fact is that the Army is organized and equipped for sustained combat. The Marine Corps is organized and equipped to sustain itself for only a short time on the battlefield, with a smaller proportion of service and support troops. Yet the Marines were employed in the same way as the Army.

March 24- About this time I went on R&R to Thailand. I took a CH-46 helicopter from Vandergrift back to Da Nang, flying very low the whole way, providing a fascinating view of the country. We went southeast to the coast and then down the beach. There were an amazing number of shell and bomb craters everywhere. When I got to Da Nang, I was, of course, dirty and disheveled and felt very out of place and unwelcome amidst all the spit and polished types in the rear. A major chewed me out for my appearance, increasing my resentment of the pogues.

Pogue is a derogatory term for the people "in the rear with the gear." The infantry regarded everybody else, including artillery, engineers and supply people, as pogues. Within the infantry, Marines regarded anybody further up the chain of command than themselves as a "pogue". To the company commander, the battalion commander and his staff were pogues. To the platoon commander, the company commander and his minions were pogues. To the squad leader, the platoon commander and his minions were pogues. To the man on the point, the squad leader was a pogue. The infantry or 'grunts" resented the people in the rear who did not share their hardships and danger. Curiously, the grunts had a respect for the enemy, who shared their hardships and danger.

While in Bangkok, I bought three sets of black star sapphire earrings for my mother, my girlfriend Paula and my sister-in-law. I took them back to the bush with me and later gave them to one of my rotating Marines to mail for me. They never arrived.

Chris
March 24 – Private Hendry , 2nd squad, was KIA. He didn't make a lot of friends while he was here. He didn't mingle with the guys, so not a lot of attention was directed his way. He was always falling asleep on the lines at night, which really turned the guys off. He was the closest guy I know to being shot by the guys around him. He didn't seem to care. I don't know much about him or his family, no one did. We lose another one from the second squad. The rest of the guys in 2nd squad took care of each other and always helped each other when needed.

Bob Dunbar
March 27 - I was WIA on this day. I was trying to recover Marine KIA's from a surrounding mountain top on the way to the Khe Sanh base. They took me to the Battalion Aid Station for treatment. I was able to return to duty in time for Operation Pegasus.

Lt. Suydam
March 27 - While climbing up one of these hilltops, we found it was occupied and fortified. Our troops attacked it upon discovery, without waiting for orders. They just overran the place and killed all the bad guys. When the firing started, I

started climbing forward. When I got to the top, it was all over. One Marine said, "Look out for the trip wire." There it was about six inches off the ground. Several other Marines started disassembling the explosive. The mine was a Chinese Claymore called a Dinner Plate Mine. Molten TNT can be poured into any shape. This metal shape was round and about thirteen inches in diameter. It was four inches thick on the outside and shaped down to two inches in the middle. The backside was flat. While a round explosive energizes in all directions thus dissipating its force quickly like a light bulb, a shaped charge channels force in a single direction like the parabolic shaped headlamp of an automobile or flashlight. A pull-friction fuse and explosive cap were found in the center of the mine. If it exploded, it would have thrown shrapnel like a giant shotgun wherever it was aimed or in this case, along the trip wire.

We were going to destroy the mine by placing it in one of the bunkers, thus destroying the bunker in the process. The bunker roof was unusually heavy with at least a foot of timber, rocks and dirt. One Marine scoffed that the mine would not lift that roof. I said, "Yes, it will." One lb. of TNT will cut a railroad rail in two. A half-pound is sufficient to lift a roof off a bunker. The dinner plate mine had to have three lbs of TNT. We argued back and forth. When the mine exploded, I looked up to see logs and rocks twirling up about 30 feet in the air. We were about 25 feet away from the bunker. Then, it began to rain logs and stones. No one was hurt. But, it was an impressive explosion and shower.

House
March 28 - Khe Sanh is the biggest battle and the detail map of how this firebase is holding out against serious attacks is of the biggest interest. The NVA is taking a beating trying to take that base.

Chris
March 29 - We now understand that the guys that relieved us at Con Thien are at a minimum of troops holding the Hill. We had a battalion of men plus a lot of attached units, including artillery and tanks, which was way over 2,200 troops. Now, the 3rd and the 9th Marines are there and have far less men to support each position of Con Thien and the neighboring DMZ front-line installations of A-1, C-1 and C-2 installations.

The attitude and direction of defensive Marine positions is beginning to change to a more offensively minded and mobile force.

Note: Con Thien and the northern defensive positions were more vulnerable than at any time. Lieutenant Colonel Kurth devised an ingenious plan to change the enemy's evaluation as to the overall strength of The Hill. The basic concept was to mislead the NVA/VC into believing the forces at Con Thien and C-2, which was three miles to the south, were fully manned and also being reinforced.

The plan was this: They employed three 6x6 trucks to conduct troop movements that appeared to be reinforcing the two bases. They loaded about 18 Marine infantrymen with weapons and gear onto benches lining each truck. The three truckloads equal 54 men, which is a reinforced platoon. They then drove the three trucks from the southernmost position at C-2, up the road and into Con Thien (A-4). Upon arrival at Con Thien the trucks pulled out of sight and left the benches in the truck beds. The men lie face down in the truck beds covered with tarps. Their rifles and other equipment is hidden in the cab of the trucks. This way you cannot see the men and the trucks look empty as they race down the road back to C-2. When they arrive at C-2, they pull out of sight and again the men take their upright seating positions. The trucks once more head northward to Con Thien. They did this twice so that it appeared over 100 Marines were transported to Con Thien as reinforcements. Lt. Col. Kurth knew Con Thien, as well as the other posts, were under constant watch by the NVA. Whether or not the NVA were fooled, they did not attack Con Thien or C-2.

Chris

March 30 – We continue to receive incoming artillery and mortar fire in the rear area at night, but not nearly the amount and not as often as everywhere else I've been. The new guys are so immature, so green, so young. They don't seem to realize what they are in for. All the new guys are just out of boot camp, which doesn't give them much of a chance to learn about the Marine Corps and war zone they are approaching. It will all be learned under fire from here on.

One of the guys here in the office, just wrote a "war story" to his girl friend. Man, what an imagination some people have. I suppose his girlfriend thinks he's a hero now. Either that or she knows better. Probably, the latter.

Note: March 30 - Khe Sanh Combat Base. Co. B, 1st Battalion, 9th Marines attack enemy in trenches and bunkers surrounding the outpost, and drive them off or kill them Marine casualties at Khe Sanh from November 1, 1967 to April 1, 1968 are reported at 205 KIA and 1,668 wounded by Colonel Lownds, commander, 26th Marines. However, others, including the Rev. Ray W. Stubbe, a Lutheran chaplain with with 26th Marines, dispute these figures. In a book he wrote, Stubbe records the names, ranks, service numbers and dates of death for 441 servicemen at Con Thien. And it should be noted that these figures do not include: the 51 KIA during Operation Pegasus, the casualties incurred by the Special Forces on the southwest perimeter of the base at Khe Sanh, 49 personnel killed in the shooting down of a C-123 Provider on March 6 or the many ARVN soldiers of the 37th Regiment killed at Khe Sanh. Nor does it include thousands of Bru Montangnards in the area who died during the siege. Another terrible waste to hold a piece of worthless ground that we later abandon. Marines counted 1,602, enemy dead. It is likely that 10,000-15,000 total enemy KIA.

The March Command Chronology for 2nd Battalion, 1st Marines reports moderate enemy contact and 100 rounds of incoming received during the eight days the battalion was at Con Thien. On March 9 the battalion moved to C-2 and C-2 bridge. The battalion received only 15 rounds of incoming during its two weeks there. On March 22 an Echo Co. killer team had a firefight with 13 NVA - 10 were KIA. On March 23 the battalion moved to Ca Lu. 2nd Battalion, 1st Marines casualties for March: 11 enlisted KIA, 3 officers WIA, 28 enlisted WIA.

On March 31, Johnson stunned the nation in a televised address by declaring a partial bombing halt, calling for peace talks and announcing that he would not run for reelection.

A historical note: An article by Peter Brush brings into focus the horrors suffered by combatants at Khe Sanh. He writes in an article for Vietnam magazine: "On February, 25, a two-squad patrol, instructed not to venture farther than 1,000 meters from the base perimeter, vanished. Two weeks later, casualties of the so-called ghost patrol were established as nine dead, 25 wounded and 19 missing. A company-size patrol on March 30 had as one of its missions the recovery of the bodies of the ghost patrol. This second patrol suffered three dead, 71 wounded and three missing before being ordered to pull back. Only two bodies from the ghost patrol were recovered at that time."

Paul Rangel, Golf Co.
April 1 - Operation Pegasus begins as the largest operation in Vietnam. The 1st Marine Regiment was responsible for assaulting along Highway 1. Golf Company of 2/1 spearheaded the operation in the hills, providing cover for those coming down the road.

Lathan Williams, Echo Co., 1st Platoon

April 1 - We kicked off Operation Pegasus, which was to reopen the Highway 9 to Khe Sanh. We assaulted 12 hills in 7 days – a bad firefight on one of them — several artillery barrages during this time. It's been a bad operation. We are all exhausted, climbing through the thick jungle canopies and hills around Highway 9.

Lt. Suydam

April 1- The 26th Marines were surrounded at Khe Sanh. The NVA intended to cut them off, starve them, infiltrate them and annihilate them. It was part of General Giap's plan to defeat the American forces in Vietnam. By surrounding and threatening to destroy the Marines at Khe Sanh, he had hoped to draw off significant resources leaving the southern portion of the country vulnerable to the countrywide attack he planned for TET. As it turned out, General Giap lost both battles but won the war nevertheless. The siege lasted for ten weeks beginning January 21, 1968, and was declared officially over April 5, 1968. The 6,000 Marines were surrounded by 20,000 North Vietnamese troops. Eventually, it became too dangerous to leave the base of operation. During the siege, the NVA fired more than 40,000 artillery, rocket and mortar rounds into the Marine positions. However, American air power dropped 80,000 tons of ordnance amounting to more than the non-nuclear tonnage dropped on Japan throughout WW II.

There was still plenty of enemy activity when we got involved. The east-west highway out to Khe Sanh is called Route 9. It is a narrow winding road perched precariously on the side of a mountain range that dropped off into an east-west river valley, the Song Roa Quan. It was easy for the communist to disrupt traffic on the road. All you had to do was drop a hand grenade from the steep banks on the north side. The communists had cut the road to Khe Sanh with repeated ambush and the emplacement of troops. Without the only overland route to the base, there was no way to haul the heavy munitions necessary to keep the artillery batteries resupplied. Air power was not suited for this kind of work. Without the road and the truck convoys of munitions, the artillery batteries were effectively shut down, thus allowing enemy forces to encroach on the perimeter of the Khe Sanh base.

The joint Army-Marine operation to re-open Route 9 was called Operation Pegasus. On the sweep out to Khe Sanh, the First Air Cavalry Division took the south side of Route Nine; the First Marines (First Marine Regiment) took the north. It took several weeks of mountain climbing and intermittent fighting to get there.   The idea was to engage and destroy enemy units, to relieve the 26th Marines and to replace them with us, the Second Battalion, First Marines (2/1).

We believed that the Air Cavalry had it easy, flying from mountaintop to mountaintop each day while we, Marines walked hill and dale. It seemed like we Marines always got the short end of the stick, the toughest assignments the worst supplies and equipment, but I tell you that we wouldn't have had it any other way.

Lt. Kirk

April 1 - The battalion's initial mission was to provide security for the 1st Air Cav and LZ Stud. At the end of March, 1/1 took over those responsibilities and 2/1 participated, for the next two weeks, in Operation Pegasus for the relief of the Siege of Khe Sanh with the 1st Air Calvary Division and 2/3. 2/1's mission was to secure the high ground north of Highway 9 and west of LZ Stud and provide security for engineers working on Highway 9 and then to provide security for the relief convoys into Khe Sahn.

April 2 - In the late afternoon, we made a helicopter assault onto a hill west of Vandergrift. The hill had a saddle shape to it, with two knolls and a draw or little valley in the middle. I was in the first helicopter and we landed at the southern knoll. I was with the first squad and we went through the draw to the northern knoll. The 2nd and 3rd squads arrived in two more helicopters. The 3rd squad moved into the draw and the 2nd squad set up in the southern knoll, as planned. Then, maybe 10 mortar rounds landed on the southern knoll. I went running back there and found disaster. We later learned it was our own 81mm mortars. They were firing over our heads from Vandergrift and had short rounds. Corporal Tilo Osterreich of Philadelphia, known as "T" was killed. He was an immigrant from East Germany. He and his parents had come over the Berlin Wall. T had extended his tour by six months and received an R&R before beginning his extension. For some reason, T had a pistol with him when he went on R&R and was turned back on the steps of the airplane, so he never got his R&R. T was normally the 1st squad leader, but he had returned unexpectedly from R&R and I temporarily put him in the 2nd squad. Pfc. Thomas Nash of Atlanta was also killed and two others wounded, including Corporal Dennis Knobloch, the second squad leader. Years later I saw a message on the 2/1 website from T's nephew, a Marine major who was a helicopter pilot. He was looking for information about the death of his Uncle T. I responded and told him the story. He was very grateful.

Note: Lt. Kirk - I wrote Corporals Tilo Ostereich and Dennis Knobloch, up for medals (I think it was for silver stars, but it might have been bronze stars) for stuff they had done under me but more for stuff they had done before I arrived on Operation Medina. I never heard a word about my recommendations. These guys were very deserving, both fearless and very cool under fire.

Note: I recently learned that Lt. Lee Suydam, my predecessor as 3rd platoon leader, wrote Tilo up for a silver star, but in spite of extensive efforts by Lee and Dennis Knobloch after the war, Tilo never got it.

Corporal Tilo Osterreich, Philadelphia, Pennsylvania
(panel 48E, line 45 on The Wall)

Private First Class Thomas S. Nash, Atlanta, Georgia
(panel 48E, line 45 on The Wall)

Lt. Suydam

April 2 - Tilo and his family were refugees from East Germany. He was later killed by friendly mortar fire. Our captain was firing 81 mm mortars around our position before setting up the company. Four of the captain's shells came in on top of 3rd platoon. Two died instantly, Tilo and Pfc. Thomas Nash. Two, including Knobby, were wounded. Every man of ours was a comrade, whether he was personally known as a friend or just another brother in uniform. When a brother fell, it was a time for remorse. If the brother was a dear friend, all the more reason for anguish and bereavement. But I tell you, there were not losses more bitterly suffered than the loss of those dear friends and comrades that fell to friendly fire. All too frequently, and because of the lethal nature of all tools in combat, men died from the killing power of our own weapons misdirected by accident or used too close to our forces.

Lt. Kirk

April 3 - The company was ordered to assault a hill to the east and get to the top by mid-morning. I warned the company commander we would never make the objective by mid-morning. The grid lines on the map were very close, indicating very steep terrain. Maddeningly, we were ordered to carry out the big, heavy (but now empty) water cans that were delivered to us by helicopter the day before, along with big sacks of mail we hadn't had time to distribute. A new guy in my platoon died from heat stroke. We stripped him down and poured water on him, but the heat, humidity, steepness of the hill and a fast pace were too much for a guy who wasn't acclimated yet. We took salt tablets every day in the belief that it prevented heat exhaustion and heat stroke (this is now generally regarded as useless). We had a brief firefight near the top and finally made it to the crest at dusk. In addition to the one man who died, we had two other heat casualties.

Chris
April 3 – I just got word that our company was hit bad as they continue their push toward Khe Sanh. Lots of WIA/KIA. – Being in the rear area office, typing and doing paperwork has been driving me crazy. I spoke to the first sergeant and explained I absolutely couldn't stand being in the office, filing papers and making reports. For being such a tough nut, he listened to me. I have been re-assigned. I am now in charge of the rear area personnel, supply and a ton of other stuff. It gets me out of the office and being more active doing numerous chores outside. When I figure out what all the duties are, I"ll give you a better idea of what I'm supposed to be doing.

House
April 3 - We are preparing all the main battle maps for 1st Division for Khe Sanh. It is a huge effort. We are plotting all the information on the enemy and our attack plans to prevent the base from being surrounded and wiped out like they did to the French at Dien Bien Phu in 1954. The Joint Chiefs of Staff and President Johnson gets some of my stuff direct in his morning briefings, along with the other G-Sections data to make his decisions. They use my maps!

Our main briefing officer, Major Owens, with two officers from the Pentagon, (One is President Johnson's son-in-law, Captain Charles Robb). asks me to give Capt. Robb one of my maps and he shakes my hand and says, "Thanks. I'm sure this will come in handy."

He was accompanied or guarded or shadowed by a couple of guys, who sure did not look like regulation Marines. They looked more like CIA or Secret Service. They had camouflaged safari vests on with shoulder-holsters that showed underneath and they carried a new short version carbine of the M-16. I remember seeing the rifle in *Popular Mechanics* called the "XM-17", with a folding/sliding wire stock and long 30-round banana clips. Hardly what we could consider to be "standard issue".

Chris
April 3 - I live in a hard-back tent – wooden, hot, 40' x 20', tin roof and screens all

the way around.   It's built two feet off the ground - as protection from the monsoons. I'm stationed across from the airstrip.   We're attached to the 1st Air Cav, which puts the Army in charge of us.   This is good, as we get supplies we could never get our hands on before.   The Army has everything and in great quantities.   We get ammo, chow, clothing, medicine, and everything else we could want.   Yes, once in a while, something appears "like magic" in our hands (nighttime recon).

You ought to see the jeep I drive around, no windshield, hardly any paint, but it runs, barely.   I sent some pictures home, mostly pictures of Hue City and Phu Bai.

Note: April 4 – On this day, Martin Luther King was shot and killed in Memphis, TN, leading to riots in Washington DC and other cities.

Lt. Kirk
April 4 - As part of another action during Operation Pegasus, my company made a helicopter assault onto a hill. We came in at dusk. We were hit by artillery or mortars. The next morning all we could find of one of my Marines was part of his hand - he had been hit by an enemy shell.   Somebody put his hand in a plastic bag.

Note: Lt. Kirk - The Command Chronology says Echo Company received five rounds of artillery that day and one man took a direct hit.

Lt. Suydam
April 4 - On one mountaintop, we were busy setting up our perimeter for the night when there was a terrific explosion close to us. We all hit the dirt expecting the worst. A little time passed. Finally, someone said that a Marine was missing. We began to search. Eventually, we found his pistol, hot and twisted, and the thumb and forefinger of his right hand; that's all. I medevaced his remains, with a note of identification. I placed the remains in one of those foil lined K-ration pouches.   I've always wondered what the helicopter crew and the morgue thought about that.   I have wanted to write to his family too but, I can't even remember his name. I believe that an 82mm recoilless rifle killed him.   These weapons fire a straight trajectory for miles. We never heard the report of a gun and there was no shell crater.   Someone way off saw movement on our mountaintop and graced us with a shot.   The round came screaming in just

above ground level and impacted on this unfortunate Marine. Rest assured, he never knew what hit him.

Chris
April 5 – Just got mail and I received my "college cut" papers, which I will submit immediately and hopefully I'll be able to leave this damn place early and get back to college. I only have a short time left and can think of nothing else. I spent some time thinking about college, playing football again and getting my position back on the team. I can't wait to see all my friends, especially Mary Jo. When I think of her, I always see a beautiful, smiling face, and so kind. She's back in San Jose, California now, but I'm sure she'll return to college in southern Oregon when I get back home. So many great memories.

Note: April 5 – General Davis decides to form a Mobile Strike Force of at least regimental size. In order to get the needed men to do this, he raids the defenses of several static positions that currently are being manned by battalion size. He does this so he can initiate offensive actions, when deemed appropriate. He wants to carry the battle to the enemy. Be nimble! This force will then be ready and reactionary to immediate offensive needs. It's probably better than just sitting in a defensive position, which we truly hated when we were at Con Thien. However, now the remaining troops on the Hill are very open to attack and to being overrun.

Lt. Kirk
April 6 - A B-52 (arc light) strike dropped bombs that seemed to fall very close to us. In fact, they were probably 1000 meters away, as that was the minimum distance from friendly troops the B-52's were supposed to maintain. The ground shook so much I fell down and landed in a shell hole.

At this point there was hardly anyone in my platoon who I started with. I had lots of replacements for people who had been wounded, gotten sick or rotated home. I had lost two of my three squad leaders, T and Knobby, and lots of others. Some military experts believe that if more than 1/3 of a unit is lost to casualties its unit cohesion is gone and its effectiveness as a fighting force is destroyed. I no longer wanted to be with the platoon. I didn't want to start over.

April 7 - One night south of the Quang Tri River near Vandergrift, we thought the bad guys were throwing grenades at us. But they all seemed to be duds. We opened fire. The following morning we found we had killed monkeys (we called them rock apes). Were they throwing rocks at us?

April 8 - I was with my platoon south of the Quang Tri River near Vandergrift. Elephant grass around there was head high and sharp. I got a call from the company commander on the radio telling me my platoon should cross the river and wait on Route 9 for a convoy. We waded across the river, which was almost shoulder deep and waited on Route 9. We were told this was the first convoy into Khe Sanh since the siege began. My platoon provided security. The engineers were still working on the road and bridges just ahead of us and we had many delays. We encountered a 26 foot python on the road. Someone shot the snake and we laid it out and measured it.

When we turned north off Rt. 9 onto the road leading into Khe Sanh and looked down Rt. 9 as it continued towards Lang Vei, the Special Forces camp that had been overrun a couple of months earlier, and Laos. A chill ran up my spine.

This was the same day the 1st Air Cav linked up with a Marine company that came out from the base at Khe Sanh.

Chris
April 8 – The first sergeant came back today. He complains all day, every day. He's a pain. Man, he gets on my nerves and everyone else's. I'd like to tell him a few things, but I think he'd disapprove.

At the present, 2/1 Echo Company is 1-2 miles from Khe Sanh. The operation has been going pretty well, contact has been made with the NVA. The 1st Air Cav got quite a few confirmed kills in the last day or so.

Echo Company got hit by mortars last night in the rear area, over 100 rounds. The mess hall took three direct rounds - not good. No matter what happens it's so much better than where I came from. I never say anything, as the guys around here are scared shitless.

Lt. Kirk
Apr 9 - My platoon spent the night in Khe Sanh and went back on the trucks to Vandergrift the next day.

Note: The U.S. objective in Operation Pegasus was to re-take Route 9, destroy NVA units along the way, which would open up supply lines to Khe Sanh Combat Base and end the siege. A 77-day battle, Khe Sanh had been the biggest single battle of the Vietnam War to that point. The NVA lost over 1,600 killed with two divisions all but annihilated. Thousands more were probably killed by American bombing.

The Siege Is Over! Khe Sanh is relieved after 77 days. When the 1st Air Cav soldiers entered the base, they saw Marines in beards, clothes dirty and torn, all in need of haircuts, showers and clean uniforms..

Lt Kirk checking lines before dark.

Machine Gun Bunker on Front

11

OUR TURN AT KHE SANH

The Siege of Khe Sanh and the Tet Offensive, although military defeat for the NVA and Viet Cong were shocking to many Americans. This was a turning point in support for the war.

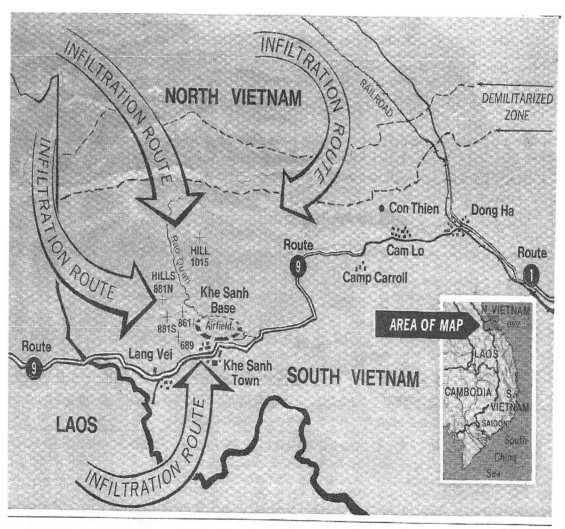

The Marine bastion at Khe Sanh: 'For those who fight for it, life has a flavor the protected never know'

Newsweek—Ritte

Lt. Kirk

April 12 - We returned to Khe Sanh by helicopter a few days later. We moved to a hill to the northwest of Khe Sanh and received mortar and artillery, resulting in four WIA, as we went. There were dead NVA around the perimeter from a firefight the night before. The 1st Air Cav had occupied the hill and the ground was strewn with all kinds of relatively new web gear, including Army packs and belt suspenders ("doggy straps"), which were better designed than Marine stuff. We used to say that Marines were re-supplied on contact (meaning we got our supplies from the enemy) or after relieving an Army unit. The next day we moved into Khe Sanh and took up positions on the perimeter facing west. It was the dirtiest, most God-forsaken series of trenches and bunkers I had yet seen. The following day we were re-supplied by a parachute drop, which took place north of the perimeter, just outside the trench line. We had to go out and get the supplies, while the bad guys rained down artillery and rockets, most of them air bursts. The base at Khe Sanh was decimated. It once had a mess hall, an actual wooden building, now in ruin. There was a post office, actually what we called a Conex box, a metal shipping container. This too was in ruin. There were several downed aircraft. In addition to the Marines, there were ARVN soldiers, Montagnards, Special Forces (I think this was the reinforced remnants of the unit that had been overrun at Lang Vei) and a small Air Force detachment that brought in Air Force supply planes. The Air Force guys lived in a large Conex box and had an air conditioner. They told me they received sub-standard housing pay. I wonder what the Air Force would have thought of the bunkers and trench lines the Marines lived in.

Lt. Suydam

April 12 - When we arrived at Khe Sanh, I was amazed by the number of bomb craters and their proximity to the wire. The total landscape was pocked marked for miles with these enormous bomb craters. Also, there were enemy trench works dug out like blood vessels heading toward the wire. Many were close enough for the enemy to throw grenades into our trench lines. The 26th Marines had only narrowly escaped annihilation and capture. There were reportedly 7,000 enemy troops still operating in the area.

During the next ten weeks, until the base was officially abandoned, U.S. forces operating in and around the Khe Sanh base lost 400 KIA, and 2,300 WIA.

We were on a hilltop watching Marine helicopters come into Khe Sanh. One set down in a minefield. The first few troopers out of the chopper touched off a mine. The crew chief panicked, thinking they were taking incoming artillery and pushed all the Marines off the chopper. Five died. Another CH-46 copter was coming in and the prop wash blew up a poncho liner (like a plastic blanket). It arced over and came in on top of the front rotor. The weight of the poncho liner in the prop caused the prop to become unstable and smash through the cockpit, killing the pilot and co-pilot.

Khe Sanh was a ghostly place with damaged aircraft bulldozed off to one side of the runway. CH-53 "Jolly Green Giant" helicopters would contour fly about 50 feet off the ground to Khe Sanh to avoid being seen by enemy artillery spotters. They would drop their under slung net of cargo and depart just as artillery would come crashing in. We got a barrage nearly every time a chopper came in. One of the most heroic things I have ever seen was a black Marine driving a giant forklift machine. He would unload the recently-dropped supplies left in the landing zone (LZ) between artillery barrages. He was fast. When you heard the guns go off, you had about four seconds before the shells landed. As soon as the shells exploded, he would dash for his running machine and move cargo until he heard the guns. Then he would dive for cover. What good were the supplies just delivered if they were to be destroyed by artillery in the LZ?

Bob Dunbar
April 12 - We humped our way to Khe Sanh and relieved the Marines under siege and our battalion wasn't even through the gate when we got hit with artillery and took numerous casualties. It was Con Thien all over again.

Chris
April 12 – I'm really feeling great about coming home and expect to hear about my college cut and a departure date soon. It seems like so long ago that I left home and came over to Vietnam. What a place to come. I remember I wanted to come over here when I signed up for the Marines. I think I got more than I had asked for.

Lt. Kirk
April 13 - A couple of days after we arrived at Khe Sanh, the battalion commander asked me to take over the 81 mm mortar platoon, thinking I would be highly motivated after my 2nd squad was decimated by friendly mortar fire from this same outfit – I was. I had little connection with the new guys in my rifle platoon. The guys I had led and fought with all these long months were gone. The loss of these fine men left me with an empty feeling.

The table of organization for the 81mm mortar platoon says it has 2 officers and

94 enlisted men, organized into a headquarters group, four sections and four forward observer teams, each of which was with one of the four rifle companies. Each section had two squads. Each squad included a gunner (who used the sight to carry out elevation and deflection instructions), an assistant gunner (who dropped the rounds down the tube), radio operators and wiremen, who laid communication wire between the guns and the Fire Direction Center. The NCO's should have included a gunnery sergeant and four staff sergeants. In fact, I was the only officer, and I had only one gunnery sergeant and two staff sergeants. But, unlike the rifle platoon, we were usually at full strength.

The mortar tube is a little over four feet long. The mortar, including the base plate, weighs 136 pounds. The 81mm mortar high explosive rounds have a maximum range of about 3½ miles. Mortars are "area" weapons, not precision weapons, so firing them close to friendly troops is dangerous. The effective bursting area of a high explosive round is about 35 meters. In addition to high explosive rounds, there are illumination rounds and white phosphorous rounds. There are different kinds of fuses: impact, proximity (time and variable time).

Fire missions are requested by the forward observers who are positioned with the rifle companies. Coming up with what is called a firing solution is complicated. First, every time you change position, you have to use what is very much like a surveying instrument called an aiming circle to "lay" in all eight mortars and put out two aiming sticks for each mortar. You use a plotting circle and firing tables to determine the elevation and deflection of the mortar tubes (dialed in by the eight gunners using the sights on the mortars) and the number of charges or fuse bags to attach to the rounds. I trained the heck out of my mortar men. I held competitions between gunners to see who could sight in their mortar the fastest (this was an art, requiring the gunner to dial in the required elevation and direction, sight on two aiming posts and get the liquid in two bubbles level. Within a month we fired over the heads of and within 35 meters of troops from Fox and Echo companies after Fox was ambushed just outside Khe Sanh. I relied heavily on a young corporal who had a degree in math. He helped me run the fire direction center.

Knobby (Post injury – 4-2-1968)
I should be at Great Lakes in about 10 days to 2 weeks. I can't make any phone calls from here because they won't let me get up and around very much yet. They'll be cutting the lights off any second.

Chris

April 18 - Unbelievable! Absolutely, unbelievable! Our company has been hit hard lately and lost quite a few men, many of them senior in the field. So, the first sergeant sees how well I run the rear area and decides I am needed in the field and he volunteers me for the front lines, again. I've been lucky to have had some time in the rear area and escape most of the bad stuff lately, so I pack my gear, rifle, pistol, grenades and ammo – lots of ammo. I took some favorite C-rats. I really thought when I returned to the rear area this last time, I would be staying, but I do understand. Actually, I am looking forward to getting back with the guys. It just seems better than being in the rear area. I feel confident in the bush and know I'll do a good job. Actually, I find I miss being in the action. I'm comfortable going back. There's a thrill of anxiety that goes with me.

I hop a copter to where the company is located, deep in the bush. It all comes back so quickly. It's all about Khe Sanh now. Sure, I'm scared, but so is everyone else. Gotta a job to do.

Note: April 18- The 26th Marines, who defended Khe Sanh during the siege, are heli-lifted out of Khe Sanh to Quang Tri.

Lt. Suydam

April 21 - Put your hand flat on the table and then draw up your fingers and lift you palm. Now you have a hilltop with fingers. The fingers are ridges that run to the valley floor. Sometimes the fingers are long and straight. But, sometimes the elevation drops off sharply at the knuckle. This was like the mountainous terrain surrounding the high valley of Khe Sanh. Situated on the northwest extremity of McNamara's Demilitarized Zone (DMZ), Khe Sanh could be fired upon from Laos and North Vietnam. The 26th Marines at Khe Sanh had almost become America's Dien Bien Phu. The French were surrounded in Dien Bien Phu by the Viet Mien in 1954 and forced to surrender after a terrible siege. I'm told that France lost more men fighting in Vietnam (French Indochina) than did America.

I was the executive officer of Echo Company, 2nd Battalion, 1st Marines. Our mission at the time was to attack and reduce an anti-aircraft battery on Hill 527 that had been downing our planes. We had seen the Sky Hawks trailing smoke and pilots bailing out over Khe Sanh. The enemy was some distance from Khe Sanh otherwise we would have walked out to the fight. As it was, we planned a helicopter-borne assault using the Marine workhorse, the CH-46 copter that carried about 9 Marines. The 46 had two equal sized rotor blades and a back door that let up and down for loading.

Hill 527 is seven kilometers due West of Khe Sanh, near the Laotian boarder. Perhaps you've heard of the Special Forces camp at Lang Vei that was overrun during the opening days of the battle of Khe Sahn.   Hill 527 is about three kilometers north of Lang Vei.

My captain was on Rest and Recuperation (R&R) in Australia, so I was acting company commander. I was called to a briefing. The assault would be two companies with Echo in the assault and Hotel in reserve. When I saw the map of the landing zone (LZ), I was horrified. The LZ was the only good-sized clearing and reasonably flat place for many kilometers in any direction. I felt that every enemy mortar and rocket for miles would be registered on this spot.

When I briefed my platoon leaders, I told them that the LZ would be hot. My instructions were for every man to get down hill and out of the LZ as soon as possible. I figured that men might not know north from east but they surely would know down. The LZ was on a step on the side of the mountain so that there was only one direction for down.   I wanted no lolly-gagging in the LZ because I believed it would be a place of death. As it turned out, I was right.

344

Echo landed in two waves of six choppers. That's 12 X 9 or about 108 bodies. I was in the first wave. We dashed downhill almost falling and tumbling. As the second wave came in low for touchdown, I heard the mortars firing from the surrounding mountainsides. Dozens of mortar shells were in the air and arcing over to the LZ as the second wave touched down. The choppers were out and the LZ almost cleared as the LZ exploded with black smoke and earth. The third and fourth wave with the back-up company and battalion commander were waived off until air support could be brought to bear and quell some of the fire on the LZ. Charlie Davis from Houston, Texas who was with Hotel Company, told me about the hot LZ. He said that Cpl. Strong was KIA and that Boykin and Cosnahan were wounded by mortar fire. When his Lt. Haaland asked to fire upon the mortars with 3.5-inch rockets, they were denied permission due to the proximity of Echo Company.

Private First Class Gridley Strong, Ontario, California
(Panel 51E, Line 25)

The enemy anti-aircraft position was immediately in front of us, down the ravine and up the finger ridge in front. It was the wrong way to approach the enemy and it would have been suicide. We swung to the left and began to climb. I wanted to swing the company around behind a hilltop that was between us and the objective, and then attack down the finger ridge toward the enemy position.

A4 Sky Hawks were working the position with daisy-cutters. These close air support bombs have enormous tail stabilizers that pop out to slow the bomb and eventually become part of the shrapnel.

We made our left flanking movement and used the terrain to shield our approach. The battalion commander, Lt. Col. Duncan, was on the radio now ordering me to swing right; to not go behind the hilltop. The top of the hill was a jurisdictional dividing line on the colonel's map. By going to the left, we would be passing into another commander's territory and could be subjected to friendly fire. I deliberately disobeyed the order. Friendly fire was the least of my concern at the moment. All I wanted was an opportunity to line up our platoons under cover before releasing them in the assault. It worked perfectly. Sometimes I think the easiest job I ever had was being a Marine infantry officer. Marines don't need to be pushed. They only need to be held back until the critical moment. Once you

345

release them, they know instinctively how to attack and pour fire on the enemy. They are energetic in the face of danger and ruthless killers in the heat of battle.

It only took a moment to line up. I called off the A4's and gave the order to attack. It was beautiful. It was textbook combat just like the exercises we practiced at Camp LeJeune and Quantico. It was probably the only time in Vietnam that I was involved in such a precision ground operation. My Marines charged into the enemy bunker complex like screaming hellions blasting everything in sight. We swept through in only a few moments. The enemy, already shaken by the A4's, chose to skeedaddle down the finger ridge and abandon the position. We found plenty of dead and plenty more blood spots indicating wounded. Among the bunkers we found several doughnut shaped trenches that had been used for the anti-aircraft guns.

It occurs to me now that the enemy must have evacuated their anti-aircraft guns immediately. Otherwise they would have been brought to bear upon our choppers, which were only 700-900 meters away across the chasm. Had this happened, many would have died in the Landing Zone.

Echo took no casualties that I can remember. I do regret the casualties suffered by Hotel Company in the hot LZ. Lt. Colonel Duncan forgave me for my temporary mutiny. He chalked it up to the fog of war and he put me in for the Bronze Star. It was one of the finest experiences of my life to command a company of Marines in combat and to be so successful in the mission.

Note: The citation reads, (please take with grain of salt, these things are a little fluffy):

First Lieutenant Glen Lee Suydam, United States Marine Corps Reserve CITATION: For Meritorious service in connection with operations against the enemy in the Republic of Vietnam while serving in various capacities with Company E, Second Battalion, First Marines, First Marine Division from 23 June 1967 to 21 July 1968. Throughout this period, yatta, yatta, yatta, ... On 21 April 1968, First Lieutenant Suydam's company was conducting a helicopter-borne assault when the Marines suddenly came under a heavy volume of mortar fire from a large enemy force. Realizing the seriousness of the situation, he boldly maneuvered his unit against the hostile positions, shouting words of encouragement to his men (that one always gets me) and directing their fire until the enemy was forced to flee in panic and confusion. More yatta, yatta about being a goodie two shoes and helping out etc., in keeping with the highest traditions of the Marine Corps and of the United States Naval Service.

Lt. Haaland, Hotel Co., 2nd Platoon Commander

April 21 - As usual, our platoon was the lead element for Hotel. I was the fourth man off the first helicopter, with Davis' squad. Like me, he always wanted to be in the lead. I was even upset that Echo Company got to go in first. Helicopters were instructed in which direction to land and as I got off the helicopter, I luckily glanced at my compass and yelled for the point man to turn right as we were going in the wrong direction in relation to our first objective. Everybody turned and ten seconds later our original path erupted in mortar explosions, because the NVA shot a fire mission as soon as they determined the direction of the helicopter's offload. As we moved to our objective, we were exposed for a long time and our only cover was a series of bomb craters. We hop scotched from one to another, until we finally reached cover. Two interesting images come to mind during that scamper: (1) I watched an offloaded helicopter lift off with a reluctant warrior hanging from the ramp by his fingers. The crew chief stomped on his fingers until he dropped off from about six feet in the air. Even in that stressful moment, I had to chuckle at the one sane man on that mission. (2) Believe it or not, a tiger ran right past me and through our men; it was also trying to get out of the kill zone. He had evidently heard the gunfire and came looking for food, as they often did, but got there early. I questioned several men later and I think no one else saw this cat except me, although I am not surprised as like many other times, I had an overview of events and saw many things my men did not see because their view was squad or fire team oriented at best. Despite the terrible conditions (which genius dropped us off in the hottest part of the day?), the Marines did not panic and we finally reached cover with minor casualties, which is pretty amazing when you look back at the event. The guys were terrific fighters and always followed orders - something that I rarely tried to do, as usually the orders were stupid that came to me. We also discovered a bunker complex and destroyed it, although it only had ammunition in it. Moments later, mortar explosions walked over the hill and wounded one or two of my men. I think it was friendly fire, but I did not say anything to my men as it stopped right after I yelled over the battalion net to cease fire. We had to carry them out, also. I knew when we got the order of battle, that it was going to turn into a ridiculous mess. Unfortunately, we were saddled with commanders who learned their lessons in Korea. They just did not understand the jungle. I would have blasted ten LZs to land in before we left Khe Sanh, and then I would have picked one at random - certainly not for its strategic position.   I would also have put in a blocking unit in Laos to catch the bad guys when they hatted out, but then what do I know?

Lt. Suydam

April 21 - After Echo Company had secured Hill 527 outside of Khe Sanh by driving off the enemy from their anti-aircraft batteries, we set up a perimeter and began a search of the bunker complex. The account that follows has continued to haunt me and I tell it with such a mix of emotions that I cannot fully convey. The consolidation of the enemy's position was routine until I was informed that Marines had found a bunker entrance that was filled in with dirt.   They were already digging into it when I got there.

Why fill in a bunker entrance with dirt? It took someone hours of backbreaking labor to dig the bunker by hand and cover it with logs, stone and earth. To fill it in with dirt was pointless, unless......................

More digging, then there were feet, jungle boots, U.S. issue jungle boots and stench.   The stench of rotting human flesh is overpowering and uncontrollably nauseating. The rope around the ankles of the dead Marines had dug deep into their flesh. Their hands were bound in front. These two had been dragged from a battlefield, perhaps wounded, but still alive to this place, perhaps tortured and finally after they died, thrown into this bunker grave and covered with dirt. Why would you drag a dead Marine miles up a mountain? No. These Marines were taken alive.

We don't leave our wounded on the battlefield. We don't leave our dead in some forgotten Asian country to rot in an unmarked grave.   This isn't written somewhere in a training manual. It's just part of the bond between fighting men. Even though we weren't taught it, we all believed it and were prepared to die in the effort to keep this commitment to our brethren.   These two had become separated from their unit or perhaps their rescuers were killed in the struggle. The discovery of these bodies was both a blessing for their recovery and a haunting question as to how they could have been taken alive by the enemy and what horrors they endured before they died.

Perhaps these bodies were from the ghost patrol or from the recovery party. Their rings, watches, wallets and dog tags were gone...souvenirs. I know this because I have taken the same from captured North Vietnamese Army (NVA) soldiers. It's what young combatants do when they have captured their enemy. But, the graves registration people would be able to identify these men from the list of missing in action and their dental records. Several began to wrap the bodies in rain ponchos and to secure them to carrying poles. Others were now opening marked graves around the bunker complex. The logic wasn't clear. If there were some dead Marines, then maybe there would be more, but in the marked graves of the enemy? We weren't thinking clearly.

Several graves contained what we believe were Chinese judging from the enormous size of their bodies. The Vietnamese people are small. One grave was marked with a cutout portion of a gallon tin can. I took it. It is one of the few souvenirs that I kept from the war. The soldier's name is Ngo Van Tu. His unit? U-40. This information is nail punched into the tin. But, the reason I kept the marker is because of what was on the back, which would have been the outside of the can. It reads, "Soybean Salad Oil, Donated by the People of the United States of America, Not to be sold or exchanged." There is a picture of hands shaking over a red, white and blue shield. I feel guilty to this day that because I took his marker, Ngo lies in an unmarked grave perhaps never to be identified for his family. I felt this guilt at the time, but I took it nevertheless. I didn't think that people would believe me without the souvenir.

Suydam Note: In the forty plus years until today, I never told anyone about it. It is hard to work these details into a conversation.

April 22 - We couldn't leave the area from the LZ we had come into. It was hot and there wasn't another flat place for many miles. So we began to walk........... up and down, up and down. The heat was unbearable. No one had to ask that the body carriers be relieved. We were going to return these honored dead to their mothers for proper burial and not a man among us flinched or shirked this duty in any manner. I couldn't have been more proud of these Marines.

Finally, we arrived at a place that could be used for a landing zone. It was like the knuckle of a finger, a grassy knoll that was just about big enough to call in a single chopper to take the bodies away. Our people were dragging with exhaustion and thirst. There are no streams of water in the mountaintops and our canteens were almost empty. The grass was head-high elephant grass. As the chopper waddled in trying to set down, a fire broke out in the grass and everyone in the LZ ran for their life. It was a hot, fast fire with flames reaching up twenty feet or more. We believe that the smoke grenade we used to mark the LZ for the chopper pilot to see from the air started a small fire which was fanned into a roaring blaze by the prop wash of the chopper. A radio operator dashed up the hill with only the hand set from his AN-PRC 25 radio. His radio and rifle burned to a crisp in the LZ. The bodies were smoldering. I watched with sadness as the fatigued young men of Echo Company poured their last dribble of their water onto the smoldering corpses. We wrapped them into new ponchos and began anew looking for an LZ and for water.

The LZ we sought now had to be big enough to accept six choppers at a time. With two companies, about 200 men, we had to load up fast and get out before we could be bracketed by artillery. The battalion operations officer, Major Wright, was directing me by radio and binoculars from the rear. He ordered me to a distant place that I thought improbable. I defied him. I told him his orders didn't make sense. He got hot with me over the radio. But, I could not understand the logic of going to the place he directed me to. After he saw where I was going, he called back and apologized. He said his map had slipped in his map case and that we were going to the right place after all.

Somewhere in America, two mothers would bury their missing sons. Echo Company had performed like champions. We were due some rest and relative safety before the next mission. It was time to clean weapons, read and write mail, bathe and cut each other's hair. Can you imagine? Inside the wire at the most exposed firebase on the DMZ was home and relative safety for our Marines.

Bob Dunbar
April 23 - I was with Echo Co until a couple of weeks after we had gotten up to Khe Sahn. I got hit the same day as when Fox Company all but got wiped out in an ambush, just outside the main gate. That was my 3rd PH (Purple Heart) and I was sent to Japan.

Knobby
April 25 - I'm feeling pretty good now, in fact the Doc let me have liberty last night until 11 PM. I went over to the enlisted man's club and met a couple of war buddies I hadn't seen in about 7 months. There was a movie showing at the club last night, Summer Place. I can have liberty this Saturday and Sunday from 12 AM to 11 PM, but I'm hoping I'll be medevaced instead.

They didn't put any stitches in my hand. They put a drain (like a plastic tube) through each one of the 4 holes and then they wrapped a big bandage around the hand and the drains. They had some type of disinfectant (I would guess) fluid running through the drains continuously for about a week. There was also a drain running through my liver and out my side, and another that came out of my jaw. When they took the bandage off my hand they put a cast on. Yesterday they took two more x-rays and changed the cast. The only stitches I had were along the bottom of my jaw and also where they made an incision starting at my belly button and going straight up to within about an inch of my breast bone. I forget the technical name of the operation – some type of "onomy" or "ectomy" – not a hysterectomy. The wound on my liver is just to the left of the operation scar. That is the one that kept me off my feet for so long.

Today was my last day in the field – I can't legally be killed anymore.

Lt. Kirk

April 28 - Khe Sanh was a very forbidding and ominous place – surrounded by high hills, many infested with NVA. The topography was similar to that of Dien Bien Phu, the site of the disastrous French defeat, and many comparisons were made to it. Hill 950, infested with NVA mortars, looked down on the base from the north, only two miles away.

We spent two and a half months at Khe Sanh. We received heavy artillery and rocket fire from Co Roc, a mountain just across the border in Laos. The bad guys had their artillery pieces on tracks so they could pull them in and out of caves quickly. We had to get permission from higher headquarters (some said Washington, DC.) to fire back into Laos, a foreign country, and by the time we got permission, the artillery pieces were back in their caves.

In Max Hasting's <u>Inferno: The World at War</u> 1939-1945, he writes:

> "Enforced passivity in the face of bombardment was among the most dismal predicaments of every soldier. "Give a Jock a rifle or a bren gun and allow him to use it, and however frightened he may be he will face up to most things," wrote Capt. Alastair Borthwick of the 5th Seaforth Highlanders. "Put him, inactive, in a trench and danger becomes progressively more difficult to bear. Fear is insidious, and it grows in inactivity."

That was my experience at Khe Sanh. At Con Thien I was going out on patrols, but at Khe Sanh I was, with few exceptions, sitting there, day after day, enduring incoming fire.

I lived in the fire direction center bunker, which was maybe about 12' long and 10' wide. At one end, we had a dirt shelf on which we placed our two plotting boards and our firing table books. Two people (usually I was one of them) would work out the firing instructions on the plotting board. On the rare occasion that we didn't get the same answer, we did it again. Two or three of us slept in this bunker. We had scrounged up some wooden pallets, which we placed on the floor, so that we could stay out of the mud. As at Con Thien, we made beds out of Marston metal matting and sandbags.

Marine F4 Phantom jets sometimes made bombing runs in support of us, at Khe Sanh and elsewhere. We knew the bad guys would keep their heads down and wouldn't be firing at us when the planes were going after them, so we felt safe. We would yell "Get some!" We had a feeling of joy and temporary respite. The roar of the engines and the smell of napalm were exhilarating. We would speculate as to whether the pilots were bachelors or married depending upon how low they came to the ground. They would drop what we called "snakes and nape", the nape meaning napalm and the snakes some kind of bomb.

The April Command Chronology for 2nd Battalion, 1st Marines says the battalion participated in Operation Pegasus for the first two weeks. Two companies made ground contact with the enemy, resulting in 11 enemy KIA. The battalion moved into Khe Sanh Combat Base on April 17. The battalion left the base on the 21st to conduct an operation and received heavy mortar fire upon touchdown by the helicopters. The battalion returned to the base on the 23rd. Enemy KIA for the month totaled 53. 2nd Battalion, 1st Marines casualties for April: 14 enlisted KIA, 2 officers WIA, 79 enlisted WIA.

Note: May 1968 would be the bloodiest month of the war for the U.S. with 2,371 Americans killed.

Chris

May 1 - My 21st birthday and I'm in a hole, somewhere in the jungle around Khe Sanh. Since it was my birthday, the guys gave me a C- rat fruit cake to take the place of a birthday cake. I hate these fruit cake things as much as the next guy and gave it right back. They thought it was funny. Actually, it was a great gesture.

We were deep in the bush and dug foxholes. As night began to fall, we realized that the NVA were directly across from us, less than the width of a football field away. We could hear them and knew that something was going to happen and soon, probably as soon as dark came on. Our position was elevated a bit from the brush on the other side of the ravine. Our fighting holes, for once, were fairly good size. We all prepared for a long night, as the fighting was soon to begin.

Dodd showed me how to get them to expose themselves at night. He lowered himself into his foxhole, covered his head with a poncho and lit a cigarette. He then tied the cigarette onto a long stick, which he pushed along the ground out to his right side. He put his rifle on automatic and instructed us to do the same. He then raised and lowered the cigarette stick slowly with his left hand, always keeping his eyes on the area directly across from us. Wait and try it again. Night has fallen and it's pitch black out. This time it works. The VC has spotted the cigarette from his hiding place. When his rifle fires at the cigarette to our left, we opened up with full automatic, as did our buddies. Actually, this was fairly effective. The only problem was you never knew if you hit him. Number one, it was too dark to go looking around and if he was hit, he was probably in very small pieces. Move your position and get your four hours of sleep. More rocks thrown by both sides and grenades. All safe.

Great birthday!

Note: From April 30th through May 2nd there was a battle at Dai Do, near Dong Ha. Two Marine company commanders, Captain Vargas and Captain Livingston, were awarded Medals of Honor for their part in forestalling a Communist attack at Dai Do, 2500 meters north of the Marine base at Dong Ha. This attack was part of a series of attacks throughout the country that came to be called "Mini-Tet."

Chris

May 3 – We were hit again last night, about 100 rounds of mortars – that'll keep your head down. It's still hard to believe I am here. I'm a grunt by every description in the book. My only connection to the outside world was in letters I received from home, or new guys that came in, but normally we didn't talk to them until they'd been here for a while. It's just the way it was. Too many times, guys would be killed on their first couple of days. No use to make friends. After a while, the guys would prove themselves by doing what they were supposed to do and friendships would happen. No one was ever really left out. Just part of the process, I guess.

Re-supply copters have been coming in every 4-5 days, bringing in C-rats and ammo, taking away our dead and wounded and maybe picking up our letters going home.

We truly became part of our environment. The better you did that, the better off you were. You didn't think about home too much, as there really wasn't anything there except a distraction. The better you were in analyzing the surrounding terrain, the better prepared you were to live.

Unable to truck in supplies to the Marines at Khe Sanh, planes flew overhead and dropped the needed ammo, food/water and medical supplies.

You learned to endure the rains and the damn cold they brought. The heat was the same. You lived with it. If guys started bitchin' about it too much, you told them to shut up. We all hated the bush. Some were better than others in how they dealt with it, day after day. Mosquitos, leeches, ringworm, it was all there. It was the bush. At times we looked so bad: dirty uniforms, dirty faces, no toothpaste, soap, no haircuts. The bush brought us together. We all shared the bad times, we shared the victories. We became closer. The new guys were finally brought into the team.

May 5 - Met up with Corporal Mike Terry again. He's in Golf Company and from Seattle. Fairly religious kind of guy. We have lots of talks about religion and everything else. Very squared away guy. He tells me that every time his squad is going out into the bush, he says his prayers and no one gets hurt. But every time he stays in the rear area, his squad gets attacked. He has a hard time with this. He always goes to a quiet place, if that is possible, and prays for the safety of the mission of his guys. Mike has invited me to be in his wedding in Seattle when we get home. His girl friend, Nancy, sounds like a great gal.

Lt. Kirk
May 6 - Today a Phantom pilot bailed out over Khe Sanh and his jet crashed just outside the base to our northeast. Unfortunately, he landed in a minefield outside our lines. I went out to get him with two of my men along what we knew was a safe route. We yelled at him to stay put, but he kept moving towards us. Fortunately, he finally understood us and stopped. He was plenty shook up. He told me this was the second time he had been shot down and bailed out in a week.

Chris
May 8 - Doc Turner left for the states. I am so happy he made it. John put his life on the line every day. When we had our heads down, he was running to administer aid to some poor wounded Marine. H is truly one of the bravest and best. I will remember him the rest of my life. Doc didn't have the luxury of smiling much. His spent every moment showing his concern for his troops. Were they taking their malaria pills? Were they taking care of their feet? Did they have any open sores that they hadn't reported? The list goes on. He was very attentive to our needs.

Lt. Suydam
May 8 - Another time, we were atop a ridge some distance from Khe Sanh. It was very dark and I was walking along to get somewhere. Suddenly, Marines

fired a 106-mm recoilless rifle. The shells for this weapon are as big as an artillery shell, except the shell casing is perforated. This allows the expanding gasses to rush rearward from the weapon thus making it recoilless. The rearward rushing gasses go backward with such force that a man would be easily killed if he were in line with the gun and within fifty feet. Luckily, they were firing slightly down. I was about 20 feet directly behind the gun and the gasses passed over my head by about two feet. It sounded like a jet plane just missed me.

Chris

May 10 – Well, I finally got R & R. I didn't go to Australia or Hawaii for seven days as I had hoped. Since I haven't had any time out of the bush, they sent me to Okinawa for a couple days. My three day R&R was in Okinawa and it is coming to an end. Nothing like going to the other places, but the company can't handle many guys away, as we've been in very low numbers for a long time. It felt good to get out, but soon I'll be right back in the shit, again.

Dave Dillberg

May 11 - I left May 11, when I and six others were wounded just above Hill 881-N, near this place called Xa Lang Miet. After I left, the rest of the 2/1 got into some heavy battles.

May 17 - On Route 9, halfway between Khe Sanh and Lang Vei, Hotel Company, 2/1 spotted five enemy soldiers and gave chase. The five led them into an ambush, where an NVA company lay in bunkers, firing from close range and shouting "Die Marine"! Hotel withdrew slightly, and called in artillery and air strikes, then assaulted and overran the bunkers. The Marines lost 6 dead and 8 wounded in the ambush, and counted 52 dead NVA.

May 19 - Fox Company headed south of Khe Sanh, along the coffee plantation road and encountered the NVA dug in, and fired a storm of automatic weapons fire, RPG's, and grenades. The company commander had been mortally wounded and contact during the next hour was mixed with serious probes by both sides.

Lt. Suydam

May 19 - We were at Khe Sanh. Each day, a reinforced company with tanks would sweep the road for mines going east to LZ Stud about five miles to our rear. One morning, Fox Company was ambushed during the mine sweep and overrun. Then run back over. My skipper told me to go see the Lt. Col. because the Fox-trot company commander had been killed and they needed a company

Corporal Gordon Molaison, Thibodaux, Louisiana
(panel 63, line 13 on The Wall)

Cpl Gordon "Judge" Molaison
Thibodaux, Louisiana

commander. I was out of my mind with fear. When I got to Col. Duncan, I tried to tell him something that would dissuade him from sending me. I really did not feel up to the task. I was twenty-one years old, had flunked out of college, enlisted and commissioned through an enlisted commissioning program when I was twenty. I had to wait thirty days before leaving for Vietnam on my twenty-first birthday. I felt very comfortable leading a platoon, but a company in combat? I was past scared. Col. Duncan stopped me after several words with........"I'm sure you'll do fine, Lieutenant." I had the last words,............................ "Yes, Sir."

The fighting was over when I got there. The two M-80 tanks were burning. What a sight. They use an RPG-7 rocket. It is a short metal tube with bamboo on the outside for a heat shield. The fins of the rocket fold up into the tube. The heavy large rocket explosive is outside of the tube. Our 3.5-inch rocket launcher held the whole rocket so it was large and heavy.   Their's has a percussion firing mechanism instead of the complex magneto of ours. Their's required one man to fire.   Ours required two.   Like most of their weapons, they were simple and effective and could run rings around ours.   Even today, the Russian invented, Chinese made AK-47 is sought after because of its durability, effectiveness, ease of maintenance and killing power. I would choose the AK-47 over the M-16 any day of the week.

Hotel Company had observed the ambush from a nearby mountain perch. They dropped down and closed in from the south, thus trapping the remaining NVA soldiers between the two Marine rifle companies. A4 Sky Hawks were dropping napalm between us. Each time they dropped the napalm, there was firing, as the bad guys tried to run out.   The Fox troops were pretty demoralized and very happy to see me because I had bars, I guess. I was finally glad to have been given the assignment because of this. There was nothing for me to be afraid of and I felt that my just being there helped the others.

At the end of the day, we piled weapons (our's and their's) on a duce-and-a-half truck with trailer.   On top of the weapons, we piled dead Marines so high I thought the truck would tip over when it moved (about 20 Marines, I'm told).   It was the saddest day of my life. The next day we were mopping up and captured two NVA survivors who were badly burned. They were young conscripts. It had been their first battle.

Note: Lt. Suydam - I learned that on the day before the battle, Hotel was in a defensive perimeter on a hilltop overlooking the road. The road from Khe Sanh runs south from the combat base approximately 3-5 miles until it joins route 9. The communist infiltrated into the valley below Hotel Company between the hill and the road. During the night, they quietly dug fighting holes about 100 meters from the road and on the west side. On the morning of the ambush, the enemy was completely hidden from Hotel Company by the early morning fog.

As Foxtrot Company came south with their mine sweep, a sapper came forward with a satchel charge that put the first tank out of commission. As the sapper retreated, Marines of Foxtrot chased him, not knowing they were running directly into the enemy lines. This was the cause of the greatest loss of life. The second tank came along side the first and was destroyed by a rocket. As the battle raged and the fog lifted, Hotel began to fire down on the enemy preventing them from retreating from their positions. With Marines on both sides, it made a perfect path for close air support to rain flaming death upon them. Enemy losses were substantial.

Capt. Eagan
May 19 – My radio operator, Judge, was killed on this day, as we were going out of the wire at Khe Sanh to help Fox Co on the mine sweep ambush. Great guy: after many months as my radio operator, he made corporal and wanted to be a squad leader. He only had the squad a few weeks before he was killed.

Clinton Davis, Echo Co., 1st platoon
May 19 - We took over Khe Sanh. It was tense, with continuing artillery incoming, and we took turns manning the hills around there, assaulted hills 881N and 881S and retook them in one day – a bitch. So many dead NVA around there it stunk of death, and the rats were insane. Every time we went out, we saw chunks of the NVA enemy laying around—a head here, a torso there, a half buried skeleton there—gruesome. Got hit on a road sweep by dug-in NVA. We had to fight from about 0600 hours in the morning until after dark—those little bastards wouldn't give up even when we had F-4 Phantom jets dropping napalm (a highly flammable sticky jelly used in incendiary bombs and flamethrowers, consisting of gasoline thickened with special soaps) right on top of them. I remember almost suffocating because we were so close to the napalm and it burned all the oxygen out of the air. I stayed in one place for six hours, firing back and hoping not to get hit. At the end of the day I had left only a half a magazine of ammo, 9 rounds, and one grenade. I usually carried 400-500 rounds and 4-6 grenades. We also got a few hundred rounds literally thrown to us so we could keep fighting. We had 19 killed and a bunch wounded. We were helping Fox Company, who got hit first.

Note: 8 Marines died, including the CO of Fox Co., Captain T. R. Oliver, and 34 were wounded in the ambush of Fox company and the subsequent action. The battalion captured 3 NVA and reported killing 66. Lieutenant Colonel Duncan said the NVA troops killed by 2/1 were "clean, were dressed and neatly groomed."

Captain Troy R. Oliver, Boise, Idaho
(panel 63E, line 15 on The Wall)

<u>Chris</u>

May 19 - I learned that Judge died today. I am so torn up. I was told that he stepped on a tomato can (USA-made) mine, a three prong mine. I could have dropped to the ground and cried. He was really my last true friend in Vietnam. My sister, Sherri, had been writing to him. Now, I would have to write and share this news with her. Another close friend killed. It hurts every time. I so wish I could tell his parents, how good a Marine and friend he was. Everyone enjoyed Judge. Captain Eagen had just promoted Judge to corporal and he was finally a squad leader, which is what he always wanted to be. He wanted to dump the radio he had been carrying for so long and take command of men. I'm sure he made a great squad leader.

This one really hurt. House was gone, Herfel was killed, Estes rotated to the states, Judge was killed, Gunny was killed, Doc was gone...I feel very alone. I still have three months to go. I just need some time and I'll be okay. It's a lot to absorb.

Note: Lt. Suydam - Depression was a problem for some, particularly those who were "short-timers". Marines who had put in their time and were about to rotate back to the States (we called it the "World") were often out of their skin with nervous energy. Almost every Marine that served in a 2/1 rifle company was either killed or wounded. The lucky ones, like me, were wounded. No one survived thirteen months of combat unscathed. The mental torment of calculating the odds could drive a man insane, if he would let it. We had a fellow who was quite popular and "short" too. He was due to rotate within ten days. Yet, he was beside himself. On the day he died, his fellow Marines saw him playing Russian roulette with an empty revolver. Minutes later, a shot was heard and he was discovered alone and dead by his own hand, a victim of the storm that raged within him.

I received a letter from his family routed through division headquarters. They had only been told that he died in combat in the Republic of Vietnam. They wanted to know about his death. I tried to explain the best way I could and I related all the details that were known to me. I hope and pray that I did the right thing.

Lt. Kirk

May 20 - During this time at Khe Sanh I was also given responsibility for the 106mm recoilless rifle platoon. The lieutenant who had this job had finished his tour. A 106 is an 11 foot long tube with a tripod. There are six of them in a platoon. The rifle weighs almost 500 pounds. It is transported on a mechanical mule (sort of a big wagon, powered by a gasoline engine). The 106's were scattered around the perimeter. The first day I had this responsibility I fired a 106 for the first time since Quantico. The way you fire it is to push a big button in the middle of the elevation wheel (pulling the button fires the spotting rifle mounted on top of the barrel). The troops learned to fire it by hitting it with their knee while they held their ears. I didn't know that and nobody told me. I hit the button with my hand. The noise was incredible.

One of the sergeants in the 106 platoon skedaddled (ran away and hid) one night when we were probed. When it came time to write a fitness report on him I gave him a very unflattering one and I told him in person that he ought to get out of the Marine Corps when his enlistment expired. To my surprise the battalion commander and the sergeant major put an enormous amount of pressure on me to revise this fitness report. I told the colonel and the sergeant major that the guy was a coward, no good to the Marine Corps and a hazard to his fellow Marines. But eventually, I relented.

Chris

May 20 – I'm back, I'm back, I'm back! In the rear area, again and out of the bush. What a thankful feeling to be called back to company headquarters. I'm not only NCOICOT (non-commissioned officer-in-charge of troops in rear), but also, supply sergeant, again. Now, try to get me out of here. It was on this day that Cpl. Mike House, G-3 section chief draftsman, departed Vietnam.

May 25 - I borrowed a mule, loaded up with ammo and drove where I shouldn't have been. I was going to far away from our compound area, which was not secure. I missed home so much and wanted to spend some time with my friend, Clark Poole. I spent an hour with my high school friend. He's a dental tech/ assistant with the Army and has life pretty nice with a room to sleep in, sheets, a pillow, books, etc. Clark gave me a 6-pack of beer before leaving. When I returned to camp the guys swarmed me and drank the 100 degree beer. I may have had 1/2 bottle to myself. It's good to share.

May 26 - I was sent back into the field today. Damn! I felt like a yo-yo. I know I shouldn't get too comfortable in the rear area, especially with all my guys still in the field. So far, I had been lucky. I had been medevaced 2-3 times. I became stone-deaf two times from the continuous firing of weapons, incoming rounds and the placement of our own 105 mm artillery position (40 yds directly behind our trench) at Con Thien. I was medevaced when my feet, up to my calves, were bleeding, my bout with malaria two times, my back injury two times and everything else. Everyone had the same amount of war. I was still here. I said my prayers, just like the next guy.

The May Command Chronology for 2nd Battalion, 1st Marines states that ground combat and shelling increased during the month. Approximately 600 rounds of incoming artillery, rocket and mortar shells were received at the Khe Sanh Combat Base. The battalion conducted several operations outside the base during the month, including one near hill 881 north and another along the Main Supply Route involving heavy ground contact with an estimated two companies of NVA. The battalion accounted for 137 enemy KIA for the month. 2nd Battalion, 1st Marines casualties for May: 2 officers KIA, 26 enlisted KIA, 2 officers WIA, 96 enlisted WIA.

Note: June 6 - Robert F. Kennedy was assassinated in Los Angeles while campaigning for the Democratic Presidential nomination.

Note: Capt. Eagen - Our corpsmen have always left me feeling intensely proud of them. I know of no other "marriage" between men of different services that has inspired such total devotion as exits between our Corpsman and Marines. I saw them act in such totally selfless and heroic ways as to humble any warrior. Lord knows they took care of me each time I was hit, gathered my wounded, treated them and saved most. They went out there EVERY TIME, regardless of the danger, despite being as tired and worn down as any other guy who'd been humping the hills, sweating across the paddies catching six hours sleep a night, two hours at a time, sharing radio watch, ambush duty, patrols and assaults. I hope I have never failed to try to repay them in whatever way I can because there is nothing sufficient to the debt I owe.

Lt. Kirk

June 17 - Several times at Khe Sanh, Puff the Magic Dragon (Peter, Paul and Mary song) came to help us. Puff is an aircraft (C130) equipped with automatic weapons (quad 50 caliber machine guns, I believe). Puff lit up the night sky with tracers, which looked like rain. Puff made a steady, very loud roar. It absolutely devastated the NVA.

Chris

June 19 – I'm down with malaria again and have a temperature of 105. I'm very cold, but sweating like a pig and delirious. This is my second time with this malaria stuff.

Lt. Suydam

June 20 - When we arrived at Khe Sanh, there were reportedly 7,000 enemy troops still operating in the area. During the next ten weeks, until the base was officially abandoned, U.S. forces operating in and around the Khe Sanh base lost 400 KIA, and 2,300 wounded. These numbers were more than double the casualties sustained by the 26th Marines during the siege.

Chris

June 22 – I'm back at my old job in the rear area and should be here for the duration. The amount of time we spent fighting and chasing down the NVA has been incredible. The continuing loss of lives has been so sad. The battles have intense and long. The struggles the guys have been under is truly showing the best we have.

I'm too short to get shot. I've been in and out of the bush lately like a yo-yo, etc. I know not to complain, as many have it much worse. We all do our job and like Doc Turner always said "We just leave it God's hands".

June 23 - Days are the same up at 0600, down at 2300 hours. I hold formations for all our personnel, sergeants and below. I hold rifle inspections, hold classes on guerrilla warfare, test-fire weapons and play housemother to all the "boots" (new guys). Since my promotion to Corporal, I get NCO base pay of $238, plus combat pay of $65 and overseas pay of $13, for a total of $316. Geez, I'm rollin' in the dough.

June 24 – Just received my orders marked "RELAD" – Release from Active Duty. It's so hard to believe that I'll be going home in two months. I don't get to do the college cut deal, but I have in my hands actual orders to leave this forsaken country and this friggin' war. I want to forget all I have seen and been through.

June 27 – I came over with 15 guys and left with only 4 going home after a full tour. I had 14 in my squad. Three returned home after a full tour and I was only 1 of 3 not WIA/KIA, Estes, House and myself. What a lousy deal. We have lost so many friends. It is so very sad.

Lt. Suydam

June 28 - Although we spent ten weeks at Khe Sanh, we didn't seem to spend much time inside the perimeter. We went on many patrols and we sat on many mountaintops overlooking Khe Sanh. We didn't want the enemy closing in on us again.

I recall one happy day when we were assigned demolition duty. There was a fortified Montagnard village just outside the gate of Khe Sanh. Actually, I think it was the village of Khe Sanh, long since abandoned. Intelligence was concerned that infiltrators and forward artillery observers were coming into that village and using the bunkers there for cover. We took lots and lots of explosives, TNT. We would make up charges and then go destroy a bunker. By the way, a bunker is a hole in the ground with a roof made from logs and dirt. In one bunker we found a small cross bow, a decorative piece of cloth and two old swords. They were flimsy and rusty, probably used for ceremonial purposes. I have several photos as we staged sword-fighting scenes. Everybody got a kick out of this horseplay and wanted their picture taken.

Lt. Kirk

June 30 - I went into a Montagnard village one day with a patrol. These people, who we called "yards" and also, as I remember, "Bru", although I don't know why, were indigenous people who lived in the mountains. Reportedly, they hated the Vietnamese, who, centuries before, had driven them into the mountains. They were small, wiry and dirty.

Note: Chris - Drugs – I have only seen pot twice in my time in Nam. I knew one guy that bought pot already rolled and re-packed in cigarette packs and then a carton, as often as he could. Commercialization of drugs and its use occurred mostly in the larger cities. After I arrived in Da Nang, I never again would travel through a large city, other than a few trips to the hospital and a trip to the morgue. The cities had a large group of U.S. troops from all the services. Supply guys always were being asked to trade. Guys on ships had their ways of getting what they wanted. The story is all day long.

Religion – Religion was something that didn't come up often. Everyone knew that we all believed in God. His name came up every time we got seriously hit or when the incoming rounds lasted a long period of time. One particular event comes to mind. A new guy commented loud and clear as he stood up after surviving his first firefight and said "That made a Christian out of me, right there, buddy".

Politics – We didn't talk much about politics. Most guys were young and didn't care. They didn't talk about politics with their friends back home. They didn't read about the government in their local newspaper. They only knew they were in a war because of politics. That leaves a bad taste in one's mouth.

The June Command Chronology for 2nd Battalion, 1st Marines   says enemy contact was light to moderate.   438 rounds of incoming artillery, rockets and mortars were received by Khe Sanh Combat Base. The battalion accounted for 30 enemy KIA. 2nd Battalion, 1st Marines casualties for June: 10 enlisted KIA, 30 enlisted WIA.

Chris
July 1 - Spoke to my family ...over. A quick conversation on a ham-type of radio, ...over. The sweetness quickly left, as the real world of ugly returned quickly. They knew I was okay and that's the only important thing for now.

Lathan Williams
July 2 -_The last few weeks at Khe Sanh were tough as they kept taking out more and more men. We only had a company left when we evacuated. The enemy could have overrun us in an hour if they knew that. Some scary downsizing.

Lt. Kirk
July 2 - We destroyed the base and the retrograde at Khe Sanh began today with an advance party leaving for our new base near Qua Viet. It was difficult for us to understand after all the blood that had been spilled defending it. The explanation was that we were adopting a mobile strategy.

Our battalion destroyed the Khe Sanh Combat Base. We emptied all the sandbags and filled in all the bunkers and trench lines. We burned the rats and mice and their nests that we found in the bottom of the trenches and bunkers underneath the wooden pallets and other material we had put there to keep our feet dry. At the bottom of the bunker I had lived in there were at least five nests. We knew we had rats because they would run over you at night, but it was disgusting to see how many of them there were.

There was a delay of a couple of days in our departure and we had no protection from bunkers or trench lines during those two days. I remember how beautiful the stars were at night, something I hadn't really seen for several months as we slept underground. During this delay, I was summoned to the battalion command

Echo Company Commander
Capt Tom Eagen

post and told to stand by to go up by helicopter to a hill (881N, I believe) where a Marine company had been in contact and unable to extract its dead and wounded for several days. They had gone through five company commanders, all killed or wounded leading their men down the hill into a draw to retrieve the dead and wounded. I stood a short distance away from a Marine general and a three star Army general, Richard Stillwell, Deputy Commanding General, III MAF, and listened to them talk about what to do about the situation. The Marine general wanted to send me up there and keep trying to recover the dead and wounded in the same way. I don't think he felt the situation was serious enough to call on the Marine Corps' limited air strike resources. The Army general thought differently. He wanted to call in an air strike – he could command the resources and he was senior. He ordered the air strike which succeeded in pushing the bad guys back and allowing the Marines to get their dead and wounded. What a relief! I didn't have to go up there! Thank God for the Army! The thing that makes it possible for you to do your duty in a dangerous situation is the bond you have with the other men in your unit – you don't want to let them down. Taking charge of a unit where you don't know anybody would be really difficult.

July 5 - Most of the battalion walked out, heading east along Rt. 9 towards a landing zone where helicopters picked them up. Some units, including mine, choppered out at about 1700 hours. I was in charge of the group. I executed a plan to gradually collapse our lines and get to the helicopters as they came in. There was only one tree standing on the entire base. I used it as a rallying point. Navy doctors and corpsmen were supposed to go out towards the end, but they raised such a stink, I let them go out early.

Note: Lt. Kirk - Westmoreland wanted Khe Sanh, in part, as a jumping off place for an invasion of Laos. General Lewis Walt of the Marines and General Creighton Abrams, Westmoreland's deputy, disagreed. At the end of his tour, General Westmoreland changed his mind but decided to let General Abrams, who succeeded him, make the decision about when to abandon the base.

Lt. Suydam

July 5 - In the last days of Khe Sanh, our orders were to demolish the defenses. The U. S. had decided to abandon Khe Sanh. We cut open every sandbag, we filled in every trench and bunker, we ruined, wrecked and burned anything and everything of value. Toward the end, I was called away on Company business for three days. When I tried to return, I had difficulty getting back. There were no choppers going into Khe Sanh. Finally, when I did hitch a ride on a medivac chopper, I got off at a big clear spot in a valley that had once been our base of operation. There was a line of trucks about 200 meters away and believe me there was absolutely nothing else. I ran to them and found out that they were the last convoy leaving Khe Sanh. I climbed aboard the last truck. We rolled out cautiously, south to route nine and then east. The battles of Khe Sanh were over.

Note: Chris – The last Marines leave Khe Sanh on July 5. This is so sad, that so many Marines fought and died here and then to leave the base. My good friend, Judge, died for this base.

12

QUA VIET & GOING HOME

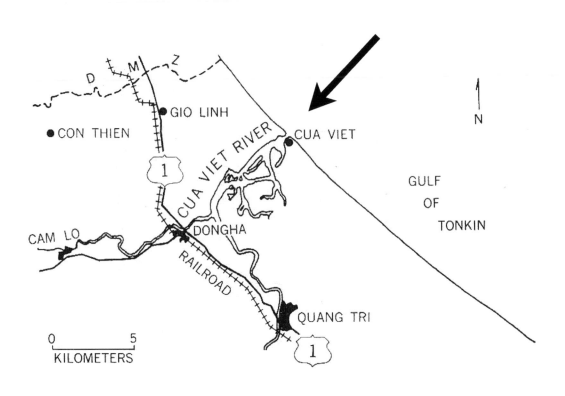

Lt. Kirk

July 5 - We were transported to Cua Viet, the southeastern corner of Leatherneck Square near the coast and just north of the Cua Viet River. Our base was called Camp Big John. What a relief! Khe Sanh was such an ominous, gloomy place and the incoming was awful. I didn't think I would make it out of there. My spirits soared when we got to Cua Viet and I started to think I would stay alive. Every day we would go down to the river and swim. What a pleasure it was to get clean and cool off.

Clinton Davis, Echo Co, 1st platoon

July 5 - After Khe Sanh, we were sent to Cua Viet, just north of Dong Ha, a dangerous place, I remember the village of Dai Do (pronounced Dye Dough). Scary - I think the villagers hated us. I think they were all Viet Cong.

Lt Jim Kirk - Clean clothes & a shower

Chris

July 6 - I am now supply sergeant, police sergeant and transit NCO. All personnel are being taken out of the rear area and sent to the front. I was one of the lucky ones chosen to stay behind. Found out that my friend Reed lost two fingers in City of Hue Battle during Tet. He was a boot camp friend. A gun just fired and I jumped. Damn - I need to get home. I've made some interesting and close friendships over here. I seem to be with guys that are my age or 1-2 years older than me and that have been to college. Good conversations. Most of the other guys are younger - 18, and I'm 21. Flight dates are due soon.

July 7 – The guns have stopped and it's quiet now. Just finished a letter to Mary Jo. I can't seem to get her out of my mind. I have been trying for 2-1/2 years. I know we'll have a good talk when I get home. I'm looking forward to seeing her and who knows?

Geez…A shot just went off and about shattered my nerves. Lots of changes the past year. I hope when I return, I'm able to adjust, remember what I've learned and forget what I've seen.

Dave Stromire, Echo Co.
July 8 – I joined Echo Company this day. You guys just returned from the bush for your first hot meal in 60 days. They arrived at Camp Big John, by the Cua Viet River, across from North Vietnam. We made a raid into the DMZ. When the choppers came to get us, all hell broke out. Saw one chopper go down, a pilot jumped out of another copter, as it was on fire and I think I saw an F-15 go down. I was busy getting on my chopper. This was my first action in 'Nam.

Lt. Kirk
July 8 - During my time in Vietnam, I corresponded with Exa Mote (unusual name, huh?), my girlfriend from when I was at Basic School at Quantico. She was a student at Mary Washington College in Fredericksburg, Va. During one of my darkest hours at Khe Sanh I wrote and asked her to marry me. I was sincere, but with hindsight I realize I was very scared and needed something to hold on to. She said yes. When we arrived at Qua Viet I felt like I was going to survive. I realized marriage would be a bad idea – I needed to finish college. I felt terrible about it, but I decided it was better to end it as soon as possible. I wrote and told her. Later she wrote to say she was engaged to marry a Marine pilot stationed at Cherry Point, NC. Exa's best friend was the fraternal twin sister of Lewis Puller, Jr., both children of the famous Marine General Chesty Puller. Lewis Jr. joined the battalion later and was severely wounded.

Chris
July 9 – I moved to a new home, the supply tent. I live alone, which is a fine. I have a work party (a group of guys), which reports to me every morning - straighten things up, clean-up the area and do any work I have for them. One more month!

It's hard not to spend a lot of time thinking about home and of course, Mary Jo. I miss her so much. I continue to think about my old college life. I had it so good then. I was now getting so close to going home. Only one more month and a few days.

Lt. Suydam

July 11 - We moved to Qua Viet, so our mail is screwed up again, as it goes to Da Nang to Dong Ha, to Qua Viet. 27 days left. One third of the month is gone, never to return.

Chris

July 24 – I just got in from the field yesterday. I had been requested to hand-cuff and take a deserter back to the company rear area. It was strange feeling to place one of our troops under arrest. The tall, large-framed negro private had refused to fight in battle and was being sent to the rear area to be placed in front of command and probably be sent to the states and placed in prison.

He was hand-cuffed to me during the daytime, as I tried to continue with my duties. When it was time for sleeping, I had to cuff him to tent post support, in my tent. In the morning, I left him cuffed while I washed up. Before going to breakfast, I asked another Marine to sit with him until I returned.

After breakfast, I returned to my tent and was immediately told that he had escaped. Geez....I was so damn mad. "Top" (name given to the highest ranking enlisted man in the company and in-charge of everyone in the rear area) jumped and screamed at me, as it was my duty to watch him and he was pissed.

I hopped in my jeep and went looking for him, .45 automatic pistol on my hip and another pair of cuffs. This is big offense, especially to those, like myself, that have served on the combat lines. I know there is nowhere for him to go, so I assumed he was still in camp, somewhere. Since he was a negro, I figured the best place to start was to find out where the negroes hung-out.

After questioning a few individuals on base, I was told where to look. I approached the tent cautiously. All the flaps were down and I was unable to see inside. Before entering, I released the flap on my holster, unfolded the flap on the side of the tent and I said out loud, "I was there to place Private X under arrest". I brought my .45 automatic pistol to my side and waited for any of the other 15 negroes to cause a problem - no one moved. They just started at the small white NCO, with a pistol at his side and an attitude. Nothing happened. The second time I spoke I said "the man I am looking for is a deserter and I have been authorized to shoot anyone that hinders my ability to take him in". I spotted him at the back of the tent, in a small group of guys. I walked into the middle of the tent and and told him to turn around, which he did. I cuffed him and led him outside.

371

Once outside, I turned him around and looked him right in the face. Looking up at this 6'4" 250 lb individual and standing erect my 5' 9", 150 lb frame I told him I had been given permission to shoot him in the front or the back, if he chose to run. He will stay with me for the next couple of days, until the MP's came for him. I expect to have no more issues. He knew I was pissed and probably thought I might shoot him. (No, I hadn't been given permission to shoot him, but I do think he believed me.

There wasn't any time while I was in the Marines that I saw negative racial issues between the negroes or blacks and the whites. We didn't seem to have to fight the racial overtones. The most popular person in our company was Gunny Weathers and he was black. He knew how to stay alive and taught us everything he could to help us live so we could go home. His color was never an issue or topic. We were lucky, as many units found the blacks formed their groups, which somehow sensed they were being discriminated against, whether real or imagined. It seemed ridiculous to me, as we were all bonded by the power of survival, which meant we needed to stand together and bond as a team. Color didn't seem to matter when we were in combat. Maybe that was the common link - combat. We needed that person next to us. Color wasn't an issue. Troops in the rear area had lots of time on their hands, maybe too much time. Maybe, since I was from the Northwest part of the country, I didn't see the color line. My acceptance of the negroes goes back to high school in Portland, Oregon, where everyone was treated the same. We all competed for the same positions in sports.

Note: Many years later I learned that my high school, in Portland, Oregon, was an integrated school in the 1960's, yet the classes were segregated. I didn't remember it causing any issues. We shared choir and physical education with the negroes (term used prior to blacks). All the sports in which I was involved was mixed with both the negroes and the whites. We got along great. I never saw any conflict or issues while in high school. The negro student lockers were all together down at the end of one of the halls. What's with that?)

I really enjoyed being back in the bush. What a strange thing for me to say. I just seemed so comfortable back with the guys and in that environment.

Mike Terry is going to get married when he gets home and has invited me to be an usher at his wedding on Aug 24. He's from Washington. Mike gave me a condensed bible, with some pretty good advice written in the front cover - "Keep your head up and your knee bent."

81 mm Mortar Observation Post

July 26 – I needed a few supplies, so I ventured over to the PX, which was only a 10' x 30' canvas tent, holding only a few items – paper and envelopes, shaving cream, toothpaste, etc. A small sign shows the tent as a PX, with a guard at the door. As I started to enter, through the tent flap, the guard spoke to me in a very slow and quiet tone. I asked him to repeat. "Are you Cpl. Christensen?" I answered that I was. He turned and said "I don't know if you remember me, but I'm the guy you threw over that cliff". I responded that yes, I remembered him and asked where he had been. He said "I've been in the hospital…you broke my back." Oh…I quickly did my business in the tent and left. (I'm surprised he didn't want to shoot me).

A close buddy of mine, Chuck Estes, who was our squad leader before me and that rotated home a short time ago, has written a letter to our squad. It seems he is now working in the Bahamas, to earn money to return to college. It's so good to hear from guys that have made it back home, especially Chuck. He was so squared away and sharp. Everybody enjoyed hearing from him.

July 29 - My flight date is set for August 13th. I now feel, for the very first time, that I'm going home.

Clinton Davis

July 30 - I hate this elephant grass that cuts like a razor, rain for solid weeks at a time, always being wet, c-rations for six months at a time before a hot meal, apricots, ham and mothers, chocolate powder, four cigs in a pack, matches that didn't work, spaghetti, chicken and noodles, yuk, I went from 186 lbs to 158 lbs in six months, using C-4 to cook with, being exhausted all the time, the horror of hearing those artillery shells whistling in, losing friends, trying to bandage up the hurt guys, pooping in a diesel fuel can, humping 45 lbs of gear in 110 degree weather, how tough the NVA's were, going down in those tunnels (I must have been crazy), air strikes, wow--I can't believe I did that

Note: Clinton Davis - Now, I am such a baby I don't even like to go to the mailbox after dark. Remember how dark it got over there, no lights anywhere around—I remember some of getting lost from the rest of the platoon 'cause we didn't know they had up and left.

The July Command Chronology for 2nd Battalion, 1st Marines notes that the battalion destroyed the combat base at Khe Sanh and moved to Mai Xa Thi on the Qua Viet River near the coast where it assumed responsibility for an area of operations both north and south of the river.   304 rounds of incoming artillery, rockets and mortars were received during the short period at Khe Sahn.   The battalion was responsible for 17 enemy KIA. 2nd Battalion, 1st Marines casualties for July: 5 enlisted WIA, 1 officer WIA, 27 enlisted WIA.

Lt. Kirk

August 1 - One of my Marines was killed and four were wounded while handling mortar rounds. They were transporting the ammo on a mechanical mule. The safety pins were removed, against orders. The action of the mule armed the rounds, in the same way the acceleration of the round in the mortar barrel arms it.   One guy's chest was split open horizontally and there was a huge gap between the two parts of his chest. He was still alive when we got him to the BAS (battalion aid station) and the Navy doctors worked on him, but couldn't save him. I remember my admiration for the doctors and corpsman. I had seen some gore, but I could hardly look at this guy. I don't know how they could work on him without breaking down.   I am shocked by the number of friendly casualties resulted from mishandling of 81 mm mortar ammunition before, during and after I became platoon commander.

August 2 - The Cua Viet ammo dump blew up. Shells cooked off for a couple of days. My 81mm mortar CP was inside an abandoned and half destroyed house. Shells from the ammo dump kept cooking off, flying into the air and falling on the roof, which was just about gone after a day or so of this. The engineers were loading ammo into an Otter when a trip flare was accidentally ignited. The ammunition and equipment destroyed included the following: 105 mm HE - 400 rounds, 106 mm beehive - 224 rounds, TNT - 1500 lbs, 60mm HE - 1200 rounds, 60 mm WP – 3786 rounds, 40mm HE - 2980 rounds, LAAWS - 720, 3.5 HE - 627 rounds, 106 mm Hept - 850 rounds, 106 mm heat - 600 rounds, 60mm illum - 1962 rounds, 81mm illum – 3672 rounds, 81mm WP – 1620 rounds, trip flares - 396, 7.62 link - 250,000 rounds, .50 caliber link - 20,000 rounds, Bangalore torpedoes - 60, cratering charges - 30, det cord - 600 feet, electrical blasting caps - 1000, 6x6 trucks - 2, Otters - 2, mechanical mule -1 , pallets of C-rations - 26, bulk fuel bladder - 1. I left out a lot of it because I got tired of typing. What a fiasco!

Chris

August 2 - My bags are packed! I'm ready to leave. Going to Da Nang to get some paperwork finished. I'll probably try to stretch the trip to 2-3 days.

August 3 - I just met Mike Elliot, he was the lifeguard at the Irvington Club in Portland in 1962-1963. He's an ensign with the Seabees.

August 5 - I stayed two days in Da Nang. Mike and I went swimming down at the beach. Again, I have no rifle, no pistol. The area seems secure, but that type of feeling has gotten many guys killed. It's still hard to relax and probably will be for awhile.

August 6 - My replacement came down from the hill today. I am now just one of many waiting to go home. I just started my 13th month over here. How did I make it? It has been an incredible journey and I am so thankful to be going home. I understand the tour is going to drop from 12 month and 20 days to 11 month and 20 days. I just heard from Tom Hammer and Geof Grabenhorst. They are in San Diego - Navy training. I also heard from Bill Lindstedt, from Grant HS. He's living in Aberdeen, Washington.

August 8 - I check in all my combat gear on the 9th and leave for Da Nang on the 10th. It's strange walking around without a weapon. Some guys hide a pistol in their sea bag, as they're very uncomfortable without some protection. It's tough to be transferring from a vigilant combatant, fighting every single day to stay alive to going home. I am very apprehensive, as I know others are, also.

Gunner (Marine leaning over) has removed the sight and is holding it in his hands. This is standard operating procedure so the vibration/shock that takes place in the barrel doesn't damage the sight.

Note: Cpl. Clinton Davis was wounded for the second time after the battalion moved to an area south of Da Nang in August.

August 9 - Well, we're all here in Da Nang, waiting for Continental Airlines to let us board and fly us home. We are stretched out along a fence, the sun is shinin', and I'm beat. So, I take nap and when I awake the plane is gone, my buddy to my right is still sleeping, so I awaken him. We have been left behind. Novels are filled with stories like this – (Safe for a year, killed on last day).

August 10 - We found a place to sleep - underground, of course and left in the morning for Okinawa, aboard a C-130. These planes don't have stews, we sat in sack seats and it was as cold as it could be in that plane and absolutely noisy. I went to sleep. Eventually, we got home.

August 11 – I flew into Travis AB, San Francisco. I don't have notes or letters describing the weeks that followed before discharge with two exceptions – the first was meeting my dear girl friend, Mary Jo, at the airport in San Francisco. We dated our freshman year at Southern Oregon University and had a great time. Our relationship grew during the year and we both felt close to each other by the time I left for Vietnam. Mary Jo wrote many letters to me during my tour overseas, which were always uplifting and positive. I would see her in my mind as I read each letter. Her dark hair flowing over her shoulders and the ever-continuous smile that truly had captured me our freshman year at college. It was nerve racking to have to patiently wait until we would finally meet again. It had been such a long time.

When our airplane arrived at Travis Air Base, in San Francisco, I telephoned Mary Jo. She was excited to hear from me and I was excited to hear her voice. I could feel the excitement. We arranged a time and place to meet at the airport. She said she'd leave right away from her home in San Jose.

I saw her walk into the airport. She was so beautiful. Her smile and her big brown eyes were just the same as when I last saw her. Her radiant smile from across the room told me I was so lucky. Accompanying Mary Jo was her best friend from high school, Pat. Mary Jo walked up to me and with a big smile, a hug and a kiss, we sat a table. She immediately placed her left hand on the table, displaying a diamond ring and announced that she had gotten married while I was gone. I was numb.

13

AFTERMATH & THE EFFECTS OF THE WAR

Each of us had experienced the war in our own way and had been affected differently. The following few paragraphs share some of how we felt about the war, after coming home, some 44 years ago and how the war may have altered our lives.

Doc Turner (written prior to our gathering at the beach in Oregon)
My wife, Donna, has her doubts about us all getting together in a group. She thinks that all of us getting together may do more harm than good. Of course, she is more worried about me than the rest of you. I personally think we all need closure of a miserable time in our lives and I think that together we can get it done. I have always felt a kinship towards you, Chris. You were always a gutsy type of guy that looked out for everyone you could and did it without being over bearing and bossy. I felt you you did your job and did it well. And I had great respect for you.

Chris
In July of 2008, as five of us gathered in a small Oregon beach town, we easily shared what we had been doing with the time that had lapsed since "Nam. Luckily, we were all with the arms and legs that we left the States with. No artificial prosthesis. How lucky we were. And, we knew it.

What wasn't so easily seen was the impact that the war had taken on our lives, mentally. I believe four of the five of us that met at the beach in Oregon suffered from Post Traumatic Stress Disorder (PTSD). We had seven marriages, three divorces, 45-50 jobs, alcohol and drug issues and much, much more...recurring nightmares, flashbacks, insomnia, irritability, anger, hypervigilance, excessive startle response, and anxiety. All symptoms of our engagement in war.

Back at college, I earned a bachelor's degree and entered the business world in the area of sales/sales management. I spent my best years selling to hospital surgical units. I did well during my working years, but seemed to change jobs often, creating a stressful life for my family. Life was more difficult for me than it should have been. I had all the right tools, but I just couldn't keep the train on the tracks. The war was having its effect on me, I just didn't know it. Only because I was so competitive was I able to pull myself through life.

I still fight the war each day. It's easier now, but it's still there. People don't seem to understand, whether they try or not, I don't know. My life is not as I imagined or hoped it would be, but I'm physically fit, have my wife and family. I know I am much luckier than so many others. Only though the patience and love from my wife and family and through the grace of God have I been able to enjoy my life today.

Injuries from the war, both physical and mental, take their toll, daily.

Lee Suydam

When we Marines left Khe Sanh, we didn't know it then, but the American hope of winning in Vietnam was over too. Early in 1968, on the Vietnamese holiday, Tet, when the ARVN troops were all standing down from their duties, the communist launched a combined Viet Cong and NVA countrywide attack on South Vietnam. It was the worst military defeat of communist forces ever suffered in the 87-year history of communist aggression anywhere in the world. The siege of Khe Sahn started just prior to Tet, perhaps as a diversion for Tet. During the heavily televised accounts of the communist defeats during Tet and the siege of the 26th Marines at Khe Sanh, public sentiment in the U.S. about obtaining victory in Vietnam slipped from slightly positive to slightly negative and would never recover. Even though American forces soundly defeated the maximum thrust of the enemy on a countrywide basis and the Marines had withstood and survived victoriously over the worst that the enemy could throw at them, America had lost its stomach for war in Southeast Asia.

The American public viewed the willingness of the communist to sustain unspeakable numbers of casualties as a threat they no longer wished to face because it meant a continuing stream of US casualties. President Johnson announced that he would not run for reelection. Richard Nixon ran for President on a campaign promise to end the war. He was elected; he spent two more years seeking a victory, then he withdrew our troops, leaving Vietnam to fall to communism.

We vets didn't talk much about Vietnam. It was so unpopular and nobody wanted to be reminded of the pain associated with the brother, neighbor, uncle, father, husband or boyfriend that was ruined or lost. So, Vietnam era veterans mostly just kept quiet. This story telling all started when I found the 2nd Battalion, First Marine web page on the Internet. A few who had been where I had been swapped stories and before it was over, I had dredged up so many recollections that I wanted to write them down.

After the Union disaster at Fredericksburg Virginia in 1862 where Federal troops were slaughtered before the stone wall at Mary's Heights, General Robert E. Lee remarked, "It's a good thing war is so terrible, otherwise we should grow fond of it." When I read this, I knew exactly what he meant. Vietnam, forgetting the bad things, was the most exhilarating experience of my life.

Doc Turner

Vietnam was difficult for all of us. I left most of it in God's hands…tried to remember the good times…did a lot of rationalizing. Just by his Grace alone, that our names are not on that marble wall in Washington, DC. In short, I put that, for the most part, behind me.

Don't get me wrong, I still have nightmares and am taking medication to reduce my anxiety. I've led a very interesting life and have achieved most of my goals. Obtaining a BSN, after Nam, was the hardest thing I did. I couldn't concentrate on learning and remembering. Almost flunked out until my senior year, then I

made the Deans List both semesters. On my State Board Exams for a license I achieved very high passing grades. I was one of the first RN's in Louisiana to become a surgical assistant. I have assisted in open heart, chest and lung, OB/GYN, vascular surgery on legs, plastic and orthopedic surgeries. I guess I substituted losses in Nam with successes in the operating room at home.

I worked on an Acute Psych Ward for about four years before returning to the OR. Most of the problems there were substance abuse related. A few cases were because of PTSD. I could tell the ones with PTSD from the others and could relate with them much better. Because of experience in surgery, I could tell if a patient was in real pain or was faking it to get drugs.

I live in a small community 18 miles north of Alexandria, Louisiana. I have a 35 acre place and was training horses for a while. The jockey became a dope head and I couldn't find a replacement, so I shut it down. I put a telephone tower in the hay field and turned the racing track into a roadbed of an eight unit RV park. I'm doing fairly well with it. I have two daughters and five grandsons, married once for 13 years once 32 years, as of 2011. I ride a Harley Davidson and belong to the Combat Vets Motorcycle Association.

I feel blessed to have so much good in my life and to have survived the war.

Mike House

My return to the U.S. from Vietnam was also the end of my two year enlistment, and it was a bitter ending that left me angry for years to come. I had ten days remaining until my official discharge date when we landed in El Toro, California. There was no duty station for me since I was so "short", so, I was assigned to a filthy, huge, and unused barracks with ten other Marines, none of them having been in the infantry or combat, but from many bases all over Asia. I ached to talk

to other combat veterans, but there were none, and I felt very alone there. The base enlisted man's club was only full of air wing pukes, and I refused to drink with those prima-donnas. I spent as much time as possible on the phone with Nancy to try to stave off the boredom and my hostility, burning the days and hours remaining until I could get on my way home.

I was ordered to form clean-up teams from the "Unwilling Ten" to pick up cigarette butts, rake leaves, mow lawns, and paint rocks along walkways with whitewash to make the base pretty for those superior jet jockeys of the air wing! This was like a slap in the face for me. Rather than being welcomed home by my Marine Corps and a grateful nation, I felt spit on, reduced to the roll of groundskeeper/babysitter. It was impossible to get those guys to do anything. Since we were all so short, nobody cared, and the question repeated back to me many times was "What are they going to do, send me to Vietnam?" All the "Gung Ho" attitude was gone. I was finished. I had done my duty, and felt I had done so much more than anyone around me, and I DESERVED to go home with dignity. I never expected to get the back of the hand from my Marine Corps, but to them it was just a date to release me, and I hated them for that. Receiving my discharge papers, I walked out the gate in my dress green uniform (I could not afford the $85.00 dress blues on my pay of $165.00 per month) with all my medals and ribbons, and $75.78 travel pay for a Greyhound bus ticket to Seattle. That was six cents per mile for 1,263 miles.

My real welcome home was simply returning to my wife and my baby boy, who had grown-up so much without me. I was twenty two years old and had "seen the elephant", and was so very glad to have survived the ordeal. I had been one of the lucky ones. I was certainly no hero. All the guys we left behind that gave their last full measure were the real heroes in my book.

I finished my apprenticeship, and became a journeyman fitter, working at the trade for ten years in the Naval shipyard, repairing many of the warships that returned from deployments off Vietnam. I became a shop trade instructor, and was a certified reactor plant worker on surface ships and submarines. I got fed up with Civil Service, and went to work for a local private steel shop for five years, building major bridges, ferry terminals, and nuclear waste containers, eventually purchasing the business with partners for a couple more years. We built two of the largest rail shipping containers ever made for the damaged radioactive nuclear fuel rods from the reactor plant at Three Mile Island, and then went bankrupt. I ended up as a Professional Project Manager for the largest engineering, machining and fabrication shop in Tacoma, Washington for twenty-five years, retiring in 2010. My wife retired a year before me after twenty-three years as a registered nurse in surgical recovery.

Nancy and I have three children, two sons and a daughter, all very successful, and we now have five grandsons. The oldest has his eye on my '34 Ford, but grandpa Mike ain't done yet!

Steve "Bernie" Bernston (the Storyteller)

"Going back to the World" Reflections by Steve (Bernie) Berntson, USMC, SGT Combat Correspondent, First Marine Division in RVN 1967-68.

All of us grunts and "Docs" commonly referred to our RTC (Return to CONUS) date as "going back to the World." We talked about, bragged about it, told each other about it repeatedly but if the truth be told, many of us had some fears about going home from the war.

For me, "going back to the world" involved a detour to 106th General Army Hospital in Japan where I underwent a couple surgeries for "holes and fractures" I received in Hue City.

After nearly a month, I was air lifted by USAF to CONUS, specifically Long Beach Naval Hospital, Long Beach, CA. The hospital was the closest to my wife and baby daughter whom I had never seen. In April 1969, I was temporarily medically retired from the Marine Corps and my life was suddenly changed to a disabled Vietnam Veteran with no job and a wife and daughter to support. I was scared then and stayed that way for the next 17 years, as I pushed my life in warp speed to "normalize" and prove that as a disabled person I could do as good if not better that the best, whether it was working as a newspaper reporter, college undergraduate and upper graduate student, and all my professional pursuits.

PTSD caught up with me in 1985 when I was experiencing a relapse of hereditary depression. Over the next year, I worked weekly with the first VA Outreach Storefront clinic in Seattle. From there I struggled for next years to balance the war experience with the hereditary tendency of clinical depression. I don't know the day or the year exactly, but sometime about the year 2000 most all of the angry, animosity, fear, and flee or fight parts of my life went away. Age? Medications? Or maybe just time and distance has finally brought me peace over my Vietnam War ghosts. And for that, I'm one lucky SOB. Every day I hope that my journey to peace can be repeated over and over for my brothers in arms who still face the struggle to "going back to the world."

Chuck Estes

When I returned from Vietnam, I obtained a construction job in the Bahamas and started saving for my return to college. I graduated with a Bachelor of Science in engineering and pursued my career in engineering by building energy plants. I presently supervise the construction of new gas-generated energy plants throughout North Texas.

When I returned from Vietnam, I was so upset with everything that I wrote a 350 page document, telling of my total disgust with the politicians, the generals and everything else about the war. The war was wrong on so many levels. I think of Vietnam every day since and can't get rid of the war.

Jim Kirk

I finished my tour in November, 1968. After a month of leave at home, I reported to 1st Battalion, 27th Marines at Kaneohe Bay, Hawaii . I was a platoon leader for a while and then became company executive officer. I was discharged in January 1970. I served in the active reserves with 3rd Battalion, 25th Marines in Cleveland for a couple of years and was promoted to captain.

I finished college, getting a bachelor's degree in economics from Case Western Reserve University. I enrolled in the MBA program, graduating in 1972. I earned the Chartered Financial Analyst (C.F.A) designation. I spent the next 36 years working in investment management for banks in the Cleveland area, managing pension, endowment and mutual funds as well as personal accounts. I was the president of the investment management subsidiary at KeyBank and executive vice president and chief investment officer for the Private Client Group at National City Bank later on. I retired in 2008 and spend a lot of time on the golf course and on my 31 foot Tartan sailboat on Lake Erie. I read a lot (I have nearly 1300 books), particularly history, and work on my family tree, which now contains more than 3000 ancestors and other family members. My wife, Jean, and I spend the winter at our condo in Naples, Florida. We have five children and twelve grandchildren. Life is good.

As I look back on my experience in the Marine Corps, I am grateful to have come through thirteen months in an infantry battalion with hardly a scratch. Based on the casualty figures reported in 2/1's Command Chronology from October, 1967 through October, 1868, I calculated that a Marine with the battalion for an entire thirteen month tour had a probability of being killed of 12% and a probability of being wounded of 58%.

I'm also grateful for the privilege of having served with some of the finest people I've ever met.

I believe we had a noble purpose in Vietnam. I believe the military succeeded, in spite of some mistakes, in the sense that we won the battles. The ultimate outcome in Vietnam was due to a failure of will on the part of the American people and Congress, not a failure on the part of the soldiers, sailors, airmen and Marines who fought there. It was a political defeat, not a military defeat.

A Washington Post survey of Vietnam veterans found that 91% are glad they served their country. So am I. 56% said they benefitted in the long run by their service in Vietnam and 74% said they enjoyed their time in the service. So did I.

Dennis K. Knobloch

When I returned to the world I decided it was time to get serious about my education. Having switched majors three times during the two years prior to joining the Marines, I chose accounting and stuck with it. It worked out well and I landed a job with an international CPA Firm upon graduation. Six years later I contributed to the formation of what is now Striegel Knobloch & Company, LLC CPA's, with four different offices in Illinois. I have been blessed to have eight great Partners and over 35 employees that are second to none.

I am proud of my service, but it took me over forty years to dig the memories of the war out of some deep hole where it was kept out of sight, but never really out of mind. General Patton said, "Compared to war all other forms of human endeavor shrink to insignificance".

The older I get the more I see the truth in his quote. We were led by some very good officers and the men I fought beside will never be forgotten. Many died so I could come home.

I was married, divorced, and have two children and three grandchildren. I bought my first boat ever four years ago – an old 1987 forty two foot Carver. I had to replace the generator, water heater, some plumbing, and with the help of two very close friends, we redid the wood. Someday my dream is to do America's Great Loop.

On the Confederate Memorial in Arlington National Cemetery
a shortened saying of Dr. Randolph Harrison McKim...

*"Not for fame or reward, not for place or rank,
but in simple obedience to duty,
as they understood it."*

Glossary

0311 – rifleman's military occupational specialty (MOS)

1/ 1, 2/1, 3/26, etc. – 1st Battalion/1st Marines, 2nd Battalion/1st Marines, 3rd Battalion/26th Marines.

1 o'clock am or? – If it's one in the morning, it's 0100 hours; if it's any time after noon add 12 hours, so 1 pm becomes 1300 hours.

6 X 6 – A "six by"; a 2-1/2 ton truck, used to transport up to 18 troops, the workhorse of the motor pool.

A

AK-47 – Russian or Chinese manufactured semi/fully-automatic combat assault rifle, with a characteristic explosive popping sound when fired; it would fire when wet and dirty; designed by Mihail Kalashnikov.

Amtrac – Amphibious armored vehicle used by Marines to transport troops and supplies, armed with a .30-caliber machine gun.

Arc Light Operations – overwhelming aerial raids of B-52's Bombers against enemy positions carrying a mixed load of 500 and 750 pound bombs. These operations shook the earth for ten miles away from the target area.

Arty – artillery

ARVN – Army of the Republic of Vietnam (South Vietnamese).

B

Bandoliers – belts of ammunition.

Base Camp – a base for field units; the location of headquarters

Bn – Battalion; a subdivision of a regiment, consisting of four rifle companies and a headquarters and service company; commanded by a lieutenant colonel; about 1100 men.

Body Count – the number of enemy killed; used by generals and Washington politicians as a measure of the progress of the war.

Booby Traps – an assortment of grenades, mines, and explosive devices and punji stakes; one out of ten battlefield casualties was the result of booby traps. Examples include:
- a makeshift bullet buried straight up with its firing pin on a bamboo stub, activated when someone stepped on the bullet's tip
- hollowed-out coconuts filled with gunpowder and triggered by a trip wire
- walk bridges with ropes almost cut away so they would collapse when someone tried to cross them
- underground and hidden punji stakes
- bamboo stakes connected to grenades and planted at helicopter landing sites
- the "Malay whip"; a strong sapling bent back into the brush alongside trail; a string is run across the trail which, when tripped, releases a sapling with pungi stakes.
- a grenade inside a tin can; a wire was tied to the grenade, stretched and tied to something across the path; the safety pin on the grenade was then pulled; a Marine catches the wire on his foot, pulling the grenade out of the can, letting the spoon fly and the grenade explodes.
- bamboo vipers and deadly cobras were often attached to the roof of a cave, awaiting the next person to enter the cave

Boo-Coo – Slang for many or lots of (something), a mis-spelling of the French word "beaucoup".

Book – to go or to leave.

Boot – A Marine in boot camp or a new guy.

Bouncing Betty – an antipersonnel mine with two charges: the first propels the explosive charge upward, and the other is set to explode at about waist level.

Brother – black Marine, also splib, negro

C

CAP – Combined Action Platoon

Capt - Captain

Chicom - Chinese Communist

Cigmos – Vietnamese kid's name for cigarettes

C-4 – High explosive used to blow up anything from spider holes, bridges, huts, captured ammo and weapons.

C-Rats – Combat rations; canned meals for use in the field; each meal contained a can with some basic course; some had a can of fruit; a dessert was included plus a packet of powdered cocoa or coffee, a small pack of cigarettes, two pieces of chewing gum, plastic utensils and toilet paper.

Claymore Mine – Antipersonnel mine filled with heavy explosive and ball bearings. Often the Vietcong would sneak up on our lines and attempt to turn the claymore around, facing the Marines.

CO – Commanding Officer

Co. – a Marine company, a subdivision of a battalion; it includes three rifle platoons and a weapons platoon.

Col - Colonel

Concertina Wire – Coiled barbed wire used as an obstacle

CP – Command Post

CT – Con Thien Combat Base

D

DMZ – Demilitarized Zone, the area between North and South Vietnam.

E

E-Tool – Entrenching tool. Folding shovel carried by infantry for digging foxholes to sleep/fight in.

Elephant Grass – tall, razor-edged tropical plant.

F

F-4 – Phantom jet fighter/ bombers with range of 1,000 miles, capable of speeds up to 1,400 mph, the workhorse of the tactical air support fleet.

Fatigues – The Army's term for the standard combat uniform, green in color with pockets; Marines called them utilities.

Firefight – a battle, or exchange of small arms fire with the enemy.

Flak Jacket – heavy fiberglass-filled vest worn for protection from shrapnel

FO – Forward observer; coordinates artillery, mortars, naval gunfire or air strikes.

Free-fire Zone – an area where everyone was deemed hostile and a legitimate target by U.S. forces.

G

Graves Registration – mortuary unit

Grunt – infantryman; also ground pounder; only about 1 of out 10 of the troops in Vietnam were fighting on the ground.

H

Hamlet – a small rural village.

Hammer and Anvil – a pincer movement by two units, where one is stationary (the anvil) and one is mobile (the hammer).

Ho Chi Minh Trail – complex web of jungle trails that enabled NVA forces to travel from North Vietnam down to South Vietnam and transport supplies; the NVA used porters, bicycles, ponies and trucks; in the early days of the war it took six months to travel from North Vietnam to Saigon; by the 1970's the trip took six weeks.

Hooch – A straw or wooden hut family dwelling.

Hot LZ – a landing zone under enemy fire.

HQ – headquarters

Huey – UH-1 series helicopters used primarily by the Army.

Hump – To walk or hike

Hwy 1 – a paved, two-lane highway that runs along the east coast of Vietnam.

I

I Corps – the northernmost military district in South Vietnam

Immersion Foot – a condition resulting from feet being submerged in water for a prolonged period of time, causing cracking and bleeding.
Our feet were so bad they would crack and bleed. Skin would fall off the legs and feet, exposing raw skin – often requiring a medevac to a hospital.

Insert – to be deployed into a tactical area by helicopter.

J

Jungle Boots – footwear that looks like a combination of a boot and canvas sneaker used by U.S. troops; leather rots when wet; canvas dries fast; there are thin metal plates on the sole for protection.

K

K-Bar – combat knife

KIA – Killed in Action.

Killing Zone - the area within an ambush where everyone is either killed or wounded.

Kill Zone - the radius of a circle around an explosive device within which it is predicted that 95% of all occupants will be killed should the device explode.

KSCB – Khe Sanh Combat Base

L

LAAW Rocket – light anti-tank/assault weapon; a shoulder-fired, 66 millimeter rocket made of fiberglass and disposable after one shot.

Lifer – a career military man. The term is often used in a derogatory manner.

LP – Listening post. A two-or-three-man position set up at night outside the perimeter away from the main body of troopers, which acted as an early warning system against attack.

Lt – Lieutenant.

LZ – Landing Zone - A cleared area where a helicopter can land.

M

M-16 – the standard U.S. rifle used in Vietnam from 1967 on; it fires a maximum rate of 150-200 rounds per minute (45-60 rounds per minute on semi-automatic), with an effective range of 460 meters; mis-firing/jamming were constant problems for the combat Marine, attributable to the powder used in the rounds.

M-60 – the standard lightweight machine gun used by U.S. troops.

M-79 – a U.S. military hand-held, breech-loaded grenade launcher that fires 40mm projectiles; range of 375 meters.

Medevac – evacuation of wounded or sick troops from the field, often by helicopter.

MIA – Missing in action

Mortar – an indirect fire weapon that fires explosive projectiles at high angles; 60mm and 81m mortars were taken into the field, with a range of 2,000 and 3,650 meters, respectively; Larger 4.2" mortars were also employed.

MOS – military occupational specialty.

Mule – A small, flatbed motor-driven four-wheel vehicle with a driver-seat and steering control suspended over the forward edge of the seat.

Mustang – A slang term used to describe Marine officers who were commissioned from the enlisted ranks, quite often coming as battlefield promotions.

N

'Nam – Vietnam.

Napalm – a jellied gasoline dropped from aircraft in large canisters, exploding on impact, it engulfed large areas in flame, sucking up all the oxygen and emitting intense heat, thick black smoke and an unforgettable smell.

NCO or **Non-Coms** – Non-commissioned officer, having a rank of corporal (E-4 or higher); NCO's are squad leaders, platoon sergeant or higher.

NVA – North Vietnamese Army; supplied by China, Russia and University of California, Berkeley students.

O

OCS - Officer Candidate School

OP – Observation post, also operation plan

OR - Operating Room

P

P-38 - a tiny collapsible can opener, also known as a "John Wayne".

Perimeter – outer limits of a military position. The area beyond the perimeter belongs to the enemy.

PFC - Private First Class; enlisted rank E-2

Platoon – a subdivision of a company; consists of three rifle squads; usually a machine gun, rocket and mortar squad from the weapons platoon were attached

Point Man - the first man on a combat patrol.

Poncho Liner – nylon insert to the military rain poncho, used as a blanket.

Pop-Flare/Smoke – smoke for marking a spot for helicopters, strike aircraft or friendly troops.

PRC-25 - Portable Radio Communication, Model 25 or "prick 25"; a back-packed FM receiver-transmitter with a range of 5-10 kilometers, depending on the weather; the standard radio carried by each squad's radioman.

Probables – enemy soldiers believed killed but not confirmed by actually seeing bodies

PTSD – post traumatic stress disorder; development of characteristic symptoms after experiencing of a psychologically traumatic event or events outside the normal range of human experience; symptoms include re-experiencing the traumatic event, lack of responsiveness to, or involvement with, the external world, exaggerated startle response, difficulty in concentrating, memory impairment, guilt feelings, and sleep problems.

PX – Post Exchange ; on-base store selling such items as toothpaste, cigarettes, writing paper, candy, etc.

R

Rack - bed or cot

R&R – Rest and Relaxation, a week of rest to one of many destinations including Japan, Hawaii, Singapore, Bangkok; normally each Marine received a seven day pass but sometimes only a three day pass if the company was in need of men to fight

ROK – Republic of Korea troops; they were damn good

Rotate - to return to the U.S. at the end of a year's tour in Vietnam.

RPG – Rocket propelled grenade.

RVN – Republic of Vietnam

Sapper – a Viet Cong or NVA armed with powerful explosives/satchel charges

Search and Destroy – an operation in which troops search for an destroy the enemy and then withdraw.

Sea Tiger – A weekly newspaper published by the Information Services of the Marine Corps

Short-timer – a solider or Marine nearing the end of an enlistment period; short timers had some funny sayings like "I'm so short I can sit on the edge of a dime and swing my legs" or "I'm so short I can walk under doors."

Shrapnel – pieces of metal sent flying by an explosion.

Shitter – 55 gallon drum, cut in half, with a board across the top with a hole cut in it; the toilet; it might have walls, like an outhouse.

Sick Bay – clinic or hospital.

Sit Rep – A situation report.

Six-By - a large flat-bed truck usually with wooden slat sides enclosing the bed and sometimes a canvas top covering it. Used for carrying men or anything that would fit on it.

Smoke Grenade - a grenade that released brightly colored smoke. Used for signaling.

Soul Brother - a black Marine

Spider Hole - camouflaged enemy foxhole.

Squad – a small combat unit consisting of 3 four man fire teams, plus a squad leader and a radioman.

Starlight Scope - an image intensifier using reflected light to identify targets at night.

Stars & Stripes – a newspaper put out by the Armed Forces and distributed to the troops.

Syrette - collapsible tube of morphine attached to a hypodermic needle. the contents of the tube were injected by squeezing it like a toothpaste tube.

T

TAOR – Tactical area of responsibility

Tet - Buddhist lunar New Year

Tracer – a round of ammunition chemically treated to glow so that its flight can be followed.

Trip Flare – a ground flare triggered by a trip wire used to signal and illuminate the approach of an enemy at night.

Tunnel Systems – During the Vietnam War, the tunnel system, which was initiated at the time of the French occupation, were enlarged and used as hiding places, hospitals, storage facilities and booby trap manufacturing; the Marines used "tunnel rats" to explore these caves and tunnels, armed only with a .45 automatic pistol and a flashlight; the tunnel rats were normally smaller in stature, as the tunnels were quite small

United States of America – "The World", land of the great PX,

USO - United Service Organization. Provided entertainment to the troops in the rear areas and was intended to raise morale.

Utilities – – standard combat uniform, green in color with pockets. Also called fatigues, especially by the Army.

VC – short for Viet Cong.
Viet Cong - The Communist-led forces fighting the South Vietnamese government and the U.S.-led forces.

W

Wake-Up - as in "13 and a wake-up" or "a wake-up and a duffle bag shuffle;" refers to waking up on the last day of a Marine's Vietnam tour.

WIA – Wounded in Action.

Z

Zero DarkThirty – pre-dawn, very early

Appendix I: Major Operations

Echo Company
2nd Battalion, 1st Marines

Operations vs Viet Cong	DaNang area TAOR	10Aug67
Operation Shelbyville	Go Noi Island	22Sep67
Operation Medina	SW Quang Tri Province	11Oct67
Operation Lancaster	Secure Rt 9 Cam to Ca Lu	3Nov67
Operation Kentucky	Con Thien/ DMZ	10Nov67
Operation Kentucky V	Tet Offensive	20Dec67
Operation Pegasus	Siege of Khe Sanh	1Apr68
Operation Scotland I	Khe Sanh/ DMZ	16Apr68
Operation Scotland II/C	Khe Sanh Area	22Jun68
Operation Napoleon Saline	Cua Viet River	7Jul68

Appendix II: Some Facts About the Vietnam War

About 8.7 million men and women served in the U.S. military during the Vietnam era. About 2.7 million of them served in Vietnam. About 10% of those who served in Vietnam were infantrymen.

Though the draft was on, 3/4 of the troops in Vietnam were volunteers. Almost all draftees went to the Army. The Marines were overwhelmingly volunteers.

2,594,000 American soldiers, sailors, airmen and Marines served in Vietnam. 58,220 were killed in action and 153,303 were wounded.

391,000 Marines served in Vietnam. 14,844 Marines were killed in action and 51,392 were wounded.

Volunteers accounted for 77% of total combat deaths, 52% of U.S. Army deaths and 95% of U.S. Marine Corps deaths.

The typical infantrymen serving a twelve month tour had a 3% chance of dying and a 25% chance of being wounded.

Of those killed, 82.5% were white, 12.5% black and 5% Hispanic.

In 1967 and 1968, the Marines saw their highest casualty numbers of the war, with 8,833 killed in action (3786 in 1967 and 5047 in 1968).

The average age of Marines killed was 21 years, 6 months. The youngest Marine killed was 17 years and 9 months old. The oldest Marine killed was 57 years and 7 months old.

The average age of those killed from all services was 22.8 years.
1 soldier was only 15 years old.
5 were only 16 years old.
12 were 17 years old.
3,103 were 18 years old.
8 women were killed in the Vietnam War.
The largest group was the 19 years old cohort, with 8,283 dying.
39,996 of those killed were 22 or younger.
997 soldiers were killed on their first day in Vietnam.

1,448 soldiers were killed on the last day of their scheduled tour of duty.

Officers were 12.5% of total troop strength and accounted for 13.5% of deaths.

Looking at Marine KIA by military occupational specialty (MOS), the top five were riflemen (7880 deaths), assault men (1122), machine gunners (1086), mortar men (568) and combat engineers (329).

The Marines suffered more casualties in Vietnam, than in all of WWII.
The Army of the Republic of Vietnam suffered about a quarter of a million KIA's. Estimates of civilian deaths, including 164,000 murdered by the NVA/VC, are in the neighborhood of 850,000.

A tour consisted of 12 months and 20 days for the Marines, 365 days for the Army.

The average infantrymen served 40 days in combat in the South Pacific and about 240 days in Vietnam, thanks to the mobility of the copter.

The average time lapse between wounding to hospitalization was less than one hour. As a result, less than one percent of all Americans wounded, who survived the first 24 hours, died.

The Quang Tri Province, in the I Corps area, was more heavily bombed than all of Europe, during WWII, reducing the 3,500 villages to only 11, by the end of the war, as documented by Landmines Vietnam. The intense bombing campaign, combined with the use of Agent Orange, had turned the land into a virtual moonscape with only a fraction of the original triple jungle canopy forest remaining.

Acknowledgements

My deepest thanks to Mike Collins (Portland, OR) for his overall direction, to my friend, Michael "Spanky" Fassett, (Bend, OR) and Bruce Bendinger who encouraged me to bring this story to press.

My special thanks to Jim Kirk (same Lt. Kirk in story) for his exhausting final review. Without his help, this book may not have been printed. He made it possible.

My friend, Rosalie Nelson (Dundee, OR) offered the final touch. Her company, Anchor Printworks, Inc., gave me professional direction when it came time to go to press.

I thank every one for their help throughout the last few years as the book was getting closer to the finish. I also want to thank everyone else that I have spoken with since 2003, the year that started me off on my book.

And my special thanks to my wife for her help during the last few days before going to press.

IN MEMORY OF WALT PITTMAN

Corporals Christensen & Pittman

We had a great time. I think it's the way we both lived life.

Walt and I entered the United States Marine Corps, in San Diego, California, on August 29, 1966. We were thrown into a billet, housing approximately 15-20 new recruits, everyone looking weird in their new haircuts (bald), baggy pants and baggy shirts. The whole lot would be named "Marines" on graduation day. Sure, it was tough, but with Walt as a friend, the journey was made easier.

We ate chow together, when we could, we attended Mass and spent most of our spare time together. We both talked about the same things – family, girl friends, college life, sports, and on. Geez...we laughed.

Word came down from the battalion headquarters for both Walt and me to report to the sergeant's quarters, which normally was a visit you didn't need. (Don't volunteer for anything). We had been picked from the entire Battalion to attend OCS (Officer Candidate School)! Wow! We were very proud, yet we had 1-1/2 years left on our two-year enlistment or three years of duty, if we accepted OCS and a commission, as a Second Lieutenant. Needless to say, we turned it down. We had so much to do when we returned from Vietnam and the sooner the better.

When we completed Boot Camp, we were transferred to Advanced Infantry Training and along with that came the opportunity to receive "leave" off base. San Diego State here we come. With our bald heads, leading the way, we headed to San Diego. We had our two day pass. We picked up a beer or two and the weekend began. We shared numerous weekends visiting his friends, drinking beer, laughing, telling stories, laughing, and laughing.

Walt and I were separated during the final phase of our infantry training. Walt went with the 26th Marines and left for Vietnam. I left a bit later and was assigned with 1st Marines.

During the first part of my tour, I met up with some guys I knew from our stateside training and asked about Walt. I was told that he received three Purple Hearts and was now in Okinawa, recuperating in the hospital. He had been hit in his arms, his legs, his head and the in the groin area.

I never gave up my search for Walt and on 11/13/2006 I made email contact with his sister, Shelia. She wrote:

"*Walt was killed on his ranch in Wyoming in 1973. His death was devastating for our entire family. He was operating a back hoe and nobody was around. When he was found, his chest was crushed and he was dead. Nobody has ever been able to determine what happened; he was only 27, and right after his death, Walt's wife discovered she was pregnant. Walt would have been so pleased to have been remembered, Gary. Walt lived his life well, and anything he attempted turned to gold. He served in Nam and was injured pretty badly. When he came back to the States, he worked for the Washington Post.*

I thank God for my time with Walt. I also know that we'll meet again in heaven. I find comfort in knowing this. Of course, I'll be old and he'll laugh at me, yes, we'll laugh again and again."

I miss my friend, Walt.

-Chris

Made in the USA
San Bernardino, CA
21 February 2017